Economic Capital Allocation with Basel II

Economic Capital Allocation with Basel II

Cost, benefit and implementation procedures

Dimitris N. Chorafas

ELSEVIER
BUTTERWORTH
HEINEMANN

AMSTERDAM   BOSTON   HEIDELBERG   LONDON   NEW YORK   OXFORD
PARIS   SAN DIEGO   SAN FRANCISCO   SINGAPORE   SYDNEY   TOKYO

Elsevier Butterworth-Heinemann
Linacre House, Jordan Hill, Oxford OX2 8DP
200 Wheeler Road, Burlington, MA 01803

First published 2004

British Library Cataloguing in Publication Data
A catalogue record for this book is available from the British Library

Library of Congress Cataloguing in Publication Data
A catalogue record for this book is available from the Library of Congress

ISBN 0 7506 6182 8

For information on all Elsevier Butterworth-Heinemann finance publications
visit our website at http://books.elsevier.com/finance

Composition by Genesis Typesetting Limited, Rochester, Kent
Printed and bound in Great Britain

Contents

Foreword

In early 2003, Dr Dimitris N. Chorafas was chairing a Capital Allocation conference in London, where I was presenting a case study on how to create an integrated capital management methodology. At this stage the banking industry was awaiting the third consultative paper to be released by the Basel Committee of Banking Supervision and Basel II/Economic Capital master-classes, workshops, lectures and panel discussions were on the agendas of quite a number of conferences to address and discuss the latest techniques in regulatory and economic capital allocation.

During the conference and in the ensuing discussion it quickly became clear to me that Dimitris Chorafas, based on his fundamental understanding of financial markets and more than forty years' experience in advising financial institutions, combines a holistic view on the impact of Basel II on the financial industry with a pragmatic sense of its implications for individual banks and their strategy.

Being responsible as a senior program manager for implementing a Basel II compliant economic capital framework at a major European bank, I have come across a number of publications and books related to Basel II and economic capital allocation. However, there are actually not that many books around which, from a practitioner's perspective, address the subject in a comprehensive and easy-to-understand manner. To that end, I was more than happy to participate in Dimitris Chorafas's research, which led to this book: *Economic Capital Allocation with Basel II: Cost, Benefit and Implementation Procedures*.

In my view the book is spot on in its content, timeliness and coverage, linking the new Basel II regulation with practical and theoretical guidance on economic capital allocation strategies. A comprehensive discussion of the political aspects of supervisory regulation and the challenges ahead concludes the book. It provides the reader with a fascinating blend of theory, case studies and views from bank experts, rating agencies and banking regulators. Dimitris Chorafas's book has all the hallmarks of becoming a reference for Basel II and economic capital allocation and I am enthusiastic about recommending it to banking practitioners and academics alike.

Eugen Buck
Managing Director
Senior Project Manager Economic Capital
Rabobank Nederland

Preface

The new capital adequacy rules by the Basel Committee on Banking Supervision, widely known as Basel II, is a set of regulatory standards targeting not only a sound capital ratio for credit risk, market risk and operational risk, but also a host of subjects relating to good governance. As is the case in engineering and in the physical sciences, the setting of standards is most important because it brings both:

- A reduction in the variability of results, and
- The localization of reasons of existing variations.

These two aftermaths see to it that standardization and regulation lead to an enlargement of the field of activity, rather than to a constrained perspective as it is often intuitively felt. They also bring to attention the need for a sound foundation for economic capital allocation. Apart from the capital requirements, which must be met, an able solution rests on three pillars:

1 *Corporate strategy.* Capital allocation should not be done on general income basis. It should follow strategic decisions, prognosticate business opportunities and promote chosen lines of activity, using income from channels with less future (cash flows).
2 *Risk management.* The amount of current and future exposure is vital input to all strategic decisions – and therefore to capital allocation. Regulatory and economic capital must assure financial staying power.
3 *Advanced information technology.* Top-tier information technology (IT) provides the infrastructure which would allow factual allocation of financial resources. Experimentation, simulation and reliable documentation are 'musts'.

A similar statement is valid about testing strategic plans, risk control policies and procedures, as well as technology and models used to help senior management to do a better job. Basel II brings into perspective the critical question of what should be settled and what should be tested in the process of regulation, standardization, and management control.

A pragmatic answer to the testing question is that new methods of risk control closely associated to the dynamic definition of regulatory capital, as well as the use of modern technology, permit us to assess a credit institutions' exposure with a higher degree of accuracy than ever before. This is fulfilling an essential condition for sound management. Risk analysis requires a lot of skill, time and data. Here, too, standardization helps.

Basel II sets standards and guidelines which reflect an increasingly sophisticated banking practice, and have to be integrated into the regular day-to-day business of credit institutions. The challenges this process poses, including its opportunities and problems, are the issues this book mainly addresses. This has been a deliberate choice, rather than focusing on the fine print of Basel II, which is anyway published by the Basel Committee on Banking Supervision.

One of the challenges, perhaps the most important, is the attention to be paid by senior management, loans officers, traders and investment experts to unexpected losses. Expected losses should be covered through regulatory capital, while the role of economic capital is to address unexpected losses and extreme events. How to allocate economic capital to the bank's business units is one of the contributions this book makes to the banking industry.

Based on an extensive research, the book is written for senior bankers in commercial and investment banking, as well as for officials of regulatory authorities, responsible for supervising regulatory capital calculations, risk management projects and economic capital allocation. The text consists of sixteen chapters which are divided among four parts.

Part 1 gives an overview of Basel II and its pillars, presents the results of quantitative impact studies (QIS) in which 350 banks in forty different countries participated, discusses the cost of Basel II implementation, outlines the benefits to be derived from such investment, including risk-based pricing and rating targets, defines the component parts of regulatory capital and outlines the global impact of market discipline.

Credit rating now plays a critical role in the definition of regulatory capital – whether done by independent rating agencies, under the standard method of Basel II, or by the bank itself under the Foundation internal ratings-based (IRB) approach and the Advanced IRB approach. Eigenmodels associated to Basel II and the need for on-line interactive datamining, add to the sophistication of required solutions.

The theme of Part 2 is allocation of economic capital to business units and activity channels. After defining the sense of economic capital and the role it plays in the management of a credit institution, the text documents how and why economic capital serves to sustain the bank's solvency, outlines the mathematical background of economic capital allocation and presents a wealth of practical applications realized by some of the best known institutions.

Entities which participated in the research which led to this book include regulatory authorities like the Basel Committee on Banking Supervision, Bank of England, Deutsche Bundesbank and Swiss National Bank, as well as commercial banks which have been active in the refinement of some of the Basel II characteristics and in economic capital allocation. In alphabetic order these banks are Barclays Bank, Citigroup, Crédit Suisse, Deutsche Bank, First Austrian Bank, Merrill Lynch, Rabobank, United Bank of Switzerland and other credit institutions.

Other major contributors to the research whose outcome has been distilled in this book have been the foremost independent ratings agencies: Standard & Poor's, Moody's Investors Service, Fitch Ratings and A.M. Best. Based on all of these research findings, the book brings to the reader's attention the evolving rules in capital allocation. It also explains, and critically analyses, strategies used by banks to increase their capital base.

Part 3 addresses three interrelated subjects: defaults and their management; the role and methods used in connection to internal ratings; and the need for a modern technological infrastructure, which must be steadily reviewed and updated. Correlations, supervisory weights and the handling of collateral are other themes covered by the five chapters of Part 3.

To help the reader get ahead of the curve in technology, the book covers the issue of off-the-shelf software, particularly solutions which can assist both in IRB implementation and in economic capital allocation – doing so effectively without having to reinvent the wheel. Three risk-pricing and capital allocation tools have been chosen: risk-adjusted return on capital (RAROC), Moody's KMV and Best Capital Adequacy Ratio (BCAR). Through practical examples, Part 3 also helps the reader to master IRB.

Part 4 treats regulatory and political issues which, for any practical purpose, are indivisible. It outlines the role played by the growing number of transnational institutions and supervisory authorities that have integrated into the global landscape of financial markets and it presents opinions which are contrary to Basel II's approach to the definition of regulatory capital.

Part 4 also explains the difference between Basel II and the third Capital Adequacy Directive (CAD 3) of the European Union (EU), as well as how and why the pending confirmation of the EU may upset the whole implementation timetable of Basel II. Part 4 also brings to the reader's attention the 2003 testimonies before the US Congress Subcommittee by regulators and commercial bankers, and it concludes with the challenge of supervising global markets.

The book has been designed to lead the reader through the ways and means to capitalize on experience so far acquired in risk management, risk-based pricing projects and initiatives associated with capital allocation, and in other activities similar to those described in the Basel Committee directives. This is largely accomplished through case studies.

The book is written in a down-to-earth comprehensible manner, yet it is both advanced and comprehensive in its coverage. To use this text and its examples, the reader needs no theoretical knowledge of finance and economics. Everything pertaining to capital allocation is fully explained, but practical banking experience *or* an academic background would help.

The benefit the reader will obtain from this book is a comprehensive presentation of the projected evolution of the banking industry in the twenty-first century; the fine-tuning of capital requirements for bank liquidity and solvency, necessary to be in charge of this evolution; an understanding of the rules elaborated by the supervisory authorities of the Group of Ten (G-10); and the technical requirements for economic capital allocation by credit institutions.

These are very timely issues because the new capital adequacy requirements by the Basel Committee on Banking Supervision, involve fairly complex new standards regarding *credit risk* and *operational risk*, altering notions familiar to banks since the 1988 Capital Accord. Moreover, credit institutions are now most interested to optimize the allocation of their economic capital in a way they can obtain at least AA rating by independent rating agencies.

As in Chapter 1, the book also brings to the reader's attention the fact that fairly significant costs are associated with the new solutions to capital adequacy promoted by the regulators. Based on intensive research in the USA, UK and continental Europe, this text outlines both the costs that would be likely incurred, and the benefits to be expected from the implementation of Basel II. Several chapters can be looked at as a 'how to' manual.

The book is designed to appeal to chief executive officers, chief financial officers, treasury executives, chief risk officers, heads of economic capital organizations and members of their staff, chief information officers, as well as systems architects, database administrators and rocket scientists who need to develop the marking-to-model and economic capital allocation aspects.

Because modern banking requires a growing amount of personnel familiar with capital allocation, internal control and risk management, the book also serves the academic market, particularly, fourth-year undergraduate and graduate students studying Finance, Banking and Business Administration in colleges and universities.

I am indebted to a long list of knowledgeable people, and organizations, for their contribution to the research that made this book feasible, also to several senior executives and financial experts for constructive criticism during the preparation of the manuscript. The complete list of the executives and organizations who participated in this research is shown in the Acknowledgments.

Let me take this opportunity to thank Mike Cash, for suggesting this project, Jennifer Wilkinson for seeing it all the way to publication, Deena Burgess and Carol Lucas for the editorial work. To Eva-Maria Binder goes the credit for compiling the research results, typing the text and making the camera-ready artwork and index.

Dimitris N. Chorafas
October 2003

Warning: Basel II, the October 11, 2003, announcement and its aftermath

1 Introduction

On October 10 and 11, 2003, a short time prior to this book going to press, the Basel Committee on Banking Supervision met in Madrid to decide on over 200 responses and comments received on the Third Consultative Paper (CP3) of Basel II. Basel Committee members committed to work promptly to resolve outstanding issues and improve the new capital adequacy framework by no later than June 2004, focusing on four themes:

- Changing the overall treatment of expected losses (EL) versus unexpected losses (UL) from credit events.
- Simplifying the handling of asset securitization, eliminating the Supervisory Formula and replacing it with a simpler solution.
- Re-evaluating the way certain credit risk mitigation techniques are being approached and implemented.
- Revisiting the treatment of credit card commitments and issues related to them.

This Warning reflects on the first of these bullets, which is at the core of the new capital adequacy, as well as on the implementation timetable and on the fact that, as one of the senior commercial bankers put it: 'Indeed, the (Basel II) process has become very political' (see also Chapter 16).

The text is based on the October 11, 2003 Announcement; the Basel Committee Bulletin 100 on home-host; a lecture by Jaime Caruana to the Seventh Annual Conference of the British Bankers Association on October 9, 2003; opinions in the City of London (practically educated guesses by bankers) in the week of October 6, just prior to the Madrid Basel Committee meeting; and interviews made with knowledgeable sources in the week of October 20, 2003.

2 Basel II implementation timetable

Good news first, by all likelihood there will be no delay in Basel II implementation. The January 1, 2006 parallel application between Basel I and Basel II and January 1, 2007 full implementation of new capital adequacy rules seem to hold. This information, which filters from the Madrid meeting, contrasts to earlier rumors in the City of London that there will be a one-year delay, and to a recent guess by one of the commercial bankers that the changes (more on them later) might mean a three-year delay.

The prevailing concept is to keep momentum in Basel II implementation. On the other hand, it cannot be excluded that some delay becomes necessary. A minor delay will not be against the banks' wishes. As a senior commercial banker put it: 'I am quite pleased that we now seem to have some more "timetable security" as far as the implementation date is concerned.' In January 2004, the Basel Committee will meet to evaluate the outcome of the consultation on:

- Change to the handling of expected losses, and unexpected losses,
- Further related work on the calibration of IRB, in light of established objectives on overall capital adequacy, and
- What should be done about the other three bullets outlined in the Introduction.

In its October 11, 2003, communication, the Basel Committee states that it does not believe that, from a conceptual viewpoint, the elements in the new approach which it has chosen would change substantially the mechanics of Basel II. Neither does the Committee expect that these adjustments will alter the new capital adequacy's fundamental structure.

Implicit, but not explicit, in the October 11, 2003, statement is that nothing will change in terms of operational risk.[1] However, an aftereffect of this October 11 announcement is that the Institute of International Finance (IIF), a Washington-based big bank think tank and lobby, sent a long memo to Basel on operational risk revision.

If (imprudently) a fifth bullet, 'Operational risk', is added to the four bullets in the Introduction *then* it will be like opening Pandora's box. This issue is so political that Basel will face 60-mile-an-hour headwinds and a very difficult landing.

Discounting such adversity, which might reach the point that the whole process collapses, the general appreciation at Basel Committee level seems to be that even if the finalization of Basel II takes place at the end of June 2004, instead of at the end of December 2003, this six-month delay will not have a material impact on the January 1, 2006 deadline for parallel implementation.

3 Changes affecting IRB, EL and UL

As it transpires from the October 11, 2003, Basel Committee announcement, there will be no changes in connection to the Standardized Approach of Basel II. All effort seems to be concentrated on the internal ratings-based (IRB) method, essentially making IRB a *Basel 2.5* solution. By all evidence,

- Economic capital and regularity capital are not merging, but maintaining their existing identity.
- Basically, what changes is the way expected credit losses are being treated and unexpected losses computed.

Basel II, as it stood prior to October 11, 2003, called for banks to hold enough capital to absorb expected losses through appropriate provisions. The approach which has been originally adopted included an EL algorithm and represented a practical compromise necessary to address differences in:

- National accounting practices, and
- Supervisory authority rules regarding provisioning.

In an implementation sense, this EL algorithm has been common to all banks. It will still be used to identify expected losses. In a nutshell, EL = PD • LGD • EAD holds. What changes is the fact that there will be no need for extra regulatory capital for EL, because banks do keep reserves for credit losses.

However, *if* the use of the EL formula ends by requiring more capital than is being effectively reserved *then* there is a case of *shortfall*. According to the October 11, 2003, document, the Basel Committee proposes that:

- *Shortfall*, if any, will be deducted from the bank's capital.

Such deduction would be taken 50 percent from Tier 1 and 50 percent from Tier 2 capital, in line with other deductions from capital included in Basel II. On the contrary, it may be that use of the EL algorithm ends by requiring less capital in reserve.

- *Excess*, if any, will be eligible as an element of Tier 2 capital, similar to the current treatment of general provisions.

Tier 2 eligibility of excess amounts will be subject to rules at the discretion of national supervisory authorities. There is, however, a limit. In no case would such excess capital be allowed to be more than 20 percent of Tier 2 capital of a bank.

An important consideration is how the unexpected loss will be computed, and which will be the necessary tests (see section 5 in the Warning, and Chapters 7, 8 and 13 in the main text). Eugen Buck, managing director, Rabobank, said in his response: 'Regarding the EL and UL separation we had discussions with our national regulator on the likelihood of a QIS 3.5 or QIS 4 exercise to review the calibrations of the IRB risk weight formulas, but they themselves are waiting for further details from Basel.'

Buck also made the point that for the handling of excess/shortfall of provisions versus EL a streamlining of T-1 to T-3 would be helpful, adding that: 'As an AAA institution we are pursuing a policy of improving, mainly, our T-1 capital base, with T-2 being quite small. Should an 'excess' be eligible as a T-2 capital element, only the proposed 20 percent limit of T-2 could become a restriction for us. In other words, we will need to take this into account when reviewing our provisioning policy and its alignment with EL.'

Rainer Rauleder, Global Head, Capital Management, Deutsche Bank, remarks that: 'In the current discussion about EL/UL treatment, the question of defining the eligible capital dimensions came up again. However, the Basel Committee was correct to avoid opening this issue during the current Basel II consultation. The capital definition is just too complex to be an add-on to the current round. Rather, capital definition deserves a separate Basel III or Basel IV (if credit risk models will feature in the next round).'

This being said, the handling of *shortfall* and *excess* leads to the notion that a new class will be created, either within or outside the hybrid T-1 and hybrid T-2 categories. As a suggestion, a streamlining of T-1, T-2, T-3, including:

- Their characteristics,
- Their role, and
- Their limits,

will be most helpful. Moreover, this streamlining should keep in mind that the distinction between EL and UL is not just a conceptual issue. EL and UL are two different areas of the same distribution.

4   Bankers appreciate crisp definitions

Commenting on an earlier draft of this Warning, one of the knowledgeable sources pointed out that there is today some confusion around the wording of two concepts:

- Provisions, which are part of P&L (income statement), and
- Reserves and allowances which find themselves in the balance sheet's liabilities side.

The opinion which has been expressed is that the concept of fixed-margin income (FMI) offsets should be retained by the Basel Committee, for two reasons:

- It constitutes first line of recourse against losses, and it is covered by the spread in pricing,
- It helps to ensure stronger incentive for adequate pricing and conservative provisioning policies.

According to this opinion, it is preferable to align the treatment of credit risk in the banking book (including dynamic provisioning) and trading book risk estimates (including VAR approaches and valuation reserves). The viewpoint of another senior banker, who contributed to shaping up this Warning, has been that conceptual differences were raised because banks look at expected loss from different viewpoints:

- Fixed margin income put in pricing, and
- Best possible ways, means and policies for provisioning.

In the October 11, 2003 document, the regulators advise that one of the grounds of a different treatment of EL than that originally projected, is that the Basel Committee recognizes that, for prudential reasons, banks may choose setting provisions in excess of expected loss amount calculated by IRB. Therefore, it wishes to promote this practice of better capitalization, where and when appropriate.

To recapitulate, under the EL headline, credit institutions will compare the IRB measurement of expected losses with the total amount of provisions that they have made, including both general and specific provisions. Such comparison may produce a *shortfall* or an *excess*. For calibration purposes:

■ Further impact assessments are planned in some jurisdictions, and
■ The Basel Committee will monitor parallel calculations undertaken by credit institutions.

One of the commercial bankers who participated to the research commented that this issue of integrating EL with loan loss reserves was first brought up three years ago by the Deutsche Bundesbank, but was not retained. On October 11 it was adopted on the insistence of the US delegation to the Basel Committee. 'My bank,' said this executive, 'is very positive to this solution.'

Other credit institutions, too, spoke in positive terms, and also underlined the importance of using both qualitative and quantitative approaches in determining capital requirements. In the opinion of Dr Harry Stordel, Director of Group Risk Management, Crédit Suisse: 'The algorithm to be used for unexpected losses needs some qualitative component, which may be scenario-based. Both EL and UL have very much to do with how the bank manages its capital.'

5 Computation of unexpected losses

The October 11, 2003, document by the Basel Committee does not make reference to specific positions taken by the different delegations. What it states is that subsequent to comments received on CP3 as well as research by the Basel Committee's working groups, the regulators revisited the capital adequacy issue adopting an approach based on unexpected losses (UL), which might also bring an improvement in handling expected losses.

The document in reference states that the method outlined in CP3 produces a statistical measurement of both unexpected and expected losses faced by credit institutions in relation to their credit risk exposures, incorporating them into the IRB capital requirement. The Basel Committee, however, has come to the conclusion that a separation of the treatment of EL and UL, within the IRB approach, would lead to a better, more consistent framework.

The statement is further made that this modified approach will see to it that the measurement of risk-weighted assets, resulting in IRB capital requirements, would be based solely on the unexpected loss portion of IRB calculations. Therefore, certain offsets within the IRB framework, such as future margin income, would no longer be necessary.

It does not take two heads to understand that if it is critical to put into place a fundamental treatment of unexpected losses, then this should be based on a sound computational approach which can be expressed in algorithmic form, plus certain qualitative factors. A factual and documented UL handling will be instrumental in assuring strong incentives for banks to provision properly against unexpected losses, but the algorithm must be:

- Mathematically solid,
- Operationally comprehensive, and
- With an output appreciated both by supervisors and by implementers.

The problem is that currently there is no valid algorithm available for the calculation of unexpected losses. One of the tools in circulation is $VAR_{99.97}$, alias $CVAR_{99.97}$ (for credit VAR) and $CAR_{99.97}$ (for capital at risk). Simply stated, this is worse than *marking to myth*, as Warren Buffett advises.[2] It is an aberration. Because of reputational risk, serious entities should not be doing silly things.

Left alone the fact that VAR is a weak and obsolete model, even for market risk[3] and that the standard VAR is mathematically incomplete as the Swiss Federal Institute of Technology, in Zurich, has demonstrated, $VAR_{99.97}$ does not make sense any way one looks at it. A factual and documented study by Citigroup found that 99.97 percent confidence requires knowledge of severity distribution in excess of 99.9999 percent quantile. Moreover,

- Direct calculation of VAR at even 99.9 percent is impossible.
- What is possible is 99 percent VAR estimates, scaling up the outcome; or stress tests.

The Citigroup study also found that sample size plays a most vital role in accuracy of $VAR_{99.97}$ results. The sample size was increased from 50 to 1,000,000 datapoints and while x̄ remained stable from the minimum to the maximum sample:

- VAR_{99} increased by a factor of 2.
- While $VAR_{99.97}$ increased by a factor of 4.8.

There is no need to make any further comment on the lack of dependability of the quantitative evidence on the instability of $VAR_{99.97}$ results. To help in finding a reliable algorithmic solution to UL, this book proposes three alternatives:

- A modified algorithm originally suggested by the Deutsche Bundesbank (see Chapter 7, section 7.7, pages 168 to 172).
- A modified algorithm originally suggested by the Basel Committee (see Chapter 8, section 8.4, pages 184 to 186).
- BCAR, the capital adequacy equation used by A.M. Best, the rating agency of insurance industry, which could be converted for implementation in banking (see Chapter 13, sections 13.7 and 13.8, pages 307 to 313).

These algorithms need to be further developed and thoroughly tested. It is not sufficient to have a dissentient voice to the use of $CVAR_{99.97}$ and similar half-baked metrics; one must also present alternatives. All tools are imprecise, but some are more accurate, while others can be outright misleading, with the result that senior management decisions based on them turn sour.

Vigorous dissent is vital in an environment of risk control. As Francis Bacon once said: 'Books speak plain when counselors blanch.'

6   The home-host issue

According to Basel Committee Publication No. 100, of August 2003, the Supervisors of the Group of Ten recognize that the new capital accord will require more cooperation and coordination between *home* country and *host* country authorities, because:

- The new rules will be applied at each level of the banking group, and
- This poses significant technical requirements in providing Pillar 1 and Pillar 2 assessment.

One of the commercial bankers, whose input helped in shaping the Warning, pointed out that the banking sector has made constructive proposals on the home-host issue. These include:

- A college of supervisors, per bank, and
- A lead supervisor to co-ordinate, preferably the home supervisor.

However, the supervisory authorities did not embrace this proposal, probably because of problems with responsibilities from the national legal mandate of the host supervisor. In the aftermath, credit institutions believe that the ball is on the side of supervisors. Leaving things as they now stand, generates:

- Huge uncertainty,
- Risk of divergence, and
- Burden for both banks and supervisors.

There is, also, need for global coordination regarding Pillar 3 (see also the concluding remarks in Chapter 16). The principle of consolidated supervision sees to it that a banking group which has operations in a country other than its home base, may need to obtain approval for its use of certain approaches from both host country and home country regulators. While the 1996 Market Risk Amendment involved similar requirements, Basel II:

- Creates some new implementation challenges, and
- Significantly extends the scope of multiple approvals, with evident aftermath on the transborder credit institution.

This runs contrary to the Basel Committee's wishes to promote the ability of all host supervisors to exercise effective supervision over foreign institutions operating in their jurisdictions; also to strengthen the coordination between host and home country supervisors of these institutions.

Both strengthening the coordination and exercising effective supervision over foreign banks are excellent aims, but it is no less true that companies like Citigroup which operates in 101 countries, and Royal Bank of Scotland, which operates in 80 countries, will be faced with a long list of challenges. To comply with different versions and interpretations of Basel II rules, would mean both red tape and an inordinate amount of costs. Neither should be the case.

The home-host issue is not linear. ABN Amro operates in 60 countries, but also has three home markets: The Netherlands, the US, and Brazil. Crédit Suisse operates in almost 100 countries and also has three home markets: Switzerland, the US and UK. Down to basics:

- Sovereignty,
- Legislation, and
- Differences in interpretation of rules

create severe problems for all multinational commercial and investment banks. This is no more globalization, but fragmentation of the global market. The Basel Committee looks at this as an implementation issue, but in reality it is one of streamlining legal mandates.

Notice that there exists, as well, a difference in viewpoints. The home supervision approach is better served by Basel II, because the financial staying power of the institution depends on its exposure and capital adequacy. By contrast, host supervisors are particularly concerned about the protection of depositors (and about deposit insurance) rather than about an institution's standing as a lender. Such differences in viewpoint lead to asymmetric home-host approaches.

In a nutshell, as far as the home-host challenge is concerned, the overarching question is: Are we really moving to more international standards and convergence with inevitable compromises, mutual recognition, and alignment to prevent international crises – or divergence because of national interests and other reasons which create a non-level playing field?

7 A preview of Basel III

The changes to the original Basel IRB solution discussed in sections 1 to 4 should be examined under the perspective of new regulation, which will be most likely forthcoming by the end of this decade. A hint on what it may contain is provided by a lecture given to the Seventh Annual Supervision Conference of the British Bankers Association[4] by Jaime Caruana, governor of Banco de España and chairman of the Basel Committee.

In his lecture, Caruana made reference to *full credit risk models* to be used in the calculation of minimal capital requirements. The implication is that through more accurate risk-based pricing, a bank's capital requirements would reflect in a more exact manner the economic benefits of diversification in the institution's balance sheet.

A further reference, found in this same lecture, has been that while some banks are making commendable progress in thinking about ways to estimate the value of diversification, regulators remain concerned about the degree of confidence one might have in those estimates. The lack of data on which to base, and subsequently verify, such calculations is one of the reasons for this regulatory concern.

Indeed, as one of the senior banker commercial bankers who participated in the October 20, 2003, research pointed out: 'One of the key benefits of Basel II has been that it pressed banks to focus on data.' This has been a dramatic swing from past information technology practices, to a new era of database-oriented solutions.

However, it takes ten years or more to develop detailed and reliable time series. This may be the reason behind Jaime Caruana's statement that today regulators are concerned that it would be difficult for third parties to validate diversification estimates, particularly if they are not convinced about the consistency of application of assumed diversification effects.

For instance, regulators are not certain that banks today consistently adjust the value of all of their assets based on each asset's contribution to diversification. Therefore, according to the chairman of the Basel Committee, regulators have decided to:

- Establish standard estimates of diversification banks would apply,
- Move forward with an approach that is more consistent with the existing treatment of market risk, and
- Pay a great amount of attention to risk-based pricing and capital allocation.

To a significant extent, this is in the process of being achieved. As Jos Wieleman, senior vice president, group risk management, ABN Amro, puts it: 'I am under the impression that Basel II already works: (it) gives incentive to banks to invest to enhance their risk management systems. However, they prefer to invest in economic capital (and) portfolio management; less (so) in Basel II regulatory compliance.'

During a meeting in Paris – shortly after the Madrid meetings – between representatives of the Basel Committee and a limited number of IIF members, it has been discussed to still look for an opportunity to recognize portfolio diversification under Pillar 2. The fact that this issue can be treated within the context of Basel II is a new development.

As Wieleman points out, the idea is that Basel II will formally allow to take into account diversification under Pillar 2, in the evaluation of overall risk profile and a holistic judgement of capital adequacy. This could open the door for an evolutionary process to gradually increase the impact of internal economic capital measures.

The Basel Committee and IFF decided to establish working groups to make an inventory of current best practices, and prepare a proposal on how a method could be implemented in the final Basel Accord. Notice that a similar effort was considered at the start of Basel II development, but at that time the regulators concluded that:

- It was too early to use those models for regulatory/supervisory purposes,
- But banks were encouraged to work along this line for internal purposes.

A valuable input to the *Basel 2.5* reference is the fact that, in a recent study, the Gartner Group said that it expects an integrated enterprise-wide risk management to be 'best practice' in 2006.

It is unavoidable that as more experience is gained with IRB, and generic credit risk algorithms are developed – rather than being carryovers – credit, market, and operational risk models should at some point in time merge. This will provide the tools for an integrated real-time risk management. Regulators, Jaime Caruana concluded in his lecture of October 9, 2003, are ready to start moving towards an advanced solution as soon as it is possible. This statement is the closest preview available today on Basel III.

Notes

1 D.N. Chorafas (2004). *Operational Risk Control with Basel II*. Butterworth-Heinemann.
2 Warren Buffett (2003). 'Avoiding a megacatastrophe'. *Fortune*, 17 March.
3 D.N. Chorafas (2002). *Modelling the Survival of Financial and Industrial Enterprises. Advantages, Challenges, and Problems with the Internal Rating-Based (IRB) Method*. Palgrave/Macmillan.
4 London, October 9, 2003.

Abbreviations

A&L	assets and liabilities
ABA	American Bankers Association
ABS	asset-backed securities
ACE	adjusted core equity
AIB	Allied Irish Banks
AIG	Accord Implementation Group
AIS	audit issue score
AMA	advanced measurement approaches
ATE	adjusted total equity
BCAR	Best Capital Adequacy Ratio
BI	business issues
BIA	Basic Indicator Approach
BIS	Bank for International Settlements
bp	basis points
BQS	business quality score
CAD 3	third Capital Adequacy Directive
CBO	collateralized bond obligation
CDO	collateralized debt obligation
CDR	cumulative default rate
CEO	chief executive officer
CFO	chief finance officer
CFTC	Commodities Futures Trading Commission
CGFS	Committee on the Global Financial System
CL	current liability
CMO	collateralized mortgage obligation
COB	Commission des Operations de Bourse
COO	chief operating officer
COSO	Committee of Sponsoring Organizations
CP	consultative paper
CPA	chartered public accountant
CPV	Credit Portfolio View
CR	concentration ratio
CRO	chief risk officer
CSFB	Crédit Suisse First Boston
CTF	Capital Task Force
DG	directorate general

DP	default point
DSGV	German Savings Banks and Giro Association
DSS	decision support system
DT	Deutsche Telekom
DTA	deferred tax assets
EAD	exposure at default
ECB	European Central Bank
EDF	expected default frequency
EDP	electronic data processing
EL	expected loss
EMU	European Monetary Union
EU	European Union
EVT	extreme value theory
FASB	Financial Accounting Standards Board
FDIC	Federal Deposit Insurance Corporation
FHC	financial holding company
FMI	future margin income
FOREX	foreign exchange
FSA	Financial Services Authority
FSAP	Financial Sector Assessment Program
FSF	Financial Stability Forum
FSI	Financial Stability Institute
G-7	Group of Seven
G-10	Group of Ten
G-20	Group of Twenty
GAB	General Arrangements to Borrow
GAAP	Generally Accepted Accounting Principles
GARCH	generalized autoregressive conditional heteroschedasticity
GDP	gross domestic product
GI	gross income
GLBA	Gramm-Leach-Bliley Act
GMA	general management account
HVCRE	high volatility commercial real estate
HF/LI	high frequency/low impact
HHI	Herfindahl-Hirschmann index
HLI	highly leveraged institution
IAIS	International Association of Insurance Supervisors
IAMIS	internal accounting management information system
IAS	International Accounting Standard
IASB	International Accounting Standards Board
IC	internal control
ICAR	Insurance Capital Adequacy Ratio
IIF	Institute of International Finance
IMA	internal measurement approach
IMF	International Monetary Fund
IOSCO	International Organization of Securities Commissions
IPO	initial public offerings

IRB	internal ratings-based
IRS	Internal Revenue Service
ISDA	International Swaps and Derivatives Association
ISMA	International Securities Markets Association
IT	information technology
LAS	Loans Analysis System
LC	letters of credit
LD	loss distribution
LEQ	loans equivalence
LF	liquid fund
LF/HI	low frequency/high impact
LGD	loss given default
LLP	loss on the loan portfolio
LSE	London Stock Exchange
LTCM	Long-Term Capital Management
MBI	major business issues
MBS	mortgage-backed securities
MIS	management information system
MOU	Memorandum of Understanding
MQS	management quality score
MRA	Market Risk Amendment
MRMS	Moody's Risk Management Services
MVA	market value of assets
NAIC	National Association of Insurance Commissioners
NASD	National Association of Securities Dealers
NRC	net required capital
NPV	net present value
NYSE	New York Stock Exchange
OC	operations characteristics
OCC	Office of the Controller of the Currency
OECD	Organization for Economic Co-operation and Development
OFC	offshore financial center
OTC	over the counter
OTS	Office of Thrift Supervision
P&L	profit and loss
PD	probability of default
PIS	preliminary issues score
PPP	personal purchasing power
QAF	qualitative adjustment factor
QRRE	qualifying revolving retail exposures
Rabo	Rabobank
RAROC	risk-adjusted return on capital
RBA	ratings-based approach
RC	regulatory capital
REC	return on economic capital
ROA	return on assets
ROE	return on equity

ROI	return on investment
ROSC	Report on Observance of Standards and Codes
RoVAR	return on value at risk
SEC	Securities and Exchange Commission
S&Ls	savings and loans
SCM	state, county and municipal
SEC	Securities and Exchange Commission
SFA	supervisory formula approach
SFAS	Statement of Financial Accounting Standards
SFBC	Swiss Federal Banking Commission
SFRC	Shadow Financial Regulatory Committee
SI	Sharpe index
SIV	special investment vehicle
SME	small and medium-size enterprise
SOAP	simple object access protocol
SP	special provision
SPV	special purpose vehicle
SR	Sharpe ratio
SRP	supervisory review process
TL	total liability
UDDI	universal description, discovery and integration
UL	unexpected loss
VAR	value at risk
WSDL	web services description language
Y2K	Year 2000

1
Commercial banks and the new regulation

1 Basel II, impact studies and cost of implementation

1.1 Introduction

A first draft of the New Capital Adequacy Framework (Basel II) by the Basel Committee on Banking Supervision[1] was released in June 1999. This was a *consultative paper* (CP), containing general outlines of proposed regulations. Known as CP1, it has been destined to affect capital requirements of credit institutions at Group of Ten (G-10) countries and beyond. Capital adequacy rules established by the Basel Committee are eventually to be adopted by central banks and supervisory authorities of the majority of countries in the world. The timetable of CPs, *quantitative impact studies* (QISs) and implementation deadlines is shown in Table 1.1.

Members of the Basel Committee have agreed on year-end 2006 as the common implementation date of Basel II. Notice that credit institutions adopting the most advanced methods for credit risk and for operational risk, are required to run them in parallel to Basel I for one year. This means that in 2006 capital adequacy will still be based on the 1998 accord (see section 1.3).

In terms of added value, Basel II establishes in the best possible way what is currently feasible, capital requirements for an economy dominated by service industries and financial instruments. It should escape nobody's attention that the change from a manufacturing to a service economy has profound consequences on the role of capital, the importance of capital reserves, as well as current and future problems the financial world faces in:

Dates	Actions
June 1999	First consultation paper (CP1)
July 2000	Quantitative impact study (QIS1)
January 2001	CP2
April 2001	QIS2
November 2001	QIS2.5
October 2002	QIS3
April 2003	CP3
October 11, 2003	Announcement changing the rules
June 2004 (probably)	Finalization of Basel II regulations
January 2006	Parallel running of IRB approaches with Basel I
January 2007	Implementation of Basel II (see Warning)

Table 1.1 Basel II timetable of consultative papers, quantitative impact studies, parallel run and final implementation

- Funding business growth in a virtual economy
- Promoting competitiveness and flexibility
- Keeping assumed exposure under control
- Having in place a mechanism for absorbing unexpected losses, and
- Assuring public confidence at large among investors, business entities and the general public.

In the modern economy, capital is increasingly used for guaranteeing future performance on which depend not only the dividends of shareholders and interest stream for bondholders, but also the means for funding pensions, health costs and environmental and social risks. Another contribution of capital is that of making possible compensation for future damages which often involves litigation. The asbestos and tobacco cases are examples.[2]

In the real economy we invest for building up production tools through the traditional industrial method. In the service economy the system of capital accumulation and utilization is utterly different. Services cannot be stored or inventoried like industrial produce, and this has a profound influence on the functioning of the financial system and the social system. It also has an impact on economic cycles.

A service economy brings up the need to face longer-term future uncertainties seriously; which means accounting for them ahead of time. This is behind the difference between expected losses (EL) and unexpected losses (UL). To achieve workable solutions requires rethinking and re-evaluating the risk management policies we have in place, including policies and methods for damage control. Capital adequacy, as defined by Basel II, is a way to reach such a goal.

An integrative solution requires the introduction into economic analysis of both future risks and future cash flows, instead of emphasizing past costs as is presently done. Therefore, a great deal depends on prognostication, which is the essence of differentiating between expected losses and unexpected losses, with particular attention paid to the latter – one of the main themes of this book.

It is no more possible to prosper when past tendencies continue to prevail, than it is to defer complex decisions till crises arise. Also, as this and the subsequent chapters will document, past concepts regarding capital reserves are looking worryingly inadequate under modern business conditions. Capital adequacy is part of corporate culture – and corporate culture has more to do with top management's mind, and the policies which it follows, than with anything else.

1.2 The three pillars of Basel II

Basel's new capital adequacy framework rests on three pillars. Pillar 1 addresses capital adequacy. It also makes commercial banks partners to regulators in computing *individual capital adequacy* – or, more precisely, minimum capital requirements – under three solutions: *standardized*,[3] *foundation* IRB method and *advanced* IRB. The latter two are respectively known as F-IRB and A-IRB.

The basic objective of Pillar 1 is that credit institutions are well capitalized. Today, many analysts consider as *well-capitalized banks* those with capital equal to more than 10 percent of their assets, provided both capital and assets are weighted for risk. *Adequately capitalized* banks are usually those with capital of 8 percent to 10 percent of assets under the same conditions.

Below the 8 percent level comes the class *undercapitalized* credit institutions, while below 5 percent are those *significantly undercapitalized*, with equity of less than 2 percent of assets. These definitions look clear enough, but what exactly constitutes *capital* is not. There is Tier-1 (T-1), hybrid Tier-1 (HT-1), Tier-2 (T-2) and Tier-3 (T-3) capital. There are also plenty of exceptions. (More on this in Chapter 3.)

All three Basel II methods, designed to gage capital adequacy and promoted under Pillar 1, target financial staying power. Internal ratings-based solutions differ substantially from the standardized approach, because the banks internally assess their own key risk drivers, which serve as primary inputs to their computation of capital requirements. The same reason sees to it that IRB solutions have a much higher risk sensitivity, which benefits senior management and the bank as a whole. A practical application is that of *risk-based pricing* of financial products, discussed in Chapter 2.

Pillar 2 is the steady review of capital adequacy, along with other criteria of *prudential supervision*, by national regulatory authorities. The more freedom credit institutions are given in computing their capital requirements, the more regulators need to inspect the bank's procedures, systems and models used to establish their capital adequacy. This responsibility comes over and above already existing supervisory duties.

To serve in an efficient manner the requirements of Pillar 2, as well as the application of Basel II as a whole, the Basel Committee on Banking Supervision has established the Accord Implementation Group (AIG). Its goal is to provide a channel for national supervisors:

■ To exchange information on practical implementation challenges, and
■ To discuss strategies to address different issues as they evolve.

The Accord Implementation Group will collaborate with the Committee's Capital Task Force (CTF) whose aim is to consider interpretations of or modifications to Basel II. The Basel Committee has asked a group of supervisors from several countries around the world, with International Monetary Fund (IMF) and World Bank participation, to develop a framework for assisting regulatory authorities from non G-10 countries, as well as credit institutions, in the transition from Basel I to Basel II.

Pillar 3 is an active use of *market discipline* to encourage reliable financial disclosure. The basis for market discipline is *transparency* in financial accounts. Not only the regulators but also the market as a whole – including shareholders, bondholders, corresponding banks and other *counterparties* – will be looking over the shoulders of financial institutions, scrutinizing their dependability.

The term *counterparty* denotes an entity or person to whom the bank has an on-balance sheet and/or off-balance sheet credit or market exposure, or a potential exposure of another type. That exposure may, for example, take the form of a loan, a derivatives transaction or other commitment.

The common ground of Basel II's three pillars is the credit institution's own internal control (IC) system.[4] Without open feedback channels and unbiased information

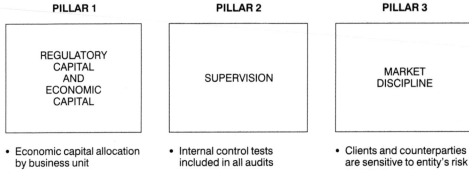

Figure 1.1 Internal control must be present with all three pillars of Basel II

reaching all levels of management, particularly the board and the chief executive officer (CEO), the notions and systems underpinning the three pillars will not stand. As Figure 1.1 suggests, internal control must be present in all three pillars of Basel II. It is a basic principle of management that of all manifestations of power, timely feedback and focused corrective action counts for the most.

As we saw in Table 1.1, it took several years, successive versions of consultative papers by the Basel Committee, and tests made by a growing number of commercial banks (see section 1.4), to converge towards a solution acceptable to the majority of credit institutions, even if certain players still have reserves of their own (see Chapter 16). A snapshot of what is and is not covered by the new regulations is shown in Figure 1.2. The following are the highlights.

■ Basel II integrates credit risk, market risk and operational risk, into a comprehensive system of supervision.

Banks must assure the capital adequacy for every one of their exposures along these three lines of reference. Provisions for operational risk are a new requirement. To face the challenge, credit institutions need to analyze their operational risks, identify the losses and provide adequate capital for future op risk events. This expands the domain of management control.

For counterparty risk, banks choosing the standardized approach will use external ratings by reputable independent agencies such as Standard & Poor's (S&P's), Moody's Investors Service, Fitch Ratings and other firms.[5] Alternatively, they will have to develop and use internal ratings, if they choose either F-IRB or A-IRB. Within limits, Basel II recognizes credit derivatives[6] as a means of managing credit risk volatility (see the discussion on securitization in Chapter 9).

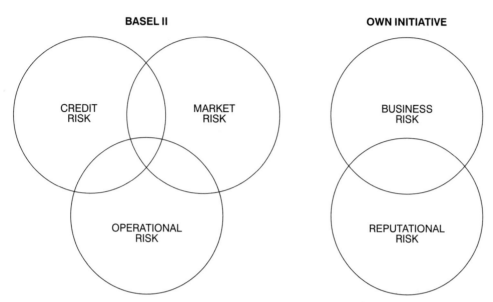

Figure 1.2 Risks covered by Basel II and what an institution must look after on its own

It is appropriate to bring to the reader's attention the fact that a rating system is not just grades and thresholds. As the Basel Committee aptly suggests, it comprises all methods, processes and controls – including data collection, datamining and other IT supports vital to the assessment of credit risk and the dynamic upkeep of grades pertaining to every rated entity or issue. Therefore, Basel says that, to qualify, an IRB solution must have two distinct dimensions:

■ Risk of borrower default (see Chapter 10), and
■ Transaction-specific factors influencing creditworthiness.

In regard to market risk, Basel II maintains the policies and methods advanced with the 1996 Market Risk Amendment (MRA).[7] Indeed, it capitalizes on the experience credit institutions have gained with the use of mathematical models in controlling market risk, and transfers that experience to the control of credit risk.

Figure 1.3 presents to the reader a snapshot of the credit risk, market risk and operational risk control methods, and their requirements. These will be discussed in greater detail in section 1.3. (In Figure 1.3 PD stands for probability of default, LGD for loss given default and EAD for exposure at default. Also VAR, is an abbreviation of value at risk, MRA of Market Risk Amendment, GI of gross income and IMA of internal measurement approach.)

■ At least for the time being, the Basel Committee leaves the control of business risk and of reputational risk to the bank's own initiative.

Business risk and reputational risk correlate. The former has many components which, though they do have financial impact, are not included in Basel II (see also section 1.7):

METHOD	CREDIT RISK (MAIN EMPHASIS)	MARKET RISK	OPERATIONAL RISK[1] (NEW EXPERIENCE)
STANDARDIZED	• INDEPENDENT RATING AGENCIES • PD, LGD, EAD BY REGULATORS	STANDARD METHOD BY 1996 MRA, WITH OFFSETS AND WEIGHTS	GLOBAL GI, OR • 8 BUSINESS LINES • 7 OPERATIONAL RISKS
FOUNDATION	• OWN RATINGS[2], OWN PD • LGD, EAD PARAMETERS BY REGULATORS	VAR, A LAGGING INDICATOR ANSWERING ONLY 35% TO 65% OF REQUIREMENTS	IMA IS NOT APPEALING. OPERATIONAL RISKS BY BUSINESS LINE ANYWAY NEED PLENTY OF DATA
ADVANCED[3]	• OWN RATINGS[2], PD, LGD, EAD	DERIVATIVES OF VAR, EIGENMODELS, STRESS TESTING	• LOSS DISTRIBUTION (BOTTOM-UP) • SCOREBOARD (TOP-DOWN)

NOTES:
1 THE TREND IS TO GO EITHER FOR STANDARD OR ADVANCED, NOT IMA.
2 BANKS SHOULD INCREASE GRADING TO SCALE OF TWENTY TO MATCH INDEPENDENT AGENCIES.
3 ROGER FERGUSON, FEDERAL VICE CHAIRMAN, SAID US SUPERVISORS INTEND TO APPLY ONLY A-IRB.

Figure 1.3 Standardized, foundation and advanced methods

for instance, misjudging evolution in the market environment, misappreciating the competitors' strengths and weaknesses, and miscalculating *our* bank's own strengths and weaknesses; also, falling behind in innovation of financial products.

The fact that with Basel II capital allocation and risk management correlate, increases the challenges faced by the board, the CEO and the executive committee. *Economic capital allocation*[8] must not only account for identified major areas of risk but also reflect on business perspectives. (Practical examples on economic capital allocation, which is the main theme of this book, are presented in Chapters 7 and 8.)

■ All risks faced by a bank are business connected, and
■ Economic capital allocation is indivisible from the management of risk.

The reasons which have been outlined, plus the amendments to the original Basel II consultative paper, made through the collaboration of big commercial banks, saw to it that the IRB method has become a sophisticated structure, and regulators try to simplify it. For instance, the definition of default has been reduced to two criteria:

■ More than 90 days past due, and
■ Unlikelihood to pay in full.

But new treatments have been added to meet the banks' concerns that the initial IRB correlations and weights were too onerous, and that too many reasons for capital requirements were included in Pillar 1. Regulators made some changes. Among these changes, residual risk on collateral and hedging has been moved to Pillar 2, project financing and specialized lending have been redefined, and so on The irony is that the more exceptions are introduced, the more complex tends to be the end result. These are some of the issues examined in the four chapters of Part 1.

1.3 A bird's eye view of standardized, foundation IRB and advanced IRB methods

The concept of global regulatory capital requirements has been first implemented with the Basel Capital Accord of 1988 (Basel I), which addressed exposures arising mainly from credit risks. It also specified that these must be backed by the bank's own funds (Tier 1) and some other eligible funds (Tier 2). Tier 1 and Tier 2 are discussed in Chapter 3. With the 1996 Market Risk Amendment, the algorithm became:

$$\frac{\text{Own funds} + \text{Other eligible own funds}}{\text{Risk-weighted exposures from credit risk} + \text{Charges for market risk}} \geq 8\% \quad (1.1)$$

This 8 percent has been a compromise which made possible the 1988 Capital Accord (Basel I). The question of how much capital should be reserved by banks for prudential management reasons has not been raised. Among European banks, between 1840 and the late 1870s, the average ratio of capital over assets fluctuated between 24 percent and 36 percent, with a mean value slightly above 30 percent. In the following twenty years, however, it dropped steadily and by 1900 it broke the 20 percent level.

In the inter-World War I/World War II years, the capital ratio stabilized in the 12 percent to 16 percent range, with a much smaller volatility than in the mid-nineteenth century. Then, it took a dive again during World War II. In the post-war years, and prior to the 1988 Capital Accord, the *average* capital ratio held was within a narrow 6 percent to 8 percent band – less than a quarter of what it was 100 years earlier, and half of what it had been in the inter-war period.

By itself, of course, the average does not mean much. Because for some banks the capital ratio had fallen below 4 percent, regulators had to act. Negotiations among Group of Ten supervisory authorities helped to establish a policy mapped into the equation we looked at previously.

The careful reader will appreciate that this equation contains several variables: own funds, other eligible funds and weights. To determine the risk-weighted exposures, the credit institution must establish on-balance sheet asset and off-balance sheet positions, and then apply regulatory weights. These are classified into risk buckets subject to prudential reference levels: 0 percent, 10 percent, 20 percent, 50 percent, 70 percent and 100 percent (Table 1.2 presents, as an example, risk categories according to the 1986 US Federal Reserve Proposals, which preceded the 1988 Capital Accord).

1 **Cash and equivalents (risk weight 0%)**

   1.1 US currency, coins due from Federal Reserve Banks
   1.2 Cash items in process of collection and transaction accounts, due from US depository institutions
   1.3 Short-term US Treasury securities in investment account
   1.4 Foreign currency and balances due from central banks in immediately available funds

2 **Money market (risk weight 30%)**

   2.1 Long-term US Treasury securities held in investment
   2.2 US Government agency securities held in investment
   2.3 Portions of loans fully guaranteed by US government
   2.4 Short-term claims on US depository institutions
   2.5 Acceptances of other US banks
   2.6 Federal funds sold
   2.7 Loans to brokers/dealers collateralized by US Treasury
   2.8 Assets held in trading account
   2.9 Legally binding loan commitments, including note issuance facilities

3 **Items with mortgage risk (risk weight 60%)**

   3.1 All state, county and municipal (SCM) securities in investment, including industrial development bonds
   3.2 All other claims on US depository instruments
   3.3 All other claims from governments and banks of industrial countries
   3.4 Acceptances of banks in industrial countries
   3.5 Local currency claims on governments and banks of non-industrial countries, funded by local currency
   3.6 Loans to brokers/dealers collateralized by other marketable securities
   3.7 Commercial letters of credit (LC)
   3.8 Standby LCs backing SCM securities, excluding those backing industrial development bonds

4 **Class of standard bank risk (risk weight 100%)**

   4.1 All assets found in a typical bank loan portfolio, including: all commercial/industrial loans and leases; residential real estate and individual loans; loans to non-depository financial institutions
   4.2 All other claims on foreign obligors
   4.3 Corporate securities and commercial paper, industrial development bonds
   4.4 Customers' acceptance liabilities, including liabilities associated with acceptance participations
   4.5 All other standby LCs (net), including those backing industrial development bonds
   4.6 Loans sold with recourse
   4.7 All assets not included elsewhere

Table 1.2 Risk categories according to the 1986 Federal Reserve proposals, and associated weights

Risk weights may change over time, but whatever their value might be they are always present because this is a way of expressing risk sensitivity. A classification in terms of weights is consistent with the fact that, by using weights and correlations (discussed in Chapter 11), regulators are after a factual and documented computation of capital ratios. Behind the drive for a rigorous approach lies the issue that:

- Banks expanded their assets too rapidly in the inflationary period of the 1970s, and perhaps took on excessive risk in doing so.
- Then, in the 1990s, banks expanded most significantly their leverage (see Chapters 2 and 9) assuming an even greater amount of exposure.

A good question is *who* provides the risk weights. Banks will slot exposures into bands according to whether the counterparties, or issues, are rated or unrated. For both the wholesale and retail market, weights are set by type of risk. For evident reasons, short-term exposures of less than three-month maturity receive preferential treatment. One of the aims of Basel II is to align risk weightings with the actual default risk in the way it is handled by the IRB methods (greater detail on weights is given in Chapter 12).

The use of the IRB approaches contrasts to the rather rigid standardized approach, where risk weights are laid down by supervisory authorities. With IRB, risk weights, and corresponding capital adequacy requirements, are computed on an exposure-specific basis, subject to a regulatory risk-weight function. Credit exposures assumed by an institution are divided into five classes:

- Corporate
- Bank
- Sovereign
- Retail, and
- Equity exposures.

Under the *foundation* IRB approach (F-IRB), banks assess the probability of default (PD) of their borrowers but regulatory capital for those PDs will be determined according to a formula set by Basel. The end capital requirement is the charge from this function multiplied by loss given default (LGD) and commitments included according to probable exposure at default (EAD). In brief, with F-IRB:

- The bank sets the PD,
- But Basel lays down LGD and EAD to be used.

By contrast, with the *advanced* IRB approach (A-IRB), the bank establishes all three parameters: PD, LGD and EAD. Retail exposures will be covered by A-IRB for all banks adopting this method. Also, with A-IRB, for the corporate, sovereign and interbank transactions, charges are adjusted for maturity. For all exposures to firms with an annual turnover of over $500 million, an explicit maturity function is compulsory.

A snapshot of differences characterizing the standardized, F-IRB and A-IRB methods is presented in Figure 1.4. As will be appreciated, IRB provides significant

METHOD / OBJECT	STANDARD METHOD	IRB FOUNDATION	IRB ADVANCED
RATING	EXTERNAL	INTERNAL	INTERNAL
PD ESTIMATE	NONE	OWN	OWN
LGD ESTIMATE	NONE	DEFINED BY SUPERVISOR	OWN
EAD ESTIMATE	NONE	DEFINED BY SUPERVISOR	OWN
MATURITY	NOT RECOGNIZED	NOT EXPLICITLY RECOGNIZED	DEFINED BY SUPERVISOR
RISK-MITIGATION FOR COLLATERAL AND PRODUCT CHARACTERISTICS	DEFINED BY SUPERVISOR	BY SUPERVISOR, THROUGH LGD AND EAD	OWN ESTIMATES, THROUGH LGD AND EAD

Figure 1.4 Credit risk measurement under Basel II (*Source*: Deutsche Bundesbank, Monthly Report, January 2003)

flexibility for measuring credit risk and this gives banks an incentive to progressively change their approach according to guidelines laid down by regulators. Nevertheless, whether the standardized, F-IRB or A-IRB approaches are used,

■ The resulting capital ratio to be observed by the bank may be no less than 8 percent.[9]
■ The 8 percent constitutes, so to speak, a floor. *If* the computed regulatory capital is less than 8 percent, *then* the difference might be seen as being part of economic capital (see Chapter 5).

Part of the value differentiation with new regulations comes from the fact that a risk-sensitive treatment of the bank's exposures is assured under Basel II by enlarging the recognition of guarantees and collateral (see Chapter 12). Eligible collateral and guarantees, including their range, depend on which solution a credit institution decides to use. With the advanced IRB approach, for example, banks may themselves determine:

■ The range of their eligible collateral, and
■ Loss rates resulting from mismatch between assumed collateral value and fair value.

In conclusion, both the foundation IRB and the advanced IRB approaches make use of credit risk models to calculate capital requirements. Such eigenmodels, however, must be granted prudential recognition by regulators. Some financial analysts expect that problems will be posed by stability of default correlations (see Chapter 11), modeling of portfolio effects, lack of market data on fair value of assets from lending business, and other factors. Another challenge is that of incorporating a multi-year time horizon rather than the one year classically being used by banks.

With the implementation of Basel II, each regulatory authority will have direct responsibility for validating the models developed and used by credit institutions under its authority. The challenge is that, unlike market risk where VAR is still king, there exists insufficient know-how on credit risk models as well as an incomplete pool of data for backtesting credit risk algorithms. This will change with time, as credit institutions gain experience with IRB.

1.4   Quantitative impact studies and capital adequacy

Basel II has been by no means a flat order given by regulators to bankers for immediate execution. Not only it has been the subject of extensive consultations with the banking industry through successive CPs, but it has also benefited from real-life tests whose results led to refocusing of norms and weights.

The first *quantitative impact study* (QIS) of Basel II took place in July 2000, following the June 1999 release of the original consultative paper (CP1). QIS2 followed QIS1 after the release of CP2, in April 2001. The objective of each of these QISs – and of those which came subsequently – has been to assess the likely effects on regulatory capital requirements for credit institutions.

The collaboration of the banking industry, which has been extended in connection with the quantitative impact studies, should in no way be underestimated. The last QIS (QIS3) has involved 350 credit institutions of varying size and levels of complexity, from more than forty countries.[10]

Results obtained through successive QISs indicated that there have been substantial differences in the impact of new capital adequacy regulations across the banking industry. Each QIS led to a revision of some of the rules steering capital adequacy computations. (A synopsis of the CP dates and QIS dates has been presented in Table 1.1.)

Each successive quantitative study had specific objectives and a more extensive impact than its predecessor(s). The aim of QIS2 was to look in detail at the effects of changes in risk weights and other variables. It involved 138 banks in twenty-five countries and, like QIS1, it showed substantial variation across institutions regarding the effects of both standardized and IRB approaches. As shown in Figure 1.5, in terms of overall results:

- The largest expected increase in regulatory capital under IRB was roughly 140 percent.
- By contrast, the biggest reduction for any bank was nearly 40 percent.

QIS2 involved fewer than twenty-four banks on the advanced IRB solution – where, as explained, the credit institution computes its own probability of default (PD), loss

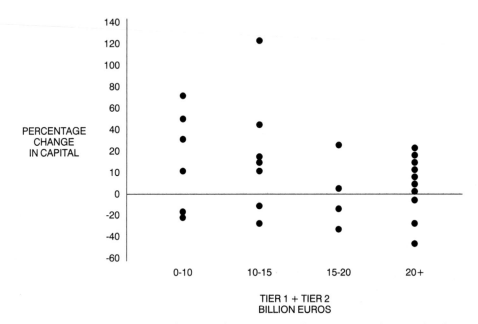

Figure 1.5 Original simulation of overall change in capital requirements for sample of G-10 banks with Tier 1 capital of at least 3 billion euros (*Source*: presented by the Bank of England at 'Capital allocation 2003' conference by IIR, London, 20–21 January)

given default (LGD) and exposure at default (EAD). In terms of an average in capital requirements, of the three methods – standardized, F-IRB and A-IRB – the latter came closer to the 8 percent of Basel I.

The higher capital requirements reached with the standardized and F-IRB approaches led to rethinking of risk weights. The new weights have been subsequently experimented with in the third quantitative impact study (QIS3). Notice that between the three major QISs there has been one, known as QIS2.5, whose objective was an early test of the effect of bending the risk-weight curves. In terms of capital requirements, the QIS2.5 outcome is presented in Figure 1.6.

Of these four quantitative tests – QIS1, QIS2, QIS2.5 and QIS3 – the most important has been QIS3. In the aftermath of QIS3, many analysts said that the universal banks in Europe passed the capital adequacy test on the strength of their retail books. On the contrary, the wholesale and investment banks had problems.

- Wholesale financial institutions were hurt because of loan losses.
- The challenge investment banks faced has been the loss of fees and commission because of market downturn.

The information QIS3 provided has enabled the calibration of norms and weights, paving the way for Basel II to be finalized by the end of 2003. Figure 1.7 presents sample QIS3 results for the world's largest forty-six banks, in their use of the standardized, F-IRB and A-IRB approaches.

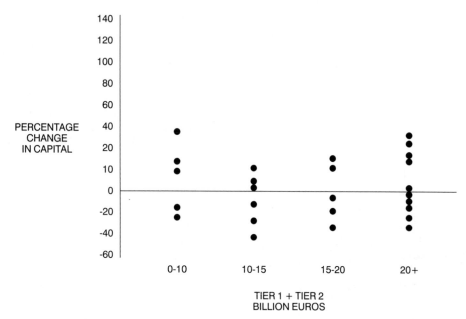

Figure 1.6 Simulation of overall change in capital requirements made after Basel's flattening of curves (*Source*: presented by the Bank of England at 'Capital allocation 2003' conference by IIR, London, 20–21 January)

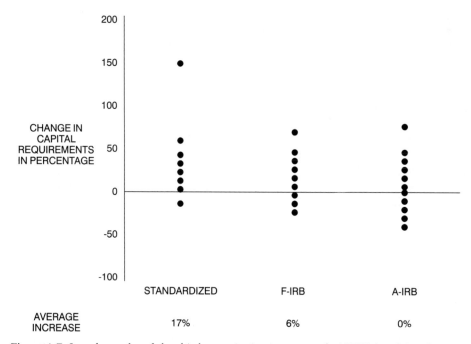

Figure 1.7 Sample results of the third quantitative impact study (QIS3) involving forty-six banks

- Overall, the outcome of the successive QISs indicates a rise in required regulatory capital, if credit risk and operational risk charges are taken together.
- The results also indicate that there are rather wide differences in capital needs between the standardized, F-IRB and A-IRB methods.

In a way, this has been inevitable because more sophisticated approaches, than a flat 8 percent regulatory capital, brought to the foreground the huge differences in counterparty exposure assumed by different credit institutions. Banks in control of their risks are rewarded. There is always an advantage to be gained with analytical approaches, particularly when they are executed with skill and dedication.

It is no less true, however, that different methods give different results as far as capital adequacy is concerned. The reader will notice in Figure 1.7 that only a few banks require less than 8 percent with the standard method, but many more banks could do with less than 8 percent with F-IRB and A-IRB, particularly in the case of the latter. At the same time, several of the banks participating in QIS3 have required much more than 8 percent in terms of capital adequacy.

- In regard to LGD, QIS3 has shown considerable volatility among credit institutions.
- Volatility has also been high in regard to exposure to default, and general commitments.

The third quantitative impact study acted as a magnifying glass of the risks taken by different credit institutions. Overall, however, results have been positive since they confirmed the regulators' aim that the new regime be more risk sensitive than the old. Some incentives for banks to progress to a more advanced method of calculating risk have also been demonstrated through the study's results.

It is appropriate to add that the early release of QIS3 output came from the Washington-based Institute of International Finance (IIF), an industry association for many of the world's big banks. As we will see in Chapter 16, IIF has been collaborating with regulators in the analysis and evaluation of quantitative impact tests.

The research meetings which led to this book have revealed that commercial bankers did not fail to notice that while, in general, with A-IRB the capital increase may be relatively small, the rise in capital requirements could be quite large for those with certain types of risky portfolios. It is inevitable that a more risk-sensitive capital framework would produce winners and losers. This is a direct aftermath of risk sensitivity, and it particularly concerns credit institutions actively engaged in:

- Securitizations
- Specialized lending
- Sovereign lending
- Interbank lending, and
- High-volatility commercial real estate.

Contrarians argue that greater risk sensitivity will establish artificial incentives for banks to structure their portfolios in ways that favor traditional lines of business and shy away from 'modern' credit intermediation activity. This is one of the arguments which does not rest on firm ground. On the contrary, as successive QISs have shown, IRB provides a useful compass in the uncharted territory of 'modern' credit intermediation.

There is no better way to document the foregoing statement than the distribution of results, as far as capital adequacy is concerned. The dispersion around the mean must always be expected in any distribution. But it is no less true that the standard deviation of QIS3 output in capital requirements is quite large.

- Table 1.3 compares the mean capital increase resulting from QIS2 and QIS3, for standardized, F-IRB and A-IRB methods.
- Table 1.4 shows the mean, standard deviation and range of results for a sample QIS3, as well as the quartiles.

	QIS2 (%)	QIS3 (%)
Standardized	+18	+17.7
F-IRB	+24	+ 6.1
A-IRB	+ 5	− 0.02

Table 1.3 A comparison of mean capital increase between QIS2 and QIS3 with the three Basel II methods

	Mean	Standard deviation	Range	Quartiles				
				0	1	2	3	4
Standardized	17.7	24.83	−9 to +150	−9.3	4.7	11.9	22.0	150.8
F-IRB	6.11	22.25	−35 to +76	−35.8	−7.2	4.8	19.5	76.1
A-IRB	−0.02	26.21	−48 to +87	−49.0	−17.6	−1.0	12.4	87.5

Table 1.4 Mean standard deviation range and quartiles for a sample of QIS3 results in capital requirements

The reader will notice that in Table 1.4 the standard deviation is too high. On the contrary, the level of quartiles is more comfortable. It is absolutely normal that banks which assume major risks will have to significantly increase their capital ratios, whereas, institutions which are well managed and keep their risks under lock and key do not have to worry about more capital. For instance, with A-IRB Citigroup will increase its funds required for capital adequacy by a mere 1 percent.

After all, what has the 8 percent of Basel I been? It has been an 'average', therefore, a compromise which rewarded highly risky credit institutions while it penalized those who were in charge of their risks. There is a joke about averages which has a biting message: it is that sort of logic which suggests that if one has one's head in an oven and feet in a freezer, 'on average he should feel alright'.

Let me repeat this reference to the effects of risk sensitivity because its message carries all the way to risk-based pricing, discussed in Chapter 2. The notion conveyed by the quartiles in Table 1.4 is that under all three methods some banks will need significantly more regulatory capital than Basel I demanded. For instance, banks falling into the upper quartile will require:

- Up to 150 percent more capital under standardized method
- About 76 percent more capital under F-IRB, and
- Some 87 percent more regulatory capital under A-IRB.

That said, there is no denying that there exist significant differences in QIS3 results between standardized, F-IRB and A-IRB approaches. These are both algorithmic and procedural. Under A-IRB banks have generally been using lower LGDs than required under F-IRB. They have been also giving more recognition to collateral.

To deal with this the Basel Committee has lowered the majority of supervisory LGDs in F-IRB by five percentage points. For instance, LGD on senior unsecured loans was lowered from 50 percent to 45 percent. Basel also recognized more forms of collateral with receivables, plant, machinery and inventory added to the collateral list. Also, commercial real estate has been included in F-IRB. But still regulatory capital requirements will not be the same as those of Basel I, no matter which method a bank chooses.

1.5   Examples of the potential sophistication of A-IRB method

As the reader will remember from the comparison of Basel II regulatory capital computation methods presented in section 1.4, one of the differences between F-IRB and A-IRB is that the latter allows banks to compute their own LGD and EAD. Another difference is that of maturity. In their advanced IRB calculations in connection to QIS tests, credit institutions have used separate maturities for individual loans. This gave a lower overall average maturity for corporate portfolios of about two and a half years rather than three years assumed in F-IRB. In the aftermath, the Basel Committee:

- Reduced to two and a half years the F-IRB maturity, and
- Left to national supervisions the option of using an explicit maturity adjustment in F-IRB.

There also exist differences in connection with instruments and the type of institution handling them. At the heart of this issue are the so-called *non-banks*, and the credit risk they represent in comparison to other counterparties like smaller, lesser known credit institutions.

There is no linear answer to the query which may be more risky – the non-bank or the small retail bank – because so many factors come into play in terms of creditworthiness. Other things being equal, on the one hand, a retail bank specializing in household mortgages is likely to have less exposure than a hedge fund. On the other hand, when it comes to credit derivatives, an institution like GE Capital gets 50 percent weighting while a small, shaky Mexican bank may get 20 percent weighting. The following ratios prevail with counterparty risk weighting under Basel I:

■ Government 0 percent
■ OECD Bank 20 percent (the Mexican bank case)
■ Other 50 percent (the GE Capital case).

Still other differences between Basel II approaches to regulatory capital relate to the calculation and use of correlations (see Chapter 11). Bringing in correlations between different underlying market factors essentially means that the bank is *netting*. The model supporting this netting operation, however, has two downsides: it might be netting asymmetric expenses, and it might become fairly complex. Therefore, its output needs to be regularly tested and calibrated.

Moreover, as far as netting is concerned, there are several general issues which must be considered. Some of these date back to the 1996 MRA and they may come up for review within a revised credit risk model, which provides bridges to market risk. An algorithm for credit add-on with bilateral netting advanced by certain institutions is:

$$A_{Net} = 0.4 \bullet A_{Gross} + 0.6 \bullet NGR \bullet A_{Gross} \qquad (1.2)$$

where A_{Net} = credit add-on with liberal netting
$\quad\quad\;\; A_{Gross}$ = original gross credit add-on
$\quad\quad\;\; NGR$ = net to gross ratio
$\quad\quad\quad\quad\;$ = ratio of $CMTM_{Net}$ to $CMTM_{Gross}$
$\quad\; CMTM$ = current marking-to-market.

What CMTM essentially means is the current market value of all transactions with the counterparty, including those involving credit risk, market risk or both. Banks are proposing to come up with a loans equivalent derivative exposure, which is a good idea.[11] An expected positive exposure indicated by 'α' can be a believable measure when:[12]

■ There are a very large number of infinitely small counterparty exposures, and
■ The average pair-wise correlation between market-driven counterparty exposures is zero, or nearly so.

Note, however, that unexpected risks and major counterparty exposures, or concentrations of minor ones, may bias netting results. The reason is that it only takes a couple of big failures to tilt the balance – thereby destroying netting hypotheses. Since this is a highly contested issue, I will keep it out of the present discussion whose objective is to explain the 'α' method.

Alpha, 'α', is the ratio of economic capital (see Chapter 5) based on the full simulation of market risk and credit risk scenarios, to economic capital based on the simulation of credit risk scenarios only. This type of simulation and associated analytical tests have been run by a few big banks, with different portfolios. They show that 'α' tends to be in the range 1.10 to 1.40, except for a few extreme portfolio configurations loaded with market risk.

The fact that this positive exposure tends to be in the aforementioned range indicates that the market add-on varies between 10 percent and 40 percent. With the exception of retail banks which shy away from market risk, the lower range seems to me to be based on wishful thinking since classically credit risk and market risk are characterized by an average ratio of 2/3 credit risk and 1/3 market risk.

The highest value of 'α', which, as I heard in a research meeting, has been calculated by an analyst at Goldman Sachs, is said to be around 2. The exact sort of portfolio it involves has not been stated. In all likelihood it is a portfolio loaded with market risk, since a ratio of 2 would indicate that exposure to credit risk and market risk tends to be equivalent.

In my research I also encountered an expanded credit risk matrix relating to different instruments and underlying market factors. This is shown in Table 1.5. However, one opinion which I greatly value has been that the pigeonholes in this credit risk matrix do not make much sense. For example, the potential exposure over the next year of a foreign exchange (FOREX) contract is the same, regardless of whether it concerns a one-year or a five-year period. No tests seem to have been done along these lines to establish the limits of pigeonhole values. The portfolios selected were fairly standard foreign exchange and derivative contracts.

Let me add that there should be no confusion between 'α' which stands for level of confidence, and is derived from an operations characteristics (OC) curve, and 'α' used with this metric. This is simply the symbol employed by the first person who proposed that there is something that should be measured in regard to the size of:

■ Credit risk and market risk
■ Versus credit risk alone.

The example I have just presented serves as another reference to the fact that the more sophisticated credit institutions are engaged in developing new models and metrics. They are also taking correlations into account to offset positions run at a confidence level of 99 percent, and involving a given holding period. Such models need to be backtested. This is what Basel wants. The banks say: 'We don't believe in backtesting,

Residual maturity	Less than 1 year (%)	1 to 5 years (%)	More than 5 years (%)
Interest rate	0.0	0.5	1.5
Exchange rate	1.0	5.0	7.5
Equity	6.0	8.0	10.0
Precious metals	7.0	7.0	8.0
Commodities	10.0	12.0	15.0

Table 1.5 Expanded credit risk matrix involving market factors

	Exceptions	Basel	ISDA
Green	0–4	1	1
Yellow	5	2	1.13
	6	2.2	1.17
	7	2.4	1.22
	8	2.4	1.25
	9	2.8	1.28
Red	10	3	1.33

Table 1.6 Multipliers for model accuracy after backtesting for repos and reverse repos

but *if* it is to be done, *then* we would like to use the multipliers proposed by ISDA.' These are different than the ones Basel has in mind, as shown in Table 1.6.

To explain the entries in Table 1.6, take as an example backtesting for repos (repurchase agreements), with the classical green, yellow and red zones defined by the 1996 Market Risk Management. In the pigeonholes of this table is the number of exceptions for each zone, as well as the penalties associated to them. Comparing the International Swaps and Derivatives Association's (ISDA's) proposal to Basel's proposal, one can easily see that the former is much more gradual.

Still another critical issue connected to the growing sophistication of modeling in the credit risk domain, is the financial industry's proposition for algorithmic solutions regarding repos and reverse repos. This is based on the notion of value at risk. The term is misleading because the algorithm in equation 1.3 has no relation to VAR classically used for market risk. The expected loss (EL) estimate is:

$$EL = PD \bullet LGD \bullet EAD, \text{ at a given confidence level, 99\% or higher} \qquad (1.3)$$

Also with this algorithm, backtesting seems to be a problem, starting with how such a backtest should be defined. Contrarians to the backtesting idea say that the bank may even buy and sell in the same day – let alone over a five-day holding period, and a 250-day historical timeframe. Some banks also add that backtesting the entire repos portfolio will be extremely difficult because of the need for clear profit and loss data. The counterargument is that models can run wild without regular and rigorous real-life tests – and this practically means backtests.

The reference just made to repos and reverse repos is so important because this market currently stands at the level of several trillions of dollars. The average volume outstanding of the US primary dealers reporting to the Federal Reserve Bank of New York is by itself almost $4 trillion. Banks say that if Basel maintains its original suggestion for high capital requirements associated to repos and reverse repos, this market may shut down overnight.

Several credit institutions suggest that repos should be treated as all other derivatives. The problem is that the derivatives market is so diverse, so complex, and is expanding so fast, that 'treating as all other derivatives' does not mean much.[13]

There is always a question of balance between cost, complexity and the absolute need for risk to be fully understood – which means that risk control must have the widest exposure.

1.6 The cost of Basel II

The methodology, models, management control and much finer mesh of credit ratings necessary for Basel II, as well as the change in internal culture, have a price tag attached to them. The object of this and of the following section is to bring to the reader's attention the most reliable guestimates for a Basel II budget. It will be left to Chapter 2 to outline the benefits credit institutions could expect for the money they will be spending in implementing the new capital adequacy framework – provided they run the whole operation in the most efficient way.

One of the first things which I learned in my postgraduate studies at UCLA, in the early 1950s, is that every well-managed project must have attached to it two very important questions, to which should be provided properly documented answers:

- How much it will it *cost*? (the subject of this section), and
- What kind of tangible *benefits* will it provide? (which is addressed in Chapter 2).

It should therefore come as no surprise that I asked both questions of every executive I met in my research. What I found in terms of the first is that nobody can answer today in a factual manner the cost question, particularly in terms of ensuring compliance with Basel II. Many experts said that, when we are going from 'here' to 'there', much depends in terms of costs and benefits on two factors:

- Where we start, and
- How effectively we conduct our business.

That said, the consensus has been that *costs matter*, and chief executives should be keenly interested in them. Like everybody else interested in cost control, chief executives are guestimating the expenditure. The CEO of Barclays Bank publicly said that:

- Basel II will cost his institution more than £100 million ($160 million) over the implementation period, and
- Of this amount about £60 million ($96 million) will be spent in 2003/04, including the cost of some fundamental studies like the one briefly depicted in Figure 1.8.

This is more than the cost of the Year 2000 (Y2K) project in some of the major financial institutions. Such Y2K reference is significant inasmuch as, according to several banks who expressed an opinion on the cost issue, the budget for Basel II implementation will probably match that of Y2K.

This is by no means money down the drain. The counterpart of money spent on Y2K has been that banks which used that budget not only to track bugs but also to renew their technology and get out of medieval mainframes and their 'legacy' (read

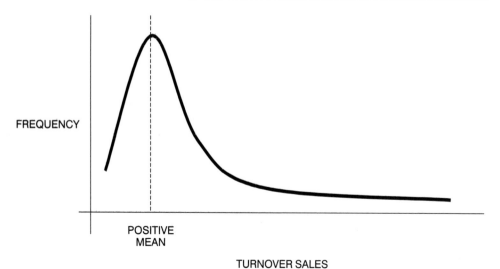

FREQUENCY

POSITIVE
MEAN

TURNOVER SALES

Figure 1.8 At Barclay's, experiments include historic turnover volatility, over a twenty-year timeframe

obsolete) software, got a great deal of benefit out of it. This benefit covered their costs and left a net profit. Therefore, it has been a good investment.

Barclays' $160 million budget is at the high end of the cost estimates I have received. Rabobank believes Basel II implementation costs will be more than $70 million, including IT. But Rabobank considers this figure acceptable because of the goals it has set itself:

- Risk-based pricing, and
- More efficient processes.

I have posed the query on better governance (see also Chapter 2) to many experts and in the majority of cases the answer has been: 'There will be a big difference in cost and benefit between banks who implement Basel II gradually, over a period of time, revamping their policies and processes along the way, and those who rush to do this job at the eleventh hour. Who does it at the eleventh hour pays top cost.'

One major bank mentioned that in the operational risk area alone, total cost is estimated between '$20 million and $50 million – double that money when the revamping of credit risk systems and procedures is included'. Other credit institutions estimated that, outside operational risk, their cost of Basel II will be another $30 million to $40 million over up to three years.

Such estimates bring total implementation costs of Basel II within the range of $50 million to $100 million and, in their way, they confirm what Barclays' CEO said. As one of my professors at UCLA taught his students: 'When you have put together your budget and double-checked your figures, double the sum you arrived at. This can give you a good indicator of what the project will cost in the end.'

- The challenge is to get significant benefit out of the Basel II investment – and, therefore, net profits.
- Economy does not really consist in saving the coal, but in effectively using the heat while it burns.

The Basel Committee, correctly, does not want to get involved in this costing issue, though the Washington-based IIF might. Here are some other opinions heard during my research meeting on the costing of Basel II: 'It does not come cheap', 'We've already spent a lot of money on it', 'Improving our bank's governance can justify the money and the effort'.

Nobody said they were afraid of the cost, and for good reason. *If* the number one goal is better governance, *then* the cost is part of the overall effort. Moreover, the by-product may also be quite important. 'Basel II may help top management in improving risk control' said one of the senior executives who participated in the research, adding that 'The fact that a financial institution is complying with the new rules is evidence that senior management is in charge, and this has a great deal to do with market discipline.'

Some vendors, too, have tried their hand in guestimating cost figures. One of the estimates I saw presented the Basel II budget as percentages related to current operating business costs per year. These percentages are supposed to run over several years. The ratios are:

- Big banks   4–5 percent
- Medium banks   6–7 percent
- Small banks   10–12 percent.[14]

It is too early to say whether this may be an underestimate or an overestimate, particularly because, as explained, opinions about budgetary requirements for Basel II range from simple to double – in connection with operational risk control and credit risk restructuring projects. Beyond this, identifying effective risk control methods and allocating economic capital will also require appropriate financing.

However, every credit institution should seek to protect itself from hype. While practically all banks, particularly the medium to smaller ones, will use consultants for implementing Basel II, senior management must be very careful as to what it pays and what it buys. There are plenty of alchemists offering their services, and money set aside for Basel II can disappear like quicksilver.

For instance, in a recent meeting, a consulting company produced the ridiculous histogram shown in Figure 1.9, which emphasized its own mythical 'best method'. This is a good example of how to lie with histograms. It introduces a new approach to the calculation of regulatory capital beyond A-IRB, vaguely labelled 'Best'. This is available to the client at the price of a long-term contract. Notice that the presenter has carefully abstained from defining what 'best' means – and for good reason.

On the other hand, lack of support by consultants will certainly put smaller credit institutions and emerging markets banks at a disadvantage because, as far as Basel II implementation is concerned, they simply do not have the data, skills and management understanding of challenges involved in implementing Basel II. They

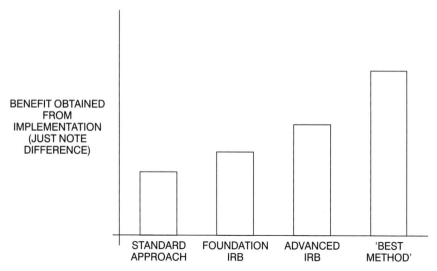

BENEFIT OBTAINED
FROM
IMPLEMENTATION
(JUST NOTE
DIFFERENCE)

STANDARD   FOUNDATION   ADVANCED   'BEST
APPROACH   IRB   IRB   METHOD'

Figure 1.9 How to lie with histograms: benefits from three Basel II approaches and a fake

need help to 'step up to the plate and play the game', but they should be very careful about what they pay and what they get in return.

1.7 Business risk and cost control

In the USA, the Office of the Controller of the Currency (OCC) has been actively discouraging small banks from using the IRB method, saying it is not applicable to them (see also Chapter 16). Some experts, however, suggest that the effort will be compensated for by the ability of smaller banks to renew and restructure their management support system, benefiting from enterprise-wide:

■ Information technology
■ Real-time solutions
■ Interactive databases
■ Credit risk control, and
■ The swamping of operational risks.

The point these experts make is that there exists a significant downside in non-compliance with Basel II. This downside can be phrased in one short phrase: 'Missing the opportunity to improve corporate governance'. In all likelihood, this failure will be manifested in a pronounced way in terms of business risk.

Section 1.1 presented a snapshot of business risks. Other business risks are erroneous estimates regarding the features of products and services, their popularity and their pricing. Pricing risk has two components. One is misjudging how much people and companies will pay for *our* bank's products. The other is failure to appreciate that *risk* is a basic *cost* component of all financial products. This is corrected through risk-based pricing, as we will see in Chapter 2. The reader should realize that:

■ Business risk is a residual risk with cyclicality, and
■ It is often expressed through fall in margin and/or loss of market clout.

While intimately relating to business risk, reputational risk has its own important characteristics, some of which have to do with market discipline. That is why in Figure 1.2 business risk and reputational risk do not completely overlap. The challenge for every risk manager is to perform the most severe and imaginative criticism of business and reputational exposures – and to do so before they get out of hand.

How can business risk be quantified and taken care of? A good example is presented through the approach taken by Crédit Suisse which accounts for business risk by reducing by 60 percent the goodwill in its balance sheet. Senior management reached this decision because goodwill is the area which will suffer the most from business risk events.

Another good example, one which is more analytical and takes costs into account, comes from Barclays Bank. The approach chosen by Barclays computes business risk through an algorithm which accounts for turnover, margin, fixed costs, variable costs and business volume:

$$\text{Business risk} = \text{Annual turnover} \cdot \text{Margin} - \\ (\text{Fixed cost} + \text{Variable cost} \cdot \text{Revenue volume}) \tag{1.4}$$

At Barclays Bank, experimentation connected to the business risk algorithm includes historic turnover volatility, margins, costs and revenues. Turnover studies are done over a twenty-year timeframe. The shape of the resulting distribution has been shown in Figure 1.8. Barclays proceeds with Monte Carlo simulation which selects values from this lognormal distribution, and applies last year's margin.

Business risk type losses may also occur, because of costs which have escaped management's attention and steady vigilance. It would be wrong to think that the more we spend on a service, the higher will be its quality. My experience tells me that quite the opposite is true. The only way to improve quality is to use a rigorous quality assurance system, like *Six Sigma*.[15]

Because of poor cost control policies inherited from the fat years of banking, credit institutions are not renowned for keeping their costs under lock and key. Documentation is provided by the cost to income ratio (also known as *overhead*) which can vary most significantly within the same institution. Take Allied Irish Banks (AIB) as an example. The cost to income ratio is:

■ 50 percent in Ireland
■ 54 percent in its operations in the UK
■ 62 percent in the US – AIB's Allfirst subsidiary.

In Ireland, the 50 percent ratio is relatively good, although below 50 percent would have been better. But 62 percent is inexcusable – even if there exist in the banking industry those that are worse than that. Apart from the fact that a high cost to income ratio means money being wasted, a critical question is how quickly can a bank adjust its cost base when revenues fall? Carelessness in cost control can be deadly – both for fixed costs and for variable costs. The ratio of variable cost to fixed cost depends on the business line.

■ Retail banking has high fixed cost because of branches.
■ Investment banking and wholesale banking have high variable cost.

Bank efficiency expressed through cost to income ratios has been an often recurring theme in my years of experience. Let us face it, banks are not very efficient. One of the reasons why commercial paper and different forms of asset-backed financing has replaced, to a significant extent, classical bank loans, is the inefficiency of the banking system. The total cost of intermediating a security over the life of an asset is:

■ Under 50 basis points in capital market operations
■ But over 200 basis points in banking intermediation.[16]

Low cost to income ratios and high efficiency correlate. To give perspective on trends and to enable corrective action, all cost management models must be calibrated to one-year and five-year time horizons. This is shown in Figure 1.10 through an example from Landsbanki, Iceland's premier credit institution. For starters:

■ The job of keeping costs under control is never ending.
■ When costs escape control the only way to right the balances is by re-engineering and downsizing, aimed at turnaround.

Commenting on the turnaround of Bethlehem Steel, an article in *The Economist* stated: 'Credit must go in part to Wilbur Ross, who played a canny hand. Although

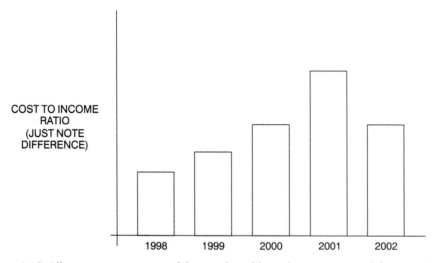

Figure 1.10 All cost management models must be calibrated to one-year and five-year time horizons: Landsbanki is an example

he made deep cuts among LTV's blue-collar workers, (he) was far more savage with
the firm's bloated corporate management.'[17] Just 15 percent of former white-collar
staff were kept on by International Steel Group which absorbed Bethlehem Steel.

Cost control, as such, is not part of Basel II, but the costs of its implementation are
an integral part of it, and such costs must be managed efficiently. This has been the
objective of bringing to the reader's attention the foregoing examples. Moreover, the
structural and cultural changes Basel II brings with it are an excellent opportunity to
revamp the credit institution's cost structure. Clear-eyed management will see to it
that such an opportunity is not missed.

1.8   Is Basel III coming at the heels of Basel II?

Last, but not least, is the issue of Basel II versus Basel I. How are the regulators
looking at Basel II compared to the capital adequacy regulations which it replaces?
'The old capital accord (Basel I) stands like an old ruin in the landscape, eroded by
many forms of capital arbitrage,' said J. Sanio, president of BAFIN, the German bank
regulator, and member of the Basel Committee. According to the Deutsche
Bundesbank:

■ Basel I is a crude measure for credit risk.
■ Basel II is better, though it may still have some shortcomings.

In his keynote lecture at the September 2003 International Capital Allocation
Conference[18], Bertrand Rime, Vice President, Systemic Stability: Research & Policy,
Swiss National Bank (SNB), and SNB's representative to the Basel Committee, said
that Basel II contributes to improving the level field because it reduces current
distortions. He also added that much will be learned with Basel II through its
implementation.

Rime's point of view has been that, as far as central bankers are concerned, Basel
II is not perfect. But, in most respects, it is the best that can be presently done to
improve the risk-sensitivity of capital requirements by commercial banks. As such, it
is an entirely new prudential instrument with two sides of important implications. For
instance, in terms of procyclicality:

■ During a downturn Basel II will impose tighter capital constraints on banks.
■ But it will also contribute to preserve the stability of the banking system during a
  downturn, which is a key condition for the availability of credit.

The benefits to be derived from the existence of sophisticated management control
mechanisms embedded in Basel II has seen to it that several credit institutions now go,
on their own initiative, for the internal ratings-based (IRB) methods. Take Switzerland
as an example. In 2000 only a couple of big banks said they would adopt IRB. In
2003, several Swiss banks are developing and implementing an IRB solution.

The way Dr David Lawrence, European Head of Risk Methodologies and
Analytics, Citigroup, looks at the rules and mechanisms of Basel II is that: 'We would
have done what we do with Basel II anyway, but at very slow timetable. Basel II

	Basel I	Basel II		
		Standard	F-IRB	A-IRB
United States	Yes	No	No	Yes top 10 only
Canada	No	Yes	Yes	Yes
European Union (CAD 3)	No	Yes	Yes	Yes
Japan	No	Different model for local banks	Yes	Yes
Australia	No	Yes	Yes	Yes
New Zealand	No	Yes	No	No
India[1]	Yes	No	No	No
China[2]	No	No	No	No

[1]This leaves open the issue on how India will manage risks taken by international banks
[2]China will have its own regulations, but experts say these will not manage the real risks

Table 1.7 Divergence in the implementation of Basel II may bring less international harmonization than Basel I

increased the pressure to do the right thing.' In other terms, Basel II has acted as catalyst of needed changes in risk management culture.

Other American bankers pointed out that even if US regulators allowed the majority of credit institutions in their jurisdiction to stay with Basel I (see also Chapter 16) the Fed, OCC and FDIC have already in place a virtual Pillar 2 – with strong regulatory supervision. The rules characterizing the risk control initiative taken by the Federal Reserve and the other US regulators include limits to leverage.

Indeed, senior American bankers have expressed regret for the Fed's decision to leave a big chunk of the American banking industry off-Basel II, and this for two reasons. First, it deprives US credit institutions from the opportunity to sharpen up their management control system through IRB and the operational risk models – improving risk visibility (more on this in Chapters 2 and 16). Second, it reduces international harmonization.

Table 1.7 gives a snapshot on this reference through a sample of eight countries and their choice of Basel I, Basel II, or other regulatory guidelines. Perhaps the greatest weakness of Basel II has been that it left too many degrees of freedom to each jurisdiction, thereby making it possible to game the system to one's own detriment.

For instance, it is said that New Zealand's regulators have told the country's banks: 'No AMA (for operational risk); no IRBs.' This is the opposite of what the neighboring Australian regulators said to that country's banks. A similar case of heterogeneity and conflict of interest between neighboring countries exists between the United States and Canada – both members of EFTA.

The issue of international harmonization would haunt regulatory authorities and commercial bankers for many years. The silver lining is that such discrepancies, and the problems they bring with them, will eventually lead to global standards. As one of the commercial bankers put it during the September 2003 International Capital Adequacy Conference: 'Basel III is coming in the heels of Basel II.'

Notes

1 A brief historical reference is in the Appendix
2 D.N. Chorafas (2004). *Operational Risk Control with Basel II*. Butterworth-Heinemann.
3 A *simplified standardized* approach has been introduced with the Basel Committee on Banking Supervision's *Consultative Document: Overview of the New Basel Capital Accord*, released in April 2003. It consists of the standardized approach for credit risk and the basic indicator for operational risk.
4 D.N. Chorafas (2001). *Implementing and Auditing the Internal Control System*. Macmillan.
5 D.N. Chorafas (2000). *Managing Credit Risk, Volume 1: Analyzing, Rating and Pricing the Probability of Default*. Euromoney; D.N. Chorafas (2000). *Managing Credit Risk, Volume 2: The Lessons of VAR Failures and Imprudent Exposure*. Euromoney.
6 D.N. Chorafas (2000). *Credit Derivatives and the Mismanagement of Risk*. New York Institute of Finance.
7 D.N. Chorafas (1998). *The 1996 Market Risk Amendment: Understanding the Marking-to-Model and Value-at-Risk*. McGraw-Hill.
8 Economic capital should not be confused with regulatory capital. It is defined in Chapter 5.
9 Basel Committee on Banking Supervision (2003). *Consultative Document: Overview of the New Basel Capital Accord*. BIS, April.
10 Ibid.
11 D.N. Chorafas (2003). *Stress Testing: Risk Management Strategies for Extreme Events*. Euromoney.
12 Do not confuse with α which identifies the level of significance.
13 See D.N. Chorafas (1996). *Managing Derivatives Risk*. Irwin.
14 Presented at 'Basel II Masterclass', an international conference organized by IIR, London, 27–28 March 2003.
15 D.N. Chorafas (2001). *Integrating ERP, CRM, Supply Chain Management and Smart Materials*. Auerbach.
16 J.B. Caouette, E.I. Altman and P. Navayanan (1998). *Managing Credit Risk*. Wiley.
17 *The Economist*, 11 January 2003.
18 Zurich, September 16/17, 2003; organized by IIR

2 Benefits from risk-based pricing and rating targets

2.1 Introduction

One of the foremost impacts of Basel II is better governance through emphasis on risk management, risk-based pricing and internal control. Other benefits are derived from consistency of client rating methods, which helps in making the governance of larger financial institutions better focused as well as more homogeneous than it used to be.

Eugen Buck, managing director of economic capital of Rabobank Nederland, mentioned during our meeting that, according to the Dutch Bankers Association, Basel II is quite a change in the development and implementation of credit risk policies and procedures. This is particularly visible in terms of:

- Credit risk modeling, and
- The way banks look at the credit process as a whole.

Other bankers have expressed a similar opinion. They are looking at Basel II as a significant improvement over the existing capital accord (Basel I), because it differentiates more effectively the levels of credit risk, reinforces trends firmly in place and obliges financial institutions to use advanced credit risk management policies and tools. Part and parcel of the latter is increased emphasis on stress testing.[1]

The upside is that by encouraging risk-based pricing, Basel II provides an advantage to banks with rocket scientists and high technology. Credit institutions which are ahead of the curve will be able to fine-tune their capital at risk. This is one of the major elements expected to change the competitive landscape of the banking industry in the coming years. By so doing, it will bring:

- Better quality management, and
- Appropriate internal control procedures.

Another advantage of Basel II is the flexibility it provides in terms of its implementation, on account of the fact that the best way to measure, manage and mitigate risks differs from one bank to the next. Hence, the need to make available a spectrum of approaches in determining capital levels, ranging from simpler to more advanced methodologies for the measurement of:

- Credit risk, and
- Operational risk.[2]

The implementation of one of the solutions promoted by the new capital adequacy rules, is subject to supervisory review. In general, however, Basel II's methodology rewards the more accurate risk measurement and management solutions. By adopting approaches which are sensitive to risks, banks can compute capital requirements that are more in line with their exposure. As a consequence,

- A credit institution becomes better able to manage risks through periods of stress, and
- This makes the banking system not only safer and sounder, but also more efficient.

To really benefit from Basel II, banks must nevertheless realize that they have to become proactive. Not only is the amount of effort required to modify existing systems and procedures to support Basel II requirements important, but also speed of action is crucial. Speed of action can be obtained only when the whole organization moves forward as one, without reserves and dispersion of effort – which in practice means when top management is in charge.

At the same time, the fact Basel II has many positive aspects, like encouraging risk-based pricing and prompting banks to use high technology for fine-tuning, does not mean that no problems or negatives exist. A major question with Basel II is the methodology associated with its implementation, which defines both return on investment (ROI) and future competitive position. It boils down to this:

- Will *our* bank operate differently in five years?
- How much better off are we going to be, compared to our competitors?

Another critical question is that of the degree of freedom left to national supervisors. In practice, the so-called national exceptions will permit national regulations to tilt the playing field. Critics say that national discretion will end up with a two-speed banking system, or a notable discrepancy between big and small banks. Time will tell whether these criticisms are well founded. This is not the present chapter's mission. Instead, its theme is how banks can be ahead of the curve.

2.2   Risk-based pricing. a major benefit from Basel II

The Introduction brought to the reader's attention that benefits from the new capital adequacy rules include, among other things, better governance, improved risk management and risk-based pricing. The better way of looking at Basel II is that it fulfills two goals. The one more commonly discussed is that of upgraded regulations which rests on the three pillars of minimum capital requirements, supervisory review and market discipline. The other goal which has received less publicity so far, yet is just as important, is that of:

- Increasing in a substantial way the risk sensitivity of senior management, and
- Leading towards an effective link between regulatory capital, risk management and economic capital.

What has been stated in a nutshell in these two bullet points provides a credit institution with the high ground in its competition with other banks. The board, CEO

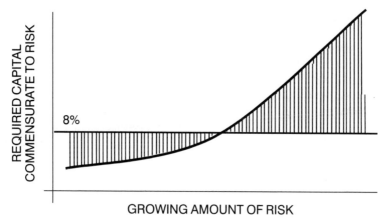

Figure 2.1 Risk-based pricing sees to it that capital requirements are dynamic, while a fixed 8 percent ratio is static

and senior executives should appreciate the advantages derived from improving management's sensitivity to risks being taken. In conjunction with the proper allocation of economic capital, risk sensitivity makes feasible credit rating targets like AA or AA+ (more on this in section 2.4).

- As Figure 2.1 shows, risk-based decision is a proactive method to compute capital needs.
- By contrast, fixed ratios like a flat 8 percent are passive, and they say nothing about assumed exposure.

Other benefits, too, are possible. Some of these are a function of the level of sophistication a credit institution chooses within Basel II. For instance, banks able to apply A-IRB may shift some of their bad risks to those who are still with:

- The 8 percent of Basel I, or
- The standardized approach of Basel II.

The A-IRB models can also serve as an early warning system, and provide the ground for flexible business policies. An example is lending for five years but adjusting the pricing of the loan every year as a function of the counterparty's credit quality. As Chapter 13 documents, this can be achieved through the use of:

- RAROC, for risk-based pricing
- KMV, for defining default points
- BCAR, for established economic capital requirements.

Risk-based pricing is a totally different method to the classical way banks price their loans and other products. The reason is that, traditionally, the lender's dependability, which has always been part of the equation, is often underestimated. Basel II changes this by obliging banks to quantify risk, as Chapter 1 has shown through the results of QIS3.

To better appreciate the foregoing statement, we should take a quick look at the origins of risk and some basic notions associated with it. One of the reasons behind risk is *volatility*, and the correlation which exists between markets and instruments. The more correlated are markets, the wider is the spread of volatility hitting a market, institution or instrument.

Another reason behind risk is *uncertainty*. In this connection a distinction should be made between expected events and unexpected events. Just as important is the frequency and impact characterizing each of these events, distinguishing between those which are:

- High frequency/low impact (HF/LI), usually expected events, and
- Low frequency/high impact (LF/HI), typically unexpected events.

A third major determinant of risk is *liquidity* in all of its aspects. Both market-wide liquidity and liquidity characterizing our bank's treasury should be considered. Based on the Deutsche Bundesbank's 2002 *Annual Report*, Table 2.1 outlines the factors determining bank liquidity. Lack of liquidity was the major reason which brought down Long-Term Capital Management (LTCM).[3]

Liquidity should not be confused with *solvency*, which is the fourth key component of risk (see also Chapter 6 on solvency management). A company is solvent when its assets, priced at *fair value*, that is, in a factual and documented manner under other

---

A. Provision (+) or absorption (−) of central bank balances by:

Change in volume of banknotes in circulation
Change in general government deposits with the banking system
Change in net foreign reserves
Other factors

B. Monetary policy operations:

Open market operations
Main refinancing operations
Longer-term refinancing operations
Other operations
Standing facilities
Marginal lending facility
Deposit facility

C. Change in credit institutions' credit balances (A + B)

D. Change in the minimum reserve requirement (according to Capital Accord)

Note: 1 Abbreviated version of a table in Deutsche Bundesbank's 2002 Annual Report.

Table 2.1 Factors determining bank liquidity[1]

	AAA	AA	A	BBB	BB	B
One-year average rate	0.0	0.01	0.04	0.22	0.98	5.3
Three-year average rate	0.0	0.08	0.19	0.77	5.27	14.9

Note: 1 Default rates for static pools, 1981–2000, by Standard & Poor's.

Table 2.2 A risk base realistically reflects the fact that default rates vary enormously by rating[1]

than fire-sale conditions, exceed its liabilities. For risk control purposes, senior management should always keep a close eye on:

- Reasons for a trend toward insolvency
- Possibility of fast realization of assets, and
- The steady tracking of default point (DP, see Chapters 5 and 9).

All the reasons briefly outlined in this text contribute to the notion of *risk-based capital* which shapes the capital requirements curve we have seen in Figure 2.1. The reader will appreciate that a risk base realistically reflects the fact that default rates vary enormously by rating, as shown in Table 2.2.

It needs no explaining that there are prerequisites to an effective risk-based pricing of financial products. The network of functions necessary to implement such policies and procedures is shown in Figure 2.2. It is important to notice that the concept of risk-based pricing, as well as the policies and procedures which should be followed, serve all channels:

- Loans
- Trades, including derivatives
- Investment decisions, and
- Portfolio management.

Therefore, risk-based pricing is a strategy which should be used throughout the bank for all its products and services, with every counterparty, anywhere it operates. The challenges are how quickly we can turn the bank around to apply it, how to use it for optimization and how to take care of after-effects.

For instance, risk-based pricing might lead to exiting some markets, or to the shifting of bad risks from A-IRB banks to others. Indeed, smaller banks are worried about being considered a second-tier institution by the market, rating agencies and sophisticated customers.

2.3 Targeting an 'AA' and 'AA+' rating

It has been a deliberate choice to follow up major benefits gained through the implementation of Basel II, like better governance, risk-based pricing and more

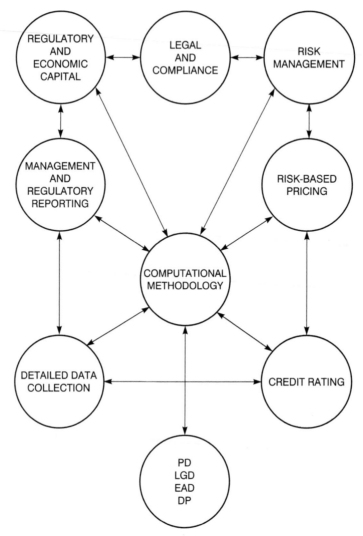

Figure 2.2 The network of functions necessary to implement risk-based pricing of financial products

focused risk management, by the theme in this section's heading. This obliges us to use the term *economic capital* before it is fully defined and discussed. (The reader will find its definition in Chapter 5.)

In the longer run, targeting a specific rating by independent agencies may well prove to be one of the most interesting, if not outright most important, aftermaths of Basel II. Ten other projected benefits which will help in the resilience of credit institutions, as well as in better governance, are:

1 Significant increase in capital adequacy.
2 Greater accuracy in calculation of capital requirements.

3 Better appreciation of need for risk control.
4 More meaningful differentiation of risk thresholds.
5 The beginning of greater emphasis on unexpected losses.
6 Awareness of need to address tail events in risk distributions.
7 Risk-based pricing.
8 Product pricing observing time horizon, and time brackets.
9 Upgrading of regulators skills, in many countries.
10 Global spread of Basel II rules and principles, as it has happened with Basel I.

There are also areas where Basel II will have little or no impact. For instance, effective diversification, across the board improvement in management quality, a 'scientific' definition of correlations and weights, as well as massive change from Paleolithic information technology culture to high technology.

A factual and documented economic capital allocation, specific targets in credit rating, models and experimentation to validate economic capital decisions are critical elements in better governance. Walter Pompliano of Standard & Poor's said: 'We don't prescribe an economic capital allocation model; we evaluate what the bank has,' adding that:

- 'Market behavior cannot be modeled
- But modeling is useful as a discipline.'

Modeling forces the pricing of risk. The downside is that clients may not pay the premium because of tough competition, they cannot afford to pay the premium because of poor economic conditions or they find other excuses to forego putting up the capital.

Neither is economic capital alone sufficient to give high credit rating; sound capitalization is a necessary but not sufficient condition for high credit rating. 'We look at capital but also beyond capital,' said Pompliano. 'For instance,

- 'management decisions
- management actions
- corporate outlook
- risk appetite
- risk control
- access to funding
- franchise
- buybacks
- diversification
- change in risk profile.'

Any one of these factors may not allow an AA credit rating. Rating has a lot to do with the dynamics of the company and of the market, and independent rating agencies have good experience in the discovery of weak spots.

Today, for practically all credit institutions, targeting a specific rating by independent agencies is a new experience. It is made feasible through appropriate financial reserves, the best possible allocation of economic capital to the bank's business units and the other factors mentioned in the previous list. The reference to 'appropriate reserves' essentially means improving the credit institution's financial staying power – and, by extension, the way its business partners look at its survivability. This can be done in different ways, as we will see in Chapters 6, 7 and 8.

The post-World War II years used to be a time when many credit institutions had a triple-A (AAA, Aaa) rating by independent rating agencies. With the exception of banks fully supported by the state, today only Rabobank is honoured with AAA. Major bad loans, project financing of deals which failed, huge exposure to derivative financial instruments and other reasons, saw to it that:

- The large majority of banks lost the triple-A.
- Many do not even command a double-A (AA, Aa) rating, and
- There is an awful lot of banks, including big ones, in the triple-B (BBB) category – with quite a few being non-investment grade entities (BB or less).

It is not the objective of this book to discuss how independent rating agencies assign a symbol representing creditworthiness to a financial institution.[4] The reader should, however, keep in mind that financial staying power – and therefore ample economic capital – underpins a high rating grade. This is precisely why Basel II helps in targeting double-A, or even triple-A.

I just mentioned that Rabobank commands an AAA. This institution has five major divisions, including insurance, but nearly 50 percent of its revenue comes from just one of them: retail banking. This is a very important factor to independent rating agencies, because well-managed retail banking gives a good cash flow and a relatively stable profit and loss (P&L) – which evidently impact on credit rating.

Another characteristic of Rabobank is that it pays a great deal of attention to economic capital and its allocation. This is tantamount to saying that it is very capable in managing its risks. Other banks, too, come close to such statement. According to Tim Thompson, head of economic capital, Barclays Bank, economic capital contrasts to regulatory capital in the sense that it is basically risk capital representing:

- Retail market risk
- Wholesale market risk
- Fixed assets risk
- Private equity risk
- Insurance risk
- Pension fund risk
- Residual value risk.

The second major difference between economic capital and regulatory capital is that the latter buys the bank a license from supervisory authorities, while the former is used for calibration to target credit rating. Economic capital also covers diversification and correlation effects (more on the contrast between economic capital and regulatory capital in Chapter 5).

As we will see in Chapter 3, regulatory capital is a subset of the broader notion of economic capital, and comprises Tier 1 (T-1 or core capital), Tier 2 (T-2) and Tier 3 (T-3) capital. The regulator defines the assets in each tier. Rating agencies said that when assessing 'A', 'AA' or 'AAA' they give high importance to T-1 capital, without hybrids and gimmicks.

At Rabobank, the capital base is pure Tier 1: Equity and retained earnings. It is evident that rating agencies appreciate this prudent policy. A good question is: 'How much more capital does a credit institution need beyond regulatory capital for 'AAA' over 'AA'?

- Should this difference be 10 percent, 20 percent or more?

There is no precise answer to this query, because other factors play a key role in financial staying power – and therefore in credit rating. It should, however, be noted that a similar critical question applies, the other way around, to downgrading. Indeed, some rating agencies suggested that:

- *If* a credit institution has only regulatory capital to cover credit risk,
- *Then* it may be a 'BB' or 'BBB' bank. (See also in Chapter 10 the discussion on the difference between bank failure and bank default.)

Targeting 'AA' credit rating is an imaginative business, but it is not an easy one. As 'AA', and even more so as 'AA+' or 'AAA', the bank must have more economic capital than otherwise. It should also appreciate that target rating:

- Is global, and
- It can be a financial burden.

Another basic characteristic of target rating is that it constitutes a moving target, since it is a lagging indicator depending on assumed risks (credit, market, operational), transfer risk(s), credit cycle, quality of management and, evidently, economic capital. Therefore, it is better to put limits – like a range 'AA+' to 'AA–' when 'AA' is targeted – or use fuzzy sets as shown in Figure 2.3.

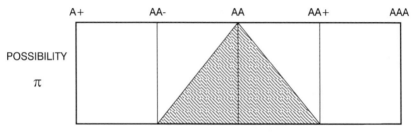

Figure 2.3 A bank should be more flexible than a single rating: targeting 'AA' is not an exact science

2.4   How will Basel II affect credit institutions?

If I were to pick one thing as the most remarkable in connection with Basel II, it would be the novelties it contains as a regulatory framework. To work with it, commercial banks have to change culture and tools. Many concepts which have over the years become familiar, will no longer apply.

Moreover, some of the old procedures will need to be reversed in order to answer in an able manner not only the new capital adequacy requirements, but also challenges associated with economic capital and its optimal allocation to the bank's business units. Nobody today can say for sure how the implementation of the rules embedded in Basel II will develop by the end of this decade as:

■ Qualitative measures guiding management's hand are redefined
■ Experience is gained with the use of advanced quantitative measures, and
■ A number of surprises develop as banks, so to speak, start marking their own financial examination papers.

When it comes to reversal of procedures which have been handed from father to son, the lawn sprinkler provides a familiar example of uncertainty: what is going to happen when it is made to suck water? Will it spin in the same, counterclockwise, direction? Will it go in the opposite direction, that is, clockwise? Or, will it behave otherwise? Look at the diagram shown in Figure 2.4.

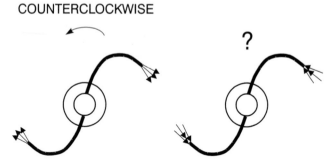

Figure 2.4 The lawn sprinkler problem: what happens if it is made to suck water?

This is a practical case. The sprinkler question was posed in 1940 at Princeton University's physics laboratory, to some of the best brains who later contributed to the Manhattan Project. 'It is clear to me at first sight,' said one of the professors. 'It's clear to *everybody* at first sight,' answered Dr Richard Feynman. 'The trouble is':

■ 'Some guy would think it is perfectly clear one way, and
■ Another guy would think it is perfectly clear the other way.'[5]

Scientists asked Dr John Archibald Wheeler, the physics department top authority, for his verdict. He said: 'Feynman had convinced me the day before that it would go clockwise (backward). But today Feynman absolutely convinced me it would still go as usual counterclockwise. And I do not know yet which way Feynman would convince me the next day.'

The next day Feynman did a physical experiment with the sprinkler. Prior to giving up the answer which is documented by this experiment, which way do *you* think that the sprinkler went:

- Clockwise (backward)?
- Counterclockwise (as usual)?
- Or, otherwise?

The answer is *otherwise*. First, when the flow was inverted, nothing really happened. The sprinkler did not move. Then, as Feynman mounted the pressure, the sprinkler exploded under the impact of two different, opposing forces. Nothing replaces a real-life test in providing evidence which is documented and indisputable.

This is precisely why the results of the quantitative impact studies (QIS2, QIS2.5, QIS3) of Basel II – which we examined in Chapter 1 – are so important. They documented which way the things fell with each consecutive consultative paper by the Basel Committee. By so doing, they contributed to:

- Improving clauses and weights of the new capital adequacy, and
- Making the new rules the outcome of an interactive process between regulators and commercial bankers.

As with Feynman's sprinkler example, different forces are at work with Basel II, finding their origin in the fact that regulators, bondholders, shareholders and managers of credit institutions do not necessarily have the same perspective. This is true even if they all look at future performance of financial entities and care for the deliverables these can offer.

- Shareholders look for quality of profits, amount of profits, dividends, increasing capitalization, and sound risk and reward tradeoffs.
- Bondholders are after good credit rating, principal protection, regular interest payments, strong capitalization and relatively low risk.
- Regulators try to keep capital requirements on a par with the evolution of the banking system and its risks, would like to see banks have 'AA' rating or better and want to avoid systemic risk, or pouring taxpayers money into defunct institutions.

Another major factor affecting the new capital adequacy requirements, and their implementation, is that the world of financial institutions is expanding, while formerly distinct areas of interest now overlap. This is indicated in Figure 2.5, which shows the major areas of finance and their common grounds eyed by all global players.

At the same time, banks with an international branch network are confronted by a horde of risks which they must monitor and control intraday on a global basis. These include counterparty risk, currency risk, interest rate risk, equity risk, position risk,

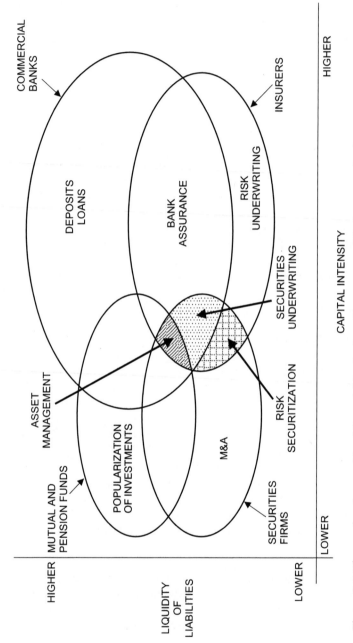

Figure 2.5 The overlapping worlds of financial institutions (*Source*: a modified version of a figure in Swiss Re's *Sigma*, no. 7, 2001)

event risk, and operational risks like transaction processing, funds transfer, sales conditions and, evidently, management risk.

As the business horizon expands and more opportunities unfold, there is no time for complacency or for taking it easy. One of the new 'don'ts' in banking is not to sleep on one's past product and service laurels, because competitors will be swinging ahead of the curve; another is not to take clients for granted, since the client can easily find a different institution with which to do business.

Chapter 1 has stated that costs matter. Therefore, banks should not let costs eat up profits, and they should never underestimate the role of high technology in finance. What is more, rigorous intraday risk control provides the best assurance for competitiveness because it exercises damage control before losses become catastrophic. This is precisely what underpins the importance of risk-based pricing.

2.5 Benefits on the road from Basel I to Basel II

To better appreciate the wider impact of Basel II, along Feynman's frame of reference, it is wise to take a quick look at Basel I and its aims. The 1988 Capital Accord had two objectives: assure sufficient capital in the global banking industry and create a level playing field for all banks. The trend line in Figure 2.6 shows that the first of these goals has been achieved. But Basel I also had some unwanted consequences. For instance,

- Banks went into more risky businesses
- Through derivatives, they assumed a growing amount of leverage
- Developed and sold some supposedly 'risk free' products
- Adopted higher risk lending practices, and
- Paid only lip service to risk-related pricing.

Since 1998, reports by the Bank for International Settlements (BIS) have offered illuminating statistics on exposures taken by credit institutions and particularly by big banks. Derivatives have been an instrument steadily used in bypassing the 1988 Capital Accord. Year after year, the trillions in notional principal amounts, in connection with derivatives products held in the portfolio of commercial banks, increased at an annual average of 25 percent to 30 percent.

Not only derivatives exposure grew by leaps and bounds but also the demodulated notional amount, to the level of loans equivalence (LEQ),[6] has been far from being covered by the capital reserves specified by Basel I – the famous 8 percent – even accounting for more reserves following the 1996 Market Risk Amendment. The years since 1988 have magnified the factor *risk*.

In 1998, the near bankruptcy of LTCM had affected bank psychology. After LTCM, many banks were writing down 5 percent of notional principal against the counterparty's credit limits – which is a way of accounting for LEQ, by demodulating the notional principal. Still, the overall derivatives exposure continued to grow as:

- Capital adequacy was exploited for loopholes, and
- Banks engaged in regulatory arbitrage.

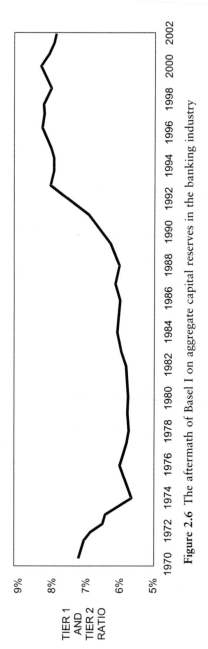

Figure 2.6 The aftermath of Basel I on aggregate capital reserves in the banking industry

At the same time, Basel I did not differentiate between high and low credit quality. The problem is that during the past twelve years credit quality continued to deteriorate. Because of this, the need for balancing became self-evident, and the transition from Basel I to Basel II is promising to give most instructive lessons.

Management can learn a lot from the implementation of Basel II because it is more comprehensive than Basel I, includes risk-sensitive clauses, is forward looking and it brings into the picture the market's reaction. It also pays attention to the fact that a risk-adjusted capital base cannot, all by itself:

■ Assure the solvency of a credit institution, and
■ Guarantee stability of the banking system.

At the bottom line, what is crucial is a bank's overall risk profile and its evolution over time. This underlines the need for accuracy in risk control. The pattern of exposure must be determined by senior management. Therefore, the Basel Committee wants to encourage further improvement in the banks' internal risk management systems – from monitoring, to database mining, and control action.

On the whole, the statements made in the preceding paragraphs show a paradigm shift towards banking supervision that is strongly quality oriented, while it uses quantitative methods not only for reporting, but also for experimentation. By all the evidence, in the coming years more extensive disclosure obligations for banks will become the rule, with market discipline employed to complement regulatory requirements and supervisory rules.

Taken together, the three pillars of Basel II determine the general framework. As Chapter 1 has explained, the standardized approach has a structure somewhat similar to the 1988 Accord but, unlike the old simple risk buckets, it provides for risk weights based on external ratings of the banks' counterparties. Behind this solution lies the fact that:

■ National authorities endorse external credit assessment, and
■ This is done in line with the broad criteria set out by the Basel Committee.

Such assessment must, however, be accomplished by reputable, well-known credit rating agencies. Chapter 1 has also explained that with the two IRB approaches (F-IRB and A-IRB), the *probability of default* is computed quantitatively by the bank, while qualitative assessments could also play an important role in its definition.

This talks volumes for the cultural change a credit institution must undergo in order to fulfill Basel II requirements even with the less advanced F-IRB method. This, too, is one of the major benefits banks get with Basel II. Understandably, banks which adopt A-IRB gain more because they must become proficient in all the qualitative and quantitative elements that underpin the method:

■ Loss given default
■ Exposure at default
■ Maturity of loans, and
■ Portfolio concentration.

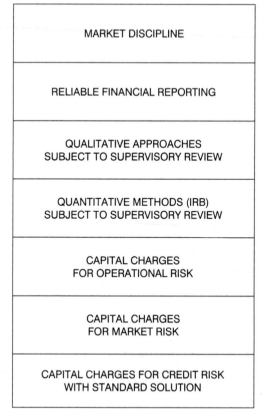

Figure 2.7 Successive layers of capital requirements and risk control according to Basel II

At the same time, as these references demonstrate there is a significant shift by supervisors towards sensitivity to exposure. The new regulations also impact in a significant way on the technology a bank uses. To appreciate the level of technological sophistication that will be necessary, one should keep in mind the different levels of reference constituting the new capital requirements. As shown in Figure 2.7, at the base is the capital ratio for credit risk to which are added higher-up layers of other capital reserves for assumed risks.

There are also domains where regulation is in full evolution. Examples are the explicit supervisory treatment of asset securitization, and recognition of a range of risk mitigation techniques. Operational risk, too, has become subject to tighter supervisory review and enhanced market discipline.[7] As the reader can appreciate, the road from Basel I to Basel II provides plenty of means to strike the right balance between:

■ The need for disciplining the risk-taking behavior of individual banks, and
■ The overall impact of regulatory capital on financial stability, including macro-economic considerations.

Part of the overall equation is the work done by the European Commission on *financial conglomerates*, which aims to establish a comprehensive regulatory framework capable of covering several issues, including capital adequacy for entities which have so far escaped supervision, intragroup transactions, risk concentration, fitness and propriety of their managers, suitability of the shareholders, role of co-ordinators in supervision of conglomerates and the exchange of information among authorities.

2.6   Basel II objectives and the effect of leverage

Part of a company's liabilities is capital defined as *equity*. It provides a permanent source of revenue for shareholders and funds further growth. The alternative is debt, or leverage. Chapter 9 discusses the Modigliani-Miller hypothesis and its weaknesses. No business person would underestimate the importance of capital. Capital:

- Is used to bear risk and absorb losses
- Is a messenger to the market, and
- Is a signal that a bank is managed in a safe and sound manner.

Capital must be calculated on the basis of both expected and unexpected losses, which have to be borne by shareholders. Rating agencies, however, and to a substantial degree regulatory capital (see Chapter 3) address expected losses. Unexpected losses are covered by economic capital (see Chapter 5).

To cover all sorts of losses, the expected net fair value of the bank's assets must exceed the expected net fair value of the bank's liabilities. At the bottom line, this is the essence of capital requirements at different levels of exposure. Therefore, as Chapter 1 already stated, any capital management model must consider by business unit and major product line:

- All assets, and
- All liabilities.

Such study should definitely include the likelihood of evolution in the institution's risk appetite over time. It must focus on the survivability of major clients, and corresponding banks, and consider risk and return by instrument within the environment in which the bank trades – including the impact of macro-markets.

These goals have not been part of Basel I but they are embedded in the conceptual foundations of Basel II, though not all of them are explicit. Currency exchange, stock index and bond futures, as well as all sorts of derivatives traded on a global scale, have been known as *macro-markets*. Though these instruments are diverse, they have in common their *macro* dimension.

The macro-markets are large enough to accommodate many investors, but there is a significant difference between maintaining momentum and gaining momentum in these wide and unpredictable markets. Each big player's size is hindered in regaining momentum after a profitless period. Moreover, momentum must be gained with profits commensurate to the risks being taken.

All this is very pertinent in the current environment of trading and investing where banks and big corporations are running the treasury for profits. Through complex derivative financial instruments it is possible to build personalized products and services which, bankers suggest, can meet any financial need. Not only bankers and institutional investors, but also corporate treasurers are attracted by them – often with little understanding of:

- What they involve, and
- The amount of exposure that is assumed.

The price of using the company's treasury *for profits* is leverage, which often gets out of control. This policy has built up momentum over the years. 'It has not yet reached epidemic proportions, but it is a growing problem,' said Robert Studer, in 1994, then president of Union Bank of Switzerland.[8] He pointed to the tendency for banks' corporate customers to:

- Run their treasury for leveraging goals,
- Rather than use it for cash management and pure risk control.

One of the unwanted after-effects of this practice has been a giant increase in the amount of gearing assumed by banks and other institutions. Etymologically, *leverage* stands for the action of a lever and the mechanical power resulting from this action. It also identifies the increasing tendency of borrowing for accomplishing some purpose, all the way to living beyond one's means.

The Basel Committee advises that when banks operate with high leverage – defined as a low ratio of capital to total assets – this boosts the banks' vulnerability to adverse economic events. It also increases by so much the risk of failure.[9] This has disastrous effects on the creditworthiness of the counterparty and, as a consequence, it increases the level of systemic risk.

The challenge for credit institutions, and all other companies, lies in the fact that while leveraging magnifies risk, it also helps to improve the entity's return on equity (ROE). The gap between leveraged and unleveraged ROE over the span of 1995 to 2003 is shown in Figure 2.8. Another point the aforementioned BIS document makes, concerns some of the effects of globalization. Banks often engage in transactions that are:

- Initiated in one jurisdiction
- Recorded in a different jurisdiction, and
- Managed in yet another jurisdiction.

This is often found to be at the origin of legal risk. Both leverage and cross-border legal risk lead to distortions in financial markets. Hans Eichel, the German finance minister, remarked in an article that offshore financial centers (OFCs) are a potentially destabilizing factor because they often have poor supervisory regimes.[10] Weak supervision of financial entities:

- Conceals risky transactions because their originators do not comply with international standards, and

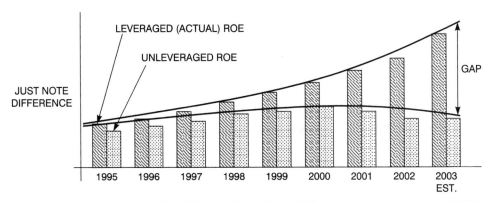

Figure 2.8 Leveraging magnifies risk, but also makes a difference in return on equity (ROE) (based on a sample of banks)

■ Permits multiple levels of leverage, creating distortion in the economic and financial landscape.

Is Basel II addressing in an effective manner these unwanted effects on leverage, cross-border legal risk and weak supervision in offshores and emerging markets? The answer is 'Not directly', but indirectly it provides means for credit institutions to take action. For instance, to manage cross-border counterparty risk in an able manner through A-IRB, banks must have a rating system that separately distinguishes borrower risk, trader risk and transaction risk. They should also feature:

■ A fine grid for performing loans and problem loans, and
■ A meaningful distribution of exposures across grades, with no excessive concentration in any particular grade.

Stress testing is integral part of this reference to improved control of exposure, and the same is true of rigorous systems able to validate the accuracy and consistency of risk factors and their values. Furthermore, the management of credit institutions needs to demonstrate that it relies on credit ratings, PDs, LGDs and EADs for key internal decisions.

Similar challenges exist with market risk. The value at risk (VAR) model for exposure reporting, specified by the 1996 Market Risk Amendment,[11] is obsolete. It is not a coherent risk measure and it only covers between half and two-thirds of financial products and services, depending on the institution and its business line. Moreover,

■ VAR shows exposure connected to those instruments which it addresses.
■ But it says nothing about the economic consequences of these exposures, the level of confidence, and likelihood of spikes.

Just as crucial are the operational risk challenges. Basel II brings forward varying degrees of sophistication in monitoring and controlling op risk. The Basic Indicator

Approach (BIA) requires banks to hold capital equal to a fixed percentage of their gross income. This is simplistic and most likely will only be used by the smaller credit institutions.

More complex is tracking key risk indicators in eight predefined business lines, with capital charges calculated along a reference frame of seven predefined types of operational risk. By contrast, three advanced measurement approaches (AMA) including internal measurement approach (IMA), loss distribution (LD) and the scoreboard, allow banks direct input into calculating operational risk capital charge.

What these methods have in common is the effort to deliver a risk-sensitive methodology, which sees to it that capital requirements may increase or decrease for an individual bank depending on its operational risk profile. Another goal these methods share with the advanced credit risk and market risk solutions is to bring along a cultural change in the way banks are managed and the manner in which they control their risks.

2.7   The need for a devil's advocate in risk management

Regulatory capital cannot effectively be computed and economic capital allocation can never be made in a factual and documented manner, unless they are closely connected to risk management. Another prerequisite is that they are steadily monitored through internal control. The Committee of Sponsoring Organizations of the Treadway Commission (COSO) defined the tasks of *internal control* as consisting of:

■ Control environment
■ Risk assessment
■ Control activities
■ Information and communication, and
■ Monitoring activities.[12]

To this the Securities and Exchange Commission (SEC) has added:

■ Preservation of assets.

The first institutions to implement COSO have been the Federal Reserve Banks of New York, Boston and Chicago. This has been followed by all other Fed banks, all regulatory agencies in the USA and financial institutions with assets over $500 million. With the exception of Canada, however, where a similar process known as COCO has been implemented, other jurisdictions have not applied COSO's principles in internal control.

Chapter 1 defined internal control as a feedback which can be effective *if*, and only if, monitoring is done steadily in real-time and the company's communications channels are kept wide open. By contrast, *risk management* is a forward-looking action with the objectives of damage prevention and, if this is not successful, of damage control.

Damage prevention and damage control are foremost risk management goals, but there is more to be said about an effective, well-rounded risk management process. Paraphrasing Dr Ben Gurion, risk management must have some brilliant operators assigned to the permanent doubting role of *devil's advocate*. Their mission should be to challenge possibly wrong hypotheses and assumptions, which might look solid but in reality they are hollow.

This role of the doubter is vital in all business activities if we wish to avoid tunnel vision. It can apply from market discipline to the different types of risk control employed by the enterprise. 'I don't believe in the single God but I believe in the single devil,' says Professor Urs Birchler, of the Swiss National Bank, adding that: 'Market discipline does not bring us to paradise, but can prevent us from going to hell.' Only wise people and well-managed institutions truly appreciate the need to:

- Challenge the obvious, and
- Turn all stones in order to find where the scorpion hides.

Warren Buffett is a good example of permanent doubter. In an article published in March 2003, on the third anniversary of the stock market's downfall, he brought public attention to the fact that an explosion in derivatives contracts may have created serious systemic risks.[13] Buffett's article underlined:

- The insanity of equity valuations reached during the Great Bubble
- The fact that derivatives contracts are sometimes running to twenty years, or more, and
- The often overlooked issue that ultimate value of derivatives also depends on creditworthiness of counterparties to them.

Buffett also pressed the point that in recent years some huge-scale frauds and near-frauds have been facilitated by derivatives trades – while making errors in the derivatives business has not been symmetrical (more on this later). What Buffett's article did not explicitly state is that derivatives exposures of trillions of dollars, in notional principal amounts, are not covered by regulatory capital, and economic capital may fall short when an LTCM-type adversity hits.

- The devil's advocate should never lose from sight this challenge, and
- Risk management should be well above the cacophony of clans and tribes in the bank's risk-taking operating units.

The reasons why risk management, regulatory capital and economic capital allocation correlate is that only when we are in control of our exposure can we be confident of having enough resources to face adversity and survive. A crucial question the board and CEO should ask themselves is 'Do we manage our assets in a way investors are willing to buy them?' The financial institution's directors must be aware of the fact that some of the reasons for high exposures are:

- Limits do not correspond to risk appetite
- Expected drawdown rates escape control

- Higher drawdown rates become a trend
- Concentrations are higher than planned.

Financial history shows that the more concentrated a big institution, the more it moves the market and the less it can get out of positions without wrecking the current values of the different instruments in which it trades. As for reasons for miscalculating expected losses, these – the devil's advocate would say – can be condensed into five points:

- Portfolio mix is poorly done
- Borrower ratings are incorrect or outdated
- Economic conditions worsen
- There is customer and/or industry concentration, and
- There are many exceptions to risk limits.

Similarly, several reasons are behind poor recoveries. They include the fact that collateral can be wrongly calculated, the borrower had pledged the same collateral to different banks (Maxwell risk), collateral value and audited value do not correspond, there is a longer time to recovery because of court action and less money is recovered at liquidation. Many reasons are underpinning the building up of financial bubbles. In order of importance, these are:

- Increased use of leverage
- A growing turnover of assets, some of which are dubious
- New issues which promise too much, yet look credible, and
- Too many new investors with too little experience joining the market.

Excessive liquidity, too, should be part of this list. In an interview, Ernst Welteke, president of the Bundesbank, was asked if, because of the low yields in bonds, the excessive liquidity on financial markets is about to jump into the stock markets again. His response was 'We have to be careful not to set the stage for the next speculative bubble'.[14]

Another factor which should trigger concern in the mind of the devil's advocate is excessive turnover. Excessive turnover of dubious assets is often orchestrated through deviations in fair value estimates. In a recent meeting in London, reference was made to a study by KPMG, which has given an interesting insight regarding differences in fair value estimates.

- These are relatively *small* for good assets
- But become *big* for assets which have turned sour.

As this study has demonstrated, computed values for traded instruments and residential mortgages, with an active secondary market, varied between 2 and 5 percent from real life. For traditional loans with good standing, the difference was about 3.5 percent, but for poor quality loans the difference grew significantly to 30 percent. That is the domain of hidden risks.

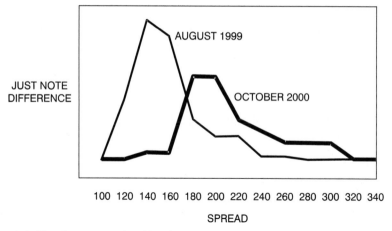

Figure 2.9 The dispersion of yields of BBB-rated bonds is very sensitive to the capital market's mood

One way to watch out for poor assets is to examine how the market is pricing them. For instance, as Figure 2.9 shows, the dispersion of yields of BBB-rated bonds is very sensitive to the mood of the capital market. At other times, however, the capital market buys equities and other assets through an irrational exuberance, as Dr Alan Greenspan, the Fed chairman, was to suggest in the late 1990s. When this happens, the conditions are set for building the bubble.

2.8 A-IRB, Basel II and the German Savings Banks: a case study

At the beginning of the research which led to this book, many of the participating experts said that Basel II may be perfect for bigger banks, but will prove to be too much of a struggle for smaller banks. 'Too much' meant too difficult, requiring highly skilled human resources and calling for an inordinate amount of development money.

This opinion now proves to be wrong, as the case study in the present section and in section 2.9 documents. In late 1999/early 2000, the German Savings Banks, which typically are of small to medium size, initiated a fact-finding project on Basel II. This project has been focusing on organizational and Basel II implementation requirements with the aim of:

■ Classifying the savings banks credit exposures, and
■ Developing internal ratings for them.

In a nutshell, the results of four years' work have proven that A-IRB is a doable undertaking at mid-range in the credit institutions spectrum, and might also be used by smaller banks. Some of these savings banks, like Sparkasse Lüneburg on which the case study in section 2.9 is based, already had in place a credit rating system but of a reduced number of thresholds. In 2001 they converted their grading system to that developed by the German Savings Banks and Giro Association (DSGV) which:

- AAA to D features an 18 ratings scale, and
- Is nearly compatible with that of Standard & Poor's, and Moody's and Fitch Ratings.

'It is very important to be compatible with the scale of the major independent rating agencies,' said Tibor Kuloge of Sparkasse Lüneburg. To provide the reader with an idea regarding its size, the assets of Sparkasse Lüneburg are at the 2.5 billion euros ($2.5 billion) level. The reason for the foregoing statement, to which I personally subscribe, is that the EU is in the process of adopting for its new Capital Adequacy Directive (CAD3, see Chapter 16) the joint use by credit institutions of an internal and external ratings approach.

'It is precisely the unlimited authorization of "partial use" for accounts receivable from states and banks that is of fundamental importance to us,' remarked Dr Holger Berndt, member of the board of DSGV.[15] 'The development of an own rating system for (many) receivables is an unacceptable cost for the banking institutions, considering the lack of histories of defaults and losses, and not necessary either.'

In my book, the regulatory permission to integrate internal and external ratings is not only sound on its merits, but also, together with the adoption of a rating scale compatible with that of S&P's and Moody's, makes possible not only joint efforts among credit institutions, but also the development of a framework which enables:

- Estimating PD, LGD, EAD
- Structuring a historical database, and
- Doing model development and testing.

Joint efforts, of course are neither painless nor do they have an assured 'happy ending'. Plenty of critical questions must be answered in a factual and documented manner: Who should be doing the internal rating? How relevant is a 'one size fits all' solution to each individual bank? How will Basel take it? The local regulators? Will they consider this effort as another kind of external rating? Answers to all these queries were necessary in order to face A-IRB challenges. Apart from the PD, LGD, EAD metrics, an integral part of an A-IRB project is *how to*:

- Conceptualize
- Design
- Develop, and
- Test the overall system.

A valid solution is not just a matter of collection of quantitative data, qualitative references, obligor information and external data. A concentrated effort also has to be made in the domain of exposure classification – and links must be provided to the credit institution's financial staying power, including:

- Its capital and reserves, and
- Maximum exposure it can take.

Within the perspective of A-IRB implementation, a framework has been developed through a joint project between Bank-Verlag GmbH, a publisher and electronic banking software developer based in Cologne, and i-flex. The latter is an Indian software company and consultancy, which specializes in IRB. The object of the framework has been to develop a method which small banks can implement.

The two projects, Sparkasse Lüneburg and Bank-Verlag, should not be confused with one another. They are different and as such help to document that IRB implementation is spreading among medium and smaller institutions. Actors in the Bank-Verlag/i-flex Basel II project – which primarily concerned itself with identifying and streamlining the IT supports – have been some fifty German savings and loans institutions, 10 percent of which are of medium size and the rest of small size.

In this particular project, system design has been characterized by two principal activities. This one is the development of a framework, whose main components are shown in Figure 2.10. The other focused on a flexible solution which may allow each individual savings bank to have and use its own rating scores, within the context of the aforementioned framework.

As was to be expected, this A-IRB effort faced both technical and project management challenges. The technical ones have been customization, robustness, scaleability, high availability, use of a flexible rating process, platform independence, as well as historical credit data collection, organization and mining. The topmost issues project management confronted, were:

- Facing changing and evolving specification requirements
- Accounting for complex non-functional needs

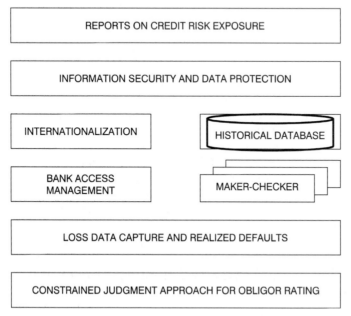

Figure 2.10 Component parts of the methodology which led to the savings banks' IRB superstructure

- Maintaining an integrative capability at implementation end
- Assuring for every saving bank well specified deliverables, and
- Keeping up with a tight timetable which saw to it that the framework was ready within one year.

The reader should take note that the Bank-Verlag has not been the only German organization addressing the Basel II implementation needs of small and medium size Sparkassen. Hannover-based Finanz IT GmbH is another example. Together, these cases document that:

- The relatively small German savings and loans have engaged themselves in intensive work towards Basel II compliance.
- By contrast, because of not adopting Basel II, much bigger American banks would fall behind in risk management, as well as in corporate governance.

David C. Furlonger, vice president and research director of Gartner Financial Services, was right when he said – during our meeting at the June 2003 Trema Monte Carlo Forum – that Basel II can be properly implemented by smaller banks without an inordinate effort. Furlonger regretted the fact that, following the late February 2003 decision by the Federal Reserve Bank, IRB does not really mean anything to the average US credit institutions, but on the contrary means a great deal to European ones.

As with practically every other advanced project, one of the major challenges faced by the German Savings Banks, in connection with A-IRB implementation, has been default data. The minimum is three years, but more, indeed much more, than that is better. However, since the savings banks have started working on A-IRB and on the credit risk database in 2000, they are well on their way to fulfilling the minimum database requirements.

Also, as everywhere else, the next major challenge is that of changing the credit institution's internal culture. The two senior executives of the American Bankers Association (ABA) whom I met in Washington in July 2001 expressed a common concern when they said that the most urgent need for their members was that of intensive Basel II education programs, but they also lamented there was no infrastructure to provide them.

Here is how DSGV has solved this problem. Every year, the Sparkassen-Finanzgruppe invests around 700 billion euros in its multi-tiered advanced training program, which is taught in different educational establishments and particularly in the twelve Sparkassen academies in the German Federal Republic. With a training percentage of about 9 percent, the Sparkassen-Finanzgruppe is the largest trainer in the German banking industry.

2.9 Looking at the Sparkasse Lüneburg project and its advantages

I asked the specialists at Sparkasse Lüneburg what motivated their bank to go for A-IRB. The central point of the answer which I have received focused on the competitive advantages gained by an institution adopting the more sophisticated Basel II approach to capital adequacy. This is a message the CEOs of all small to medium banks should convey to:

- Their own people
- Their competitors, and
- Their clients.

Lothar Arnold and Tibor Kuloge first made reference to the fact that since 1999 the organization department of Sparkasse Lüneburg has been developing an integrated system to quantify and control credit risks. This involved scoring- and rating-validation procedures, as well as instruments specifically tuned to measurement and reporting of risks.

Senior management has been of the opinion that such procedures and instruments are necessary for early recognition and estimation of credit exposures assumed by the bank. Most significant is the fact that the decision to initiate the Basel II project was motivated more by economic reasons than legal ones; in other words, by risk management rather than simply compliance. This is the number one message the reader should retain.

Worsening economic factors and an increasing number of insolvencies, which characterized the world economy in the first years of the twenty-first century made a scientifically based risk control system more necessary than ever. Therefore, Sparkasse Lüneburg got busy from the start with the projects developed by the DSGV, gradually proceeding with the conversion of its existing credit rating system to a Basel II compatible basis.

In all fairness to the reader it must be said that the German Länderbanken (central treasuries of savings banks) and Sparkassen are faced with a huge challenge. From 2005 – that is, in just one year – Landesbanken and Sparkassen, which together control about 40 percent of retail and company deposits and loans, will be forced to compete on equal terms with private banks. Therefore, they are faced with a rude regulatory awakening as the state governments which guarantee:

- Their triple-A ratings, and
- Cheap capital markets funding

must stop doing so. Here lies the challenge. The better managed of the Sparkassen are not only aware of this, but also have taken the measures necessary to significantly improve their governance. Therefore, some of them have taken the lead in implementing Basel's new capital adequacy framework which significantly improves:

- Risk management, and
- Economic capital allocation.

Sparkasse Lüneburg falls into this 'best managed' class. Its Basel II project started at the end of 1999, and the plan is to complete it successfully by December 2005. Correctly, the project has been designed for flexible implementation and, therefore, in part A-IRB is already working. For instance, this is the case of the rating for the bank's corporate customers and private customers. By contrast, A-IRB at Sparkasse Lüneburg is still in the area of real estate ratings, but it is progressing.

In another part of the project, the Credit Portfolio View (CPV), the savings bank uses data of the German Federal Statistical Office. An example is the correlation matrix. One of my questions has been whether the Basel II project is addressing internal ratings only, or merges internal and external ratings. The answer is that the savings bank distinguishes two classes of rating:

- For its credit business, and
- For its securities business.

For its loans it uses the internal credit rating system of DSGV. Borrowers are allocated a grade between 1 and 18, according to a standardized procedure. (In this scale, the higher the grade, the larger the loss probability.) By contrast, for its securities business, the bank employs external ratings from S&P's or Moody's.

The response to the query 'Does the project include risk-based pricing? has been that the bank's A-IRB project indeed incorporates a risk-based pricing approach. A system has been partially introduced to this effect and management plans to have it completely installed throughout the institution by the end of 2005.

A most interesting statement Sparkasse Lüneburg has made is the number of person-years invested and to be invested from the start to the end of the process. The answer I received was approximately *8 person years* – which essentially means a two-person team working over the four-year timeframe. Any credit institution which says that it cannot invest eight person-years to implement Basel II is either patently incapable or of very bad faith. American banks who think they are off the Basel II hook should take notice.

An evidently critical question has been how the database problem is approached: by Sparkasse Lüneburg alone or in collaboration with other saving banks? The specialists responded that a database was jointly assembled in collaboration with DSGV and other savings banks. This provided the working basis for the development of the rating system by DSGV and Oliver Wyman – leading to the credit risk control program CPV (by McKinsey) which also serves for portfolio control.

The reader will appreciate from these responses that Sparkasse Lüneburg confronted practically all the major questions which face a credit institution in terms of Basel II options, up to the final choice of A-IRB implementation. Based on references of a similar nature made by other banks, here is a list of questions which invariably come up following a decision on IRB:

- How do you develop an internal rating system compatible with external ratings?
- How do you ensure that the system is operational throughout the bank's business landscape?
- How do you address functionally specifications and other issues of daily business interest?
- How do you change the culture of the organization so that the new system is successfully implemented?
- What will be the advantages the credit institution gains against its competitors?

The last question is evidently most crucial. Senior management authorizing an A-IRB project would want to know what the bank gains from it. Advantages had better be tangible. One of them is risk-based pricing, to which reference has already been made. The specialists of Sparkasse Lüneburg particularly underline the scientific basis which has been established enabling the quantification of risk and making risk measurements transparent to all management levels.

Banks implementing A-IRB would be well advised to take note of the fact that there can be plenty of advantages from the implementation of A-IRB. Here is a list I would be inclined to add beyond that which Sparkasse Lüneburg has stated:

- Being first in the market
- Becoming profit oriented
- Restructuring business units
- Shedding non-core operations
- Providing value added services
- Assuring a flexible solution which can grow
- Developing a common infrastructure, while specializing deliverables.

One more major point was raised by Sparkasse Lüneburg in terms of obtainable advantages through the implementation of the advanced IRB method of Basel II: the better the bank's rating system is, the more easily the institution can refinance itself and offer more favorable conditions to its customers. Not many banks participating in the research which led to this book made reference to refinancing. Yet, this is a most critical issue, whose appreciation divides the banks 'worth their salt' from the rest.

Notes

1 D.N. Chorafas (2003). *Stress Testing: Risk Management Strategies for Extreme Events*. Euromoney.
2 The management of market risk is not changing with Basel II. The rules set by the 1996 Market Risk Amendment still prevail, but in all likelihood they will come under review in the next few years.
3 D.N. Chorafas (2001). *Managing Risk in the New Economy*. New York Institute of Finance.
4 For the mechanics of this, see D.N. Chorafas (2000). *Managing Credit Risk, Volume 1: Analyzing, Rating and Pricing the Probability of Default*. Euromoney.
5 J. Gleick (1992). *Genius: The Life and Science of Richard Feynman*. Pantheon Books.
6 D.N. Chorafas (2000). *Managing Credit Risk, Volume 2: The Lessons of VAR Failures and Imprudent Exposure*. Euromoney.
7 D.N. Chorafas (2004). *Operational Risk Control with Basel II*. Butterworth-Heinemann.
8 *The Economist*, 4 June 1994.
9 Basel Committee on Banking Supervision (2002). *The Relationship between Banking Supervisors and Banks' External Auditors*. BIS, January.

10 *Financial Times*, 7 February 2002.
11 D.N. Chorafas (1998). *The 1996 Market Risk Amendment: Understanding the Marking-to-Model and Value-at-Risk*. McGraw-Hill.
12 D.N. Chorafas (2001). *Implementing and Auditing the Internal Control System*. Macmillan.
13 Warren Buffett (2003). Avoiding a supercatastrophe. *Fortune*, 17 March.
14 *Frankfurter Allgemeine Zeitung*, 3 November 2001.
15 DSGV press releases 71/2003 of 3 July 2003.

3 Regulatory capital defined

3.1 Introduction

The theme of this chapter is regulatory capital. However, to put into context its definition it is necessary also to make a brief reference to economic capital (which, as already mentioned, is the subject of Part 2). Both regulatory and economic capital have to do with the bank's financial staying power; the former principally addresses expected losses (EL), while the latter has a dual *raison d'être*:

- To help the credit institution generate profits, and
- To provide a cushion against unexpected losses (UL).

The reader will recall that regulatory capital is the *minimum* amount needed to have a license. Economic capital is the *mean* amount necessary to be in business and therefore it should be computed at a 9 percent or higher level of significance. Additional capital is also necessary for:

- Extreme events, and
- In order to gain market confidence.

Regulatory capital principally consists of *Tier 1* (T-1) and *Tier 2* (T-2) capital as defined by the 1988 Capital Accord (see sections 3.3 and 3.4). Around the year 2000 two other notions came up: *Hybrid Tier 1* (HT-1) and *Tier 3* (T-3) capital. Independent rating agencies do not 'buy' HT-1 (neither do I). 'We don't consider hybrids as core capital,' said Walter Pompliano, of Standard & Poor's. Regulators, however, permit HT-1 to constitute up to 15 percent of Tier 1.

Of these two twenty-first century developments, HT-1 is hybrid in the sense that it has some characteristics of equity, some of debt and much of leveraging. As for T-3 capital, to a substantial extent it comes from trading profits. Here again, because Tier 3 derives itself, to a large measure, from derivatives trading, it is very volatile.

All these forms of capital are there to help the credit institution face expected losses. In terms of good business practice, the way to bet is that neither expected risks nor unexpected risks are instantaneous. Like business cycles and economic downturns, an entity's downs take years to develop and correct. Therefore,

- One of the challenges is the computation of the holding period of return.
- This computation is more of a management requirement, than a regulatory issue.

What the supervisors require is that within the medium to longer term the board must not only assure compliance to regulatory capital, but also have enough additional

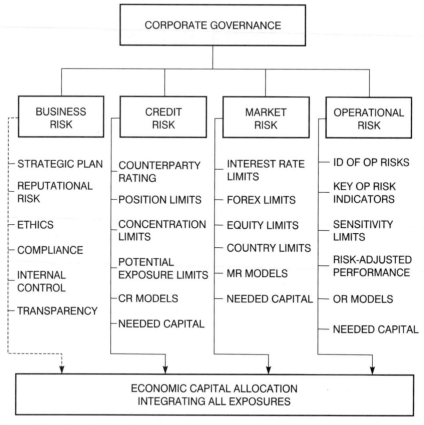

Figure 3.1 A global view of risk control and capital allocation in financial institutions

reserves to cover the bank's business channels of exposure. Of the four shown in Figure 3.1, credit, market and operational risks are closely followed up by supervisors.

The boards and CEOs of well-managed companies also account for the fact that the entity's business units, product lines and geographic locations find many ways to bypass laws, regulations, established policies and procedures. In connection to economic capital, for example:

- A popular technique is *multiple gearing*.

It consists of counting the same capital twice or more, in different entities in the group, as well as raising capital through leveraging (see Chapter 9).

- Another approach is *downstreaming* of capital.

A company issues debt and then uses the proceeds as equity for its subsidiaries. This enlarges its reach, but also increases its underlying exposure – and therefore its vulnerability to gyrations of the market.

Quite often, top management only pays lip service, or even no attention at all, to the fact that financial might can quickly turn to ashes. In 1989, at the apogee of the Japanese banks' brief rise in the world's financial capitalization, the Japanese financial industry had an impressive $400 billion in unrealized profits. Then, this turned into a $1.2 trillion torrent of red ink – which is very serious because:

- Japanese banks were never strongly capitalized, and
- Their special reserves were trivial or outright non-existent.

Not everybody appreciates the importance of special reserves, which go well beyond regulatory capital, and in some countries they are even illegal. Yet, they can be lifesavers. On 15 November 2002, after injecting another $1 billion in Winterthur, Crédit Suisse exhausted its special reserves. On Wall Street, some experts said that this completely changed its risk profile.

3.2 The role of regulatory capital

Regulatory capital and economic capital are two concepts key in managing a bank's business activities and in prudential regulation. They are also closely linked to one another (see Chapter 5). Adequate regulatory capital cushions individual credit institutions against expected losses, and it contributes towards the stability of the banking system as a whole. Moreover,

- The amount of available capital limits the extent of risk being assumed through operations.
- A bank's risk position determines the level of capital it needs from both an economic and a regulatory perspective.

At the same time, however, regulatory capital and economic capital requirements differ in several ways. One of them is shown in Figure 3.2 based on the concept of the German Bundesbank.

- Regulatory capital requirements are minimum requirements imposed on credit institutions by the banking supervisory authorities.
- A bank's economic capital represents equity and other financial resources, which the credit institution itself deems necessary in the light of prudent risk management.

As cannot be repeated too often, regulatory capital corresponds to expected losses which are of higher frequency but are less in terms of impact, case by case, than unexpected losses. Economic, or internal, capital allocated to cover unexpected losses can extend all the way to extreme events:

- Extreme events most often lie at the tail of the distribution.
- The way to bet is that they are low frequency but high impact.

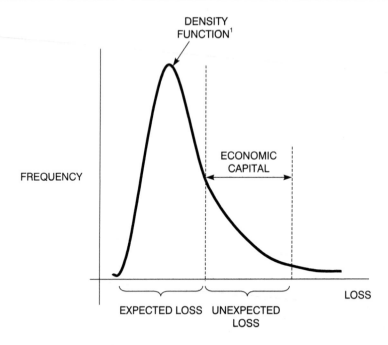

NOTES: 1 MONTHLY REPORT, JANUARY 2002

Figure 3.2 Probability distribution of future losses of a loan portfolio by the Bundesbank (*Source*: Deutsche Bundesbank, *Monthly Report*, January 2002)

Even if this contrast between HF/LI and LF/HI, which was brought to the reader's attention in Chapter 2, were the only difference, it would have been enough to signal that economic and regulatory capital requirements are not identical. The reader should, however, bear in mind that regulatory and economic requirements also differ with respect to measurement of risks to be backed by capital.

Another major difference between regulatory and economic capital is customization to each individual case. This is changing with the new regulations because, in contrast to Basel I, Basel II provides the rules and algorithms to evaluate the risks of different events. This is a way to customize. For regulatory capital, however, customization is made through a general frame of reference expected to be valid for all credit institutions that choose one of the methods offered by Basel II.

As we will see in Chapter 4, the aim of the Basel Committee on Banking Supervision is to align the regulatory capital in a way that creates a level playing field. It is up to each bank to fine-tune its economic capital and associated financial resources. To the extent that losses can be absorbed by equity capital and reserves, the credit institution's continued existence is assured.

■ Theoretically, a bank could ensure its perpetual solvency by relying totally on equity financing.
■ Practically, a certain degree of debt financing is unavoidable, but also implies a default probability commensurate with the credit institution's risk position.

It is important as well to note that the capital measure which institutions themselves use for managing their business operations, is not necessarily identical either to the capital shown in their balance sheet or to the definition of regulatory capital. It often depends on the way banks assess their liabilities, maturities, reserves and other factors which may differ from regulatory provisions.

A major role in this allocation is played by the fact that many institutions are keen to clearly signal their creditworthiness to outsiders. In Chapter 2, we have seen an example on what it takes to gain a rating grade such as AA, and of the contribution Basel II makes in this process by increasing senior management's risk sensitivity.

Accounting rules also play a major role in this connection. Under the International Accounting Standards (IAS) rules, capital is derived as a residual after subtracting from total assets. However, each country has its own accounting rules and the assets and liabilities shown in annual accounts drawn up according to the national framework may differ from the same accounts compiled in line with IAS.

- Some are methodological differences in distinguishing between equity and debt items.
- Others are due to divergent disclosure and valuation rules, which lead to differences in the amount of equity shown in the balance sheet.
- Still other differences are the result of valuation at current market or fair value, versus use of accrual method and book value.

There is no one-to-one correspondence between accounting standards and supervisory requirements. Therefore, there is no unique format for reliable financial reporting. Much depends on the jurisdiction, even if Basel II rules are global. Figure 3.3

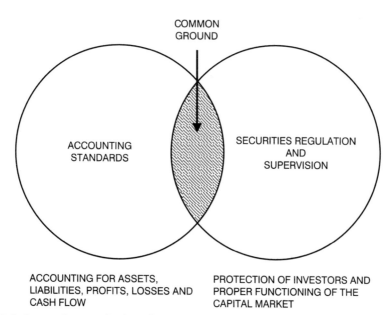

Figure 3.3 Accounting standards and supervisory requirement correlate, but they also cover different functional areas

emphasizes the fact that while regulatory and accounting standards overlap rather significantly, there exist also significant deviations in the level of detail as well as the functional areas which they address.

In the USA, for example, accounting standards are established by the Financial Accounting Standards Board (FASB), which depends on the Securities and Exchange Commission (SEC). Bank supervision is done by the Federal Reserve, Office of the Controller of the Currency (OCC) and Federal Deposit Insurance Corporation (FDIC). In the UK, accounting standards are established by the Accounting Standards Board; and bank supervision is done by the Financial Services Authority (FSA), a different entity.

Let me give some insight into the detail. Accounting for items at their fair value has implications for equity capital. The marking-to-market valuation method under IAS is increasingly used with financial instruments in the banking book and trading book – apart from self-originated loans and refinancing liabilities in the banking book, which have to be valued at amortized cost, and those items in the trading book which it is management's intent to keep to maturity (Statement of Financial Accounting Standards [SFAS] 133, by FASB).

In the USA, Generally Accepted Accounting Principles (GAAP), developed by the FASB, are binding on all firms that have to draw up independently audited accounts. Some large companies in the EU also apply US GAAP, mainly prompted by the desire to be listed on US exchanges and to have access to American capital markets.

The International Accounting Standards Board (IASB) is active in ironing out the differences in accounting formats prevailing between different countries, and some of the details characterizing different jurisdictions. But it is not possible to say at this moment if this integrative work on international accounting principles will be accepted by every country, and made the law of the land. The problem is political, rather than technical. To a lesser extent, political problems also exist in connection with Basel II, its rules and the extent of its implementation. We will look into these in Chapter 16.

3.3 Components of regulatory capital

The regulatory definition of capital requirements in the banking industry has been established with the 1988 Capital Accord. Basel I was the starting point but, as we have seen since Chapter 1, this definition has expanded. Basel II identifies three categories of own funds. They differ in their ability to cover losses:

- Core capital, Tier 1
- Additional capital, Tier 2, and
- Tier 3 capital.

Core capital is in some cases also called 'economic capital' and this leads to confusion, because (if this title is retained) it would mean that economic capital is at the same time a subset of core capital and a superset of it. The term is used in two different ways because terminology is not always clear cut.

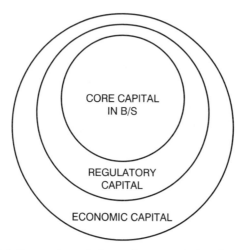

Figure 3.4 Economic capital, regulatory capital and core capital

- The practice with Basel I to call 'economic capital' the core capital, has slowly faded away.
- With Basel II, the banking industry switched terminology. 'Economic capital' now identifies what in the past was sometimes called 'entrepreneurial capital' (see Chapter 5).

The definition of *economic capital* is not cast in stone. The October 11, 2003 announcement by the Basel Committee introduces the concepts of *shortfall* and *excess*. This may eventually impact the notion of economic capital.

For the time being, to avoid misunderstanding, in this text the term *economic capital* will be used in the sense of the onion-skin diagram shown in Figure 3.4, while the term *core capital* will be restricted to what shows as equity in the balance sheet. In this sense, core capital is a subset of regulatory capital, while regulatory capital is a subset of overall economic capital.

- Core capital (Tier 1) and additional capital (Tier 2) constitute the liable capital of the institution.
- Tier 3 capital is still a minor player. The statistics in Figure 3.5 come from the Monthly Report by the German central bank.

Most credit institutions participating in the research which led to this book commented that at the moment regulatory capital is not a constraint on them: 'We have much more capital than regulatory capital,' said the senior executive of a global bank. 'For us, return on economic capital is the criterion.'

The European Central Bank (ECB) defines Tier 1 and Tier 2 capital as consisting of assets important for national financial markets, such as equities, marketable debt and non-marketable debt. Their eligibility criteria are established by national central banks, in line with minimum ECB-approved eligibility guidelines.[1]

Tier 1 assets consist of marketable debt *only*, made up of government securities issued by:

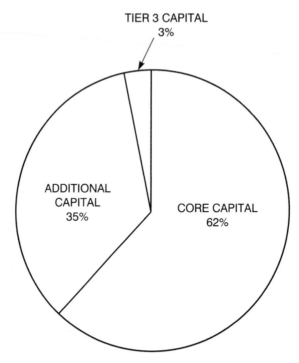

Figure 3.5 According to the Bundesbank, core capital is only part of regulatory capital (the institution's own funds) (*Source*: Deutsche Bundesbank, *Monthly Report*, January 2002)

- Central, state and local governments
- Social security funds
- Securities issued by banks, backed by residential mortgages or by public sector debt.

Within the Eurosystem, ECB-approved Tier 2 capital includes bonds issued by corporations, asset-backed securities other than mortgages and public sector debt, and non-marketable instruments such as bank loans, trade bills and mortgage-backed promissory notes.

Other jurisdictions, however, have added more instruments in T-2. Examples are:

- Preferential shares, less own preferential shares
- Liabilities represented by participation rights
- Longer-term subordinated liabilities.

Changes in T-1 and T-2 capital can have an impact on the functions performed through economic capital and its contribution to the institution's financial staying power. As a reminder, since the 1988 Capital Accord, 50 percent of regulatory capital must be T-1, and this constraint has an impact on the capital base. It is appropriate to keep in mind that:

- T-1 does not necessarily increase efficiency, and
- It can be open to abuse, like the so-called 'Hybrid Tier 1' (HT-1).

Basel II clearly specifies that HT-1, which is also called capital from 'innovative instruments', will be limited to 15 percent of T-1 capital *net* of goodwill. (This decision was made in 1998 by the Basel Committee.)[2]

'Hybrid T-1 capital is an innovative instrument with some characteristics of equity and some of debt,' said one of the regulators. 'A key question is what kind of obligation is created with Hybrid T-1,' suggested one of the experts. 'We don't have any Hybrid Tier 1,' pointed out an executive of a major British bank. 'If we had we would run into trouble with FSA.' This reaction comes from the fact that HT-1 is a double-edged knife.

- Apart from other risks HT- 1 may increase market expectations, in an undocumented way. Hence a bank must be cautious in its usage.
- Several credit institutions, however, seem to like HT-1 not only for beefing up their capital base, but also for tax reasons.

The professionals pay scant attention to the fact that regulators and rating agencies dislike HT-1, which is a creative accounting gimmick used since the late 1990s. Credit institutions employing it are the same ones that go for leverage. One of the means to do this is mandatory convertible bonds which cost below equity, but present a number of other problems. For instance,

- Inherent complexity, and
- The fact that they dilute in a significant way the existing shareholders' equity.

Moreover, whether or not the use of HT-1 capital is a lawful exercise, depends on the jurisdiction. Here is a real-life example from France and Germany – therefore, from two different jurisdictions.

In late February 2003, at 2.3 billion euros, Deutsche Telekom's (DT's) mandatory convertible bond has been the biggest of its kind. It also rekindled doubts about the wisdom of a type of issue that within the EU French regulators have already called into question following deals of this kind from Vivendi Universal and Alcatel. In December 2002, a couple of months prior to DT's issue, commenting on the convertible issues from Vivendi and Alcatel, the French Commission des Operations de Bourse (COB) said that the potential consequences of these instruments are still difficult to gage, be it:

- On the secondary market in the issuer's shares,
- Or, regarding the ability of the public to take part in transactions that are inherently very complex.

Subsequently, COB has banned further issues of mandatory convertible bonds, where the coupon on the bond is paid in advance. It also expressed concern at the high level of interest from hedge funds for such instruments, which reflects a common feeling that long-term shareholders are losing out as companies go in desperate search of a quick capital fix.

The good news is that, as indicated by the previous quotations from regulators, analysts and bankers who respect themselves and their clients, serious financial institutions are not expected to fall into the trap of HT-1. They appreciate that not everything that is novel is sound, and they can see that HT-1s:

- Are looked down upon by many supervisory authorities, and
- Have as an aftermath that the equity of companies passes into the hands of highly leveraged hedge funds at shareholders' expense.

Neither is the case of DT of any comfort, because it is no different to other entities greatly loaded with loans who do not 'see the light at the end of the tunnel' – for instance Vivendi, Alcatel and, among banks, Suez which features a huge debt of 28 billion euros. With about $68 billion of debt, DT is under pressure to raise capital, and it goes for *mandatories* as a desperate measure.

Further to this point of HT-1, there is at present limited assessment of various hybrid capital characteristics. As my research has documented, serious banks do not want to dilute their capital base through hybrid instruments. Moreover, as I never tire of repeating:

- Hybrid T-1 is not appreciated by independent rating agencies, and
- There is the added problem of much greater volatility with Hybrid T-1 instruments.

The weight of IAS 39 accounting rules should also be given due consideration. Under the new IAS, some of what are currently shareholder funds will be classified as liabilities. For instance, if a bond pays no cash but offers shares, it will be seen as liability. This changes significantly the method of meeting T-1 requirements. Like SFAS 133 in the USA, IAS 39 expands the use of fair value for measuring and reporting on:

- Financial assets
- Financial liabilities, and
- Derivative instruments.

It provides for limited use of hedge accounting, but sets criteria for recognition and derecognition. This comes beyond IAS 32 which requires compound instruments, such as embedded derivatives, to be split into their components and accounted for accordingly.

In conclusion, with the 1988 Capital Accord, the definition of T-1 capital was simple and straightforward. Developments which took place in the years since see to it that this is no longer the case, and Basel II is in no way responsible for the resulting complexity. The regulatory capital picture has been muddled in the financial bubble of the late 1990s, through the exploitation of loopholes. Derivatives and creative accounting had much to do with this.

3.4. Beyond Tier 1: the Tier 2 and Tier 3 regulatory capital

Sections 3.2 and 3.3 should have left no doubt in the reader's mind that regulatory capital definition is in full evolution. It is influenced, among other things, by the ongoing international development of accounting standards which impacts on the notions underpinning both economic and regulatory capital. Another major impact comes from the way in which different jurisdictions look at recognized own funds.

A standard recognition of own funds which fits all legislations, regulators and credit institutions is by no means an easy matter. It is an issue at the heart of convergence between regulatory and economic capital requirements, but it is impeded by limitations arising from divergent goals of national banking regulators and the commercial business of credit institutions. To be meaningful, regulatory capital requirements have to be:

- Coherently established
- Generally objective, and
- Verifiable at any time.

To provide a level playing field, regulatory capital must be comparable throughout credit institutions, able to satisfy prudential minimum requirements. A good way to appreciate the difference between two main components of regulatory capital, T-1 and T-2, is to understand the philosophy behind them and the criteria used to distinguish between them. These criteria are:

1 Performance. Shares are permanent; subordinated debt is not.
2 The possibility of stopping payment. Dividends can be stopped; interest to bonds and loans cannot.
3 The possibility of write-offs. We can write down equity without being sued in court. We cannot write down debt without court decision, bankruptcy or filing for protection from creditors under Chapter 11 or similar law. Criteria 1, 2 and 3 document that T-1 can only include what is generally known as paid-up capital:

- Equity
- Endowment(s)
- Published reserves
- Profits for the year
- Paid-up co-operative society shares
- Contributions from silent partners.

Tier 1 capital, however, excludes preferred shares – and this is only one of the reasons why HT-1 with interest paid upfront, is a fake core capital. Moreover, from the amount specified by the above six bullet points should be deducted loss for the year, withdrawals by and loans to proprietors, net debt in personal assets of proprietors, reclaimed amounts paid up by co-operative society members, intangible fixed assets and different adjustments.

The fact that each national supervisor has the freedom to define, within his jurisdiction, the meaning of certain components of regulatory capital, leaves the way open to abuses – and therefore to systemic risk. For instance, in the late 1990s, the Japanese bank supervisor (Financial Services Agency) unilaterally allowed the country's banks to use as capital the so-called deferred tax assets (DTA). Deferred tax assets are a pure oracle; they are also an example of the fact that since the 1988 Capital Accord, the broadly defined asset categories created opportunities for banks to play the system,

- Reducing their burden of regulatory capital for any given level of risk, or
- Increasing their exposure to risk for any given level of capital.

Plenty of gimmicks became possible as managing a portfolio to reduce risk involves combining assets with different risks in such a way that, at least in theory, the hazards offset each other. In practice, that is a myth which produced a great number of opportunities for creative accounting in financial reporting. The latest scandal concerns Resona, the fifth largest Japanese bank. When the DTAs were excluded, its capital reserves fell from 6 percent to 2 percent.

A great deal of manipulation reduces the bank's capital to ashes. As one of the regulators suggested, all potential expected losses should be covered by equity and items entering this broader definition of T-1, not Hybrid T-1. But in his jurisdiction it is admissible to cover goodwill with HT-1. And there is always the need to take a close look at T-2 capital which has been a compromise among central bankers at the time of the 1988 Capital Accord.

For any practical purpose, T-2 is supplementary capital, including some kinds of debt, loan-loss reserves, and up to 45 percent of unrealized gains on securities (paper profits). Paper profits are extremely volatile and, although they were included in T-2 to please the Japanese in the late 1980s, today, with the Tokyo and Osaka exchanges struggling, this clause turned around and hit the Japanese banks on the head. T-2 divides into two parts:

- 'Upper Tier 2, which is perpetual subordinated debt, and it can be up to 100 percent of Tier 2.
- 'Lower Tier 2', which is dated subordinated debt and it can go only up to 50 percent of Tier 2.

The next question is 'What about outright sales?' Provided that assets for which there is a market do exist, this is indeed one of the options for meeting capital adequacy requirements (see also Chapter 9). But the sale of assets must be a strategic top management decision – not a hit and run policy with the sole objective of obtaining some cash. And there should be willing buyers for these assets, rather than having them marked down in a fire sale.

A strategic decision by top management practically means that the assets to be sold are *not* core. Non-core assets may be around for two reasons. Either they should not have been acquired in the first place, or there is a change in strategic orientation. For instance, when in the late 1970s Bankers Trust decided to concentrate in merchant banking, it sold its fifty-seven branches in Manhattan and the rest of the State of New York to Leumi, NatWest and the Royal Bank of Canada.

Also, in general lines of reference, additional capital entering into regulatory capital includes contingency reserves, preferential shares (minus own preferential shares), unrealized reserves (up to a maximum of 1.4 percent of the weighted risk assets), liabilities represented by participation rights, longer-term subordinated liabilities and an additional sum of uncalled commitments. From these must be *subtracted*:

- Market management positions in securitized own participation rights
- Longer-term subordinated liabilities, and
- Certain adjustment items.

As contrasted to T-1 and T-2 defined by Basel I, T-3 is *not* long-term capital. It does not even have a unique definition, among bankers. Some credit institutions include insurance in it; others do not. Tier 3-based capital came up as an option mainly in the twenty-first century:

- It is mostly trading book P&L
- It is too volatile to count on, and
- It consists of short-dated instruments.

Rating agencies will not go for T-3 because trading gains can turn into trading losses at a moment's notice. The regulators take a cautious approach to T-3, and so do several senior bankers. Here in a nutshell are commentaries I heard from different experts regarding the ways they look at T-3 capital:

- 'It is available to cover market risk.'
- 'It is contingent capital and insurance.'
- 'It is largely illiquid assets.'
- 'We don't need it.'

As these comments suggest, today T-3 is neither generally liked nor widely used. Trading assets come and go, changing the base on which regulatory and economic capital are computed. Since its inception in 1998, only big banks with significant trading books tend to favor T-3. It is as well to take note that T-3 usage leads to pricing differentials. Tier 3 maturity is up to two years, and this contrasts to five, ten and fifteen years for loans.

- The pros say T-3 means greater flexibility.
- Contrarians answer that volatility sees to it that this can be an oracle.

Oracles cannot be pillars of the capital base. Contrarians to T-3 also add that updating for profits from trading, minus losses from trading, opens the balance sheet to a wave of creative accounting exercises – masking the fact that, in several cases, T-3 may have a negative value because it includes:

- Net profit in close-out of trading book positions, less probable expenses and less potential liquidation losses
- Short-term subordinated liabilities, and
- Some additional capital above defined ceiling.

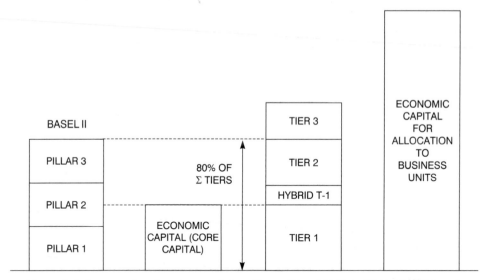

Figure 3.6 A comprehensive picture of the pillars of Basel II, T-1, HT-1, T-2, T-3 and economic capital

Notice also that from T-3 capital must be subtracted market management positions in short-term subordinated liabilities, illiquid assets and losses of subsidiaries (for securities trading firms). When all this is done, what remains stands a good chance of being of questionable value to the institution.

In conclusion, keeping in mind the definitions of component parts of regulatory capital, plus the fact that economic capital has a double meaning (as explained in section 3.3), it is possible to draw a comprehensive view of capital reserves behind Pillar 1 of Basel II – including T-1, HT-1, T-2, T-3 and progressing towards the higher threshold of economic capital to be allocated to the bank's business units. This is shown in Figure 3.6. I am indebted to Tim Thompson, of Barclays Bank, for helping to draw up this picture.

3.5   Pricing assets in Tier 1 and Tier 2 capital

The money embedded in core capital and in additional capital is invested in assets whose fair value is volatile. For assets and liabilities (A&L) management reasons, these assets have to be priced. The adopted solution must be within directives set by regulators. In general, there are two alternatives:

- Book value, and
- Marking-to-market.

Using both methods indiscriminately can lead to trouble. For instance, *if* capitalization is $30 billion and book value stands at $50 billion, *then* the regulators will ask senior management to explain the reasons for the difference. The better solution is to use *management intent* (as specified by SFAS 133):

- If assets are for trading, mark to market
- If for long-term holding, use accruals method.

In the aftermath of requirements posed by the 1996 Market Risk Amendments, credit institutions have learned to mark to model. A major Swiss bank, for example, is marking-to-model its loans portfolio based on the:

- Characteristics of the loan
- Dependability of counterparty
- Prevailing market value, and
- A number of probabilities,

for instance, the likelihood that a loan would not default in the first year, as well as an overall default probability characterizing market conditions. The loan is valued on expectation of cash flows – which is essentially *intrinsic value* – and it is discounted at the appropriate interest rate. A risk premium is added to cover potential surprises.

This example conveys a couple of messages. One is that modeling is becoming the focus of valuation methods and of risk management strategies. With Basel II we can expect the development of state-of-the-art approaches to computing fair value, as well as economic capital requirement to support credit risks resulting from the likelihood that the borrower will default.

Since the mid-1980s, top-tier banks have recognized that expert systems can be instrumental in this solution, because they help to value a client firm on the basis of accumulated knowledge and experience.[3] In the 1990s, the German central bank developed and implemented a sophisticated expert system to judge the quality of loans which it accepted in repo agreements. Among the main inputs of expert systems for loans clearance are:

- The quality of the company's management
- Its capital structure
- Its product line, market appeal and profit outlook
- The volatility of its earnings, and
- Quality of its collateral.

This methodology can be applied with significant returns, with Basel II, for instance, in connection to assessment processes which assign a credit score, probability of default (PD), migration of credit risk probabilities, loss given default (LGD) and exposure at default (EAD). Notice that PD is in percent and LGD is in percent, while EAD is in monetary units: $, £, euro, etc. (PD, LGD, EAD are discussed in detail in Part 3.)

Nearly every company has its own default pattern. Therefore, wholesale clients should be studied on a case-by-case basis – albeit sometimes grouped into small homogeneous groups with nearly common characteristics. This is what Basel II says, as shown on the left-hand side of Figure 3.7. By contrast, medium-size company loans and retail loans can be pooled.

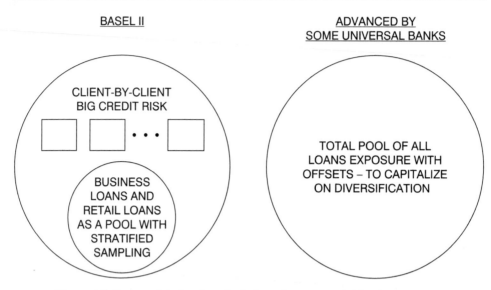

Figure 3.7 Two models for the calculation of a commercial bank's exposure

Many big banks contest this. To minimize their capital requirements they prefer to do total pooling of all exposure associated with their loans, with offsets, as shown on the right-hand side of Figure 3.7. This is not a sound strategy and can lead to many unpleasant surprises. Apart from the fact that extreme events have the potential to significantly weaken the bank's capital base, as a senior central banker was to comment:

- In wholesale banking, these risks are managed in different ways depending on client relationship, and
- Diversity of contractual conditions makes it appropriate to look at big clients separately.

It is always a good credit risk control policy to look carefully at big names and potentially major exposures. This helps the bank in its efforts at diversification, as well as in computing correlations in a factual way.

Moreover, all economic capital allocation essentially deals with risk capital and, therefore, it should be risk adjusted. Details of clients and their loans are most helpful in this procedure. The best managed banks calculate ratios for risk-adjusted returns which are used for:

- Measuring performance, and
- Managing risk of individual business units.

Ratios such as risk-adjusted return on capital (RAROC) and return on economic capital (REC) have become market benchmarks, replacing more traditional ratios like return on equity (ROE) and return on assets (ROA). For starters, return on economic capital identifies the yield represented by the net result in relation to the allocated economic capital K_i, by business unit i or channel (major product line). The algorithm is:

$$REC_i = \frac{Net\ result_i}{K_i} \tag{3.1}$$

and for all business units:

$$REC = \sum_{i=1}^{n} \frac{Net\ result_i}{K_i} \tag{3.2}$$

For each business unit, if the net result is negative, then the corresponding REC_i is negative. A similar formula applies if instead of business units the REC is computed by channel j. In both cases:

$$Total\ economic\ capital = \sum_{i=1}^{n} K_i \tag{3.3}$$

Crédit Suisse differentiates between *economic* net income and *accounting* net income because, in the opinion of its management, the difference between the two can be significant in some product lines. An example is the insurance business. The algorithm used for economic net income is:

$$\begin{aligned} Economic\ net\ income\ = \ &Accounting\ net\ income \\ &+ Adjustment\ for\ fair\ value \\ &+ Changes\ not\ recognized\ in\ income \end{aligned} \tag{3.4}$$

The risk-adjusted return on capital is more sophisticated than REC in the sense that it tunes income to the level of risk being assumed. For instance, it adjusts the interest rate to the likelihood of default, by upping the demanded interest rate. (More on risk-adjusted return on capital in Chapter 13.)

Some banks use a different metric for risk-adjusted return on capital. They take account of the target rate of return in connection with the capital they employ, which essentially means the opportunity cost of capital allocated to a business line or channel. In this case, the algorithm is:

$$RAROC^4 = REC - R_t \tag{3.5}$$

Where R_t stands for target rate of return on the economic capital employed. Notice that such a target rate of return can be computed either on the basis of market comparison, such as taking as reference risk free treasury bonds, through use of one of portfolio theories, or by employing some other standard as target rate.

Furthermore, a sound policy in measuring REC, RAROC, ROE, ROA or any other performance standard, will account for the fact that nothing moves in a straight line. Today, what most graphical presentations offer to the reader is a mean or median, which can be misleading. My advice is to use either:

RETURN ON EQUITY

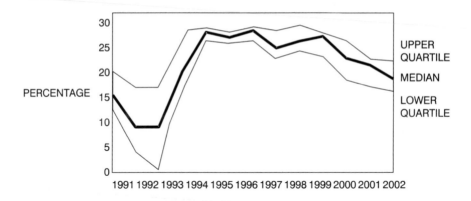

TIER 1 CAPITAL/RISK-WEIGHTED ASSETS

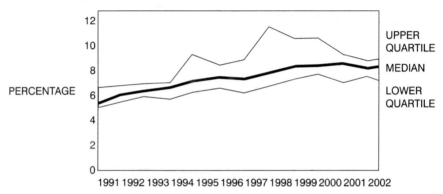

Figure 3.8 Twelve years' return on equity and Tier 1 capital risk-weighted assets of UK banks

■ Mean and 99 percent or 99.9 percent confidence intervals, or
■ Median with upper and lower quartiles.

An example of the latter is shown in Figure 3.8, which presents statistics on twelve years return on equity and T-1 capital over risk-weighted assets. Statistics in this figure come from the 1991 to 2002 timeframe and they characterize the behavior of these two variables in the British banking industry.

In conclusion, the presentation of financial results to senior management, the regulators, and for market discipline reasons, must be both comprehensive and comprehensible. In general, REC and RAROC can be a better gage of operational performance than traditional ratios like ROE and ROA, because they relate return to risk incurred. It should, however, be appreciated that rates of return say nothing about the absolute level of exposure – unless we price in a documented way the risk(s) being assumed. Risk control is a more complex enterprise than the adoption of some ratios.

3.6 Accounting for risks assumed with lending

Default and its consequences are defined in Chapter 10. The purpose of this section is to bring to the reader's attention the fact that different sectors of the industrial and commercial market do not have the same characteristics of exposure. Therefore, any serious study on regulatory capital, and on allocation of economic capital (see Chapter 6), must account for these differences.

Take as an example the retail customer portfolio, which includes mortgage loans. The input parameters are PD, LGD and EAD. One of these parameters may be derived from expected losses (EL). As a rule, exposures to retail borrowers carry a much lower capital charge than exposure to companies – but this may not be true about mortgages,

■ If the bank has a concentration on them, and
■ If it specializes in commercial real estate.

The savings and loans (S&Ls, thrifts) in the USA, and building societies in the UK, are examples of institutions with significant concentration of exposure related to mortgages. Because they finance their mortgages through deposits, they are constantly faced with *mismatch risk* between:

■ The fixed interest rate of long-term mortgages, and
■ The variable interest rate offered to their clients to attract deposits.

This mismatch risk led to the mammoth $800 billion loss by the US thrifts industry in 1989–1991. To assure such failure is not being repeated, the Office of Thrift Supervision (OTS), the regulator of savings and loans in the US, requires that the entities which it supervises submit daily simulations of their financial position with changes of ±100, ±200, ±300 and ±400 basis points (bp). The ±200bp is the benchmark.[5]

Another challenge faced by lenders is the control of loans exposure associated to small and medium-size enterprises (SMEs, see also Chapter 12). The big unknown is the quality of their risk management. According to a 2001 survey by KPMG and Lloyds TSB, most mid-market financial companies have no proper system of risk control, let alone a rigorous system which:

■ Is designed to identify and manage the risks of their various activities, and
■ Is able to inform their board and CEO in a rapid, action-oriented manner.

The lack of a risk control infrastructure puts the banks lending to SMEs in an awkward position because, as every company should appreciate, there is plenty of scope for risk control, and for steps taken in due time to avoid financial disaster. For instance,

■ What will happen if an SME's supplier goes into liquidation?
■ What if a client given a credit line files for bankruptcy?
■ What are the consequences of an investor failing to deliver the funds promised?

Usually the lack of alternative plans and absence of preparedness for adverse conditions, which characterize many SMEs, sees to it that bank loans are used as a buffer. Therefore, vigilance is always essential on the credit institution's part. Once the risks have been identified, managers must be assigned the job of monitoring them. If a problem occurs, there must already be a solution in place, so that the business can continue with minimal disruption – or the bank immediately exercises damage control.

The presence or absence of risk control procedures at loan clients should be reflected into the credit risk model used by the bank (more on this in Chapter 12, section 12.5). The world of insolvency is littered with companies that did not pay sufficient heed to the risks their businesses faced. To avoid disasters, senior management must be ready, in a proactive manner, to:

- Identify the significant risks that could hit the company and, then, arrange these in order of urgency and importance
- Check if the company is fully exploiting its intellectual property and its technology for risk control reasons, and
- Assure board level participation to assessing risks, approve corrective measures, and take needed steps to redress the situation.

This is tantamount to having an early warning system, which does away with the 'fire brigade' approach. Which are the clients to whom we lend that have provided evidence of being in charge of their risks? Which have in place a sound and functioning internal control system? Has *our* bank a system of early indicators which enables it to safeguard its assets?

Given the aforementioned reasons, it is not surprising that the Basel II formulae for credit risk are based on credit ratings applied to company debt, either by rating agencies or internally by banks themselves. The problem is that few of the smaller companies are rated, although in some countries the reserve bank has been giving a helping hand. As mentioned in section 3.5, in Germany the Bundesbank uses expert systems to rate the creditworthiness of loans that commercial banks discount.

According to German law, all loans of DM3 million ($1.5 million) or more must be registered with the Bundesbank. This system could be used effectively as the way to a solution to some of the credit rating problems. A little more complex is the issue of greater risk being assumed with longer-term loan maturity.

Aware that if many loans unravel they put at stake the stability of the financial system, regulatory authorities have taken some proactive steps. Because the large majority of smaller credit institutions are not equipped to rate the companies to whom they lend, on 5 November 2000 the Basel Committee posted on its website new suggestions that include:

- Risk weightings for smaller companies, and
- Proposals that physical collateral, receivables, and leased assets be used to lessen a particular company's credit charge.

These were interim approaches, the Committee said, which needed to be tested and eventually revised. Critics comment that slowly the Basel Committee is starting to micro-manage credit risk by trying to address every issue affecting banks and their loans – or other exposures (more on this in Chapter 16). Another example is the so-called *w-factor* concerning the possibly unquantifiable residual risk in credit derivatives, and setting minimum risk weights for unrated securitized assets.

Because, as section 3.5 explained, T-1 capital is often invested, equally important to the credit institution is its ability to control equity exposure. Notice that for a maximum of ten years, supervisors may exempt from IRB particular equity investments held at time of publication of Basel II. However, if an acquisition increases the proportional share of ownership in a specific equity, this add-on will not be exempt. Internal ratings-based banks are required to separately treat their equity exposures. Basel II offers two alternatives:

- The one builds on PD-LGD-EAD for corporate exposures, requiring them to provide theirown PD estimates for equities
- The other allows them to model potential decrease in market value of equity holdings over a quarterly period.

For both, a simple method exists by which set risk weights are laid down by regulators. Using the more advanced PD-LGD-EAD method banks may use their own estimates. Using the market-based approach, internal models or a scenario analysis may be implemented. Stress testing should also be part of the bank's evaluation toolkit, with the outcome of experiments immediately brought to senior management's attention through the institution's internal control system.[6]

3.7   Provisioning for bad loans under the new framework

Impaired obligations are those where losses are probable and estimable. A loan is classified as impaired if the book value of the claim exceeds the discounted value of the cash flows in future periods, including interest payments, scheduled principal repayments and liquidation of collateral. The nature of accounting and regulatory rules affects the way in which financial institutions:

- Respond to changes in perceived risk, and
- Establish provisioning strategies.

Provisioning for bad loans is part of the regulatory framework. It is also an important factor in credit management, influencing bank profitability and its volatility. In many countries, accounting rules only make feasible a provision to be created after there is a clearly verifiable deterioration in credit quality.

To make matters worse, there are often restrictions on tax deductibility of provisioning expenses, with the result that it is difficult for a bank to increase provisions in an economic boom even if it believes that the future ability of its borrowers to repay has deteriorated. This leads to procyclical effects which are discussed in Chapter 8. In principle,

- Additional profits that arise from underprovisioning could be retained on the bank's balance sheet, rather than paid out as dividends.

- But this is not always possible given the pressures on bank management to maximize return on equity, or because of tax constraints.

Therefore, Basel II correctly aims to bring forward a solution which is rational and at the same time reflects the fact that globalization requires the creation of a level playing field. An effective solution, however, requires the support of many jurisdictions – in view of the fact that it will affect the dynamics of financial cycles in certain countries.

The principle is that a regulatory system built around globally applicable minimum capital ratios and ways which can avoid procyclicality, can contribute to better stability of the financial system. However, critics say that under certain conditions it might also exacerbate economic downturns, as widespread losses from bad loans and/ or equity investments can cause a number of banks and other financial institutions, like insurance companies, to significantly change their behavior. For instance, banks may cut lending,

- To avoid further financial difficulties
- Or simply to pump up capital ratios.

This tightening of lending standards might amplify a downturn, as occurred in Japan in the 1990s and which continues to the present day. A similar situation, in terms of major defaults, developed in America and Europe during the early twenty-first century. At the end of February 2003 Moody's Investors Service gave a warning that corporate defaults in 2002 were higher than at any time since the Great Depression.

The independent rating agency said 141 companies defaulted on $163 billion of debt in the twelve months till end of February 2003, and more than twenty borrowers reneged on debts of $1 billion or more. But Moody's also noted the silver lining: that the market weathered the largest bankruptcy in history when WorldCom defaulted on $23 billion of bonds.

The fact that the market weathered the $163 billion storm *and* WorldCom's mega-bankruptcy has been good news. The bad news is that even though the money will not all be lost, with creditors eventually receiving an average of 20 to 30 percent of their loans, that leaves a huge amount of bad debt, which has not all shown up yet. There are fears that, when it eventually does, too much of it will be on the books of insurers, pensions funds and mutual funds.

The new capital adequacy rules attempt to correct this through a dynamic solution. Basel I capital rules required an increase in the level of capital in a boom if lending is expanding, but they did not call for an increase in the ratio of capital to assets. In other words, the capital requirement for a given portfolio did not change through time as the riskiness of the portfolio changed. This seems to be taken care of in Basel II.[7]

Because, as pressures from impaired loans mount, regulators may be induced to lower the capital standards to avoid procyclical effects or take off the pressure from the banking industry, a proactive evaluation of exposure taken by the banking sector is a 'must'. Particularly important is to know the weight of big banks, given their impact on the global market structure. A metric is the *concentration ratio* (CR), measuring the market share in percentages, of the biggest three to ten credit institutions (depending on the total number of banks), relative to the total banking market (see Chapter 5).

Notes

1 European Central Bank (2002). *Annual Report*. ECB.
2 Basel Committee on Banking Supervision (2003). *Consultative Document: Overview of the New Basel Capital Accord*. BIS, April.
3 D.N. Chorafas and H. Steinmann (1991). *Expert Systems in Banking*. Macmillan.
4 The concept underpinning RAROC is explained in Chapter 13.
5 D.N. Chorafas (2002). *Liabilities, Liquidity and Cash Management: Balancing Financial Risk*. Wiley.
6 D.N. Chorafas (2001). *Implementing and Auditing the Internal Control System*. Macmillan.
7 For greater detail in the calculation of expected loss see Chapter 3, page 75 and Chapter 6, pages 133 and 134.

4 Market discipline and its global impact

4.1 Introduction

The global financial environment has evolved tremendously in the post-World War II years, and most particularly during the last three decades. It has changed from one dominated by banks to one that is increasingly based on liquid capital markets. With this evolution, however, credit risk became a greater issue than it used to be, because of its potential to change into a market-risk tide. The new environment:

- Has increased price volatility, and
- It has made more painful transborder financial losses.

New rules and regulations must therefore account for the ongoing change, as well as for the fact that greater volatility in assets and liabilities can be costly in capital adequacy terms. Beyond this, experts think that some of the more classical issues underpinning prudential capital adequacy, such as loan loss provisioning, may themselves become unstable because of market risk embedded in new financial instruments invented to relieve credit risk, such as credit derivatives.

An integral part of the new market environment is the polyvalence of regulatory action (see Chapter 15) and evolution in regulations. Basel I was a capital accord while, as has been explained in Chapter 1, Basel II is an accord having three pillars: *capital requirements*, *regulatory validation* and *market discipline*. The latter should induce banks to self-discipline with regard to:

- Being in charge of the exposure they are assuming, and
- The computation and maintenance of adequate capital ratios, to face expected and unexpected risks.

In all likelihood in the longer term, the most important innovation brought by Basel II – one with global impact – is that of *market discipline*. As has been explained, market discipline is the target of Pillar 3. Adjuncts to this are issues like reliable financial reporting and transparency, but there are also global-type questions. For instance, is closer alignment of regulatory capital with economic capital good public policy?

To promote market discipline banks must make their accounts available for inspection (I do not mean double books), avoid creative accounting practices, have well-documented reserves and be able to convince the market that they possess financial staying power. The reference to transparency applies to all three main exposures: credit risk, market risk and operational risk – and it requires that the board and CEO provide regular public attestations as to:

- Soundness of the bank and of its assets
- Quality and depth of its managers and professionals (see Chapter 14)
- Robustness of its systems, including information technology, and
- Existence of rigorous internal control (see Chapter 1).

In connection with the first of these points, it is beyond doubt that there must be strategic reserves to face developing imbalances in the banking book and the trading book. The challenge is to provide the *evidence* of such reserves, accounting for the fact that internal and external auditors will not in the future be the only parties directly responsible for market discipline. Corresponding banks and other stakeholders will also play a role. This expands the sense of auditing as well as of what regulators can do.

- Some regulators like the Fed, the OCC and the FDIC have their own examiners.
- Others, like the FSA, are not resourced to do this, and they depend on the audit by chartered accountants.

At the same time, the role of auditing is expanding to include intangibles, like quality of management and internal control. The soundness of the bank's assets and quality of its management correlate. The former is the body of and the latter the mind of the bank, and as an ancient Greek proverb put it: 'A sound mind can only exist in a sound body.' In finance, this proverb works both forwards and backwards.

There is as well much in common between quality and depth of management, on the one hand, and top tier systems support, on the other. High technology sharpens the sensitivity and attention of the bank's management (see Chapter 11). A similar statement is valid in regard to the proper functioning of internal control. Internal control contributes to market discipline when it enables senior executives to have at their fingertips information updated in real-time, as shown in Figure 4.1.

	FOREX	MONEY MARKET	FIXED INCOME	EQUITIES	EXCEPTIONS*
FRONTDESK					
RISK CONTROL					
BACKOFFICE					
MANAGEMENT REPORTING					
AUDITING					

Figure 4.1 Internal control requires five levels of functions to be interactively supported in real-time

*For instance, client suspended after downgrade

Finally, to really contribute to Pillar 3, the auditors (internal, external and of the regulatory agency) must themselves be disciplined and they should use an analytical form of evaluation – from balance sheets to internal controls. The methodology advanced by Basel II can be of service in reaching this goal, and there should also exist transborder consistency. Today, all four remaining big chartered public accountants (CPAs) are global, but they should also be convincing when they act as an arm of the regulators.

4.2 Market discipline and enhanced financial disclosure

The Basel Committee has been encouraging market discipline by developing disclosure requirements allowing market participants to assess key information, which describe the financial health of other market participants. This process will be more effective if it is supported by accounting standards that are global and broad in scope – an issue on which both Basel and the IASB are currently working (see Chapter 3).

Basel II also specifies that for disclosures that are not mandatory under accounting for other requirements, the management of a credit institution may choose to provide Pillar 3 information through means such as publicly accessible Internet websites. Moreover, in observance of the principle of materiality a bank should decide which disclosures are relevant for public information. In principle, data is regarded as material if its omission or misstatement influences or changes the assessment or decision of its reader.

As these two paragraphs document, Basel II has moved way ahead of the 8 percent capital adequacy ratio developed by the Basel Committee in 1988, to provide a level ground for all global banks. (A 4 percent capital adequacy level was retained at the same time for local banks.) Equally important is the fact that the implementation of capital standards is spreading. Subsequent to the 1988 Capital Accord, some eighty countries subscribed to its clauses – representing more than six times the equivalent membership of the Basel Committee. Experts think that Basel II will have wider implications – with market discipline being a key reason.

As we have seen in Chapter 1, however, solutions will not come cheaply. An integral part of enhanced market discipline is the challenge of cross-border consolidation of balance sheets. This adds to supervisory responsibilities because the real problem is that of legislatory differences prevailing in each jurisdiction – as well as lack of homogeneity in law enforcement procedures. These kinds of difference have a significant impact on:

■ Global market discipline, and
■ Transparency in financial statements.

Jurisdictional differences make compliance with Basel II that much more complex and expensive. Citibank has to worry about 101 regulators, in an equal number of countries in which it is active around the world. The Royal Bank of Scotland has to deal with eighty regulatory environments. Similar statistics prevail for many other banks.

Part of the challenge lies in the fact that, in terms of constitutional grounds, there are as many national regulators as countries. There are also regional groups interfacing between the Basel Committee and national regulators, like the EU and its Capital Adequacy Directives (CAD, see Chapter 16), as well as G-10 regulators who are not part of Basel but of the International Organization of Securities Commissions (IOSCO). An example is the Securities and Exchange Commission (SEC) of the USA. All this adds to the challenge to the banks, which must assure capital reserves are:

- Realistic in exposure terms
- Robust in their computation, and
- Reflecting strong governance.

The good news is that the able use of statistical measures may help in conveying a message of confidence to the market, one which abstracts from local legislatory differences and enforcement procedures. Market discipline in a global market can capitalize on the fact that thanks to the 1996 Market Risk Amendment both regulators and commercial bankers think in terms of confidence intervals which qualify the level of reserves. Based on statistics by A.M. Best, the independent rating agency, Figure 4.2 provides an example which links confidence levels to:

- Capital reserves, and
- Company ratings.

Pessimists say, 'The whole regulatory capital problem is not solved by Basel II'. I disagree with this statement, though a great deal depends on what one means by 'the whole'. The whole problem is vast, and under no condition it can be solved by means of one set of rules. For instance, the treatment of capital to guarantee insurance company solvency is now being approached by *Solvency 2*, elaborated by European insurance industry regulators. Solvency 2 is not the objective of Basel II in its current state.

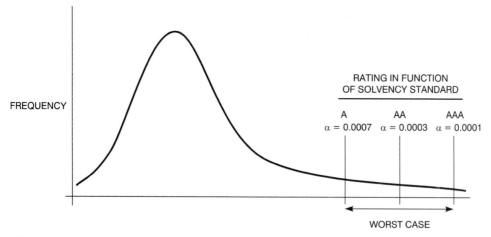

Figure 4.2 Economic capital, solvency standard and level of confidence, according to A.M. Best

One of the salient points of market discipline is that governance is strengthened through financial disclosure practices designed to permit a complementary use of market mechanisms for regulatory objectives. The reader should appreciate that the concept of market discipline is based on the expectation that well-informed market players will find it to their advantage to reward counterparties which are ahead of the curve in:

- Keeping their exposure under control, and
- Having risk-sensitive senior management, as well as effective risk management mechanisms.

Alternatively, market players will be ready to penalize riskier behavior, particularly if the entity's financial resources are weak. This is expected to provide corresponding credit institutions with an additional incentive to control and efficiently manage their exposure. The way to bet is that when market participants find out that discipline is wanting, they will exercise a downward pressure on the culprit financial institution(s). An example is *Japan Premium* which has hit the Japanese banks.

A crucial element in this connection is that of developing a flexible strategy for achieving market discipline and for taking due account of the interests of the different market players. At stake is the scope, depth and frequency of disclosure. For instance, in a fast-moving business environment the classical annual financial statements are too sparse to provide lenders, investors and other counterparties with information regarding the risks they are taking.

- Today, even quarterly financial statements, as practiced in the USA, are not enough.
- The Basel Committee does not say so, but with intraday virtual balance sheets now being feasible, more frequent financial disclosures may be both practical and welcome.

Banks with top-tier technology will not find it difficult to meet such a call, at a certain admissible level of accuracy – say 3 percent. Precision is not important in this case. What is vital is the order of magnitude in marking assets and liabilities, supported by the principle of materiality, as well as means for:

- Confirmation of authenticity and accuracy of financial reports, and
- Protection of confidential information when determining a bank's individual disclosure practices.

In principle, the distinction between core and supplementary capital discussed in Chapter 3, allows financial reporting consistent with the bank's own risk profile. Notice, as well, that virtual financial statements can always be subjected to *backtesting*, in a way similar to that which regulators require with VAR. Accuracy checks are necessary to convey confidence regarding the reliability and quality of chosen:

- Financial information
- Classes of risk, and
- Risk management methods.

For evident reasons, it is wise to maintain a significant degree of homogeneity between the supervisory disclosures, disclosures forming part of external accounting, internal and external accounting practices, internal and external auditing practices, procedures put in place for risk containment, and the institution's system of internal control.[1] This is written on the full understanding that in the corporate world some things are not quite black and white when it comes to accounting procedures and financial statements.

What has been stated in the preceding paragraph is just as valid with internal financial reporting as it is with public disclosures. Both contain qualitative and quantitative information (see section 4.3), and in both exist some 'fuzzy' items. The difference is that an internal accounting management information system (IAMIS) incorporates confidential issues not released in public disclosures. Beyond this issue of confidentiality, however, there are many similitudes between internal and external financial reports – as demonstrated in the next section.

4.3 Qualitative and quantitative information in financial reporting

There are several critical questions connected to financial reporting practices. Some obvious ones concern compliance with new regulations; others focus on the evolving way of doing business: Have *our* accounting standards kept up with changes in lending, trading and investing? Are *our* standards of disclosure and risk assessment well defined? Are they rigorous enough? There are also some crucial queries never really answered through typical financial reporting. For example:

- How well have board members planned and controlled company activities?
- Who profited from the company's complex business structure?
- Who should have been policing the firm, other than the auditors?
- Is there evidence of rule- or law-breaking by directors, managers, traders or loans officers?
- Do corporate governance rules need to be tightened in order to assure sufficient independent scrutiny of management?

Practically all of these questions have to do with market discipline and they should be treated in qualitative disclosures. Taking a leaf out of regulatory reporting requirements connected to credit risk, I am outlining, in four points, some of these issues that help in qualitative disclosures for market discipline:[2]

- Definition of past credit risks, market risks and operational risks (and their frequency)
- Assessment of impact of each of these risks, and of the way in which it has been controlled
- Identification of specific and general allowances for these risks, and their sufficiency
- Types of statistical methods used for quantitative disclosures and their relation to qualitative disclosures.

According to Basel II, qualitative disclosures should be taken very seriously. Nearly all national regulators have the authority to conduct administrative proceedings that can result in censure, fines, issuance of cease-and-desist orders, and suspension or expulsion of the bank or broker, its directors, officers and employees. What is new is that the market has now been given privileges of oversight which, although not yet statutory, has considerable weight because the market can exercise downward pressure when it becomes unhappy with an entity.

In late July 2002 Ericsson's credit rating was cut to junk status in a move that threatened the Swedish telecommunications equipment maker's plans for a heavily discounted SKR30 billion ($3.2 billion) rights issue. Right after, Ericsson said the financial impact of the decision would lead to an increase in the company's financing costs by about SKR100 million ($10.5 million) a year, this being the cost of a one-notch downgrade from BBB– to BB+.

To act in a way to keep the market at ease, different companies have come up with solutions which permit their management to be ahead of the curve. In the early 1990s, for instance, JP Morgan developed what became the VAR algorithm to provide its CEO and senior management with a daily snapshot of market exposure at 16.15 each day. In the late 1990s Prudential Securities designed an executive scorecard which provided the investment bank's senior management with a snapshot of risk and return. Austria's Creditanstalt said that:

- Information on positions for risk categories and counterparties is in real-time, and
- Reports like P&L, trading activities and VAR, are produced and given to senior management daily – though credit reports are still monthly.

Virtual balance sheets available in real-enough time are a good solution. In the late 1990s, Boston's State Street Bank provided itself with the capability of a balance sheet covering its global operations, which could be compiled in thirty minutes. Its accuracy has been at a 96 to 97 percent level – enough for management information on exposure, and for a decision on whether the institution is on the right or the wrong side of the balance sheet. This is what I mean by order of magnitude reporting, which is an engineering term.

The steps necessary to attain such proficiency in financial reporting are very similar to those needed for being in charge of Basel II. The latter are shown in a comprehensive way in Figure 4.3. Notice that they start with top management implementation decision, and they end with compliance and a report to the board. In between lie qualitative and quantitative aspects connected to measurement of counterparty risk. This is the nature of disclosures which helps in improving market discipline. In connection to credit risk, for instance, quantification can be broken down by:

- Aggregate amount of credit, market and operational risk
- Details on instrument exposure which has been assumed
- Geographic distribution of this exposure, and
- Industry/counterparty distribution, including appropriate analyses.

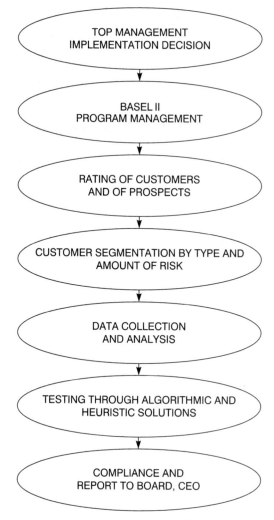

Figure 4.3 Steps necessary for being in charge of Basel II, in counterparty risk

Taking operational risk as an example, an integral part of this quantitative evaluation is allowances for operational risk losses, recoveries, charge-offs, exposure covered by insurance contracts on-balance sheet, exposure covered through derivatives off-balance sheet, possible risk transfer through securitization similar to credit derivatives, and identification of results of operational risk control enhancements.[3]

Along this same frame of reference, just as important is comparison of projected operational risks, frequency and impact documented through real-life data, and the identification and analysis of outliers. Similar references are valid in connection with risk indicators. To be understood by the market, their choice must meet many criteria such as:

- Risk sensitivity
- Relative importance, and
- Management control action.

Risk sensitivity can be tested through analysis of variance (chi-square) and correlation between risk indicators and actual loss experience. For instance, some indicators associated with reconciliation of nostro accounts have higher correlation with loss experience than other indicators. By contrast, there is evidence that risk indicators like client disputes have a rather low correlation with past losses.

On the side of credit risk management, one of the more significant correlations is between credit ratings and loss experience. Both the banks themselves and independent rating agencies watch for this factor. It needs no explaining that timely corrective action promotes market discipline.

For these reasons, the credit institution's senior management should always be informed about the distribution of exposures across rating grades, the associated PDs, LGDs and EADs. Internal and external ratings must be explicitly linked with the bank's internal assessment of capital adequacy, profitability analysis, management of strategic resources and incentive compensation plans. This should be done:

- Comprehensively
- In a homogeneous manner
- On a global scale, and
- In a way to satisfy the prerequisites for market discipline.

There are, however, domains where classical risk calculation methods are ineffective. For instance, current approaches do not cover project financing, which is different to classical issues connected with credit exposure. The risk revolves around the likelihood of the project being completed with assumed credit. Hence, the need to follow up quite closely the progression of the project, milestone by milestone.

A success story in using technology to achieve the aforementioned goal has been Securum, the financial company set up by the Swedish government in the early 1990s to absorb the huge losses of Nordbanken. A negative example of being in control in project financing came a few years later when the Deutsche Bank failed in this task, and the result has been a rumoured DM5 billion (2.5 billion euros) loss in the Schneider affair.

4.4   Credit ratings are a tool of market discipline

Chapter 2 has looked at the drive for higher credit ratings by financial institutions as one of the major benefits of Basel II to the banking industry as a whole and to each individual entity. There are several reputable independent rating agencies, and they all take care to provide investors with reliable information on creditworthiness, which is assessed in a consistent and appropriate manner.

The reader's attention has also been drawn to the fact that another important benefit derived from, or at least assisted by, Basel II is risk-based pricing of financial products and services. In terms of credit risk control, this revolves around the active use of credit ratings – both internal and external – which substantiates F-IRB and A-IRB.

As my research has revealed, opinions differ as to what constitutes the kernel of IRB. The majority opinion has been that it is not models but *ratings* per se whose aftermath is amplified by the dual impact of capital adequacy dynamics and assumed risk. Barclays Bank has given an excellent example of how far the rating issue goes in both directions:

- Ratings of counterparties done by the bank, and
- Rating of the bank's own creditworthiness by independent agencies.

Well-managed credit institutions seem to have taken both points, and most particularly the second one to heart. Speaking at the 'Capital Allocation 2003' conference in London,[4] Tim Thompson and Peter Goshawk said that Barclays has chosen for itself an AA rating target because a double-A is necessary:

- To act as a depositor of funds in the UK, and
- To be a reliable trading partner for corresponding banks and client companies worldwide.

There is no better evidence that Basel II will have an influence on market discipline than this drive by credit institutions to obtain higher ratings from independent agencies – or, for that matter of the fact that credit ratings have become a means of communicating to counterparties an entity's creditworthiness. This is shown in Figure 4.4 which brings to the reader's attention the transition:

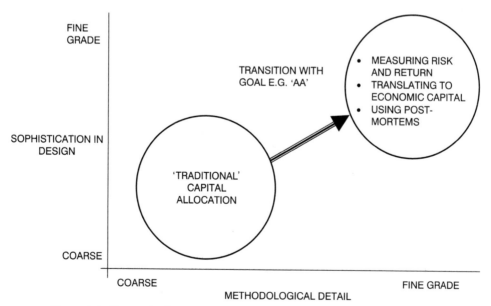

Figure 4.4 Change in the top management view of capital because of Basel II

- From classical capital allocation
- To one which accounts for target ratings, by focusing on the sufficiency of economic capital and on risk and return.

As with every coin, this has two sides. On the one side is that each legal entity to which a loan is made must first be rated, and such rating should be subject to approval by an independent department within the institution that does not stand to benefit from the rating being assigned. The other side of the coin is that banks must keep a close watch on the ratings they themselves are allocated by independent agencies.

- Beyond doubt, ratings must be subject to steady review, and this review process should be documented.
- Borrowers have to be rerated at least annually, as well as within ninety days of receipt of new financial information.

The caveat here is that banks themselves are borrowers. They buy money from correspondent banks, and from capital markets by issuing bonds. Therefore, similar principles apply to the review of the bank's own rating by its business partners, and independent rating agencies as well. Market discipline is a two-way process; it is not just one way.

It follows that each and every bank should have effective ways and means to obtain and update relevant information on its borrower's financial condition. Higher-risk or problem credits have to be updated both more frequently and through a more rigorous method, corresponding to *tightened* inspection. This, too, contributes in a significant way to market discipline.

Higher-risk or problem credits should be reviewed more frequently and with more urgency, particularly when new information comes to light. Figure 4.5 suggests that

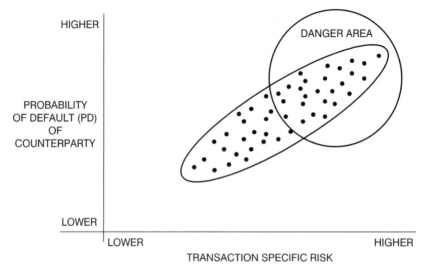

Figure 4.5 Solution space for a valid internal rating system

the bank's internal rating system, which defines the solution space for creditworthiness, must have at least two dimensions:

- An estimate of the risk of borrower default, and
- An estimate of transaction-specific, or facility-specific, risk.

Regarding the first of these, the best IRB approach is not to have just two-tier yes/no sort of answers – which is approximated by the usual limited range of five credit grades or so – but to have wide risk-sensitive answers. This calls for a scale of twenty thresholds corresponding to rating by independent rating agencies: from AAA to D.

Market discipline is enhanced through greater detail because it limits the effects of chance, oversight or slippage from a coarse lower to a coarse higher grade in a way that poor management is rewarded. Associated with a fine-grain rating policy should be a directive by the board that in no case, in this scale, should more than 10 percent of the counterparties fall within the same threshold – and fewer than 10 percent should be in all of the non-investment grades taken together.[5] (Basel's viewpoint is covered later in this section.)

Speaking from experience, some of the experts I met in my research pressed the point that a credit rating scale of twenty is better than one of ten. But others thought that a scale of ten in internal ratings is anyway an improvement over current internal credit rating practices. I do not agree with this viewpoint. A scale of ten grades would group two by two the finer level of thresholds. For instance AAA and AA+, the best in creditworthiness, would correspond to just one grade. That is not enough.

Ten-grade scale	Rating scale	Probability of default: 1 year	Probability of default: 5 years	Management quality[1]
1	AAA, AA+			
2	AA, AA-			
3	A+, A			
4	A-, BBB+			
5	BBB, BBB-			
6	BB+, BB			
7	BB-, B+			
8	B, B-			
9	C			
10	D			

Note: 1 This can be used only to decrease the grade scale classification, not to increase it.

Table 4.1 A ten-grade credit risk classification: rating buckets must be calibrated to default

The usually practiced rating buckets for a system of ten grades are shown in Table 4.1. Even with such a reduced scale, each threshold should be assigned a probability of default in one year and in five years corresponding to the *worst* of the two ratings grouped at the same grade level. An added feature of accurate rating is that of accounting for the quality of management, which has become a 'must'.

A matrix like the one in Table 4.1, or better still one of twenty grades, is part of the domain of counterparty risk control practices. With Basel II, banks are required to derive a one-year PD for each grade. To my mind, the five-year DP is a 'must'. Notice that with any scale, senior management must ensure that the distribution of loans and other transactions is not skewed towards lower ratings.

The Basel Committee says that there should be meaningful distribution of exposure across grades, with no more than 30 percent of gross exposures in any single borrower grade in the performing loans classes of a ten-grade scale, which essentially means grades 1 to 5 in Table 4.1, since 7 to 10 are non-investment grades.

Whether a twenty-grade scale or a ten-grade is chosen, it should also be appreciated that ratings are never black and white. They come in tonalities of grey, which means in 'fuzzy' sets. An example is provided in Figure 4.6, with a scale which goes from A– to AAA. An entity rated at triple A has a high possibility of being of that grade, but also a low possibility of being AA+. Similarly, one rated at AA– has a high possibility of being either A+ or AA.[6] Markets, and therefore investors, lenders and other parties should be accustomed to this notion which underpins 'fuzzy' engineering.

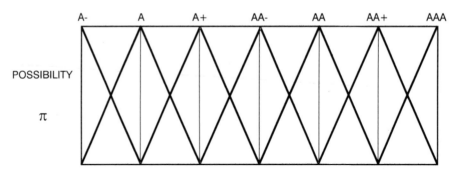

Figure 4.6 Whether they concern bonds or counterparties, ratings come in fuzzy sets

4.5   Important notions about risk grades and rating systems

Every financial transaction involves risk, but some do so more than others. For obvious reasons, counterparties, financial instruments and transactions involving higher exposure should be the subject of greater attention. An evaluation of risk grade should incorporate the bank's conservative expectations as to the borrower's ability to:

- Withstand normal business stresses, and
- Meet future contractual obligations.

Because risk ratings are usually mapped into the one-year PD, as has been emphasized, the Basel Committee advises that the probability of default should be reviewed at least annually and more frequently for higher-risk borrowers. Also, both regulators and the market as a whole expect each credit institution to be able to demonstrate the criteria it uses to cover all credit risk factors. Such criteria should be:

■ Relevant to the analysis of borrower risk
■ Both plausible and intuitive
■ With predictive and discriminatory power, and
■ Used to distinguish risk, rather than minimize regulatory capital requirements.

A basic demand by the Basel Committee, in connection with IRB, is that all material aspects of rating and probability of default estimates (see Chapter 10) must be understood and approved by the board of directors, CEO, executive committee and senior management. Market discipline requires nothing less than that. Senior managers should receive at least monthly reports including risk profiles by:

■ Major counterparty
■ Distribution of grades
■ Migration across grades
■ Quantification of loss estimates per grade, and
■ Comparison of realized default rates against expectations.

While these are elements of internal good governance, they also impact on market discipline. The same is true of assurance by the bank's senior management that the rating process, criteria being used and outcome are comprehensively documented, to facilitate auditing. When and where statistical models are used in the rating process, management must see to it that the credit institution has in place a methodology which facilitates the understanding of model development and usage, including:

■ The hypotheses being made
■ The mathematical and empirical basis of assigned PD estimates to grades for individual obligors
■ The data source(s) used to make these estimates
■ The out-of-time and out-of-sample performance tests.

The methodology to which I am referring should provide a sound basis for validating the selection of explanatory variables, indicate circumstances under which the model does not work effectively and document that the bank is fully aware of the model's limitations. Everything facilitating the market's appreciation of an institution's methods and models helps in terms of discipline.

Along this same line of reference, the regulators' message is that there are prerequisites to a valid IRB implementation. These start with risk grades, proceed with modeling and end with information which can be understood by the market – and evaluated in terms of accuracy.

A sound and properly maintained system of counterparty risk rating is invaluable in securitization, and in the evaluation of collateral. Several studies have demonstrated that the hypothesis, 'If one has sufficient collateral, he does not need to care about rating', is wrong. Every bank must appreciate that:

- The quality of collateral varies from one case to the next, and
- Management must always expect loss connected to collateral (see also Chapter 12).

Beyond this, the methodology being adopted, the hypotheses being made and the deliverables obtained with Basel II, whether the standardized method, F-IRB or A-IRB is implemented, have to be regularly audited. For such purpose, the bank must internally audit and document the performance of its rating system at least annually, including its quantification of internal ratings. An external audit can also provide valuable insight.

It is no less important to emphasize that rapid innovation in financial services has made static approaches to valuation akin to driving at 100 miles per hour but looking only through the rear-view mirror. Figure 4.7 says as much about the estimation of risk. The upper half of the figure, though common practice, is an aberration. The lower half suggests a dynamic valuation approach where:

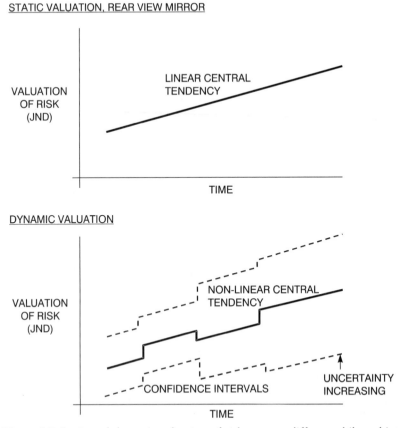

Figure 4.7 Static and dynamic valuation of risk are two different philosophies

- The central tendency is non-linear, and
- Confidence intervals are always computed, preferably at 99.9 level of significance (more on this later).

Notice that in the second half of Figure 4.7 the first three distributions are normal, but the fourth is skewed with tendency towards a higher valuation of risk. The reader will also recall, from section 4.4, that the shape of risk distributions, too, must be audited.

To ensure that the audit of credit risk distributions, as well as that of the credit risk model as a whole, are dependable, policies established by the board should feature an independent credit review function responsible for taking a critical view of the design, implementation and performance of the internal rating system. Market discipline is improved when this unit:

- Makes stress tests on internal ratings
- Analyzes reports on the outputs of the bank's internal rating system, and
- Evaluates historical data on the performance of credits by internal grade, including migration analysis.

Other functions of the aforementioned control should be to assure that procedures are in place to check regularly that ratings are consistently assigned according to established policies and criteria, and to review as well as to document any changes to the rating process – including the reasons for these changes, and their aftermath.

Finally, corporate policy should clearly state that risk assessments must always be conservative and, as we have seen, extend beyond accounting information. In line with the concept of tightened inspection, introduced in section 4.4, market discipline requires that the depth of credit analysis should increase as:

- A borrower's financial condition deteriorates, and
- The default point approaches (see section 4.6).

Credit institutions must always be ready to take all relevant information into account in assigning and testing ratings. Data should be current, the methodology being used clearly specified and the hypotheses being made well documented. As a minimum, both in evaluation and in re-evaluation, a bank should consider the borrower's historical and projected capacity to generate cash to repay debt and support other capital expenditures, and the likelihood that unforeseen circumstances could exhaust the capital cushion and result in insolvency.

4.6 Market discipline and the management of default risk

Sections 4.4 and 4.5 have presented a long list of critical factors to be evaluated in establishing the borrower's quality and dependability. Other criteria are the stream of earnings, the degree to which revenue and cash flow come from core business operations (as opposed to unique and non-recurring sources) and the availability of reliable, audited financial statements. These should conform to applicable accounting standards. Still other factors that have significant impact on credit risk patterns are:

- The possibility of accessing debt and equity markets
- The degree of operating leverage, and susceptibility to interruption in revenues
- Risk characteristics of the country in which the company operates, including cross-border transfer risk
- The borrower's position within the industry and pragmatic future prospects
- The depth and skill of management to effectively respond to changing conditions and deploy resources.

All five items in the aforementioned list, indeed all variables used in modeling a company's survivability, must have statistical power. There is also critical information of a qualitative nature which must be captured by the bank's analysts, informing senior management for appropriate action to be taken.

Regarding the last point in the list, which refers to management quality, it is quite interesting to notice that as a recent study by Moody's Investors Service documented, the most significant factor affecting the probability of default had to do with quality of management. The importance of this factor has already been brought to the reader's attention in connection with Table 4.1.

Because banks (and investors at large) typically make more money from credit risk than from market risk, the control tools should be chosen most carefully on the credit risk side. The able management of default risk has a long list of prerequisites. When all of them are fulfilled, we position ourselves in a way enabling us to address two of the IRB milestones:

- *Definition of default point*, or asset value at which the company will default, a metric which must be dynamically recomputed for every medium to major counterparty.
- *Default correlations* (see Chapter 11). These measure the degree to which are related default risks of various borrowers and other parties in the portfolio.

Default rates, default points and correlations change over time, sometimes significantly so. Figure 4.8 documents this statement with statistics from US junk bonds in the 1972 to 2002 timeframe. Default volatility characterizing junk bonds is *Milken risk*, named after the man who discovered that between 1972 and 1984, fallen angels (formerly competitive companies which went bankrupt), and their bonds, had only an average 2 percent probability of default.

Market dynamics, however, saw to it that the massive exploitation of junk bonds radically changed this 2 percent statistic and led to an 11 percent default rate; a 550 percent increase in non-performing bonds below investment grade. With such high default rate, plus mismatch risk, the savings and loans (S&Ls, thrifts, building societies) which had invested in junk bonds collapsed. As a result, for five or six years junk bonds went out of favor – but then they zoomed up again as favorable instruments in the bubble years of the late 1990s.

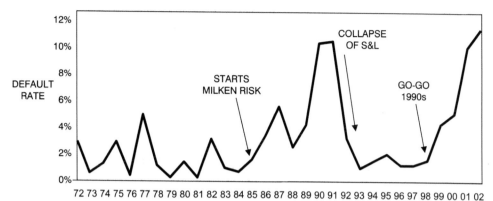

Figure 4.8 Default in rates in US junk bonds, 1972–2002, and Milken risk

One of the issues many banks and investors fail to appreciate is that there is a lack of upside with liabilities. Unlike equities, loans have no upside potential, while bonds have a rather limited upside conditioned by interest rates. Therefore, the case for managing default risk in diversified portfolios is truly compelling, both:

- To the individual credit institutions for reasons of good governance, and
- To the market as a whole, and all of its players who must be able to gage the amount of credit risk outstanding.

These two points give a hint of how polyvalent the perception of risk necessary for enforcing market discipline needs to be. Several preparatory steps, including a rigorous conceptual framework, should be fulfilled to create a sound credit risk modeling methodology that can stand the test of time. The use of IRB for market discipline is not for the faint hearted. A sound methodology would proceed through milestones:

- Creating a master credit risk scale
- Associating probability of default to this master scale
- Proceeding with definition of default point for each major relationship
- Establishing appropriate default correlations
- Pricing to risk, rather than to market
- Introducing a factor representing quality of management, and
- Making capital allocation according to the shape of the risk distribution (see Chapters 5 to 7).

What market discipline requires is dependable information on all these milestones. When default categories are established involving several clients, there must be an adequate number of loans in the sample, the data period used should be relevant and the underlying statistical analysis robust. It is also advisable to consider the economic and market conditions for the period from which historical data was taken, and to account for the fact there is volatility in credit risk.[7]

Conditions underpinning default and its default point, the product of the *probability of default* and *loss given default* gives the quantitative estimate of *exposure at default*. For corporate, business, mortgages and personal loans, EAD provides a good reference measure *if* brought to level of:

- Loan pricing, and
- Loan approval.

This is part of risk-based pricing (see Chapter 2). Just as important is the process of computing *loans equivalence* – which essentially amounts to demodulation of the notional principal amount characterizing each derivatives instrument, down to the level of capital at risk.[8] The integration of credit risk with market risk, resulting from trading and derivatives exposure, makes mandatory demodulation to LEQ, followed by Monte Carlo simulation. Loans equivalence should also be used in conjunction with limits. Still more metrics are needed for letters of credit, overdrafts and other instruments where there will be drawdown of unused lines as default approaches.

4.7   Winners and losers with the new regime

Neither historical earnings nor dividends provide a satisfactory explanation of how the market (as contrasted to independent rating agencies) grades a credit institution. Perceived financial staying power as well as prospective growth in earnings and dividends are probably more influential criteria than economic equity per se. Current market prices of stocks are supposed to reflect stockholders' expectations of future cash flow, or *intrinsic value*, although few equity investors take care to study them analytically.

The immediate aftermath of mergers and acquisitions on an equity's price is an example of the market's sway by the event itself, rather than its fundamentals. Nor are book values so important in determining the price of an acquired company, or for that matter of an investment. Book values merely represent historical values; money that has been poured into assets maintained through accounting in the books in a way that may have little relation to current prices.

The operational value of an acquired or merged company is more relevant when counted in terms of its business contribution to joint activities. The problem is that acquisitions have embedded in them a significant element of prestige, as well as a goodwill component which reflects familiar clichés but has limited understanding of the acquired or merged entity's strengths and weaknesses. This contradicts the principle that the ultimate test of any business operation is its ability to predict its own outcome.

Predicting or estimating the outcome of an operation is by no means an easy job. The financial industry is particularly difficult because the rules of the game allow a great amount of leveraging, both of the assets of the institution itself and the economy as a whole. This may lead to bubbles and instability in the financial markets – which is the antipode of market discipline.

Marriner Eccles, the chairman of the Federal Reserve in the Franklin Roosevelt years, phrased the risk to which I am referring in a beautiful way: 'There is no limit to the amount of money that can be created by the banking system. But there are limits to our productive facilities, and our labor supply, which can be only slowly increased and which at present are being used to near capacity.'[9]

Up to a point a limit to leveraged growth and its unexpected consequences is put through market psychology. When market psychology turns negative towards a company, investors punish it by hitting hard its capitalization, and by refusing to buy its debt without a significant premium to the interest rate, and some covenants.

Psychology is a virtual component of market discipline. The real component, particularly in regard to a credit institution, is capital adequacy. However, as we have seen, a static capital ratio such as the 8 percent of Basel I, does not account for the dynamics of the economy and for the risks taken by the financial institution to which it applies. This can be corrected through the IRB method of Basel II – which is in the process of becoming an internal risks-based method for greater market discipline.

But there are prerequisites. The Basel Committee has advanced some fundamental requirements for banks to be eligible for the IRB approach. Each of these is relevant to some aspect of market discipline, like the meaningful differentiation of credit risks, completeness and integrity of rating responsibilities, and criteria and orientation of the rating system. Other rules address:

- Minimum requirements for estimation of probability of default
- Oversight of the rating system and associated processes
- Reliable data collection and information technology systems, and
- Factual and documented internal validation, as well as dependable disclosure.

Several experts participating in the research expressed the opinion that, as far as market discipline is concerned, for every credit institution the ultimate test will come post-mortem. This is strengthened by QIS results (see Chapter 1) which indicate a high degree of dispersion in capital requirements between banks. There is also procyclicality (see Chapter 8), which affects the cost of capital acquisition as banks find themselves obliged in time of distress to liquidate certain assets to meet capital requirements.

In fact, results obtained through successive QIS led analysts to the conclusion that because IRB allows certain freedoms to banks, and no two institutions have the same risk profile, it will be very interesting to study the resulting differences in due course, and the regulators' reaction to them. Already, Basel has moved some of IRB's constituent elements from Pillar 1 to Pillar 2 and streamlined market discipline (Pillar 3).

For instance, Pillar 2 will pick up legal differences existing in jurisdictions, like the one concerning bankruptcy protection. The contrast between countries can be easily seen by comparing bankruptcy protection in Germany, where the law is tough, with bankruptcy protection in the USA in Chapter 10. Loss given default depends a lot on national bankruptcy laws.

Analysts to whom I spoke on the issue of risk patterns to be revealed through IRB, think that for reasons of market discipline regulatory capital requirements will generally increase over time with Basel II – but this will also improve bank dependability. The way to bet is that banks that will profit from Basel II are those with sound corporate governance *and* with sophisticated solutions – including rocket scientists and high technology. In short, credit institutions able to:

- Show the up-marking as *signaling capital* (therefore benefiting from market discipline), and
- Willing to establish rigorous risk management methods, as well as hold open their internal control channels.

Another element which will divide winners from losers is that the greater skills and risk sensitivity of some of the banks will favor them in the sense of creating barriers to entry into their territory for other credit institutions. By contrast, the penalized banks will be those with a weak capital base, wanting skills, low technology, primitive risk databases and unable to show that market discipline is among their foremost objectives.

Notes

1 D.N. Chorafas (2001). *Implementing and Auditing the Internal Control System.* Macmillan.
2 Basel Committee (2001). *Working Paper on Pillar 3 – Market Discipline.* Basel Committee, September.
3 D.N. Chorafas (2004). *Operational Risk Control with Basel II.* Butterworth-Heinemann.
4 Organized by IIR, 21–22 January 2003.
5 D.N. Chorafas (2000). *Managing Credit Risk, Volume 1: Analyzing, Rating and Pricing the Probability of Default.* Euromoney.
6 D.N. Chorafas (1994). *Chaos Theory in the Financial Markets.* Probus.
7 D.N. Chorafas (2000). *Managing Credit Risk, Volume 1: Analyzing, Rating and Pricing the Probability of Default.* Euromoney.
8 D.N. Chorafas (2000). *Managing Credit Risk, Volume 2: The Lessons of VAR Failures and Imprudent Exposure.* Euromoney.
9 William Greider (1987). *Secrets of the Temple: How the Federal Reserve Runs the Country.* Touchstone/Simon and Schuster.

2

The allocation of economic capital to business units

5 Economic capital defined

5.1 Introduction

There is no uniform definition of economic capital. According to a survey by the Bundesbank, many institutions use core capital as their gage, though others also incorporate components of additional capital such as preferential shares, unrealized reserves and so on. Dutch regulators want to see exposures like transfer risk, interest rate risk, FOREX risk and insurance risk covered by economic capital.

A broader approach to economic capital than the one just mentioned looks at it as a reserve or cushion for unexpected losses. This is in contrast to regulatory capital which, as discussed in Chapter 3, primarily addresses expected losses. In this sense, economic capital's role is to assure that even under extreme conditions the credit institution:

- Attracts counterparties
- Remains solvent, and
- Stays in business.

These two examples show that the borderline between regulatory capital and economic capital is not cast in stone. This book looks at economic capital as going well beyond regulatory capital, which is necessary to get a license. Taken together, regulatory capital and economic capital are the bank's comprehensive financial resources in a form that is liquid or easy to realize. Together, they cover all significant risks. 'Business risk is an implicit capital,' said one of the regulators.

With only a couple of exceptions, the outcome of the meetings I held in my research on the theme of this book can be phrased in one sentence: while regulatory capital is the *minimum* amount needed to have a license, economic capital is the amount necessary to be in business – at a 99 percent or better level of confidence – in regard to assumed risks. This leaves room for further capital reserves to cover the 1 percent at the tail of the distribution.

- Capital additional to that required by regulators is necessary for unexpected risks, including extreme events, and for gaining market confidence.
- But economic capital is a *management requirement*, not an issue of compliance with regulations – and this largely explains why there are different viewpoints regarding its definition.

These different viewpoints have a common background, which looks at economic capital as a performance measure. They also pose challenges such as fair value of assets and liabilities; identification of risks, correlations, weights and effective resource allocation (see Chapter 7). The latter must satisfy a number of requirements, having to do with the three different approaches to which I have already referred in Part 1:

1 *Shareholders' perspective.* Shareholders watch if capital is calibrated against market prices. Notice however that, as the market rises and falls, an entity's capitalization is volatile.
2 *Bondholders' perspective.* As far as bondholders are concerned, intrinsic value is just as important as capital reserves. The same is true of the entity's liquidity and of the value of its assets.
3 *Regulators' perspective.* According to the viewpoint of supervisory authorities, risk weighting of assets serves regulatory capital purposes, and this contributes to financial stability. Nevertheless many regulators want to see additional capital addressing unexpected risk and extreme events, along the pattern shown in Figure 5.1.

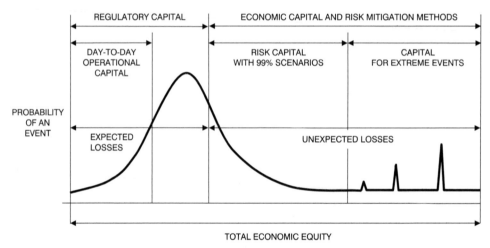

Figure 5.1 Classification of a bank's capital requirements according to risk

This is the evolving general direction. Regarding regulatory guidelines in connection with economic capital, the details are still being worked out as everybody – from central bankers to commercial bankers – gains experience with Basel II. For instance, what should be done to avoid procyclicality (see Chapter 8), or how should equity, loans and investments be priced in a way to account for volatility in fair value, and for associated uncertainty in net worth.

5.2 A close look at economic capital

The statement was made in the Introduction that, so far at least, the regulators have not established a unique definition nor set global rules for economic capital. 'How to handle it' remains the privilege of each jurisdiction and, to a significant extent, of each bank. Based on the majority of expert opinions obtained in my research, I look at economic capital as being a major component of *total economic equity*, which includes:

■ Regulatory capital
■ On-balance sheet assets and liabilities, and
■ Off-balance sheet assets and liabilities.

An integrative pattern is presented in Figure 5.2. Total economic equity is divided into these three classes, each having its own characteristics. Different component parts, like contingent capital and insurance, are playing an increasingly important role in financial support of institutions and might be looked at as weak members of the economic capital family.

Much of what comes into the right-hand box in Figure 5.2, however, represents largely illiquid assets. At least so far, in general, it has been available to cover market risk. This right-hand box contains elements of both T-3 and contingent capital. (More on total economic equity in section 5.3, and on contingent capital in section 5.4.)

Another problem with off-balance sheet economic equity is that a great deal in fair value has to do with derivative financial instruments in the bank's trading book. While the majority of derivatives tend to be short to medium term, some are long

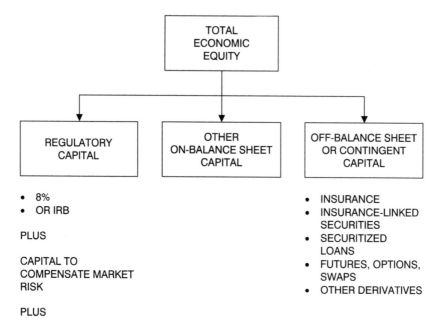

Figure 5.2 A comprehensive definition of total economic equity under current conditions

term. Interest rate swaps may go up to thirty years, which is not rational but that is the reality. To make matters more complex, the fair value of these instruments is tied to several variables.[1]

Some regulators permit valuation of derivative instruments kept to maturity through accruals, while those for trading purposes must be marked to market. According to the SFAS 133 by the Financial Accounting Standards Board, the difference is made by *management intent*. As already stated, provided the board clearly defines its intent to the regulators,

- *If* derivatives assets are for trading, *then* they must be marked to market
- *If* for long-term holdings, *then* the institution can use the accruals method.

In addition to the difference that exists between regulatory capital and economic capital, there is a distinction to be made between economic capital and entrepreneurial capital. It has been a deliberate choice, in preparing an integrated view of expert opinions on economic capital, that this distinction should not take center stage, for the following reasons.

In the late 1990s, the notions of economic capital and entrepreneurial capital were coexisting but were not clearly defined. Often, when one bank told me something constitutes economic capital another bank said, 'This is entrepreneurial capital' and described something different – and vice versa (more on this confusion in section 5.3). As we have already seen, even this one concept – economic capital – does not mean the same thing to all people because its criteria vary from one entity to the next. The choice of criteria is influenced by the:

- Institution's internal culture
- Nature of unexpected losses
- Risk-weighted approaches
- Granularity in measurements, and
- Type of risk-based modeling.

Other reasons why different entities have distinct ways of looking at economic capital are relative cost of equity and cost of debt (see Chapter 9), policies in regard to solvency and liquidity and attention paid to the so-called signaling capital. Signaling capital tells the market whether *our* bank has financial staying power and, in principle, it goes beyond economic capital to cover tail events. Tail events are events which happen at the tails of a distribution, particularly those beyond three standard deviations. They are very interesting because they may hide spikes, also recurrent events as in the case of a leptokyrtotic distribution (Hurst exponent).[1]

Still other criteria used by credit institutions in framing an economic capital definition are the capital allocation methodology they are adopting, risk-based evaluations which they are doing, the assets they keep in their economic capital equation, and what they leave out of these assets and how they allocate them. For instance,

- Share buybacks consume economic capital.
- Goodwill also consumes economic capital, therefore, it has an impact on capital allocation decisions.

'Economic capital is the amount of capital required by a financial institution to achieve its target solvency standard,' says José Sanchez-Crespo, general manager of A.M. Best European Operation, adding that, 'The solvency standard is expressed in terms of company default probability.' A.M. Best, an independent rating agency specializing in the insurance industry, characterizes as economic capital all capital available to offset the company's liabilities, including:

- Shareholder funds
- Discounting of reserves to their economic value, and
- All other forms of capital that can be used to pay policyholders (in insurance).

A.M. Best incorporates into economic capital part of the debt when the length of borrowing is twenty years. This is also known as 'hybrid capital' (see Chapter 3). Altogether, the Sanchez-Crespo definition, as well as the others we have considered, is in contrast to that of regulatory capital which, for an insurance firm, is:

- The minimum solvency margin, and
- What an insurer needs to get a license and operate.

'Economic capital is an amount such that any loss in value larger than this amount has a really small predefined probability,' suggests Walter Pompliano of Standard & Poor's. This means sufficient capital reserves are required to absorb all risks, even with a market that does not support capital replenishment. Standard & Poor's advances four criteria for sound economic capital provisions:

- Three years without access to capital markets
- Forced rollover of maturing loans
- No way to attain liquidity of loans
- Enough capital to continue making loans.

As an independent credit rating agency, Standard & Poor's uses two core capital metrics, in contrast to equity and T-1: *adjusted core equity* (ACE), equal to permanent equity minus goodwill and minus reserves, and *adjusted total equity* (ATE), which tracks the hybrid T-1. There are three conditions for hybrid capital instruments to be included in ATE:

- Permanence
- Loss absorption
- Cushion to debtholders in liquidation.

'Ideally, the level of economic capital should be the same as the level of own funds,' said the Austrian National Bank. According to the Austrian central bank, own funds consist of paid-up capital, which is share capital, disclosed reserves (that is, open reserves), funds for general banking risks (provisions with reserve character), hidden reserves (which in Austria and Switzerland, but not in the USA, are lawful), supplementary capital, subordinated capital, revaluation reserves and short-term subordinated capital.

One of the challenges posed by this outline of own funds' components is that of proper valuation of equity. The classical book equity is not a good measure because, as we have seen, book value rarely, if ever, corresponds to market value. Also, book equity has a weak correlation to risks actually faced by the credit institution. For this reason, many banks working with the A-IRB method consider the broader definition of economic capital as a better framework for calculating operational risk reserves.

5.3   Emphasizing total economic equity

Section 5.2 made a quick reference to entrepreneurial capital, stating that it has been a deliberate choice to downplay its role, if not to leave it out of the picture altogether. At the same time, however, the text introduced the concept of total economic equity into which regulatory capital, entrepreneurial capital and economic capital used to merge. As a historical reference, the pattern of the definition prevailing in 1998, is shown in Figure 5.3.

My research in 1998, sponsored by the International Securities Markets Association (ISMA), came to this distinction between economic capital and entrepreneurial capital from an internal control viewpoint. The need for an integrative approach lies in the fact that information, carried to senior management by the feedback channels of internal control, must be convergent in order to lead to corrective action.

Let me make at least one reference to how, at the time of the 1998 ISMA-sponsored research, regulators looked at entrepreneurial capital. 'Most banks consider entrepreneurial capital as regulatory capital,' said Dr Susanne Brandenberger of the Swiss Federal Banking Commission. By way of contrast, in the course of that same meeting, the internal allocation of economic capital was defined as:

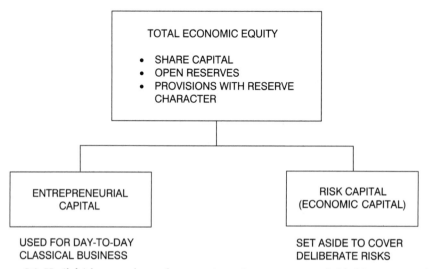

Figure 5.3 Until fairly recently total economic equity was seen as divided into two major classes, each with its own risk management prerequisites

- Typically done for trading reasons, and
- Followed up by the calculation of value at risk.

These definitions have significantly evolved over the elapsed years, and this is a talking example of the dynamics of the financial industry. During a recent meeting in London, experts said that as long as one accounts for such evolution in concepts, and one can find a reasonable convergence of opinions, the exact definition is not that important. They also added that whichever way economic capital's definition goes, the fact remains that today there is a multitude of forms linking:

- Capital allocation, and
- Risk control.

One of these is the strategy chosen by the credit institution for *capital management* and it is connected to the effectiveness of measures, metrics and policies adopted for that specific purpose – with exposure being a major input. Responding to the needs of the market, in which an institution operates, involves risk. Therefore, to a large extent, 'the capital the bank puts at play is risk capital – no matter how it is called,' suggested one of the experts. Risk capital serves three principal purposes:

- Establishing an operational base
- Funding ongoing operations, and
- Protecting against adverse financial results.

The third point enhances the company's financial staying power, and supports its longer-term survival. Therefore, through both on-balance sheet and off-balance sheet instruments, banks try to give more substance to their capital base. They also use different forms of debt which contribute to leveraging and, by extension, to the credit institution's exposure, as we will see in Chapter 9.

In terms of total economic equity, Prakash Shimpi, of Swiss Re, distinguishes three classes: operational capital, risk capital and signaling capital.[3] He also makes the point that the cost of operational capital for a risk-free project should reflect only the time value of money. By way of contrast, the additional risk capital a company requires depends on its risk appetite.

One way of looking at the synergy (some people would say tautology) between economic capital and risk capital – and their correlation – is to keep the company's likelihood of ruin below an acceptable reference level. In this sense, Shimpi says, operational capital and risk capital are two legs of *economic capital*, while the *signaling* capital is needed to assure all stakeholders that the firm is sound and well managed. In essence, the signaling capital is a message-giver.

Prakash Shimpi expresses his view of what lies beyond risk capital through a pattern similar to that in Figure 5.4. This provides one more definition of economic capital and its role, which, as the reader will appreciate, is incompatible with the other definitions we have examined so far. Notice that signaling capital consists of financial resources beyond the level of significance obtained at $\alpha = 0.01$, therefore beyond the 99 percent confidence level. As such:

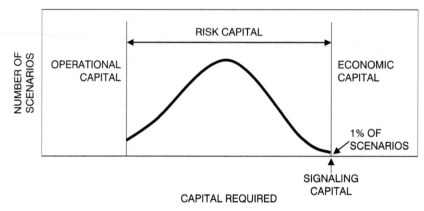

Figure 5.4 A view of the role played by risk capital and economic capital, according to Prakash Shimpi

- It addresses the tail of risk events distribution, and
- It could be looked at as *respectability* capital.

End to end, the graph in Figure 5.4 represents the entity's total economic equity. As such, it finds a certain place in the bank's balance sheet – into which integrate all off-balance sheet items, as *other assets* and *other liabilities*. Since the late 1990s, in Switzerland, such integration is specified by regulatory requirements for financial reporting.

The reader should nevertheless appreciate that an allocation of capital at the 99 percent level of confidence will leave 1 percent of all cases outside its limits. Extreme events may upset the balance sheet, and even cause default, if they are not provisioned. Solutions that go beyond the 99 percent and, even better, the 99.9 percent levels are proactive; they significantly enhance the bank's financial staying power.

In order to obtain a comprehensive view of economic equity rather than the aforementioned integration, I would choose a restructured balance sheet which assigns capital by level of confidence, as shown in Table 5.1. This solution has been suggested by Dr Werner Hermann of the Swiss National Bank. Notice that:

- Both assets and liabilities need to be reported at fair value, and
- The allocation of capital must go beyond the 99.9 percent level of confidence.

Some of the experts participating in this research suggested that a 99 percent level of confidence could be enough, since this is what regulators are asking with value at risk. Others, however, pointed out that the 99 percent level of confidence cannot handle outliers. It leaves no capital coverage at the tail of the distribution of risk events. Dr Hermann's solution is much more fundamental than current procedures and most of the alternatives being suggested.

Assets		Liabilities	
Current, medium, and long term at fair value	100	Current and medium-term liabilities	50
		Capital at 90%	20
		Capital at 90%–99%	10
		Capital at 99%–99.9%	5
		Capital >99.9%	15
			100

Table 5.1 A restructured balance sheet by Dr Werner Hermann, of Swiss National Bank

5.4 Economic capital, contingent assets and contingent liabilities

Sections 5.2 and 5.3 have demonstrated that every financial institution's capital and the risks it is taking are related through a multitude of forms, one of the most important being the level of confidence. It has also been emphasized that, within this perspective, a critical role is played by the strategy chosen for capital management, the entity's risk appetite and the effectiveness of solutions it adopts for risk control. The capital which *our* bank decides as being appropriate to its operations, serves purposes such as:

■ Establishment of an operating base
■ Funding ongoing operations, and
■ Protecting against adverse financial results.

If the economic capital corresponds to the 99 percent level of confidence, *then* beyond this should come financial resources kept in reserve to address extreme events at the queue of the distribution (see Figure 5.1). Having available resources with which to face the outliers in losses enhances the bank's survivability, and it is instrumental in promoting its longer-term market appeal.

In my research, I did not find many contrarian opinions to the concept just outlined. The question which came up time and again, however, is where would this extra money come from? Some experts have been suggesting that on-balance sheet, paid-up capital can be increased through contingent capital.

Contingent capital has significant roots in banking. Banks use various lending-related instruments to meet the financial needs of their customers. For instance, they issue commitments to extend credit, standby and other letters of credit, guarantees, commitments to enter into repurchase agreements, note issuance facilities and revolving underwriting facilities.

These bank guarantees represent irrevocable assurances, subject to satisfaction of pre-established conditions. The bank offering a guarantee essentially says that it will make payment in the event that the customer fails to fulfill its obligation to third party or parties. Commitments to extend credit in the form of credit lines, typically range in maturity from one month to five years. They are available to secure the liquidity needs of customers, but are not yet drawn upon by them.

- The risk these instruments carry is similar to that involved in extending loan facilities.
- The contractual amount of these instruments is the maximum amount at risk for the bank, if the customer fails to meet its obligations.

Needless to say, this risk must be carefully monitored and be subject to specific credit risk policies as well as to limits. To mitigate risks from outstanding commitments and contingencies, banks often enter into sub-participations. A *sub-participation* is an agreement with another party to fund a portion of credit facility, and to take a share both of the profit and of the loss in the event that the borrower fails to fulfill its obligations.

Banks also hedge through derivatives, in a fast-increasing manner. Taking all these references together, we can map *company risk* – from the lender's viewpoint – and the amount of *exposure to risk*. This is done in a two-dimensional frame of reference, like the one shown in Figure 5.5. Notice that mezzanine debt is subordinated debt and, as such, it fits between equity and senior debt in terms of the priority of claims on:

- Corporate cash flows while the firm is operating, and
- Corporate assets if the company files for bankruptcy.

Figure 5.5 essentially reclassifies assets and liabilities in relation to risk. It distinguishes between forms of capital according to exposure to the entity's retained

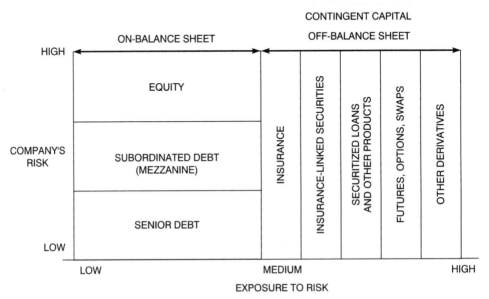

Figure 5.5 Company's risk and exposure to risk correlate, but they are not synonymous

risk(s). The senior debt providers are the least exposed, while equity investors are the most exposed, but there are also other major risks involving off-balance sheet forms of capital (more on this in Chapter 8).

The use of contingent capital and derivative financial instruments makes the economic capital equation so much more complex. This complexity is increased by the need to measure the commercial performance of individual business units, as well as the risks associated with its operations – not only those which are current, but also those that might develop in the future.

As subsequent chapters will demonstrate, prognostication of future risks is a very important enterprise. Business considerations mandate that every investment is worthwhile as long as the marginal return exceeds the marginal cost of the required economic capital *and* the risk assumed by the operation. All this ensures that calculating economic capital requirement for the bank as a whole:

- Varies from one institution to another, and
- At the same time it is a fairly complex mission.

The cornerstone of this effort is the role played by derivatives. Off-balance sheet solutions are a risk transfer mechanism. Some types of exposure are being transferred away from the firm by buying insurance or through securitization (see Chapter 9). In essence, securitized corporates, mortgages, auto loans, credit card and other receivables are not bonds but derivative contracts creating a form of contingent capital which:

- Is largely off-balance sheet
- But through creative accounting it could be made to show up *as if* it were a capital base.

The second point in the list describes a frequently used policy. There is also the leveraging of economic capital by means of multiple gearing and downstreaming. In the background of both of these lies the fact that companies find many ways to bypass laws and regulations, including those involving compliance with capital requirements. An example which has been already mentioned is HT-1 capital (see Chapter 3).

The reader is already aware of the fact that *multiple gearing* is another popular technique in strengthening economic capital. It consists of counting the same capital twice or more, in different entities in the group – constructing a sort of a pyramid. Another gimmick is *downstreaming* capital. To do this, a company issues debt and then uses the proceeds as equity for its subsidiaries.

The reason why it is important to bring all these creative accounting strategies into a discussion on total economic capital, is that in all likelihood they will find their way into the calculation of capital adequacy for the different forms of risk assumed by the credit institution. If and when this happens, it will be synonymous with driving nails into the coffin of regulatory capital and of economic capital.

In conclusion, whether they are made for credit risk, market risk or operational risk reasons, capital reserves must be properly calculated and funded through real, liquid assets. Creative accounting may be good for cheating the shareholders (and over a short period the regulators) but it is a cheap way to making financial statements look good. As Abraham Lincoln once said, you can deceive all of the people some of the time, or a fraction of the people for a long time; but you cannot cheat all of the people all of the time.

5.5 Economic capital and management accounting

One of the most interesting functions of economic capital is that, once it has been admitted as a concept and unit of measurement, it facilitates the functions of management accounting and internal financial reporting. This comprehensive view supports the fact that its internal allocation to business units enables board members, the CEO and senior executives to analyze each product line's performance and its exposure.

- Economic capital is a management tool for capital allocation, said Rainer Rauleder, of Deutsche Bank.
- Other senior executives suggested that it helps the chairman, the board, the loans officers and the traders to focus on risk and return.

As the subsequent chapters of Part 2 will document, monitoring and evaluation of risk and return are best performed when we have in-depth knowledge of the work we are doing. The allocation of economic capital to business units (see Chapter 7) serves this purpose, because once this is successfully done, it can be brought down to finer business segments in a way associated to prudential limits. This promotes transparency because eventually everything – including the exposure being assumed – is costed and priced at the market rate.

A factual and documented economic capital allocation improves senior management's watch over regulatory capital, not just on a one-year basis but over a ten-year framework, as shown in Figure 5.6. Experience with management planning and control demonstrates that better results are obtained when we consider the longer-term perspective. Economic equity requires a time dimension to become a meaningful tool.

In planning terms, senior management decisions regarding this time dimension can be guided with the use of certain crucial ratios. As we will see in Chapter 7, economic capital is not distributed evenly by product line. In general, in the 1980s and through most of the 1990s economic capital tended to be allocated in the following proportions:

- 2/3 to credit risk, and
- 1/3 to market risk.

Among major money-center banks these proportions have changed, tilting towards market risk. By contrast, among conservative retail banks credit risk represents much more than 2/3 of exposure. The reason why in several big banks market risk tends to match credit risk is securitization, and particularly credit derivatives.

The fact that among credit institutions with major product lines in trading, investment banking and insurance, market risk now gets a bigger share of total

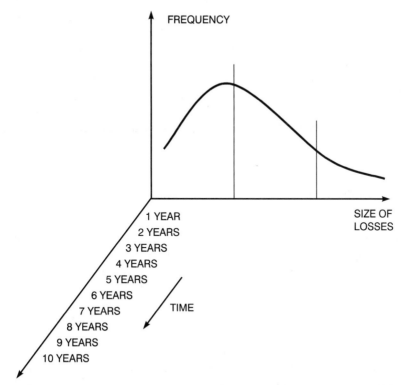

Figure 5.6 Economic equity requires a time dimension to become a meaningful tool

exposure, is a different way of saying that, when it comes to economic capital allocation, great attention must be paid to the risk appetite of product lines, and which one is 'major' depends on the type of institution. One of the universal banks, for instance, allocates 6 percent of its economic capital to private banking but 30 percent to investments, with derivatives trading being the second largest capital-intensive sector.

For internal management accounting purposes, several banks estimate their economic capital requirements by marking-to-model their portfolio of assets. This is a common enough policy, but modeling and hypotheses associated with it can lead to surprises. A test done by a group of Wall Street firms, in collaboration with the SEC, has shown that:

■ While all participating banks used the same model portfolio of assets,
■ They ended with risk calculations that were up to 35 percent apart in capital needs.

This test focused on capital requirements for market risk. On Wall Street, some analysts suggested that *if* capital needs were also added for credit risk and operational risk, *then*, other things being equal, bank-to-bank differences might have been characterized by a ratio of 1:2 mainly due to model risk.

Model risk has many reasons. One of these is inaccuracy. It is nobody's secret that VAR has many weaknesses as an exposure measurement tool. Neither are the different derivatives of VAR really helpful in economic capital calculations as far as realistic risk estimates are concerned.

Value at risk models are supposed to reflect market risk factors, including their volatilities and dependencies. Experience, however, demonstrates this is not necessarily so. Market risk is underestimated by VAR. Apart from the mathematical fact that VAR is not a coherent risk measure, its methodology does not constitute a rigorous approach to market risk estimates because:

- VAR has a strong distributional dependence
- Assumes normal market conditions, and
- Fails to consider high-impact outliers.

The so-called return on value at risk (RoVAR) does not carry much weight, nor are other VAR derivatives helpful in developing a factual and documented top management view of economic capital allocation. In contrast, what is helpful is the development and use of effective capital management methods which:

- Are paying full attention to strategies for maintaining the franchise, and
- Assure that higher rating can continue with low cost funding.

Two other important requirements in properly positioning a credit institution are the a priori investigation of deviations and inaccuracies that might happen sometime in the future in the aftermath of current decisions, and the ability to remain one step ahead in business development and its funding. Practically, this is tantamount to following the advice of an executive of the United Bank of Switzerland, who said during our meeting: 'To maintain our business we have to be seen as extremely stable.' Then he added: 'An AA+ rating is like a market variable.'

5.6   Synergy between economic capital and risk management[4]

Factual and documented economic capital allocation is a significant improvement in risk control. It is not a 'new religion in town'. 'Economic capital allocation is also an exercise in compliance', said a senior executive of one of the money-center banks. 'As the requirements come out, we will restructure our portfolio.' The message has been that this financial institution:

- Can comply with anything the regulators specify
- Regulatory capital is just part of the cost of doing business, and
- The bank has already reduced the credit risk in its portfolio by shifting to higher credit rating.

Of course, in the very competitive markets of the twenty-first century shifting to a higher credit rating is easier said than done. Credit risk and market risk are multidimensional, and economic capital is only one of their dimensions. Masters in risk control appreciate that they need a polyvalent approach, including liquidity at:

■ The bank's treasury, and
■ The market at large.

Another important dimension is top management's ability to take corrective action at a moment's notice, to redimension risk exposure. The chief risk officer (CRO) should regularly check with the CEO on all lines of exposure: credit risk, market risk and operational risk – doing so with all instruments and with all counterparties.

The CRO and his/her immediate assistants should regularly control risk management methods and tools, to assure that nothing and nobody 'drops into the cracks of the system'. One of the weak points to watch out for is risk concentrations. As the CRO of one of the money-center banks had it:

■ 'The total distribution of economic capital is subject to limits to concentration
■ We look carefully at big names and major exposures, and
■ We stress test positions with major counterparties across instrument classes.'

The same executive was to add that the fact his institution is very sensitive to concentrations is what has kept them out of Enron, Worldcom and similar types of trouble. Concentrations are also what regulators watch out for – albeit for different reasons: runaway concentrations lead to systemic risk.

In evaluating exposure to systemic risk, it is important to know the weight of large institutions in the economy. In this connection, it is wise to use the concentration ratio (CR) which measures big banks' market share as a percentage compared with the total banking market in the country.[5]

$$CR(n) = \sum_{i=1}^{n} MA_i \qquad (5.1)$$

where   n   = number of biggest banks (3, 5, 7 or 10)
        MA = market share in percentage points.

In implementing equation 5.1 several credit institutions take as proxy for market share the lending volume, volume of deposits or balance sheet. An alternative to equation 5.1 is known as the Herfindahl-Hirschmann index (HHI) which uses squares, with the result that larger shares are weighted more heavily. The algorithm is:

$$HHI = \sum_{i=1}^{n} MA_i^2 \qquad (5.2)$$

where   n = total number of banks in a given market.

Whether at central bankers' level or that of commercial bankers, new tools are in the process of establishing themselves in banking culture. Models for credit risk and market risk are increasingly used as planning and control tools (see in section 5.7 the outline of a default model).

It is only reasonable to expect that in the coming years a new, more sophisticated family of models will address economic capital allocation, monitoring of results and post-mortem analysis. This is a basic requirement because as several cognizant people remarked during our meetings: 'Today economic capital calculation is much more intuitive than it should be. It's like forecasts on annual profits.'

- Revenues are relatively easy to establish,
- But costs and risks are elusive, influenced by subjective judgment.

The crux of the matter is that to establish a sound methodology for economic capital allocation and performance control, we must know what exactly we wish to achieve. We must start with our operating margin, then bring in assumed risks, as well as be able to cope with intangibles like goodwill.

For instance, what Crédit Suisse is doing for business risk purposes in connection with goodwill is to write off a priori 60 percent. In this manner, business risk which has to do with banking products, their pricing and the market's response will not upset its capital base. Other banks have chosen different approaches to handling goodwill.

As these and the preceding examples document, a milestone in effective economic capital allocation is that of choosing the tools and the benchmarks. In the final analysis, benchmarks must be sophisticated enough, represented by a function that scales, and make it feasible to establish a pattern of results. Both strategic plan and clearly established performance criteria connected to deliverables should be part of the picture. This is what the snapshot in Figure 5.7 suggests.

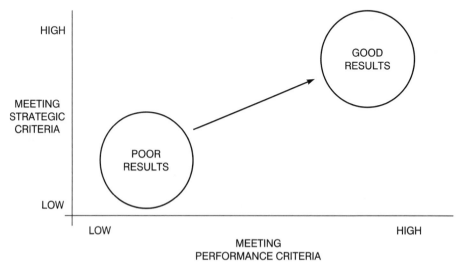

Figure 5.7 Strategic criteria credit rating targets and risk adjusted return on capital characterize top tier results

5.7 Economic capital and the impact of default models

As documented through first-hand references in sections 5.1 to 5.4, there is no uniform definition of economic capital. Chapter 7 will explain why there is neither a single best way in regard to its allocation to business units. Modeling fills the gaps. For instance in connection to credit risk, economic capital should be computed with the help of models which lead to capital charge able to cover individual exposures in loan-specific criteria. Three notions already introduced in Chapter 4, with reference to Basel II are:

- Borrower's probability of default (PD)
- Bank's loss given default (LGD), and
- Bank's exposure at default (EAD).

Within the more general frame of reference, default models aim to capture borrower-specific characteristics, at company and industry level, including systematic risk factors. They target market-wide parameters in a statistical loss distribution of a loans portfolio, including DP, LGD and EAD, but also:

- Maturity (M), or time horizon, and
- The correlation ρ between defaults of different borrowers.

An important element is the characteristics of the overall portfolio, of which the loan forms part, including default correlations (see Chapter 11). When correlations are estimated in an able manner, then the better way to look at economic capital is as capital against a position examined under a dual perspective:

- Correlated risks, and
- Uncorrelated risks.

Because of default correlations, and other reasons, the economic capital of a portfolio generally differs from the sum of its individual parts. One of the weaknesses of simplifications associated with modeling is that most credit risk artefacts assume a constant, non-probabilistic bankruptcy rate. This is, however, inadequate. Each major borrower should be given the PD corresponding to his/her rating.

Loss given default is the other side to the bankruptcy rate, calculated from bankruptcy costs incurred, and level and quality of collateral. With A-IRB, LGD should be specific to each major client, while minor clients are pooled and LGD is calculated at a level of significance $\alpha = 0.01$ percent, or better.

The reader will recall from Part 1 that exposure at default is the sum of current exposure and loan commitments taken up until the time of default. As with PD and LGD, for major counterparties this, too, should be specific by client relationship; and it should reflect exposure of a pool for minor accounts at the 99 percent level of significance.

Default probability is the subject of Chapter 10. This chapter has no intention of duplicating or pre-empting what is said there. Instead, the reason for bringing to the reader's attention matters concerning the computation of PD, LGD and EAD at this point, is to underline the importance of assumptions made with models – as well as the vital role played by correlations (see Chapter 11) and weights (see Chapter 12).

For instance, one of the key assumptions with many default models is that a counterparty's returns are determined by a systematic risk factor, while the loans portfolio is taken as being sufficiently granular. Under these general type approaches, risk weights are often derived based on a value-at-risk type credit risk model. As already stated, this is fairly inaccurate.

Moreover, in terms of algorithmic solutions, an assumption is frequently made that *if* the loans remain in the banking book throughout the contractually agreed period, *then* the value of a loan when the contract expires – in relation to the present time – can be expressed as a binomially distributed random variable.

- The full loan amount will be characterized by a probability of (1-PD).
- While with a probability of PD, the bank will receive only (1-LGD)•EAD.

This, too, is an approximation and the premises on which it rests are not fulfilled in every case. When they are, the loss on the loan to counterparty i (L_i) is also taken as being binomially distributed. Generally, this is specified per unit of exposure at default. Based on these assumptions, expected loss on a loan can be algorithmically expressed.

The Basel Committee says that with F-IRB and A-IRB, banks can recognize provisions in offsetting the expected loss of risk-weighted assets. For most exposures, the EL of risk-weighted assets is defined by the formula:

$$EL = 12.5 \bullet PD \bullet LGD \bullet EAD^6 \tag{5.3}$$

Beyond expected loss is the unexpected loss on the individual loan. One of the algorithms being suggested uses the standard deviation, s, of the distribution of L_i. This is of course another approximation, which makes sense only when we can establish the shape of the distribution of losses – and the hypothesis of a normal distribution can be sustained.

Notice that one of the algorithms advanced for UL accounts for only $1s$ as measure of volatility. This is inadequate. The algorithm should consider a confidence interval at 99 percent, or better, 99.9 percent level of significance, with the corresponding number of standard deviations. Stress tests should also take place focusing on the tail of the distribution.

An algorithm for evaluation of UL, by the Deutsche Bundesbank, is given in Chapter 7, while the management's appreciation of unexpected losses is presented in Chapter 14. Another crucial issue is that of weights (w). The loss on the overall loan portfolio (LLP), goes beyond any single loan. It equals the sum of weighted individual losses:

$$LLP = \sum_i w_i L_i \tag{5.4}$$

where the weight is expressed by the equation:

$$w = \frac{EAD_i}{\sum\limits_{i} EAD_i} \tag{5.5}$$

The overall loan portfolio loss is a random variable that depends directly on individual losses taking place. The unexpected loss on the loan portfolio as a whole is usually smaller than the sum of unexpected losses on individual loans, when diversification effects come into play. As a result, the standard deviation for portfolio loss is determined both by the s of individual losses and by correlations between loans. Taken two loans i and j as an example:

$$s_{ij} = \sum\limits_{i} \sum\limits_{j} w_i\, w_j\, s_i\, s_j\, \rho_{ij} \tag{5.6}$$

where s_{ij} is the standard deviation of risk associated to i and j. It follows that the risk contribution of an individual loan to the bank's loans portfolio is smaller than its UL. It is:

$$RC_i = w_i\, s_i\, \rho_{iP} \tag{5.7}$$

where RC_i = risk contribution of individual loan i
   ρ_{iP} = correlation between individual loss and portfolio loss.

The algorithm is:

$$\rho_{iP} = \frac{\sum\limits_{i} w_i\, s_i\, \rho_i}{s_P} \tag{5.8}$$

where s_P is the standard deviation of the portfolio. For only two loans, i and j, $s_P = s_{ij}$.

Based on the foregoing concepts, albeit with a certain degree of approximation, it can be said that the volatility of the sum of the risk contributions reflects itself in the standard deviation of portfolio loss. The risk contribution increases directly with an increase in UL; also as the weight of the individual loan increases. Other things being equal, in general:

■ The smaller the correlation with the portfolio loss, the smaller the risk contribution.
■ A correlation coefficient between 0.1 percent and 0.3 percent is small; while between 0.6 and 0.8 is big.

Some banks define the UL for overall loan portfolio not by the standard deviation but by the VAR. This is not good practice because, as already stated, VAR is not that accurate. In many cases, it can be computed with sufficient accuracy only through default simulations. Also, VAR says nothing about future risk, has other shortcomings and it is much harder to determine than the standard deviation. Let us remember all this when, in Chapter 9, we deal with a more rigorous definition of default.

The careful reader will remember the statement made in the Warning that $VAR_{99.97}$, $CAR_{99.97}$, or as you like to call it, is an aberration as far as the computation of UL is concerned.

It is indeed regrettable that an unreliable algorithm such as $VAR_{99.97}$ is used as a tool for estimating unexpected credit losses at the 99.97 percent level of confidence. The 99.97 is chosen because of the probability of default associated to 'AA' rating (α = 0.0003), over a 1-year timeframe.

The Basel Committee notes that some banks depend on $VAR_{99.97}$ for UL while other financial institutions depend on stress tests for their estimates of unexpected loss. Still others employ $VAR_{99.97}$ but also incorporate stress tests, including scenarios.

This book proposes the use of better tools to be found in Chapter 7, section 7.7, pages 168–172 (the UL algorithm is on page 170); Chapter 8, section 8.4, pages 184–186 (notice that this needs a proxy for future margin income (FMI)); and Chapter 13, sections 13.7 and 13.8. What underpins the latter is a sophisticated equation for net required capital (NRC).

Notes

1 Chorafas, D.N. (1994). *Chaos Theory in the Financial Markets*. Probus.
2 See D.N. Chorafas (1996). *Managing Derivatives Risk*. Irwin.
3 *Journal of Applied Corporate Finance*, **14** (4), Winter 2002.
4 Chapters 6 and 7 elaborate on this issue. This is only an introductory section providing a general view.
5 Deutsche Bundesbank (2003). *Monthly Report*, January.
6 Basel Committee on Banking Supervision (2003). *Consultative Document: Overview of the New Basel Capital Accord*. BIS, April, pp. 13–17.
7 Basel Committee (2003). *The Joint Forum. Trends in Risk Integration and Aggregation*. BIS, August.

6 Economic capital and solvency management

6.1 Introduction

Chapter 5 has defined economic capital by presenting its different aspects and outlining its interpretation by different entities. The text has pressed the point that while these definitions are not the same, they tend to converge. Also part of the presentation in Chapter 5 has been the synergy which exists between economic capital allocation and exposure assumed by:

- Every business unit of the financial institution, and
- The organization as a whole, in the short, medium and longer term.

The subject of this chapter is to examine in greater detail the link between risk management and economic capital allocation. These two issues and the way in which they impact on one another will dominate senior management interest in the years to come. In all likelihood, they will also be the greatest legacy of Basel II, since clear-eyed bankers look at the new norms and directives as a process which will assist in significantly improving corporate governance (see Chapter 2).

Risk-related economic capital allocation able to assure solvency under contrarian market conditions is a new concept and, therefore, there are few precedents on how to handle it in an able manner. This lack of precedent underlines the need for rethinking first principles, as well as credit and trade approval processes. The example given in Figure 6.1 integrates responses on best practices, which have been received during my research, from different institutions.

Every bank adopting the F-IRB or A-IRB approaches, and most particularly A-IRB, must go through this restructuring process of methods, procedures and information flows connected to credits and trades. As a word of advice, revamping must be oriented not only to risk and return but also to the way which makes management control more efficient than ever before – keeping in mind that the scarcest commodity is time and attention of senior management.

Very few business leaders are able to cope simultaneously with troubles springing up on many fronts. The sophistication of financial instruments, the flood of information that now pours in and amount of risks being assumed have changed the nature of crisis management. Both proactive solutions and much more powerful tools are needed to face several issues at the same time.

That is why, when we talk of economic capital allocation, it is like returning to first principles. At the same time, the multiple links between economic capital and risk control see to it that we should go beyond the 'evident' questions like: 'What kind of factors determine exposure?' The new set of first principles must pay attention to the significant synergy existing between:

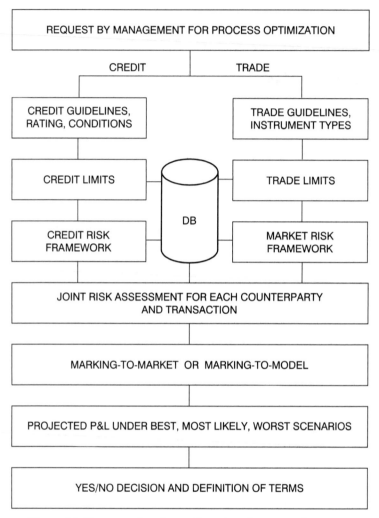

Figure 6.1 Restructuring the credit and trade approval process

- Basel II regulatory capital
- Economic capital, and
- Risk management systems.

These three elements must be considered in unison. They cannot be taken as distinct from one another. What is more, the solution we choose must be capable of embedding their concepts, metrics and synergy into computing processes. This is a key challenge over the coming ten years.

Moreover, banks should not treat the correlation between risk management and capital allocation as a 2006 problem (this is when Basel II will be effectively implemented), or as a compliance-only challenge. Rules behind capital allocation and the payoffs being expected will have an impact on the strategic upgrading of management structure, personnel skills, risk control methods, information systems, the sophistication of products which we offer to the market and, most obviously, the institution's solvency.

6.2   Practical examples with Basel II implementation

Chapter 2 discussed the benefits provided by Basel II to those institutions which know how to capitalize on what it makes available. Chapter 3 addressed the different method for computing regulatory capital: the fixed percentages of Basel I and the three approaches of Basel II: standard, foundation and advanced. It has also been stated that much depends on the jurisdiction: small to medium-size banks in the USA may keep on using Basel I but their counterparts in the EU will have to switch to Basel II because of EU directives.

The reader will also recall that the evidence shows the bigger, significant banks and those which are internationally active will be adopting the advanced method. Many big banks take it as a matter of prestige to apply A-IRB, signaling that they have the sophistication, methods, tools, money and human capital for doing so.

If experience from ongoing operational risk projects (which also come under Basel II) is of any value, *then* the probability is high that banks will go for either the simpler standard approach or the sophisticated advanced method, rather than a midway solution. They will also have to take a view which treats credit risk, market risk and operational risk as one integrated system of management controls.

This is precisely what is done by those credit institutions which are ahead of the curve in implementing Basel II. For instance, Rabobank started with A-IRB in mid-2002. The first application addressed simultaneously two of the institution's five major business units.

Another early implementer is the Erste Bank, Austria's second largest credit institution, with assets of about 121 billion euros and operations in four of the neighboring countries (Hungary, the Czech Republic, Slovakia and Slovenia). The Erste has 10.7 million customers, a large number of them in retail banking, and it has decided to implement the A-IRB approach in the retail banking domain. It will use F-IRB for its other business lines, but with the aim of moving to A-IRB within a reasonable time.

In order to qualify for A-IRB in connection with *credit risk*, and for an advanced measurement approach in what is regarded as operational risk, all members of Erste Bank Group are required to fulfil the Basel II requirements. The Erste Bank treats Basel II as a group project. The bank-wide implementation accounts for local conditions. This policy has led to:

■ Introduction of standardized rating systems for all client segments
■ Data collection and data pooling to meet IRB requirements
■ Adoption of organizational structure and interactive processes responding to Basel II prerequisites.

All business lines of the credit institution are required to compute probability of default, loss given default and exposure at default (see Chapter 5 for one of the currently available models treating these variables). Data collection targets PD, LGD, EAD and associated risk exposure. The Erste uses four interactively available information structures:

- Ratings database
- Risks database
- Collateral databases, and
- Default and losses database.

The ratings database includes rating methods, ratings history and current ratings. Because this work started in 2000, the databases contain two years of information elements or more. The risk database is also used for running credit performance tests. The default and losses database is subject to steady upkeep including default events, deals which led to defaults, losses and their aftermath.

This is a first-class A-IRB project, which proves that the board and the senior management of financial institutions are able to undertake a major cultural change. Also, it observes Dr Werner Heisenberg's famous uncertainty principle, which suggests that you cannot know both the precise location and the precise velocity of anything. The concept underpinning this principle is one of the areas that quantitative analysis in finance and physics have in common.

No two credit institutions I met with have used the same methodology in starting to implement A-IRB. This is understandable because past policies and procedures necessarily influence each bank's way of approaching Basel II applications, and because some of the aspects of such applications find themselves in between credit risk and other exposures like interest rate and FOREX risk.

For instance, one of the better known retail banks made the point that, given its long tradition in several countries, it has established the policy of funding through local capital to keep FOREX risk under control. This is not changing with A-IRB. The models it uses account for the fact that local capital requirements are driven by:

- Minimum capitalization needs
- Large lending opportunities
- Foreign exchange risk and country risk
- Taxation rules, and
- Local regulatory requirements.

Another key variable in this bank's modeling procedure is that, most often, once capital has been injected, it becomes a long-term source for other local business. Foreign subsidiaries of major clients promote the use of local capital, and hedging by local capital in non-core currencies reduces translation risk. It also fosters local focus on *risks* and *costs* associated with local capital, in each country where it has business units.

A brokerage made the point that its direct exposure to credit risk mainly results from its activities in margin lending, securities lending, investments and being a counterparty in financial contracts. Indirectly its credit risk comes from investing activities of certain of its own proprietary funds. To be in charge of such risks, the broker has established policies which include:

- Computing and regularly reviewing credit limits
- Monitoring of credit limits and quality of counterparties, and
- Increasing margin requirements for certain securities.

Moreover, most of the entity's credit extensions, such as margin loans to clients, securities lending agreements and resale agreements, are supported by collateral, subject to requirements that the client has to provide additional collateral in the event that market volatility results in declines of value of assets received (see Chapter 12).

Each counterparty's credit exposure is actively managed through individual and portfolio reviews performed by account officers and senior line management. Periodic assessment of the validity of credit ratings, and underlying credit quality, as well as the credit management process itself, is conducted by a risk review department which is separate from loan origination and monitoring operations.

Senior management regularly evaluates asset quality, including concentrations, delinquencies, non-performing private banking loans, losses and recoveries. All these are factors in the determination of an appropriate allowance to be made for credit losses, which is reviewed quarterly by senior executives.

The broker also spoke of fiduciary risk, which has the potential for financial or reputational loss through the breaching of fiduciary duties to a client. Fiduciary activities with operational risk exposure include, but are not limited to, individual and corporate trust, investment management, custody, and cash and securities processing.

One of the key issues raised by several entities, from retail banking to investment banking, is that to cover expected losses and unexpected losses the estimated net fair value of the institution's assets must exceed the estimated net fair value of its liabilities. This is the essence of capital requirements. Therefore, any IRB model must consider chapter by chapter, without netting:

- All assets, and
- All liabilities.

One of the entities defined as follows its fair value policies. Cash and cash equivalents, receivables, deposits from banking clients, payables, accrued expenses and other liabilities, as well as short-term borrowings, are short-term in nature. Accordingly they are valued at fair value, or in amounts that approximate fair value.

The fair value of its loans is estimated using discounted contractual cash flows adjusted for current prepayment estimates. Discount rates being used are based on the interest rates charged to current clients for comparable loans. The models have been designed to reflect the aforementioned criteria.

Securities owned are recorded at estimated fair value, using quoted market prices, where available, or third party pricing services. The fair value of the entity's swaps is estimated by obtaining quotes from dealers and pricing services by third parties. A portion of the company's long-term debt is adjusted for changes in the value of swaps. The fair value of its long-term debt is estimated using third party pricing services and discounted cash flows; also by using discount rates currently available for similar instruments.

In the case of off-balance sheet financial instruments which primarily consist of firm commitments, a broker noted that the majority of these mature within one year. Their fair value is estimated based on fees charged to enter into similar agreements, considering creditworthiness of counterparties, as well as computing loans equivalence.[1]

On repeated occasions, the point was made that, wherever credit risk comes into the picture, to improve the dependability of fair value calculations it is important to gage the likelihood of survivability of major clients. These are among the challenges of economic capital allocation discussed in this chapter and in Chapter 7.

6.3   Economic capital and an institution's solvency

It has been brought to the reader's attention that, whether implicitly or explicitly, executives participating in the research meetings said that economic capital is essentially *risk capital*. As such, it should not be confused with accounting loss. Economic capital is *proactive*, allocated to potential risks for *solvency* reasons (for the definition of solvency see Chapter 12). By contrast, accounting loss is post-mortem. Solvency-related economic capital:

■ Defines potential loss in economic terms, and
■ Addresses many events which may not be relevant from an accounting perspective.

An example is mismatch risk between loans and deposits. Economic capital is capital against a position (see section 6.5), and it is allocated for the specific purpose of protecting that position in case of adversity. This makes it part of a probability function of sustaining losses – in other words, of a function of risk confronting the institution.

The fact that unexpected losses are covered by economic capital does not mean these are 'unknown' losses (see also Chapter 14). Many of what are considered unlikely exposures have shown up in the past in the one, the other or several financial institutions. The problem is that very few banks have really studied their pattern – or, for that matter, were able to learn from their own mistakes, and those of others, in order to avoid repeating them.

The allocation of economic capital induced by Basel II presents the opportunity for doing so. In capital allocation the keynote is 'Learn how to learn'. A good guide is Dr Richard Feynman's 'notebook of things I don't know about'. A physicist by profession, Feynman worked for weeks in disassembling each branch of physics, oiling its parts and putting them back together. At the same time, he was looking for:

■ Rough edges, and
■ Inconsistencies.

This methodology of the physical sciences is fully applicable in modern banking, and most particularly in economic capital allocation and solvency studies. It enables the

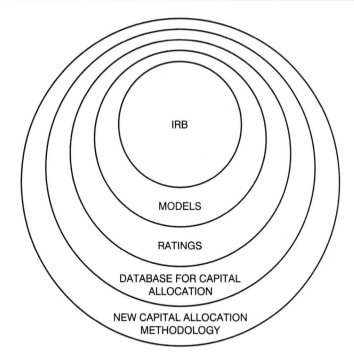

Figure 6.2 An onion-skin view of capital allocation for Basel II. The database should include all risks, all returns, all ratings

problem to be stripped of nothing but a pair of point charges, building up a method from first principles and including error ranges in all calculations.

- Such methodology is by no means a problem of algebra.
- It is a problem of understanding a situation's macroscopic aspects, and the challenges which go with it.

Therefore, the physicist method applies hand in glove to the control of risk. Indeed, what I have just described is the outer layer of economic capital allocation, which can be presented as the onion-skin view shown in Figure 6.2. An integral part of this methodology is to learn from approaches that are well established and with expected losses in order to attack the more complex unexpected losses domain. The basic equation for expected loss (EL) is:

$$EL = PD \bullet LGD \bullet EAD \qquad (6.1)$$
$$\text{in \% in \% in \$}$$

Obligor rating is the important probability of default (PD) reference, on a 1-year timeframe. *Loss given default* (LGD), for loans, should include collateral (type, amount), guarantor (if any), recovery rate, discounting in expected timeframe, bankruptcy rate, and so on.

This information is mined from the bank's exposure database, which includes all clients. Usually a reconciliation process at 98 percent is applied. While the credit risk database is common, the calculation of LGD (and EAD) is individual for big accounts, reflecting obligor, transaction (and collateral), product-specific information, and other deal-specific references

Loss given default should be individually computed for all major exposures. LGD for trading includes exposure-centered add-ons. Estimates are based on simulations. Into *exposure at default* (EAD) should be mapped: Drawn amount, undrawn but committed (converted to cash), a factor reflecting product type (converted to capital), other commitments which are applicable, expressed in financial terms.

Unexpected events are at the tail of the loss distribution. Those more worrisome to the bank are of low frequency but high impact (LF/HI). Background reasons may be:

- Event risk, like the KKR buyout of Reynolds Nabisco.
- Unreliable financial statements misguiding lenders and investors, like Enron and WorldCom.
- Conflicts of interest in financial analysis, and so on.

A careful examination of historical events by position (see section 6.5), as well as hypothetical scenarios, permit us to take a closer look at outliers. Simulation is better than ad hoc economic capital allocation, which is too subjective and fails to appropriately account for assumed risks.[2] Also, simulation provides documentation which backs up capital allocation for solvency reasons.

This is written with the full understanding that currently a great deal of economic capital allocation is ad hoc. It is often a give and take in negotiations between senior management and business units. By contrast, simulating an aggregate potential loss distribution provides evidence on frequencies, severity, and some extreme events – if it is properly done:

- By type of risk
- At high confidence level
- Over a defined time horizon.

This does not mean that simulation solves every problem. One of its shortcomings is that there is no assurance business cycles will repeat themselves. Therefore, stress tests should be made to check capital models by means of recession scenarios and other outliers (more on this later).

Moreover, within the perspective of a rigorous risk management system, the models we develop and use should reflect the fact that the economic capital each business unit needs is the amount of money necessary to remain solvent under extreme conditions and adversity connected to the bank's operations. Solvency ratios impact upon:

- Credit rating, and
- Market standing.

This is the reason why Chapter 5 brought to the reader's attention the fact that risk capital which has been calculated for unexpected losses and events towards the further-out tail of distribution can also be called *respectability capital*. Sensitivity analysis helps to identify key solvency drivers and pinpoint potential unexpected losses calling for economic allocation.

- *If* regulatory capital is the minimum amount necessary to have a license
- *Then*, respectability capital is the minimum amount needed by a unit, and the bank as a whole, to be accepted as business partner.

Up to a point, but only up to a point, the two correlate. For this reason, Crédit Suisse uses an algorithm which compares balance sheet risks, off-balance sheet risks, operational risks and business risks to available level of economic capital. The pattern is shown in Figure 6.3. Such comparison makes it possible to adjust economic capital to the necessary level.

Decision tools and patterns as in Figure 6.3 are part of the shift taking place with Basel II, and they are intimately related to the notions of risk capital and of solvency. Solvency ratios can be used effectively to study trends and lead to corrective action. Solvency tracking is performed by calculating the ratio which prevails between:

- Available economic capital at time t, and
- Required economic capital given the bank's business and risk profile.

The more the business world expands, the more the required amount of economic capital is subject to the law of polyvalence. Banking has come a long way from the time when professors of banking taught their students that loans carry credit risk, while trading instruments involve market risk. Loans have both credit risk *and* market risk, the latter due to the fact that:

- They are largely made with fixed interest rates, and
- There is plenty of market risk associated to their securitization.

The loans book is exposed to interest rate risk from changes in the interest rates on its assets, and to foreign exchange risk if it is transcurrency. There is also mismatch risk connected to funding sources which finance these assets. To mitigate the risk of loss, the institution must establish policies and procedures which:

- Set up guidelines on the amount of net interest revenue at risk, and
- Monitor the net interest margin and average maturity of its interest-earning assets, as well as funding sources.

In addition, the institution should use swaps to mitigate interest rate exposure associated with its loans book, and funded through short-term floating interest-rate

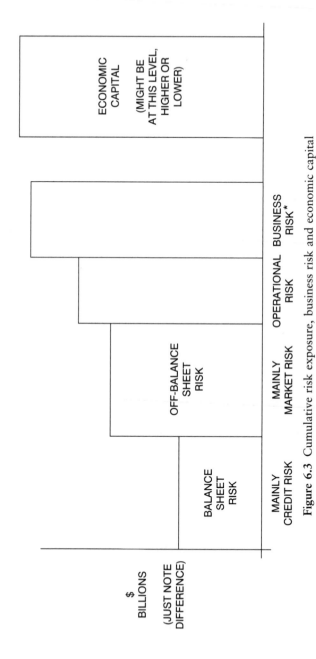

Figure 6.3 Cumulative risk exposure, business risk and economic capital

*Business risk is not under Basel II. To compensate for it some banks deduct 60 percent of goodwill from shareholder equity.

deposits. This demonstrates the need for internal swaps, as shown in Figure 6.4. Market risk is taken out of the loans book and into the trading book, by swapping fixed with flexible interest rates. Similarly, a swap can take credit risk out of the trading book.

Interest rate swaps can be first internal, then brought to the market. Their effective management requires simulation to pre-evaluate and proactively manage the effect of changing interest rates. Such models should include all interest-sensitive assets and liabilities, as well as swaps used by the institution to hedge interest rate risk assumed with the institution's customers. Key variables include:

■ Changes in the level and term structure of interest rates
■ Repricing of financial instruments, and
■ Prepayment and reinvestment assumptions.

Notice that interest rate simulations involve issues that are inherently uncertain and, as a result, modeling cannot precisely estimate net interest revenue, or precisely

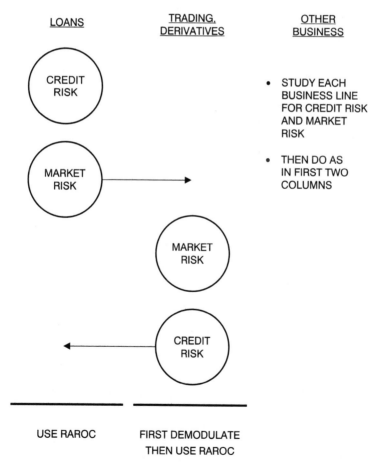

Figure 6.4 Capital allocation by channel after separating credit risk and market risk

predict impact of changes in interest rates on net interest revenue. Actual results may differ from simulated results owing to changes in assets and liabilities mix, the timing, magnitude and frequency of interest rate changes, as well as changes in market conditions and in management strategies.

Basel II does not imply that internal swaps should be done, but the separation of credit risk from market risk on a transaction by transaction basis makes the provisioning of economic capital much more accurate. In turn, this improves solvency prospects through a drive for better focused economic capital calculations. Through such a proactive approach, capital management goes well beyond the level of sophistication implied by Basel I and its risk-weighted factor targeting solvency.

6.4   Solvency and the regulation of insurance companies

This is a case study in the insurance industry on the theme of solvency, discussed in section 6.3. The regulation of insurance companies has a dual objective: it helps them survive the perils of insolvency and illiquidity, and protects policyholders from these same perils. The two latest EU regulations for the insurance industry are known as Solvency 1 and Solvency 2.

Solvency 1 aimed to review existing EU directives, bringing amendments to existing prudential supervision rules. However, it did not provide conclusive results. A new project was initiated in 2000 when the European Commission undertook an in-depth review of current EU solvency requirements. This is what today is known as Solvency II. In a way similar to Basel II, it rests on three pillars:

- Minimum capital requirements
- Rules for supervision
- Market discipline.

It is worth noting that in insurance, as in all other financial industries, solvency is a moving target. It is dynamic, changing over time, as shown in Figure 6.5 which presents data from Swiss Re, concerning insurance companies in the USA and the UK. Also, because of reasons discussed in the following paragraphs, it correlates with solvency in other sectors of the economy.

Given this correlation, it is not at all surprising that regulators of the insurance industry work very close with their colleagues in banking. The 1990s saw the emergence of large multifunctional financial groups which were very active both in banking and in insurance, while the financial instruments themselves have evolved to cover both domains.

An example of this evolution is the growth of credit risk transfer techniques, such as financial guarantees and credit insurance. Litigation, too, follows a similar path, as in the case of recent litigation in New York between JP Morgan Chase and a group of insurers, involving claims under surety bonds. These references underpin the need for a focus on the way in which capital adequacy, prudential supervision and market discipline fit together in what used to be different sectors of the financial world.

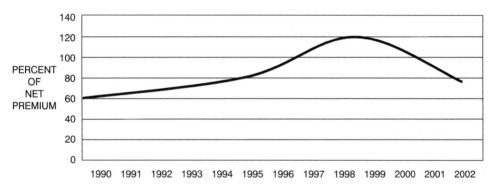

Figure 6.5 Development of US and UK solvency margins (*Source*: Swiss Re, *Sigma*, no. 4/2002, data for 2001 provisional or estimated)

Systemic risk, in a financial stability sense, is no longer confined to banks. There are growing interlinkages between financial sectors and these are giving rise to the need for close co-ordination. This should involve not only the identification of old and new insurance risks and a methodology to accurately account for them, but also generally agreed definitions of debt, equity and nature of adjustments. For instance, total adjusted capital components include:

- *Reported surplus equity adjustments*, including unearned premiums, assets, loss reserves, reinsurance
- *Debt adjustments*, like senior debt, subordinated debt with certain characteristics, hybrid equity, contingent capital, debt service requirements, and
- *Other adjustments*, necessary to cover potential catastrophe requirements, future operating losses and the like.

Regulators talk also of *further adjustments* to be included in an insurance company's capital model. Examples are assets risk factors adjusted for country risk, a reserve capital factor adjustment reflecting stability of reserves, adjusted premium capital factor for weak earnings and adjusted premium capital factor for a stable or unstable legal environment. Taken together, all these issues contribute to solvency.

Other metrics must focus on catastrophe exposure, which means extreme events. Examples with old insurance risks are the 1-in-100 hurricane and the 100-year earthquake. But extreme events also increasingly characterize new risks, such as rogue trader insurance, CEO malfeasance and huge losses connected to derivative financial instruments. The integrative model of an advanced approach, presented in Figure 6.6, reflects both of the foregoing references. Further elements are:

- Provisioning through insurance for unexpected losses, done by other financial sectors but impacting insurers solvency
- Extreme events and spikes encountered by insurance companies themselves during their operations offering coverage to their clients.

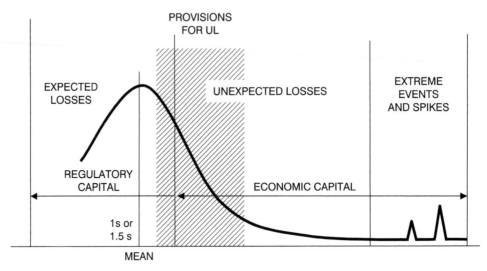

Figure 6.6 The advanced approach to regulatory capital will extend into both provisioning for unexpected loss and the unexpected losses domain

Both are addressed by Solvency 2. In the background is the fact that identification of different risks is crucial to solvency. Many experts believe that with Solvency II, Europe's insurance industry will move a step closer to a risk-based regime which, the same experts suggest, will make the insurance industry safer (see Chapter 2 on risk-based pricing).

Supervisory authorities point out that reform of the EU's regulation of insurance companies must ensure that rules designed to protect insurers reflect more accurately the risks the different firms face. This poses three challenges:

- Identify the new risks
- Classify them in terms of frequency and impact, and
- Go down to detail of the risk factors (see Chapter 13 on A.M. Best's BCAR formula).

The traditional insurance risks are fairly well known. These are based on underwriting risk and technical risk connected to reserves. This is translated into asset risk because of market values, interest rates, inflation and other factors. Like any other sector of the economy, insurance companies also assume credit risk associated with fixed-income instruments and reinsurers. But there are also new risks evolving from rapid business development, as well as operational risks with many unknowns.[3]

Defining the type of risks that need to be addressed, and agreeing on the appropriate risk factors to calculate the estimated required capital, are cornerstone to attaining the objective of establishing a solvency system that matches fairly accurately the different risks affecting a risk-based approach in insurance. Economic capital allocation will greatly benefit from this risk-based solution.

There is pressure from capital markets for greater consistency and clarity in the measurement of solvency. Apart from the EU effort, the International Association of Insurance Supervisors (IAIS) is also reviewing the supervision of insurer solvency. Another contribution is the work of the IASB. Its International Accounting Standard will impact on insurance accounting.

One of the challenges is the co-ordination between American and European standards in insurance industry regulation. The USA already operates a risk-based approach, which includes a whole series of regulatory tools that can allow risk-oriented action to be taken where a problem might arise with an insurer. Not all European regulators were initially happy to abandon the so-called 'one-size-fits-all' solvency rules, but a risk-sensitive culture can:

■ Promote better risk management,
■ Detect problems before they became fatal, and
■ Calibrate capital requirements to the risks being taken.

The drawback is that few insurance companies have the skills and technology to develop and apply such an approach. Yet, a risk-based capital adequacy solution serves the factual analysis of an insurer's financial strength rating, and it assists in determining appropriate risk factors per:

■ Line of business
■ Territory of activities, and
■ Instruments being used.

These point to the need to develop internal models for insurance risks, equivalent to the A-IRB approach under Basel II. The value-added results will be a rigorous redefinition of an insurance contract and greater visibility regarding an insurance company's solvency.

6.5 A practical look at position risk

The point has been made in Chapter 5 that the move from regulatory capital to economic capital raises the need to identify and calculate position risk. This is just as important for bigger banks who have decided to take appropriate action along Basel II guidelines, as it is for medium to smaller banks which are likely to wait till final accord is in place and tested – but in the mean time they must get ready for Basel II implementation.

Attention to position risk is part of the statement that institutions adopting the advanced IRB method have to invest in sophisticated internal risk management systems, enabling them to calculate exposure position-by-position. This promises to be a fairly complex task requiring both skills and money, because of the current:

■ Lack of methodology in calculating capital charges by channel and by business unit

- The fact that the Basel II set of rules, and details, is still expanding, and
- The need to develop and use in an interactive manner rich databases which few institutions currently have to hand.

Also, there are still inconsistencies between jurisdictions, particularly in the way they look at the liability side of the balance sheet. While these factors could be seen as negatives, they should not discourage the adoption of the A-IRB method and the widening usage of position risk. Position risk should be computed on:

- one-year time horizon, at
- 99 percent level of confidence.

But tests should also be conducted at three-year and five-year time horizons – and 99.97 percent level of confidence, which corresponds to AA rating by independent rating agencies. Moreover, methods and metrics should be chosen which provide a useful base for:

- Setting limits
- Monitoring risk, and
- Identifying risk correlations.

Apart from the fact that these are prerequisites to a successful A-IRB implementation, all three points help the institution to improve internal control and management oversight (more on this later). Take legal and compliance risk as an example: the possibility is that an institution will be found by a court, arbitration panel or regulatory authority not to have complied with an applicable legal or regulatory requirement.

It is by no means generally known at board level that any and every position in the entity's portfolio may be subject to this risk. The company may be subject to lawsuits or arbitration claims by clients, employees or other third parties in the different jurisdictions in which it conducts business. Claims against the institution may increase as:

- Clients suffer losses due to deteriorating equity market conditions, or
- The entity has underwritten some sort of guarantee connected to the nature of advice it provides to clients. (An example is the claim of Unilever's pension fund against Merrill Lynch Asset Management.)

The nature of position risk changes over time, because new rules, and an evolution in the interpretation of current rules, could affect the credit institution's manner of operations, and its profitability. That is why banks attempt to mitigate legal and compliance risk through policies and procedures that they believe are reasonably designed to prevent or detect violations of applicable statutory and regulatory requirements – or by means of insurance policies.

Alternatively, positions in a bank's portfolio may be overvalued, characterized by prices which have little or no relation to the market. A senior investment advisor of one of the brokers who participated in the research which led to this book, brought to my attention one of his findings – that many banks have lots of money in private equity positions and are unwilling to realize their losses.

Prerequisite to any analytical approach to position control is to properly identify the positions. This starts with organization. As an example, Table 6.1 presents eight trading positions and twelve portfolio positions. It has been compiled at that level by comparing and combining into one list positions identified by three different commercial banks.

Trading positions	Portfolio positions
Foreign exchange	Corporate lending
Interest rates	Business lending
Internal swaps	Retail lending
Equities	Mortgages
Commodities	Exchange-traded equity
Credit derivatives	Private equity
Other securitized products	Fixed income
Assets and liabilities management	Structured assets
	Emerging markets
	Real estate
	Insurance underwriting
	Other underwriting

Table 6.1 Trading positions and portfolio positions

Following the classification and identification efforts, each position has to be analyzed in terms of the risks involved. The best approach is by responding to crucial questions concerning the handling of position risk. How much risk can be transferred through credit derivatives? What is the worst case of using securitization as arbitrage for economic capital? What is the level of risk assumed with asset-backed securities (ABS)? Mortgage-backed securities (MBS)? Collateralized mortgage obligations (CMO)? Which are the most important criteria to be used in risk modeling in connection with different tranches in securitization? The change in relative weight credit risk/market risk due to securitization?

Similar criteria should be chosen for the test of positions. A methodology must be in place to ensure that both trading positions and portfolio positions are regularly tested, including stress tests (see section 6.6). For instance, for emerging markets, stress tests can use severity events, like South Korea in 1997 and Russia in 1998. They can also use regional and global contagion effects. The results of both classes – normal tests and stress tests – should be aggregated. This requires identification of markets and instruments that:

■ Tend to be correlated during crises
■ Or, are more or less independent.

Buckets must be defined by correlation increments: 0–10 percent, 10–20 percent, . . . 80–90 percent, 90–100 percent (correlations are discussed in Chapter 12). Identifying high correlations is a way to flush out key risk exposures. All this work must be performed to an acceptable level of accuracy, keeping in mind that in risk management accuracy is much more important than precision.

Some institutions feel at a disadvantage because they do not have the rocket scientists (and perhaps the budget) to play with complex models. In a number of cases, this is not really necessary. The 1996 Market Risk Amendment offers the possibility of using a standard method with offsets and different weights for estimating market risk.

Provided the use of this standard method meets with the agreements of supervisors in the jurisdiction where it is applied, it can serve nicely at the market risk side of position exposure. This is basically a duration approach with residual maturities. Banks employing it do not need VAR.

Even big banks can benefit from such a solution. Given the size and nature of its operations in the UK, when the Market Risk Amendment was implemented, Citibank decided to use the duration and residual maturities method, after receiving the approval of the Bank of England who, at the time, was the regulator. Citibank still uses it today in its UK operations because the FSA accepts aggregation of swaps, which implies a disallowance of 10 percent in one time zone and about 40 percent in several timezones.

In terms of equity positions, this approach leads towards capital requirements at the 8 percent level of gross positions and 8 percent of net positions, but these might shrink to 4 percent if the bank is well diversified. In fact, capital requirements can go even lower under certain conditions of rigorous risk control. Citigroup prides itself on taking very little market risk for a bank of its size.

In conclusion, computational accuracy is what we need the most in exercising effective internal control and in keeping position risk under lock and key. Internal control and position risk correlate, because the latter increases as a result of:

- Failed internal processes
- Non-performing systems
- Human errors, and
- External events to which the entity lacks sensitivity.

While capital charges are necessary, they do not represent an effective substitute for adequate internal control – and adequate internal control depends on both open communications channels and the accuracy of information brought to senior management's attention for corrective action (see also Chapter 4).

6.6 Stress testing risk positions

The classical way of handling risk positions is through what is assumed to be normal conditions, without any consideration of outliers and distribution tails which hide extraordinary events. The preference for using normal distributions of events and measurements is understandable.

- That is how people have been trained, and
- That is where a wealth of statistical tables can be found.

Yet, quite often keeping tests within the confines of linear events and using normal distributions can produce misleading results, and lead to the wrong conclusions. These can be corrected through stress testing, which accounts for extreme events that, over time, are present in any business.[4]

It should be noted that in the way used in connection to scientific investigation, stress testing is a generic term. As far as practical applications are concerned, it does not necessarily mean the same thing to different people or different companies. In general, stress testing describes various techniques and conditions employed to gage the potential vulnerability of a portfolio or transaction to simply unexpected but plausible events rather than only those which are exceptional or extreme.

An exceptional event is one that occurs once and can have dire consequences. In relation to credit risk, the effective bankruptcy of Argentina in 2001 was just such an exceptional event – though a careful analysis of trends would have revealed the country was living beyond its means for more than a decade.

An extreme event is one that can be usefully represented as an outlier from a normal pattern of occurrences. The stock market crash of October 1987, which was fourteen standard deviations away from the expected value of a normal distribution, is an often cited example of an extreme event in the area of market risk.

The collapse of Enron in 2001 was another extreme event: it was not expected or predicted by analysts or investors, for the company's creative accounting practices had managed to convey to the market the impression that it was one of the most financially robust energy companies in the USA. Stress tests are worthwhile when they are able to break this 'crust of the pie', and make it possible to look at what lies inside.

Because the Basel Committee believes that credit institutions adopting A-IRB, or F-IRB, should hold adequate capital to protect against adverse or uncertain conditions, the new regulations require the performance of meaningful stress tests. The goal is to ascertain to what extent IRB capital requirements could increase during a stress scenario, including:

- Economic downturns
- Depressing industry conditions
- Severe market risk events
- Liquidity squeezes, and
- Solvency problems facing the counterparty.

Stress tests must be meaningful and reasonably conservative. The credit institution can choose the test to be performed subject to supervisory review. The results of the stress test should contribute directly to the expectation the bank will operate above Pillar 1 minimum regulatory capital requirements, and in a way satisfying Pillar 2 and Pillar 3.

'We welcome the growing emphasis in stress testing, to make people aware of outliers and extreme events,' said Barbara Ridpath of Standard & Poor's. 'The challenge is to get consistent stress tests across all risk types,' added Tim Thompson of Barclays Bank.

A bank can be more prudent in counterparty risk by basing credit rating on stress scenarios. For instance, taking into account borrower characteristics that render a company vulnerable to adverse economic conditions. Moreover, given volatility in bank capital requirements, banks can stress test required capital needs to account for the effect of changes in:

- Probability of default
- Loss given default, and
- Exposure at default.

The importance of stress testing is further underlined by the fact that, as explained in the preceding sections, the market and its characteristic factors, like solvency, are dynamic. In many cases the use of historical precedents, particularly within narrow timeframes, is not very helpful, because the market is very different from what it used to be even just a few years ago. Historical scenarios require long-term series, including:

- Default and recovery rates
- Market panics and near panics (like LTCM 1998)
- And other significant events, which affect market psychology.

By simulating market behavior based on assumed but plausible extreme events, stress tests reveal conditions leading to scenarios which, for instance, represent intense downward pressure in the market and its most likely aftermath.

This is important inasmuch as the dynamics of the market must be fully accounted for under all circumstances. The growing variety of derivative financial instruments now enables financial institutions and investors not only to hedge some of the market risks, but also to speculate on market movements to a greater extent than ever before. Therefore, stress tests have to be devised to give insight into outliers connected to:

- Forward rate agreements
- Interest rate swaps
- Equity derivatives
- Credit derivatives
- Deregulation of markets
- Globalization of investments, and
- Other factors that can have an impact on financial results.

Stress tests are helpful in interpreting market behavior and, at times, in projecting that behavior within established confidence intervals. One of the most important developments of the last ten years has been the experimental culture associated with:

- The testing of hypotheses, and
- The notion of confidence levels.

More recently, in the aftermath of Enron, Global Crossings, Adelphia, Tyco, WorldCom, Ahold and other scandals, stress testing has become for senior management a means of preservation of company assets, given the unreliability of counterparties. Moreover, the need to test for outliers is connected to the issue of management accountability.

For instance, in late February 2003, the German government moved to prevent a local repeat of Enron-style accounting scandals by holding executives *personally liable* for misleading shareholders. The new measure is part of a plan to make German companies more attractive to investors. The blueprint, which will be enforced by 2005:

- Proposes a kind of 'accounting police' able to check corporate accounts, and
- Includes revised rules on financial analysts and rating agencies, to assure independence of opinion and unbiased research.

Stress tests help in assuring this independence, in evaluating contrarian opinion and in pinpointing trends which tend to be hidden. Failures such as Enron's tend to happen because of inordinate exposure which has not been appreciated in time. It is therefore reasonable that senior managers should seek to be informed through study of worst cases and their aftermath. Stress tests can be made at various levels through any of four methods: scenario writing, sensitivity analysis, statistical inference under extreme conditions and drills for a meltdown.

Stress test for business risk should include all business units as well as all product lines and income derived from each of them: commissions income, fees income, loans income, trading income, net interest income, capitalization income, income from insurance and income from ancillary channels. Each of these positions identifies *earnings-at-risk*.

Stress tests should also focus on expense by channel in a crisis. At the bottom line, a good part of business risk is the difference between income in a crisis and expense in a crisis – as compared with pre-crisis income and expense. Normal tests, too, can be of assistance, but in many cases they provide only low-profile help.

Stress testing financial instruments calls for establishing plausible criteria against which the different portfolio positions are evaluated in terms of margins of variation. Examples may come from real-life case studies, and give a reference to stress tests which can be made by instrument:

- *FOREX*: flight to, from the $ or other currencies
- *Fixed income*: global tightening, substantial increase (or decrease) in interest rates
- *Equities*: market crash and/or Japan-style stock market limbo
- *Internal interest rate swaps*: spread widening
- *Traded credit risk*: major increase in defaults
- *Real estate*: collapse of the market, by market sector.

One of the better known financial institutions has a policy of daily tests on FOREX exposure. For the whole entity and all its business units percent change in regard to all main currencies in trading and investment positions is computed: +10 percent, +5 percent, +2 percent, +1 percent, 0 percent, –1 percent, –2 percent, –5 percent, –10 percent.

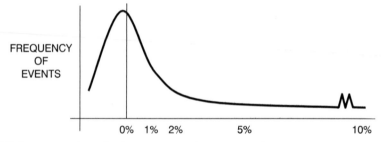

Figure 6.7 A pattern of results from stress testing currency-by-currency exposure on a daily basis

The ±5 percent represents regular stress tests, and the ±10 percent level extreme events. The latter corresponds to roughly fourteen standard deviations in the distribution of value changes in currency exchange, one-day movements. An equivalent interest rates stress test will focus on ±100, ±200, ±300, ±400 basis points – with ±200 representing the regular stress test and ±400 extreme events.

Figure 6.7 gives a snapshot of the pattern behind the daily exchange tests. A similar policy can be followed in connection with interest rates. The best example for interest rate stress tests I have seen so far is that devised by the Office of Thrift Supervision for 1100 savings and loans (thrifts, S&L, building societies) under its jurisdiction.[5]

Regulators are increasingly oriented towards the benefits derived from stress testing. A stress test from the FSA required each individual company in the UK insurance industry to evaluate its solvency in case stock market's capitalization fell by 30 percent. Cross-instrument stress tests are also important and, in this connection, critical tests are those for liquidity, volatility and solvency.

Notes

1 D.N. Chorafas (2000). *Managing Credit Risk, Volume 1, Analyzing, Rating and Pricing the Probability of Default.* Euromoney.
2 See D.N. Chorafas (1995). *Financial Models and Simulation.* Macmillan.
3 D.N. Chorafas (2004). *Operational Risk Control with Basel II.* Butterworth-Heinemann.
4 D.N. Chorafas (2003). *Stress Testing: Risk Management Strategies for Extreme Events.* Euromoney.
5 D.N. Chorafas (2002). *Liabilities, Liquidity and Cash Management: Balancing Financial Risk.* Wiley.

7 Economic capital allocation: practical applications and theoretical background

7.1 Introduction

Because this book is written for practitioners, it has been a deliberate choice to include practical applications of economic capital allocation by means of real-life examples, prior to discussing a theoretical background. The way banks, at least the large majority of them, allocate economic capital is not based on theoretical foundations but on practical needs. Yet, there is a basis for theoretical background, as the reader will see in sections 7.6 and 7.7.

Today practically every financial institution has its own process of economic capital allocation, though several of the principles which have been outlined in Chapters 5 and 6 start slipping up in a growing number of organizations. In the course, of my research several banks made the point that a sound strategy is to proceed:

- First by considering risk and return
- Then by instrument exposure, handled by each business unit
- Following up with business unit integration.

Barclays Bank says that by identifying risk and return at transaction level, it increased efficiency of management control by 25 percent. An instrument-centered approach obliges the credit institution to consider how much money should be contributed to the body and to the tail of the loss distribution shown in Figure 7.1.

As banks with experience in economic capital allocation appreciate, funding for extreme events is not the same as allocating capital for expected losses. Exposure connected to expected and unexpected losses varies tremendously by instrument.

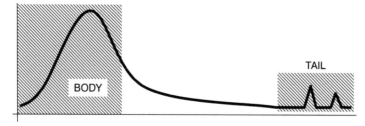

Figure 7.1 The economic capital allocation method must be polyvalent, to address both the body and the tail of the loss distribution

Derivatives add a great deal to tail risk. By contrast, American banks pressed the point that with credit card receivables nearly everything is expected risk (which is not necessarily true of European banks).

Because no senior executive or business unit will wish to be considered risk-prone, a major challenge is that of calculating risk appetite by instrument, product line and business unit. Many business unit executives and product-line managers tend to shy away from high capital allocation, because they think that:

- *If* they need substantial capital
- *Then* they will be expected to present big profits
- Or, they may be considered bad managers.

This is one of the reasons why in several cases economic capital needs tend to be underestimated. The downside of economic capital shortfalls is that business unit managers do not consider the full amount of risk they assume in their operations. Yet, their risk appetite must be fully covered – because they will be steadily faced with:

- Book leverage
- Market leverage
- Non-performing instruments
- Probability of default, and
- Liquidity challenges.

This underlines the need to define risk appetite by instrument, channel and business unit, as shown in Figure 7.2. Economic capital must be always computed in function of risks being assumed – whether the procedure we follow is based on practical

BUSINESS UNITS

	BU 1	BU 2	• • •	BU 'N'	SUM OF BU
CHANNEL 1					
CHANNEL 2					
CHANNEL 3					
⋮					
⋮					
⋮					
⋮					
CHANNEL 'M'					
SUM OF CHANNELS					

Figure 7.2 Risk appetite matrix by channel and business unit

business rules or rests on an algorithmic basis with theoretical underpinning. In fact, in the last analysis, the practical and theoretical approaches should converge, because only in this way can the process of management planning and control be properly documented.

7.2   Role of the corporate center in economic capital allocation

Whether economic capital allocation is top down or bottom up (see section 7.3), there should always be a general management account (GMA) at headquarters. The way I learned it from Dr Carlo Pesenti, the chairman of three Italian banks to whom I was a consultant for sixteen years, GMA is the internal corporate balance sheet reconciling funds and requirements for product lines and business units.

This GMA mission serves well the principle that a credit institution should manage its assets in a such a way that other people are willing to buy them. This concept goes beyond value-based management because it weights-in the risks assumed by business unit and channel, all the way to solvency as explained in Chapter 6. Moreover, the use of a GMA as a profit center independent of the corporate treasury, assists top management in its mission to actively measure and manage:

- Allocation of economic capital
- Diversification effects at group level
- Risk exposure at business unit, channel and group level.

A GMA approach to economic capital allocation also accounts for the fact that most of what is done in economic capital allocation today in conjunction to Basel II, is done for the first time. To a significant extent, the same is true of risk-based pricing. In capital allocation, many banks work by analogy, *as if* they are choosing a portfolio of investments. The better managed banks appreciate that they have to have rules which are applicable to *their* business. Therefore they concentrate on developing:

- Factual EL/UL forecasts for expected losses and unexpected losses, and
- Documented risk and return distributions which can be tested by instrument and business unit.

This raises the question of which product lines and business units should be considered for capital allocation. The general answer is all of them; there should be no exceptions. The specifics, however, depend on the organization and structure characterizing every credit institution. No two banks have the same organization or management responsibilities connected to their business units.

Figure 7.3 gives a bird's eye view of one of the organizational solutions. It features eleven divisions, each headed by an executive vice president. Seven of them represent its major product lines; four are administrative (auditing, real estate and couple of other services have not been included).

Every one of these eleven divisions should be a profit center,[1] with the four administrative units billing the seven major product lines for their services. In this

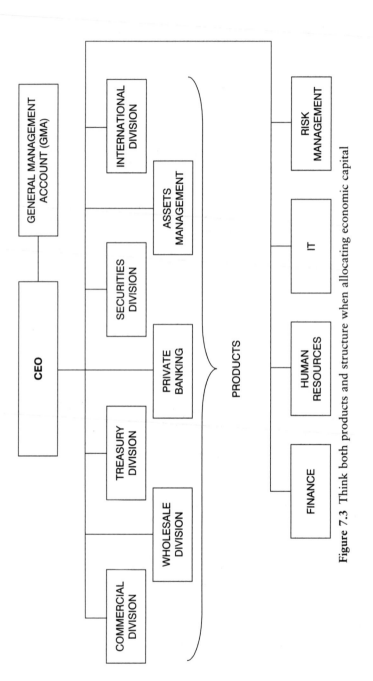

Figure 7.3 Think both products and structure when allocating economic capital

example, major risks are taken by the seven product lines – and that is where economic capital allocation should be focused.

It is not necessary that each division is taken as one business unit. Indeed, it may well be that it includes more than one business unit. Alternatively, the bank's structure may attribute business unit status to key subsidiaries – at home and abroad. It is prudent to be very careful with terminology, because it varies from one institution to the next.

An important function of the corporate center, along the GMA line of reference, is to integrate risk exposure of business units regarding corresponding banks, important clients and other clients. A matrix for database organization is shown in Figure 7.4. It identifies exposure by chapter featuring, as an example, three main business lines. Information contained in this matrix should be updated in real-time.

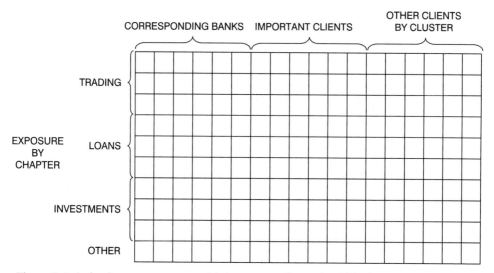

Figure 7.4 A database on exposure with important clients should be kept in a matrix form and updated in real-time

Another vital duty of the corporate center is to project, then closely follow up, return on economic capital by business unit and for the institution as a whole. The manner in which this is done varies by financial entity. One of the commercial banks says that it uses different discount rates for different product lines, with its corporate center:

■ Controlling risk and return by business unit
■ Controlling total investment for total operations
■ Calculating cash flows by business unit, and
■ Managing the capitalization of the institution.

Well-managed banks appreciate that there should be a capital charge for allocated economic capital. Given the risk exposure at product line, instrument, business unit, client relationship and group level, the institution as a whole may experience *underfunding* in economic capital, in which case:

$$\text{Total capital} - \text{Allocated economic capital} < 0 \qquad (7.1)$$

Or, there may be *idle capital*. This happens when:

$$\text{Total capital} - \text{Allocated economic capital} > 0 \qquad (7.2)$$

Strategies addressing the best use of idle capital vary from one credit institution to the next. Some banks use that excess money to buy back their equity – which is a questionable policy. Share buybacks, says Walter Pompliano of S&P, decrease the bank's core capital.

Some companies use *economic profit* and *economic value added* as a framework by which to measure the aftermath of their capital allocation. Economic profit is the income from continuing operations after taxes, excluding interest, in excess of a computed capital charge for average operating capital employed. Economic value added represents the growth in economic profit from year to year.

As with every other enterprise, it is absolutely necessary to have adequate metrics, which enable monitoring and evaluation of economic capital allocation. Properly chosen metrics help in focusing senior management's attention. They also serve in determining annual incentive awards and long-term policies for employees, by clarifying management's understanding about:

■ What creates value, and
■ What destroys wealth.

The background to these lies in the fact that risk and return should not be cosmetic words but issues with real weight, influencing executive decisions. One of the key problems in comparing risk and return distributions between different channels is that they are not designed to be comparable with one another. In many companies there is also a lack of homogeneity of risk evaluation measures, down to the business unit level. Another frequent problem is that of mixing up:

■ Criteria, and
■ Metrics.

These and other reasons underline the wisdom of post-mortem tests concerning economic capital allocation, as well as return on economic capital. What should these post-mortem tests be primarily after? An equity analyst had this advice: 'Look where banks make or lose too much money. Chances are that there is where the business unit is undercapitalized.'

The regulators are well aware that some of the credit institutions product lines or business units may be undercapitalized. Therefore, they tighten their inspection. Mergers is a case in point. After the merger of Citibank with Travelers and its Salomon Smith Barney investment bank, the Fed of New York wanted the bank to administer tests for the past five years. On Wall Street rumours had it that these tests involved some seventy different VAR models.

Post-mortems, stress tests (see Chapter 6) and feedback help in applying risk-based capital measures, and in improving management awareness, control and account-ability. In turn, this makes economic capital allocation a better structured process. Given the importance of rigorous solutions, the approaches to which I make reference should be the corporate center's responsibility.

7.3   Top-down and bottom-up identification of economic capital requirements

One of the arguments frequently heard in connection with economic capital allocation is whether it should be done top down or bottom up. This is a pseudo-problem. First and foremost, whether top down or bottom up, the study should have as a goal, to heighten risk awareness. Second, and just as important, as far as economic capital allocation is concerned:

- Top-down, and
- Bottom-up approaches

are *complementary*; they are not contradictory to one another. Both should be tried and reconciled through an iterative process in the search for an optimum in economic capital allocation. 'Bottom up is good to start with,' said Ian M. Michael, of the Bank of England, 'but it must be controlled at the top. The business unit may ask for lots of money, but might not show so much return.'

Bart Dowling, director of global asset allocation at Merrill Lynch, London, suggested that there are no blanket solutions: 'At this point of the cycle, top down is preferable. But at the end it comes to a two-way approach – with bottom up informing the people at the top.' Barclays Bank, too, uses this interactive approach:

- The top provides guidelines and gives approval
- But the parameters for economic capital allocation depend on the business unit.

For starters, *top down* means that headquarters (the corporate center, the holding company) uses its authority to allocate capital and adjust the financial structure of each business unit and major product line. In procedural terms, top down typically starts with:

- Corporate strategy
- Credit risk and market risk
- Top operational risk factors (management, legal, IT), and
- Value-based analysis.

A top-down economic capital allocation typically proceeds with global level of available economic capital. It considers capital structure, business mix and risk matrix – by channel and business unit. The mission is that of analyzing global risks reflected in:

- Volatility in profits and losses
- Volatility in capitalization
- Credit spread on subordinated debt versus treasuries, and other factors.

Moreover, crucial top-down decision elements are the ability to replenish capital within the chosen time horizon, maturity of instruments, credit risk associated with each major business partnership and with clients as a whole, market risks connected with the instruments being traded and with portfolio positions, and so on. The corporate office should take a dynamic approach to credit risk, market risk and operational risk.

With the *bottom-up* approach to economic capital allocation, each business unit, or channel, establishes its standalone financial structure. This should be done in line with a corporate target, but bottom up gives the business unit more degrees of freedom in economic capital than top down. Taking an example from operational risk control, the loss distribution method is bottom up, while the scoreboard solution is top down. In principle, bottom up concentrates on:

- Business unit goals
- Risk classification
- Data collection
- Modeling.

But as already underlined at the beginning of this section, the two methods will eventually map into one another. 'We do it both ways,' said Christian A. Walter of Crédit Suisse, adding that neither approach should:

- Be done independently of business operations
- Try to deliver everything at once
- Lead to an unbalanced assessment of risk
- Bet on quick gains, or
- Give the impression of being a one-off effort.

As George Pastrana and Dr Per-Göran Persson of the United Bank of Switzerland aptly observed, using only a bottom-up approach would hit against too many parameters and it would not allow an effective audit of the deliverables. Business lines needs guidelines from the top, and these include:

- Key performance indicators
- Revenues, costs, risks
- Present and projected exposure
- Return on equity
- Margin on assets
- Revenues and costs per person
- New money growth criteria.

The interactive procedure between top-down and bottom-up economic capital allocation is shown in Figure 7.5. A solid project which supports both senior

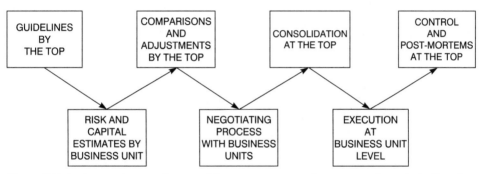

Figure 7.5 An interactive top-down and bottom-up approach to economic capital allocation

management and business unit viewpoints is not done overnight. At UBS it took three years to establish, and it involved a considerable amount of collaboration with the bank's controllers.

Interactivity requires common criteria, and the insight provided by the research which led to this book points towards some basic principles relating to calculation of risk exposure for capital allocation. Summing up the best of the results obtained from different credit institutions, I have come up with the following risk categories:

- *Credit risk*: wholesale, business loans, retail, mortgages, country risk.
- *Market risk*: structural interest rate risk, fixed income, equities, foreign exchange, derivative instruments.
- Critical factors such as *insurance risk, liquidity risk, insolvency risk, operational risk*.
- *Other exposures*, which include fixed assets, goodwill, intangibles, investments and so on.

For every risk class, the bank must account for expected losses, unexpected losses, regulatory compliance, regulatory weights, time horizons (one year, five years, maturity), tail characteristics for extreme events and solutions for extreme conditions. A sound policy is that basic criteria are established at the corporate center and applied homogeneously throughout the organization.

In conclusion, economic capital allocation is an interactive process. It cannot be effectively accomplished one way, whether this is top down or bottom up. Part of the work in establishing a rigorous allocation procedure is that of comparing the capital needs, assumed risk and return perspective of one business unit to another. This evidently involves people. For instance:

- Traders
- Private bankers
- Loans officers, and
- Asset managers.

As a project, economic capital allocation must adopt a longer-term perspective, including a close look at changes in value, in exposure(s), in cash flow and in regulatory capital. Capital allocation is a prime example of the need for a solid methodology, which makes feasible a factual and documented decision and is able to attain the most likely results.

7.4 Economic capital allocation at Rabobank, Crédit Suisse, Deutsche Bank and Citigroup

Prior to presenting the three case studies, it is appropriate to draw attention to the fact that the majority of banks who participated in this project believe an economic capital methodology is more comprehensive than one based on regulatory capital alone. Figure 7.6 exemplifies this statement by comparing the more fundamental, polyvalent approach of Basel II to the elementary solution provided by Basel I. It also suggests the need for a link between:

- Risk management, and
- Allocation of economic capital.

In line with this, top-tier banks started work on Basel II a few months after the June 1999 publication of the new capital adequacy framework, linking capital allocation, risk management and efficiency of deliverables. An example is Holland's Rabobank (Rabo), which placed emphasis on specific financial risks associated with running its banking business. Rabo's five major channels are:

- Credit risk
- Interest rate risk
- Market and foreign exchange risk
- Transfer risk (cross-country)
- Insurance risk.

Operational and business risks are taken as a non-financial risk. For all financial risks, Rabo and other banks launching into Basel II have been measuring their exposure and translating it into economic capital. This advanced methodology is in sharp contrast to the classical way of more or less seat-of-the-pants capital allocation, and it is directly connected to target rating. In Rabobank's case, this is AAA.

There is a great deal that can be learned from credit institutions which are ahead of the curve in Basel II implementation. For instance, to improve its methods and procedures regarding economic capital allocation, Rabobank has created an *internal capital market*, to be of service in:

- The pricing of risk, and
- Channeling economic capital to its business units.

The implementation of this approach requires the translation of traditional risk metrics into economic capital units. It has also called for a consistent internal risk control methodology, able to assure meaningful identification and measurement of exposures, as well as:

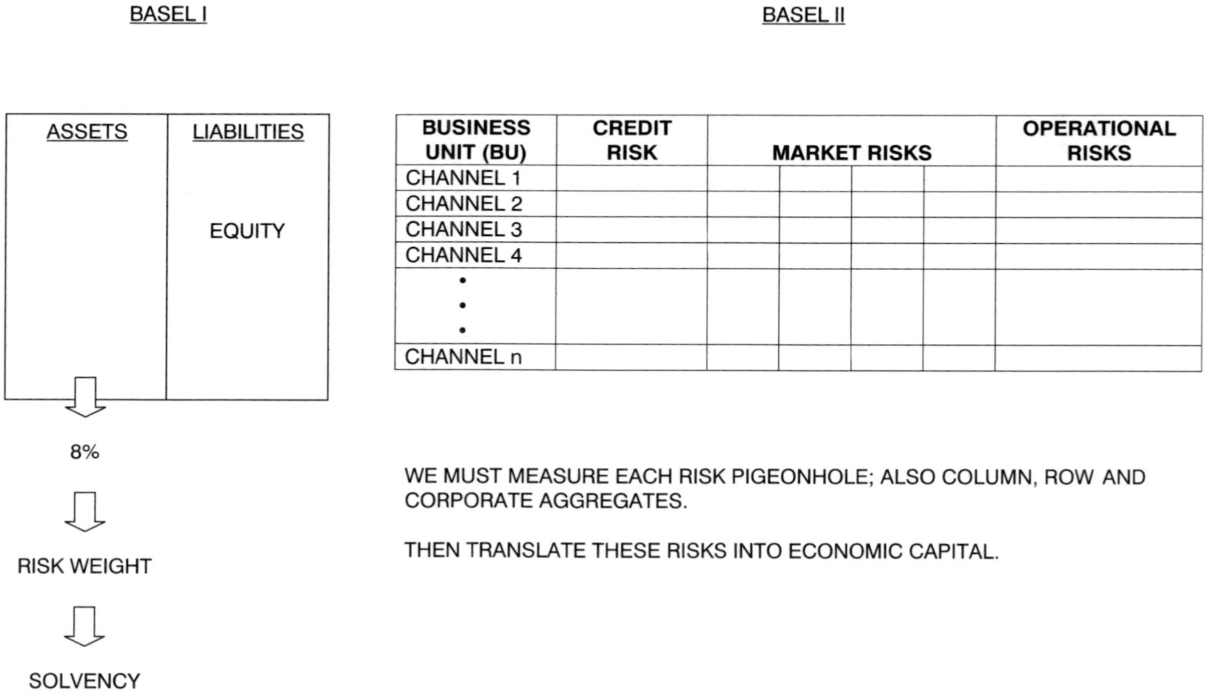

BASEL II

BUSINESS UNIT (BU)	CREDIT RISK	MARKET RISKS			OPERATIONAL RISKS
CHANNEL 1					
CHANNEL 2					
CHANNEL 3					
CHANNEL 4					
• • •					
CHANNEL n					

WE MUST MEASURE EACH RISK PIGEONHOLE; ALSO COLUMN, ROW AND CORPORATE AGGREGATES.

THEN TRANSLATE THESE RISKS INTO ECONOMIC CAPITAL.

BASEL I

ASSETS	LIABILITIES
	EQUITY

8%

RISK WEIGHT

SOLVENCY

Figure 7.6 An economic capital methodology is more comprehensive than one based on regulatory capital

- Comparison of risks among themselves
- Aggregation of risks within and across business units, and
- Aggregation of risks at group level.

Critical to this methodology has been the institution of a process able to control and safeguard consistency across the bank's business line, and to ensure that the aforementioned economic capital allocation system evolves as business realities change. Indeed, this is an explicit goal of all well-managed banks.

Economic capital allocation at Crédit Suisse follows a fairly similar procedure. One senior executive said: 'We define what we need in economic capital because of our risk profile, for instance, CHF 20 billion ($14.3 billion). We strive for AA, even if now our bank has A+ rating.' Another very interesting point has been that at Crédit Suisse:

- AA rating is like a market variable, and
- Economic capital is targeted after AA rating by independent rating agencies.

To ensure the maintenance of the right balance, senior management compares needed financial resources with what the bank has available in economic capital. 'Maybe we conclude we have taken on too much risk,' added the Crédit Suisse executive. If so, the alternatives will be to reduce the amount of risk or increase the economic capital resources. (Banks find ways to do so, as we will see in Chapter 9.)

The allocation of economic capital at Deutsche Bank follows a somewhat different procedure than the two so far examined in this section. The German credit institution takes economic capital as a starting point and as a driver for book equity allocation. The management of Deutsche Bank's corporate treasury rests on two pillars:

- *Capital*, with equity, reserves, hybrids, regulatory requirements
- *Liquidity*, with debt, senior bonds, and local funding (see Chapter 5).

The links between the two pillars are financing, leverage, debt issuance and capital requests. Capital levels have to match business needs, as well as expectations from rating agencies and equity analysts. This brings back the use of credit rating targets for establishing a balance between expected risks covered by regulatory capital – and unexpected risks addressed by economic capital.

Indeed, this balance is a policy which has all the characteristics of becoming popular among major credit institutions. There are, however, differences regarding the mechanics employed to monitor and maintain such balance. Rabobank plans to use RAROC for allocation of economic capital to its five major business units – unit by unit. This would most likely be done on a *virtual capital* basis. Rabobank has not yet decided to subsequently allocate physical capital to business units, which is what Deutsche Bank is doing.

Real *vs* virtual economic capital allocation is now one of the key issues confronting commercial bankers as well as regulators. 'For big subsidiaries commercial banks usually do real economic capital distribution,' said an executive of the Bank of England. 'They may develop reputational and business problems, unless they offer explicit guarantees.'

At Citigroup, economic capital allocation is physical within its twenty-one channels. How each main business line allocates economic capital within its operations is up to its management. For smaller subsidiaries, credit institutions may do a virtual economic capital allocation, depending on:

- Business considerations
- Accounting reasons
- Technical reasons
- Tax optimization, and
- Requirements by exchanges.

One of the positive aftermaths of real economic capital allocation to business units is a process under way, in some credit institutions, to make economic capital allocation a rigorous evaluator of managers' performance. The choice between virtual and real money allocation depends on organizational set-up, suggested Christian A. Walter, at Crédit Suisse. In this case, real capital is allocated to business units at least at the level of major legal entities, Crédit Suisse First Boston (CSFB) being an example.

The question should evidently be asked as to whether the credit rating-targeted economic capital allocation has given the results expected of it. The answer is not that clear, as Table 7.1 documents. While this is a very recent policy, and it may well be that it has not yet had the time to give the results expected from it, rating agencies have priories of their own.

'Since 1999, we don't believe banks to be overcapitalized,' said Barbara Ridpath, of S&P. 'It is rather the opposite.'[2] Ridpath made the point that while regulatory capital keeps an institution's banking license, 'more capital' means the bank is safer – as seen by:

- Shareholders
- Bondholders
- Lenders
- Depositors, and
- The capital market.

Peers	BIS Tier 1 ratio (as of 30 September 2002)	Rating (S&P's) (as of 21 December 2002)
UBS	11.6%	AA+
Citigroup	9.1%	AA+
Barclays	N/A	AA
Lloyds TSB	N/A	AA
ING	N/A	AA–
Deutsche Bank	8.9%	AA–
Crédit Suisse	9.0%	A+
HSBC	N/A	A+
JP Morgan Chase	8.6%	A+

Table 7.1 Tier 1 capital ratios and S&P ratings

As the reader will recall from Chapter 3, to make sure no entity uses 'funny money', in its rating S&P excludes all hybrid from core capital. Also, the rating agency's adjusted risk-weighted assets incorporate qualitative assessment of portfolio quality, market risk management, use of securitization and risk mitigation techniques, risk concentration, asset and liability management, inclusion of other business activities, like insurance, asset management or private equity, and operational risk.

The reader will also observe in Table 7.1 the reference to Tier 1 ratio. Chapter 3 has explained that this is banks' core capital. In the 1996 to 2003 timeframe, practically all major banks have tried to strengthen core capital, and have aimed to support business growth within risk-weighted limits. At Deutsche Bank this transition has gone from 5.9 percent T-1 in 1999, to 7.4 percent in 2000, 8.1 percent in 2001 and 8.9 percent in 2002.

What Standard & Poor's, and practically all rating agencies, are after is the ability to identify sufficient capital to absorb all risks through an economic cycle, particularly its low level when the market does not support replenishment. For this purpose, as has been already discussed, the S&P capital model incorporates a recession scenario – which practically means sufficient capital to absorb incurred risks, without going 'cap in hand' to the credit market. The cornerstone of such evaluation is the quality and composition of the institution's portfolio.

7.5 Citigroup's adjustment factor: an example with operational risk

As the practical examples in section 7.4 have documented, every credit institution has its own method of allocating economic capital to its business units. These different approaches have common notions and share common concepts. They converge on critical background issues, though they diverge in the implementation details.

No matter which solution is followed, an important common characteristic of the best economic capital allocation methods is their transparency. Full transparency benefits everybody: from business unit management to the financial people doing the final capital allocation at headquarters, and the investigating minds responsible for post-mortems. The latter must be able to:

- Spot wrong results and unwanted outcomes, and
- Do so even if they may have no precise idea of what is the 'right' figure that could or should have been allocated.

Regarding evaluations and post-mortems, both financial executives and risk controllers must be uncompromisingly frank about each misuse of resources, risk findings, underperformance or faulty steps. They must also guard themselves against self-deception that 'the right thing was done at the right time', even if obtained results show that this was not the case.

One of the experts participating in this research made the point that, sometimes, analysts and controllers believe so much in the results they are seeking, that they start to overweight favourable evidence, underweight possible counterexamples and pay no attention to error ranges. This way, they fail to appreciate a sequence leading to capital misuse. Another expert, however, suggested precisely the opposite: that the controllers may be too critical, and fail to appreciate the circumstances prevailing when the capital allocation was made.

With these reservations about post-mortem bias in the background, it is appropriate to keep in mind that a relatively new domain like that of allocating real economic capital to business units, provides a good example of a methodology in the making. One of the financial institutions said that, to start with, a good approach is to check what the regulatory charge capital may be for:

- Every business line, and
- Every product and service.

This assists in defining how much money should be put in the expected losses class, where there is more experience than with unexpected losses (see section 7.7 in this chapter, and Chapter 14). It also helps to be objective, not subjective, overcoming reactions like: 'this risk event will never happen'; 'traditionally we did not have to pay attention to this type of risk'; 'the probability is a small fraction of what it takes to control this exposure'. The crucial issue is that what we do is reasonable and, as far as possible, well documented. Let me take operational risk as an example, and with it the needed follow-up on economic capital allocation to operational risk.

If we wish to have deliverables which are commendable, we should take things that we know about operational risk, select one of the methods for operational risk control advanced by Basel II, and get down to the task of developing the appropriate method.[3] It is not the objective of this text to elaborate on operational risk, but rather to bring to the reader's attention that even the best capital allocation will be short-lived if it is not regularly:

- Re-evaluated, and
- Updated in capital requirements.

Back to basics: capital allocation should be fit for the problem we face. Money acts as a common denominator, but throwing money at the problem will not solve it. It will only make it worse.

The economic capital allocation which we make must be adjustable to changing conditions. Here, the best example that I have found is Citigroup's ingenious adjustment factor. Because the frequency of review is a compromise between precision and cost, Citigroup chose quarterly adjustment through the formula:

$$EC_1 = EC_0 \sqrt{\frac{R_1}{R_0}} \tag{7.3}$$

where EC_1 = economic capital allocated this quarter
        EC_0 = economic capital allocated last quarter
        R_1 = revenue in channel i this quarter
        R_0 = revenue in channel i last quarter.

The way Dr David Lawrence explained the algorithm, revenue is taken by channel, not on a bank-wide basis. Citigroup's studies have shown 'R' by channel to be a better metric than gross income (GI) suggested by Basel. The square root rule was adopted because the relationship between economic capital and revenue is non-linear.

This method is easy to implement, uses existing data and gives results that are sensible and reasonable, which should be the goal for all good models. This quantitative square root rule is supplemented by qualitative adjustments, through auditing, which differentiate between:

■ Business issues (BI), and
■ Major business issues (MBI), weighting $3 \times BI$.

The distinction between business issues and major business issues is made by the auditor who reviews the operations, but the head of the business unit has to agree with the assessment at the end of the audit. Another adjustment factor is *aging* which means past due date without corrective action. The algorithm is:

BI or MBI $\times$ Aging = Preliminary issues score   (7.4)

As shown in Figure 7.7, an ogive curve helps in converting the preliminary issues score (PIS) to an audit issues score (AIS). The latter is multiplied by the corresponding risk level to produce the qualitative adjustment factor (QAF). The algorithm is:

AIS Risk level = Qualitative adjustment factor   (7.5)

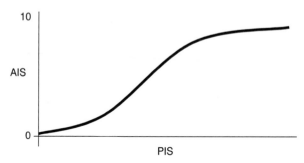

Figure 7.7 An ogive curve helps to convert the preliminary issues score (PIS) to audit issues score (AIS)

Throughout the entire corporation, there may be hundreds of outstanding business issues and operational risks underpinning them. The peak is immediately following a large merger.

While this specific example focuses on one domain, that of op risk, the concept behind it is much more general in its application, because the algorithms supporting it are adaptable. After all, a query every good manager should ask himself is: 'What are my alternatives?' So far, to my knowledge at least, no other company has come up with a more elegant solution to the necessary update of economic capital allocation than this one by Citigroup.

7.6 Developing a theoretical framework for capital allocation

The reader will recall the reference that there is currently no fundamental way to answer from first principles how much economic capital a bank as a whole and each of its business units individually require. Indeed, along Basel II principles, economic capital allocation takes second place to regulatory capital, as the latter extends to unexpected risks. The emphasis on algorithmic approaches to expected risks, however, is growing and this sees to it that:

- It makes much of current theory irrelevant
- While, at the same time, it brings a big amount of noise in the economic capital allocation processes.

Section 7.5 made reference to the need for fitting the method to the problem. In this we are confronted by two vital issues. One is to account for the credit institution's strategic objectives. The other is that of incorporating performance measurements into the capital allocation model. How to do it is explained in a snapshot in Figure 7.8. The outlined process ranges from strategic planning to feedback and it includes at its core an evaluation methodology. RAROC is taken as an example.

Yet another challenge, referred to in Chapters 5 and 6, is that of estimating fair value. Several major banks have commented that allocation decisions are largely based on a market price approach, like that prevailing between buyers and sellers. Others have said that they benchmark economic capital's discount rate for cash flow, then they use net present value (NPV).

Some of the major financial institutions have been of the opinion that while the aforementioned two approaches are today's solutions, eventually a theory will be developed that underpins and streamlines economic capital allocation to business units and channels. One way to improve upon, and formalize, this allocation process as it now stands is to establish an algorithmic procedure that aims at optimization after accounting for:

- Capital costs
- Business risks
- Expected and unexpected losses.

If we consider the different alternatives which are currently in the front line, we will see that the simplest method that can be used to allocate economic capital among business units and/or major product lines, is a standalone approach which looks at individual entities and their capital needs. According to this method, which has a fairly wide following, the bank autonomously calculates for each business unit:

- Economic investments and operating expenses
- Expected profits from operations
- Expected and unexpected losses, as well as amount of capital required to cover them.

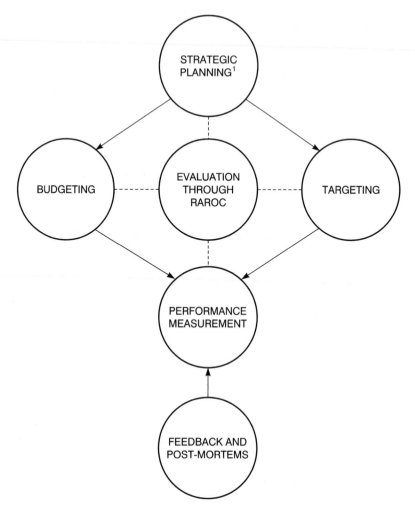

PART OF STRATEGIC PLANNING IS TARGET RATING, FOR EXAMPLE, AA+, WHICH IMPACTS
ON RISK-TAKING, TACTICAL MOVES AND P&L

Figure 7.8 Linking capital allocation to performance measurement

Economic capital will be allocated according to the numbers produced by these three points. In some institutions, through a *linear standalone method*, the arithmetic sum of economic capital needs of all business units determines the bank's aggregate economic capital requirements – which the credit institution may or may not be able to meet (more on this later).

■ *If* economic capital is allocated from the bottom up, *then* each business unit computes its own needs and submits it to senior management for approval.
■ *If* it is from the top down, as well as in the course of the iterative approval process, discussed in section 7.3, general management must have a yardstick.

The simplest yardstick is gross income (GI).[4] It has been adopted by Basel II in connection with capital requirements for operational risk with the standard method. Enterprise-wide GI is the sum of GI_i, the gross income of each business unit i. This, too, is a simple linear approach – which, however, is not without problems.

Apart the fact that GI is just a proxy of some other more accurate criterion for allocation of economic capital, this linear method has the disadvantage that it disregards effects of synergy, as well as of diversification, between business units. Its strength is that it produces without any complexity an estimate of capital requirements per business unit, and for the bank as a whole, provided that:

- Risks and returns of individual business units are not correlated
- Each business unit makes a contribution to total profits roughly proportional to its GI_i, and
- Bank-wide available economic capital is equal to what all of the business units need.

An alternative is the *proportional scaling method* which accounts for the fact that the sum of economic capital allocated to the units may not be available through bank-wide financial resources. Using this approach, a business unit's capital requirement is scaled in line with the bank's total economic capital. If a business unit reports a capital requirement of K_i under the standalone approach, it is allocated a proportional economic capital amounting to:

$$K_i' = K \frac{K_i}{\sum_i K_i} \qquad (7.6)$$

with $K \neq \sum_i K_i$

where K = economic capital of the bank
   K_i = economic capital required by business unit i under standalone approach
   $\sum_i K_i$ = sum of economic capital required by the i units

   K_i' = modified economic capital allocation per unit i, under proportional scaling.

Proportional scaling works on the hypothesis that if bank-wide available economic capital is not enough to satisfy all business units, then it must be allocated according to some proportion. This, however, is not always done linearly, because the board may decide to promote one or more business units. Hence the need to introduce weights into equation 7.6.

Alternatively, it may be that bank-wide available capital is in excess of what is currently required by all business units, but there is no need to increase proportionally the allocation. As already discussed, the board may decide to use the extra capital to buy another company (adding a new business unit, or strengthening an existing one), buyback shares or for other reasons. The reader will recall that share buybacks reduce the bank's economic capital.

A more sophisticated approach to economic capital allocation is to establish return on capital guidelines by the board which provide a frame of reference, facilitate interactive capital allocation and make feasible effective audit and management control. This, too, has been discussed, along with criteria established by one of the major banks, like key performance indicators connected to a strategy promoting new money growth.

Moreover, since economic capital is risk capital, we have first to compute the most likely exposure at a given level of confidence – 99 percent or 99.9 percent – on investment we are after. Then, we must establish return on investment criteria. The algorithm for *return on economic capital* has been already detailed. As a reminder, it is:

$$REC = \frac{Net\ income_i}{K_i'} \qquad\qquad (7.7)$$

where   REC = return on economic capital
        K_i' = economic capital allocated to business unit i.

Some banks use net income-based accounting for calculating return on economic capital. Others choose economic net income. We have already covered about the difference between the two and the reasons behind the choices being made.

A couple of credit institutions have commented that they look at capital at risk through an aggregation method which simulates the changes in their portfolio's value with predefined extreme events and correlations connected to market moves. This helps to compute maximum simulated loss.

Extreme moves in market rates and prices are computed for all products and then applied by currency to first-order risks and second-order risks – the two classes into which all exposures in the bank's positions have been divided (see Chapter 8). These extreme moves are derived using the 99th percentile, or largest move from historical data distributions, which are based on longer-term observation periods. Other financial institutions use VAR instead of capital at risk.

7.7   An algorithmic solution for unexpected losses by the Deutsche Bundesbank

The capital allocation method outlined in section 7.6 is the simplest possible. As such, it can be improved in a number of ways. Some of these improvements have been suggested by regulators. The Deutsche Bundesbank's solution for economic capital allocation to business units, is known as the *internal beta*.[5] This accounts for correlations, and it aims to allocate capital to individual business units in line with their actual contribution to the bank's aggregate risk and return.

According to this approach, a credit institution's aggregate risk exposure is determined through an algorithm that uses the standard deviation of future returns and marginal contribution of every business unit to the bank's aggregate risk. This is estimated by its beta (β_i). Let me add that it has been difficult to find the originator of this approach. Apparently, the basic concept goes back to the 1960s and it could be credited to Dr Harry Markowitz. The algorithm is:

$$\beta_i = \frac{A}{s_{BR}^2} \sum_i w_i \, cov_{ij} \qquad (7.8)$$

where   A   = assets of the bank, preferably using capitalization as proxy
         s_{BR}^2 = variance of aggregate bank's risk
         cov_{ij} = covariance between returns of business units i and j (or, alternatively, between unit i and the bank)
         w_i = weight representing the share of unit i in the bank's assets.

Economic capital will be allocated to a given unit through the algorithm:

$$K_i = \beta_i \bullet w_i \bullet K \qquad (7.9)$$

with

$$\sum_i \beta_i \, w_i = 1,$$

and where K_i = Economic capital allocated to business unit i
            K = Economic capital held by the bank.

The impact of major contribution of business unit i to returns of the whole bank is assured by the fact that the greater the correlation of its returns with bank-wide results, the higher will probably be the economic capital allocated to this business unit. This is not necessarily a cast-iron approach because, as it will be recalled, there exists the theory of *cash cows*, business lines which at present generate considerable cash flows but their future is rather bleak. Therefore, they are milked for cash to benefit other product lines or business units that are supposed to have a better future.

The reader will also remark that the beta approach does not cover the case of losses incurred by a business unit, but this could be corrected through scaling. The betas in equations 7.8 and 7.9 help to determine a business unit's provision with capital. This approach has the advantage that both correlations and contribution effects are taken into account in the allocation of economic capital to the bank's individual business units (or product channels). Notice that the beta of a business unit might be negative, which would imply a negative cost of capital.

Beyond this level, a comprehensive economic capital allocation model would put a limit on the amount of capital the credit institution could obtain through deposits and bought money. Both this limit and the cost of capital are a function of the bank's credit rating, which talks volumes for the important role independent rating agencies have with Basel II.

If we abstract from the aforementioned constraint and assume a bank has a virtually unlimited capacity to procure capital, *then* the problem becomes one of profit maximization taking the entity's risks and costs into account. This algorithm has been developed by Frank Heid of Deutsche Bundesbank. The implied constraint is that the overall unexpected losses, corresponding to economic capital, must be less than the economic capital the bank actually holds:

$$UL = a \bullet s \left(\sum R_i w_i\right) A \leq K \qquad (7.10)$$

where   UL = unexpected losses
        a   = a constant.

As multiplier of the standard deviation for one-sided distribution at 99.97 percent (corresponding to AA), under assumption of a normal distribution a = 2.75.

       s = standard deviation of the bank's aggregate risk
       R_i = outlier unexpected losses, at business unit i (defined in equation 7.12)
       w_i = weight representing the share of unit i in the bank's assets
       A   = assets of the bank, preferably using capitalization as proxy
       K   = economic capital held by the bank.

In equation 7.10 economic capital K is assumed to be fixed in the short run. Dr Heid points out that usually it is determined by the credit rating the bank wants to hold in the longer run (see Chapter 2), or by the target value established by senior management for the credit institution's own probability of default (see Chapter 10).

As Heid went on to suggest, *if* one assumes that the bank sets its probability of default at 99.5 percent, then it might choose its capital K as being equal to VAR at 99.5 percent level of confidence. But *if* the bank chooses PD at 'four nines' level (99.99 percent) – as the case should be – then, *if* the VAR approach is retained, the level of confidence would be set at 99.99 percent.

A considerable amount of research still has to be done on this issue, linking equation 7.10 and the aforementioned hypotheses to AA and AA+ rating. Also, a better method than VAR should be chosen involving demodulation of notional principal amount, or loans equivalence, and stress tests. Still, the algorithms and methodology being outlined constitute a good starting point of a method which can integrate with and enrich the tools in Chapter 13 (RAROC, Moody's KMV and BCAR).

The optimization algorithm which incorporates cost of capital may be either:

$$\max A \bullet \sum_i E_{ri} \bullet s_{ri} \bullet w_i - K(1+c) \qquad (7.11)^6$$

where E_{ri} = expected returns of business unit i
       s_{ri} = standard deviation of returns of business unit i
       w_i = weight associated to business unit i
       cK = cost of capital.

As a reminder, s_{ri} is s of business unit i returns (r); s_{Ri} is s of business unit i risks (R). Similarly, E_{ri} is expected returns of unit i; E_{Ri} is expected losses of unit I due to current business risks. Heid advises that one could envisage a two-step procedure, where the bank first determines total economic capital, as well as risk and return. Then, in a second step it allocates capital to its business units.

Alternatively,

$$\max A \bullet \sum_i E_r \bullet s_i \bullet w_i - K(1 + r_t)$$
(7.12)

where $r_t K$ = risk-free return at time t, such as interest rate of treasuries.

To be complete, an optimization algorithm should reflect the fact that expected return of a business unit i, greatly depends on risk being incurred. Optimization should therefore be subject to the constraint that economic capital may experience outlier unexpected losses. By business unit i, this is expressed as:

$$R'_i = E_{Ri} + \lambda \bullet s_{Ri}$$
(7.13)

where R'_i = outlier unexpected losses, at business unit i
E_{Ri} = expected losses due to current business risks at unit i
s_{Ri} = standard deviation of losses due to risks at unit i
λ = multiplication factor for unexpected losses.

Stress testing can be instrumental in estimating λ (see Chapter 6).[7] Outlier unexpected losses, R'_i, find themselves at the upper range of unexpected losses in Basel II. In this text, R'_i stands not only for credit risk, but also for market risk and operational risk. There are two ways to get a number for R_i.

■ Extrapolating historical data beyond α = 0.01, for example α = 0.001.
■ Using hypothetical data, based on expert opinion, preferably through the Delphi method.[8]

In the one-tailed distribution of equation 7.13, a good way to look for λ is in the range: $3 \leq \lambda \leq 15$. A multiplier λ = 3 brings the value of losses to the tail of the distribution of losses. The higher values of λ, such as $10 \leq \lambda \leq 15$ serve for testing extreme events. A worst case scenario of unexpected losses will be:

$$R' = \sum_i R'_i$$
(7.14)

where R' = enterprise-wide sum of extreme losses developed by all business units.

This is worst case because, in all likelihood, there will be a compensation of losses between business units through correlations – at least up to a point. The constraint is established by placing limits to R'_i and R'', which condition the risks involved in loans, trades, investments and other bets. For instance:

$$R'_i \leq X_i$$
(7.15)

$$R'' = \sum_i R'_i \le X = \sum_i X_i \tag{7.16}$$

where X_i = maximum of expected and projected unexpected losses for business
                unit i

       X = maximum of expected and projected unexpected losses for whole
                entity.

These maxima will curtail the business unit's, and the bank's as a whole, risk appetite. To be effective, they must be set and policed by the board. Total economic capital K, economic capital by business unit K_i, cost of capital cK and risk limits X_i and X are connected through the algorithm:

$$\max A \bullet \sum_i E_{ri} \bullet s_{ri} \bullet w_i - K(1+c) > Y + X \tag{7.17}$$

where Y is the gross profit projected by the strategic plan of the bank for the whole entity. Y is the sum of Y_i, the gross profit each business unit should target during the year in its financial plan. A sophisticated model would express Y_i and Y as a function of confidence intervals.

    Like all models this is based on simplifying assumptions, for instance, that the bank is able to set the betas and determine its optimal allocation of financial resources. Historical simulation is important but it must be enriched through simulation of future returns and future risks, helped by scenario analysis. Projections should be good approximations for a real-life portfolio, and they must be regularly backtested.

Notes

1 D.N. Chorafas (1999). *Commercial Banking Handbook*. Macmillan.
2 'Basel II Masterclass', organized by IIR, London, 27–28 March 2003.
3 D.N. Chorafas (2004). *Operational Risk Control with Basel II*. Butterworth-Heinemann.
4 See also in Chapter 16 the objection made by State Street Bank in Congressional hearings.
5 Deutsche Bundesbank (2002). *Monthly Report*, January. I feel particularly indebted to Dr Frank Heid, of the German Central Bank, for his contribution to the contents of this section, plus the fact the original algorithms are the results of his research.
6 The root of this algorithm can be found in Deutsche Bundesbank (2002). *Monthly Report*, January.
7 D.N. Chorafas (2003). *Stress Testing: Risk Management Strategies for Extreme Events*. Euromoney.
8 D.N. Chorafas (2002). *Modelling the Survival of Financial and Industrial Enterprises. Advantages, Challenges, and Problems with the Internal Rating-Based (IRB) Method*. Palgrave/Macmillan.

8 Evolving rules and procedures for economic capital allocation

8.1 Introduction

Chapter 6 discussed the synergy that exists between risk control, economic capital allocation and solvency management. Through practical examples, Chapter 7 explained how banks allocate capital to their business units, and then presented a theoretical infrastructure which may eventually characterize capital allocation procedures. The aim of the present chapter is to complement the practical side of economic capital allocation, including senior management policies and rules which promote a rational approach.

Lessons learned from the first couple of years of simulations and procedural experiences in economic capital allocation, by means of projects undertaken by major financial institutions under Basel Committee supervision, can be condensed in seven rules. The first rule is that guidelines for economic capital allocation must be established by the board, with all business units given the responsibility for calculating their own economic capital needs:

- Evaluating business perspectives
- Estimating their exposures
- Using models and observing schedules.

This may sound like a preference for a bottom-up approach, but it is only partly so. We will see why. The second rule concerns the top-down component of the iterative process, which has been outlined as the better approach. Risk management specialists, at group level, must carefully control the exposure which has been assumed, as well as the risk and return estimates made by business units and product lines. This will enable the corporate centre to establish:

- Mean value of economic capital for each type of assumed risk
- Mean value of economic capital for each business unit, and
- Economic capital at 99.9 percent level of significance, or better, for business units and major product lines.

The third rule is that detailed documentation is very important because no two business units, or product lines, have the same characteristics. The fourth rule is that the process of economic capital allocation must be steadily developed, and defined capital requirements regularly updated as business evolves. Also executives in charge of this process should always consider the time horizon. An exposure matrix by product line and business unit, with time the third dimension, is of great assistance to decision-makers.

The fifth rule is that even what we consider to be 'the best possible plan' of economic capital allocation, has to be tested under both normal and extreme conditions. For this reason, Chapter 6 advised the use of stress tests, and it has also explained their goal and the tools and results which they deliver. Destructive testing is a good option because it teaches a great deal about a capital allocation plan's weaknesses.

The sixth rule involves the need for feedback and for evaluation through post-mortems. The reader will remember the importance of open channels of communication, underlined in Chapter 1 in connection with internal control. One of the elements of great interest to the board, the CEO and senior management is failure in economic capital allocation. Their identification is necessary not to sanction, but to improve, the process the next time around.

Like its predecessors, the seventh rule is valid for every business, and it can be briefly stated in these terms: 'In order to start, you have to start.' *Where* to start, is the question. The answer given by some of the early starters is retail banking, personal loans, and loans to SMEs, then corporates. (For a more detailed discussion on SMEs, see Chapter 12.)

Only after experience has been gained with these channels, is it wise to proceed with derivatives, swaps, mortgage-backed securities, asset-backed securities, collateralized mortgage obligations and other instruments whose handling places severe demands on skills, tools and methods. The latter are the product channels which involve a considerable amount of unexpected losses, and therefore they require a great deal of experience at the junction of economic capital allocation and exposure management.

8.2 Corporate focus on economic capital allocation

Because the amount of attention (or inattention) paid by top management makes (or breaks) any approach to economic capital allocation, the first question I ask in my meetings is whether or not economic capital allocation really *is* on the board's and the CEO's agenda. If it is not, the bank will be 'spinning its wheels in a vacuum'. Provided the answer to this specific query is positive, the next steps are to:

- Ensure the collaboration of business unit and product line management
- Clearly define which channels will be first, second and third in capital allocation
- Ensure there are no overlaps among responsibilities of different business units and channels
- Focus on one objective at a time, taking a couple of selected business units as starting points
- Proceed with a couple of pilot projects, evaluate risk and return, allocate capital and make stress tests.

Chapter 2 brought to the reader's attention the role of a devil's advocate, explaining that this is an integral part of management planning and control. While each business unit may do its own evaluation of tools and methods necessary for economic capital allocation, the top-most test of each approach, and of the system as a whole, is the responsibility of the corporate center. Experts at corporate center must:

- Evaluate tools and methods
- Challenge the allocation being made
- Pinpoint its weaknesses
- Reconcile capital needs to the balance sheet
- Check adequacy of provisions, and
- Assure the framework will pass regulatory scrutiny.

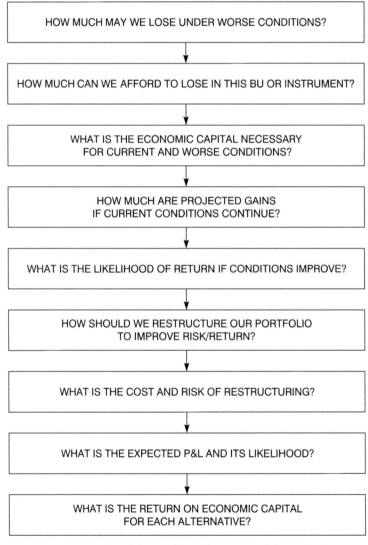

Figure 8.1 Economic capital and the analysis of unexpected losses by business unit and instrument

Evidently, all this should be accomplished within the perspective of Basel II, as well as of prevailing laws and regulations within each jurisdiction. A procedural framework is needed and Figure 8.1 summarizes in a nutshell what is necessary for the analysis of unexpected losses by business unit and instrument. Most of the elements coming into this framework have already been discussed.

Who should be the experts on whose work depends so much? In the real world of banking and finance, there are four kinds of people who come together in economic capital allocation. One group is the financial instrument designers, who are in part salespeople and in part rocket scientists.[1] They are very good at instrument design (see section 8.4) and abstraction, seeing nearly all things described by means of:

- Algorithms, and
- Data structures.

The second group is the market developers who sell the designers' instruments, or commission them to design a new financial product according to customer specifications. These are the people who really understand the market. Their downside is that they can be easily carried away towards greater and greater risks, assumed by the bank.

The third group is the risk managers, who should not only know both instruments and counterparties, but also appreciate what it takes to track exposure, control deviations and take timely corrective action – either directly or by alerting senior management. To work effectively, they must classify risks according to priorities (see the discussion on first-order and second-order risks in section 8.4).

The fourth group is the financial people, who hold the purse strings. Not only do they have to be diligent in their mission as devil's advocates, which they do together with risk controllers, but they also have to question the hypotheses made by business units and product managers as to what is the market potential – and the returns. They must always keep in mind the conflict of interest facing product developers and salespeople because of commissions.

All these people make a contribution in elaborating the conditions necessary for allocating capital to business units and for controlling this allocation. The viewpoints of experts that were provided in Chapter 7, and associated practical examples, document that there is no best method for economic capital allocation, other than the synergy of many skills, which has just been defined. A closely related query is, which tools should be employed?

- It is said that the Federal Reserve uses KMV/EDF to spot financial problems of banks it is inspecting (see Chapter 13).
- Rabobank has been using RAROC to allocate economic capital to its major business units.

Chapter 13 explains the reasons why I see these two solutions as complementary, rather than competing with one another. A commercial bank can use the Fed's approach to evaluate probability of default, and Rabo's to estimate return on assets, at each level of credit rating and loss given default, and include credit risk equivalence for positions in the bank's derivatives portfolio.

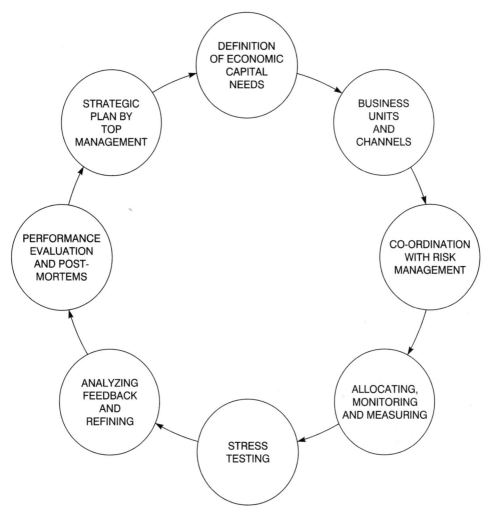

Figure 8.2 The wheel of economic capital allocation

Knowledge and skills, a sound methodology, and tested tools are so important because economic capital allocation to business units and product lines is a never-ending process. It is more like the wheel shown in Figure 8.2 which turns all the time. As the wheel turns, economic capital allocation experts at the corporate center should put themselves in the places of line executives at business units carefully watching for:

■ Strong points which promote competitiveness, and
■ Weak points which, when left unchecked, damage the enterprise.

There are plenty of strong and weak points to be found in any plan. The plan for economic capital allocation at business unit level is no exception. The *strong points* are:

- Providing transparency
- Promoting accountability
- Obliging management to price risks, and
- Increasing the focus on stress testing.

The reason behind the *weak points* can be found in the fact that, on several occasions, economic capital allocation to various units and channels still uses:

- Traditional non-analytical practices
- Imprecise and incomplete risk measures, and
- Doubtful performance metrics in terms of risk and return.

One piece of advice Dr Peter Drucker often gives is, 'Feed your strengths and strangle your weaknesses'. To strangle the aforementioned weaknesses, economic capital allocation requires a sophisticated approach, which is at the same time factual and documented. The complexity of identifying, qualifying and quantifying current and future exposures increases because of the need for dynamically linking economic capital to risk factors and to the market environment.

Along these lines of reference, a sophisticated capital allocation mission goes beyond calculating expected losses and potential unexpected losses due to business events, to include feedback and post-mortems. Another requirement is that of calibrating parameters like time horizon and confidence level, which should be part of every economic capital allocation plan. An integral part of this effort is that of looking behind the numbers into qualitative characteristics which give the numbers the right meaning.

8.3   Real-life examples with economic capital allocation to business units and channels

Chapter 7 has presented real-life references to the principles which have been guiding economic capital allocation in several major institutions, including Crédit Suisse, Deutsche Bank, the Erste, Citigroup and Rabobank. In this section we will follow the capital allocation process to a greater level of detail, including some of the problems encountered in this process. For this reason, the names of credit institutions behind the practical examples in the following paragraphs are withheld.

To focus this discussion on real-life capital allocation examples in the right way, it is appropriate to bring to the reader's attention two important issues. The first is the cultural change Basel II has initiated. Banks start to appreciate there are clear advantages in improving the quality of their risk control, since disclosure requirements for the more advanced methods under Basel II will:

- Expose the full extent of existing risks, and
- Bring into the open the institution's internal processes.

For example, is it able to collect accurate information and report on operational loss data? Can its management understand the implications of its decisions in terms of length of commitments? What is its concentration of exposures? What financial resources are needed to feed current and future strengths?

The final query relates to the second issue which impacts on economic capital allocation: what kind of proxy should be used for effective assignment of financial resources? The Basel Committee leans towards *gross income* but, as we saw in the case study in Chapter 7, Citigroup has chosen *revenue* by channel as proxy. Other major financial institutions, too, have followed the revenue choice.

Based on a sample of universal banks, Figure 8.3 shows, as an example, the mean and range of distribution of revenue among four divisions: treasury, securities, corporate finance and other commercial banking. (Some of these companies also had insurance, but this was edited out of the statistics, since it was not common ground.) The numbers in the histogram are average figures; the range is shown in the right-hand column.

A final decision on economic capital allocation will not necessarily be done along the numbers of the proxy. But we need a starting point, and this is suggested as the starting point of preference. Other factors, too, enter the allocation algorithm, including:

- Future prospects of the business unit
- Risk appetite of the bank
- Concern for the effects of economic capital allocation on stakeholders, and
- Best practices in creating scalable economic capital allocation schemes.

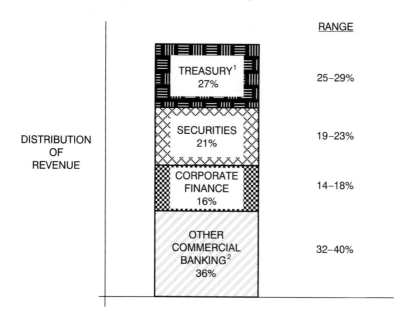

NOTES :
1 INCLUDING DERIVATIVES AND FOREX.
2 INCLUDING BUSINESS LOANS AND RETAIL BANKING.

Figure 8.3 Distribution of revenues from banking operations, based on a sample of universal banks

Supporting technology, too, plays a role because it involves mapping capital allocation onto a model which is controllable. Each of these issues plays an important role in the economic capital allocation process, beyond the proxy. Take as an example capital allocation and the stakeholders. The criteria being established must satisfy several different parties in determining capital ratio and structure: shareholders, bondholders, regulators, auditors, rating agencies and capital markets.

To make matters more complicated, the aims of these groups are only in some cases convergent. In other cases they are opposed. Moreover, objectives have become dynamic, constantly changing with market sentiment, business requirements and performance targets. Investors now take a closer look at how the bank allocates money within each channel:

- Paying attention to assumed risk, and
- Estimating the institution's ability to pay dividends.

Questions asked of money-center banks in connection with economic capital allocation, received as a reply the figures presented in Table 8.1, along six major channels. Economic capital allocated to derivative financial instruments has not been specified in these discussions. A regulator who saw the distribution of economic capital in Table 8.1 judged it as reasonable. Another global bank, not too dissimilar to those behind Table 8.1, suggested that it would:

- Allocate 20 percent to 25 percent of its economic capital to its insurance division
- Allocate up to 30 percent or 35 percent to its (major) investment banking division
- Keep corporate banking at the 20 percent level, and
- Devote less capital to asset management, corporate investments, and some other business lines.

Channel	Percentage of economic capital	Comments
Corporate banking	20–30	Tends to attract lots of capital
Investment banking	10–35	Depends on the business the bank is in
Private banking	3–10	Growth area because of wealth effect
Asset management	2–15	Growth area because of demographics
Corporate investments	2–5	High volatility, low performance. The trend is to reduce
Retail business lines	20–48	Several banks now move into the market which gives relatively stable revenue

Table 8.1 Economic capital allocation by major channel in financial institutions. Economic capital allocated to derivatives has not been specified.

	A	B	C
Corporate banking	20%	30%	30%
Investment banking	35%	20%	10%
Private banking	5%	10%	3%
Asset management	15%	2%	7%
Corporate investments	5%	3%	2%
Retail banking	20%	35%	48%
Sum	100%	100%	100%

Table 8.2 Economic capital allocation by three different universal banks

Practically all institutions which responded to queries regarding the ranges in Table 8.1 suggested that current and projected exposure plays so much of a key role in capital allocation decisions that relatively wide ranges can be justified even if the product lines are not too different from one bank to the other. Table 8.2 compares economic capital figures allocated by three different banks – identified as A, B and C – along these six channels.

How are credit institutions checking the accuracy of their assumptions which underpin economic capital allocation beyond the proxy level? Credit institutions which answered this query suggested that the validation of exposure plays a critical role, and there are essentially three ways for estimating expected and unexpected losses in a forward-looking manner:

- *Hypotheses* being made, including those which concern outliers and extreme events. Simulations, like Monte Carlo, are made to add quantitative results to qualitative assumptions.
- *Historical information.* Past risks can be used to project future risks, if they have a pattern. Through analogical reasoning and database mining, historical information helps in making hypotheses about future events or trends; while a different set of data assists in testing them.
- *Experimental approach.* Marking-to-market, then comparing to define gaps between market values and the accruals. The importance of this is substantiated by the fact that regulators start looking very carefully into discrepancies in net present value between marking-to-market and book value. The use of models and marking-to-market practices has increased the visibility of balance sheet discrepancies – which serve as an indicator that the bank's accounts may not be 'squaring out'.

Some of the meetings focused on operational risk. Table 8.3 shows a more detailed example on economic capital allocation, which includes an operational risk add-on. The institution from which these statistics come has twelve channels. Notice that operational risk capital allocation is not a fixed percentage of capital distribution for credit risk and market risk. A couple of experts who looked into these figures found them reasonable.

Channel	CR + MR distribution	Operational risk add-on
Derivatives and other trading	20	2.0
Sovereign	5	1.0
Corporate/wholesale	18	2.5
Business/SME	7	1.5
Other commercial banking	4	0.5
Financial products	17	2.5
Credit cards	4	1.0
Other retail banking	3	0.5
Insurance	14	1.5
Asset management	4	2.0
Retail brokerage	1	0.5
Payments and settlements	3	1.0
	100	18.0

Table 8.3 Corporate level economic capital allocation in conjunction to risk exposure. Operational risk has low correlation with credit risk and market risk.

Several of the banks participating in the research meetings underlined the critical role played by internal control, and the confidence management placed on organizational systems and procedures associated with economic capital allocation. One of the rating agencies suggested that the new regime (Basel II) exposes failings more harshly than has been the case so far, and this has adverse consequences for market perception.

Finally, it has been a consensus of these meetings that credit institutions, particularly those with global or multiple holdings, need to pay great attention to the topology of their risks, and to issues of consolidation in terms of both regulatory capital requirements and economic capital which goes beyond regulatory level. They must also signal to the market that they have financial staying power everywhere they operate.

8.4   First-order and second-order risks

Classification and identification of risks faced by the credit institution and its business units is prerequisite to handling them in an able manner. This is the purpose of dividing them into first-order and second-order risks, or using some other criteria with which to classify exposure. The need for a classification will be better appreciated after a brief introduction to product lifecycles.

Development work associated to new financial products has many similitudes with issues characterizing engineering design. Design work falls into a number of essential phases. In engineering, researchers typically conceive of, or envisage, a product that addresses a critical customer need or one which is able to generate new customer requirements. What is being accomplished by rocket scientists with new financial products is very similar to this engineering practice. The risks, however, are different both:

- In their nature, and
- In their magnitude.

Borrowing again a leaf from the engineering book, researchers accomplish their work by attacking its technical, business and (sometimes) legal aspects associated with designing a product. This is achieved by selecting parameters specifying the product's intended functionality, quality, cost and marketing perspectives. The legal aspects typically concern infringement of patterns and hidden issues of liability. Part and parcel of design work is that of:

- Testing to validate the product based on design specs, and
- Empowering the customer to safely and effectively operate this product.

Manufacturing is the next important phase in engineering, where quality control must hold the upper ground, and with it cost control. If the product has complex technical characteristics, sales engineers must be heavily involved in the marketing effort, which is the next phase. Their mission is to ensure that the product not only attracts the customers' attention but, also, that its implementation performs according to specifications. The final phase is after-sales service – from installation, to maintenance and disposal.

   The functional areas described in the preceding paragraphs account for much of what professional engineers do. Successful companies see to it that the tools which their designers, manufacturing engineers, quality controllers and sales engineers are using to perform the functions expected from them, are commensurate with:

- The mission they should accomplish, and
- The deliverables they are expected to provide to their company's clients.

Product lifecycles with financial instruments are fairly similar to what I have just described, though volatility, therefore assumed risk, is much greater than with engineering products. In this short paragraph are encapsulated two critical issues. One is the culture and set of skills necessary to become a successful practitioner in modern finance. The other is that special attention has to be paid to the risks embedded into the deliverables.

   In order to be handled in the most effective way, the risks associated with financial products have to be classified in terms of priorities. Such priorities are neither universal nor cast in stone. Each bank develops its own. This is what Crédit Suisse has done with its taxonomy into *first-order risks* and *second-order risks*. A classification along this dichotomy can be instrumental in setting risk limits and in being in control of their observance. According to Crédit Suisse,

- *First-order risks* are interest rates, currency rates, equities, other commodities, and credit spread.
- *Second-order risks* are option delta, gamma, theta, kappa, rho;[2] the yield curve, swap spread, cross-currency basis risk, and interest rate basis risk.

Each of these risks must be appreciated by senior management, and has to be addressed by product designers, traders, salespeople and risk controllers. Both expected losses and unexpected losses may result from first-order and second-order risks. In some cases, rapid innovation makes the task of forecasting levels of exposure a formidable one. In risk management, the golden rule is:

- Simple things should be declarative, and
- Hard and complex things should be procedural.

Properly elaborated procedural solutions make the execution of difficult and complex issues possible. This is true all the way from definition and monitoring of first-order and second-order risks, to economic capital allocation which takes them into account. As we have seen, risk management works in synergy with identification and control of exposure, therefore, it spans both inside and outside the classical boundaries of a financial instrument.

To a significant extent, procedural solutions must be automated. To do so, we need to use another engineering tool: mathematical thinking mapped into computer programming. Both can be found at the core of every modern product development and product management effort. Mathematical formulas underpin most current procedures in the banking industry and, quite evidently, IRB solutions. A Basel Committee algorithm defining regulatory capital under IRB is:

$$RC \geq UL + \max(0; (EL - SP - GP_{nonRC} - FMI)) \tag{8.1}$$

where: RC   = regulatory capital
         UL   = unexpected loss
         EL   = expected loss
         SP   = special provision or charge off
         GP_{nonRC} = general loan loss provision other than RC
         FMI   = future margin income.

Some credit institutions suggested during the research meetings that, in their opinion, future margin income (FMI) is essentially business risk. Others, however, insisted that FMI and business risk are two different issues – if for no other reason than business risk is not part of Basel II's Pillar 1, while this is the case for FMI.

This bifurcation of opinion led to a second round of talks and, in these discussions, there has been a convergent opinion that FMI is not yet clearly defined because no significant amount of research has been done, so far, on this subject. I point out this issue because it is a good example of one kind of difficulty with mathematical models: some of the factors entering the algorithm are not always clearly defined.

Regarding other factors in equation 8.1, the senior executive of one of the big commercial banks with whom I met commented that 'unexpected losses' is a biased term, because it has a lot to do with the type of accounting the institution chooses. He added that there is also the challenge of getting a number of ULs, which could be done through either of two methods:

- Extrapolating on historical data, at α level of confidence,
- Using hypothetical UL estimates, based on expert opinion.

The reader will recall the excellent algorithm developed by the Deutsche Bundesbank for unexpected losses (section 7.7 in Chapter 7). In Chapter 14, we will return to the issue of ULs from a managerial perspective. Having established a basis for handling ULs at a comfortable level of confidence, equation 8.1 can be rewritten:

$$UL + EL \leq RC + SP + GP_{nonRC} + FMI \tag{8.2}$$

Under the stricter definition whereby $RC = EL$, equation (8.2) can be reduced to:

$$UL \leq SP + GP_{nonRC} + FMI \tag{8.3}$$

Keeping within the perspective of credit risk (essentially abstracting market risk and operational risk) and introducing:

- UL_{AA} as substitute to UL, where UL_{AA} stands for targeting AA rating
- K_{EE} as proxy of capital for extreme events (a new variable)
- BR, or business risk as proxy of FMI, in spite of the aforementioned objections

equation 8.3 becomes:

$$UL_{AA} \leq SP + GP_{nonRC} + BR + K_{EE} \tag{8.4}$$

The right-hand side of equation 8.4 can be taken as a good approximation of economic capital needed to face unexpected losses, strictly at credit risk level. This and similar algorithms can become better focused by including first- and second-order risks as component parts of the unexpected losses. UL_{AA} is essentially a function of assumed risks.

$$UL_{AA} = f \text{ (interest rates, currency rates, equities, other commodities,}$$
$$\text{currency spreads; options, the Greeks, yield curves, swap}$$
$$\text{spreads, cross-currency basis risk, interest rate basis risk)} \tag{8.5}$$

Exposure due to the variables in function (equation 8.5) should be reflected in the four capital factors at the right-hand side of equation 8.4. K_{EE} might be estimated with a reasonable degree of accuracy if we have detailed and dependable time series – preferably over twenty years. The evaluation of K_{EE}, done by the bank, needs to be tested and verified by an independent entity. I asked one of the rating agencies if it would grade K_{EE} estimates. The answer has been that this job must:

- Be done case by case
- Be based on reliable data
- Account for default information
- Map all assumed risks, and
- Integrate estimates of future exposures.

What should be provided by a detailed and accurate credit database to facilitate the computation of K_{EE}? A good proxy is the contents of Moody's RiskCalc regarding a bank's credit coverage. These include financial statements, industry descriptors, ratings, other indicators that can be used to predict default, obligor level descriptive data on defaulters and non-defaulters, statistically tracked obligation details (term, type, exposure), cash flows to defaulted loans and bonds, and certain macroeconomic predictive variables.

As the reader will notice, some of these factors relate to the entity itself, others to the economy – but all of them are helping to measure loss given default. Let me repeat that, ideally, the span of time series should be twenty years, with a ten-year span as a reasonable minimum. For a reliable estimation of K_{EE}, a bank must:

- Have its own time series of credit data
- Enrich this database with industry time series, for historical scenarios
- Develop hypothetical scenarios, including worst cases, and
- Conduct plenty of stress tests.[3]

These should include rigorous analysis of commitments made, and of commitments to be made, reflected in the economic capital requirements. The way to bet is that *if* a business unit or channel needs significant capital, *then* it has assumed a great deal of risks. These exposures should be pruned out, to right the risk and reward balances.

Moreover, after the four capital factors at the right of equation 8.4 have been computed, their sum should be tested against an independently estimated UL_{AA}, to see if the resulting capital requirements are reasonable. Equation 8.5 outlined the factors entering this test. Stress tests conducted in conjunction with independent entities can help.

I asked one of the rating agencies if they would conduct such a test study, in case a credit institution asks them to do so. The answer received was that, if they do so for UL_{AA}, they will not only consider a quantitative estimate of economic capital but also qualitative factors like management decisions and actions, company franchise and outlook, risk appetite, quality of risk management, access to funding, and diversification (see Chapter 2).

As an alternative, an algorithm like the square root of the sum of squares, similar to the one used in BCAR (see Chapter 13), may provide a good approximation to the computation of UL_{AA}. Whether this or a different formula is chosen, applicable risks must be taken at 99.9 percent level of confidence to account for outliers.

The development of an algorithm which reflects the general nature of unexpected risk, and is parametric to enable its adaptation to each bank's specific business environment, might eventually lead to a fundamental theorem linking economic capital to risks and their management. We are not yet there, but we can learn a lesson from precedent in the physical sciences.

8.5   Learning a lesson from physical sciences

The lesson to which section 8.4 referred is two centuries old. In 1799, Carl Gauss, the mathematician, published a revolutionary document on the fundamental theorem of algebra. Gauss pointed to the fact that discoveries of universal physical principles cannot be found by mathematical formulas alone.

- They must be discovered experimentally, and
- Their discovery calls for great attention to stubborn, seemingly tiny, margins of error in the formulas.

The same principle has also been behind what Jonathan Kepler detailed in connection with the original discovery of gravitation in his seminal 1609 publication, *The New Astronomy*. In the late twentieth century, some of the most important sources of risk, as in the case of the O-ring on the *Challenger* shuttle, have required similar minute observations – and they led to changes in combinations of technology and materials included in product design.

This is, for instance, what Dr Richard Feynman did when he identified a minor element, the O-ring, as the reason for *Challenger*'s failure. His method has been that of applying in the process of discovery the essential scientific principle of investigating and prognosticating unexpected and unsuspected risks; in short, of exploring the unknown. Feynman aptly pointed out that:

- Relying on simplistic faith in arguably proven risks and formulas is intrinsic incompetence.
- It is not what we know but what we *do not* know, which we must always address, to avoid major failures, catastrophes, and panics.

In the context of financial risks this principle is modeled along eight axes of reference in Figure 8.4, and paying attention to what we do not know along each axis. Seen in fiat, these contribute to a risk pattern which affects the institution as a whole. In order to appreciate hidden risks we have to examine every axis of reference individually, most carefully looking for stubborn, seemingly tiny, margins which:

- Hide unexpected risks, and
- May have dire consequences.

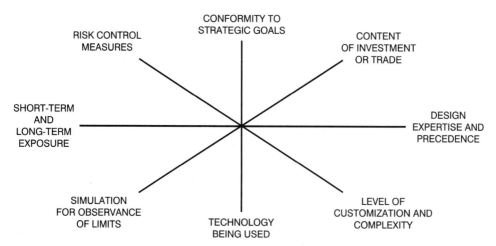

Figure 8.4 The different dimensions which make or break trades and investments

What Keppler, Gauss and Feynman did was to search for qualitative and quantitative detail *behind* both foreground and background factors. This detail is often hidden by the glare of headlines. On 29 July 2002, the headline was that Qwest Communications will review its financial statements of its last three years, and will not be ready to meet the 14 August 2002 deadline of certifying financial statements by its CEO and chief finance officer (CFO). Which were the background factors? The hidden reasons behind them? This is what investigators should look after.

Take another financial example. The headline was that, in general, executive options cream off 10 percent of a company's profits. With technology companies, what the senior executives takes home through stock options zooms up to between 20 and 30 percent of annual profits – which is roughly how hedge funds treat their investors. What are the background factors? The caveats? The aftermath on shareholder confidence in senior management?

The headline has been that by shorting stocks and playing big in options, hedge funds exert intense downward pressure on the market.[4] This is adding to sky-high volatility and it is creating some wild price swings. What are the background factors? Can we express qualitatively and quantitatively some of their details? Can we monitor them to document the hypotheses we make on the role of hedge funds in the economy?

This is the sort of investigative mind needed to find generic linkages between economic capital and risk assessment. As the previous seven chapters have documented step by step, economic capital can be properly calculated only when we understand the factors contributing to exposure, and their assessment. An investigative mind will also consider client relationships in constructing a basis for:

- Identification of risks
- Estimation of their frequency and impact
- Hidden correlations in exposure created through gearing, and
- Aggregation of risks which go beyond prudent limits.

Here is an example of the after-effect of letting background factors find their own way to the foreground. When in mid-1982 Italy's Banco Ambrosiano was approaching default, a horde of 250 corresponding banks of the parent company and its subsidiaries abroad became alarmed. In terms of risk they had only dealt with the crust of the pie, not what was lying inside. Suddenly, all 250 of Ambrosiano's corresponding banks were desperate to recover the money they had lent directly or indirectly to the defunct Italian credit institution and its subsidiaries in the four corners of the world.

On 29 July 1982, at the twelfth hour prior to the Italian bank's default, representatives from 200 different creditors got together. In a meeting held in London, Ambrosiano's permanent commissioners, who were appointed by the Bank of Italy, explained how $1.287 million had vanished through a trapdoor in Panama.[5] None among this horde of lenders seems to have bothered, till then, to:

- Find out the background reasons leading to Ambrosiano's failure, or
- Account for this not-so-unexpected risk and position themselves against it while there was still time.

It is interesting to note in this connection that the treatment Ambrosiano's corresponding institutions got has been mixed. Banks who had lent to Banco Ambrosiano in Milano, that is, the parent company, were protected under the 1975 Basel agreement which made the national bank responsible for credits damaged by default of one of the institutions it supervised (see also in Chapter 15 the discussion on the Concordat). But there was no cover for the debts Ambrosiano's foreign offshore affiliates had contracted. The money had been lost, and this money was the big part of the total sum.

Another example of the importance of investigating with an open mind the background reasons, particularly those hidden from general view, comes from operational risk. Technology has been of great help to financial institutions, but it also has the potential for loss due to deficiencies in control processes and systems. Such deficiencies constrain the bank's ability to gather, process and communicate information efficiently and securely, without interruptions.

- A modern entity's operations are highly dependent on the integrity of its technology, and
- Its success depends, in part, on its ability to make timely enhancements and additions to its technology in anticipation of client demand and/or of changes in risk patterns.

To the extent a bank experiences system interruptions, errors, or downtime, which could result from a variety of causes, its dependability as a whole is significantly reduced. The origin of these failures may be internal or external. For instance, rapid increases in client demand may strain the credit institution's computers and communications resources. Or, computer illiteracy at board and CEO level may damage the bank's ability to enhance its technology and expand its operating capacity.

It needs no further explaining that technology and other operational risks also include human error, fraud, terrorist attack and natural disaster. Banks could mitigate operational risks by maintaining a comprehensive internal control system, by employing experienced personnel and by providing capital reserves for operational risks. The lesson to be learned from the great physicists, however, suggests that this action will be so much more successful if great attention is paid to background reasons, hidden factors and their evolution.

8.6 The issue of procyclicality and its impact on economic capital

Prior to allocating economic capital to business units and channels, top management must ensure that the bank has enough of it. To do so, it has to either grow its resources to meet its obligations, or it must redimension the risks it is taking to make them commensurate to its resources. As Chapter 9 explains, credit institutions use different approaches to increase their economic capital. The other side of the equation, however, is that this money must be working – and for this reason, it is invested in bonds, equities and other commodities.

When the stock market rises, senior management is euphoric. There is good return on assets. Things are different when the stock market drops. If this happens over a prolonged period, as in the 2000–03 period, then assets are shrinking and all sorts of financial institutions find themselves obliged to sell equities and other commodities in a depressed market. This brings us to the issue of procyclicality.

Procyclicality is what happens when one or more market events can create a self-feeding cycle, for instance, selling equity in a depressed market to improve solvency. The notion of procyclicality is not necessarily associated with panics, though it might both contribute to them and be influenced by them. Many analysts think the drive to satisfy regulatory capital requirements might lead to procyclical events, *if*:

- Equity markets are weak for a long time
- Interest rates are characterized by sustained high or low extremes
- Large exposures hit the banking industry
- Capital ratios of some big banks sharply decline relative to peers
- There is a continued weakness in corporates
- Several emerging country defaults damage the treasury of their lenders.

Procyclicality issues must be examined from both a macro- and a micro-perspective. On 27 January 2003, in the UK, the Financial Services Authority was forced to tell embattled life insurers that they would be allowed to 'temporarily disregard solvency requirements', to avoid selling off stocks and so worsening the equity crisis. Behind this move is the fact that British insurers and pension funds own about 40 percent of quoted stocks at the London Stock Exchange (LSE). For the FSA, the option was between:

- Allowing the insurers and pension funds' economic capital to dwindle
- And feeding the fire of procyclicality in the equities market.

Notice, however, that satisfying capital requirements is not the only trigger. Abrupt investor reaction can be just as lethal. In early 2003, owners of insurance stocks hit the panic button and sent the equities of top European insurance firms like Allianz, Munich Re, SwissLife, Swiss Re, ING and Aegon down by 6 to 8 percent. London's big Prudential Life Assurance and Aviva Insurance each lost 7 percent of its capitalization.

In earlier times, the UK's Prudential Insurance advertised itself as being as solid as the rock of Gibraltar. But in February 2003 it was announced that Prudential's market capitalization has fallen 70 percent in two years, to just £6.5 billion ($10.4 billion). This not only significantly weakened the insurer, but also had the potential of making Prudential a prime take-over target for banks hoping to build up their life insurance businesses.

In market capitalization terms, procyclicality can become the financial equivalent of a black hole in the cosmos. On 21 May 2003, it was announced that the international hotel chain, Le Meridien, had scheduled an urgent meeting with its debtors in a last minute effort to avoid bankruptcy.

- A group of banks led by Nomura had bought the Le Meridien hotel chain for $3.0 billion in 2000.
- By 2003, Le Meridien owed its lenders $1.5 billion.

■ Its capitalization, however, had fallen to $1.1 billion – leaving it with $400 million negative net worth.

Procyclicality can be deadly to everybody, particularly to insurance companies because, typically, they collect premiums from individuals or firms and invest them in stocks, bonds or other instruments. From the booming 1990s, most insurance companies, particularly in the UK, had portfolios that were heavily weighted toward stocks. But, between the last quarter of 1999 and the first quarter of 2003, the FTSE 100 fell by half. As a result, many property, accident and life insurance companies suffered heavy losses.

Another source of a torrent of red ink for property and accident insurers has been 11 September 2001, the destruction of the World Trade Center buildings by terrorist attacks. Still another was the European floods of 2002. As of October 2002, insurance industry analysts estimated that European insurers lost nearly $100 billion in capital over 2002. Stock market losses wiped out a further big amount.

Procyclicality is one of the issues underlining the difficulty in measuring an entity's capital, as well as presenting new challenges which are not easily resolved. Some financial analysts are of the opinion that *net present value* is a better alternative in computing available capital, because it addresses both assets and liabilities, along the lines of the balance sheet structure.[6] The weakness of this method lies in the estimation of present value through accruals. It is rare that book value represents NPV. This has promoted:

■ Marking-to-market all items for which there is a market, and
■ Marking-to-model everything else, which is, in many cases, the majority of A&L.

Indeed, the problem is that many, if not most, of the positions in the bank's trading book, and a good deal of those in its banking book, have no active market. Asking other parties' opinions of NPV has its limits (and dangers), both because these are often undocumented guesses and because there may exist conflicts of interest. As for marking-to-model, the downside is what Warren Buffett calls 'marking to myth'[7] (more on this later).

Still another issue concerns the way estimated values are presented. With the exception of cash in hand, the expected value of capital can be calculated at different levels of confidence: $\alpha = 0.1$, $\alpha = 0.05$, $\alpha = 0.01$. In other words, the door is open to enhance the balance sheet even though mathematical approaches are supposed to be rigorous.

In order to compute NPV in a dependable way, for many of the items in the trading book and in the banking book it will be necessary to forecast the distribution of yield curves over time. To do so, we must project the nominal interest rate as the sum of real interest rate and inflation – using only the real interest rate for intrinsic value. But a great deal of items in the banking book could well be longer term and officially available ten-, twenty- and thirty-year yield curves are rare.

Moreover, converting every item to a discounted cash value, in order to create a vector of expected values, can become complex because of the compound effect of credit risk and market risk. To simplify the econometric model to the nominal interest rate, many banks assume a *zero risk* counterparty, for instance, the US government with treasury bills or treasury bonds as the instrument.

While these approaches address the quantitative representation of NPV, procyclicality still remains a part of the bigger picture. It is unavoidable that capital requirements will increase as the assessed risks rise. The extent of volatility in capital needs depends upon several elements, including rate of increase in the aftermath of changes in probability of default (see Chapter 10), and developments which are beyond the reach of any single institution. This brings us to the role of regulators. A case study is presented in section 8.7.

8.7 Banco de España: case study on an initiative against procyclicality

If banks are liberal in assigning credit ratings in good times, on the assumption that economic conditions will continue at the upside, *then* downturns will result in volatility in ratings, and therefore capital requirements will be difficult to satisfy in time of adversity. The risk evidently is that several credit institutions, insurance companies and pension funds sell the same asset at the same time, thereby:

- Forcing additional sales
- Destabilizing capital adequacy requirements, and
- Having a negative impact on the financial system.

Because in Basel II, along with residual risk, procyclicality comes under Pillar 2, Banco de España, Spain's reserve bank, developed a method of *dynamic provisioning* through capital buffers. The essence of this approach is to keep more capital than required when the economic cycle is in an upswing. The algorithm is linear.

$$BUF_{it} = \beta_1 BUF_{it-1} + \beta_2 ROE_i + \beta_3 NPL_{it} + \beta_4 BIG_{it} + \beta_5 SMA_{it}$$
$$+ \beta_6 GDPG_{it} + n_i + e_{it} \tag{8.6}$$

where BUF_{it} = capital buffer of bank i at time t
BUF_{it-1} = capital buffer of bank i at time $t-1$
ROE_{it} = return on equity of bank i in time t
NPL_{it} = non-performing loans of bank i in time t
BIG_{it} = big bank factor, of bank i in time t
SMA_{it} = small bank factor, of bank i in time t
$GDPG_t$ = gross domestic product growth, in time t
β_j = multipliers set by the central bank, j = 1 ... 6
n_{it}, e_{it} = other determinants set by the central bank.

There is a dual concept in the background to this framework. Capital is a costly resource and the higher the cost of capital, the less banks put aside. On the other hand, credit institutions increasingly judge one another on the basis of available economic capital beyond regulatory capital. Banco de España aptly remarks that a significant amount of economic capital reduces bankruptcy costs as well as costs of not meeting regulatory requirements in a downturn. Finally, a third factor behind equation 8.6 is that raising capital is itself costly.

To develop its model, Banco de España used data in the 1986 to 2000 timeframe, involving some 1300 banks. Its analysts looked into processes for dynamic provisioning able to counterbalance procyclicality, without losing sight of the fact that some procyclicality is unavoidable since Basel II seeks a close relationship between:

- Capital requirements, and
- Risk management, esspecially credit risk.

Central to the Spanish solution is the concept of proactive *loan loss provisions*, developed through asset classification and having three main components:

- General provision, which is a fixed percentage over total loans
- Specific provision, aiming at covering impaired assets, and
- A so-called *statistical provision* for insolvency, which is an extension of the specific provision.

The statistical provision essentially acknowledges the existence of latent risk in a credit institution's loan portfolio. *Latent loss*, says the Spanish reserve bank, should be understood as a cost which corrects the excessive cyclical bias in profits, and counterbalances the cyclical behavior of existing loan loss provisions.

Failure to account for latent loss sees to it that bank profitability and solvency may be distorted, because of overvaluation of dividends and other reasons leading to erosion of capital. Indeed, the model developed by Banco de Espana is of wider applicability. Though the Spanish reserve bank did not say so explicitly, it may very well be used with trading P&L, where so far only latent profits are guestimated with a bias for fat commissions, but nothing is said about latent losses.

To test the model in equation 8.6 Banco de Espana did a simulation which involved several Spanish commercial banks. This study distinguished between four phases of an economic cycle:

- Two years of an expansionary phase where latent risk is greater than specific provisions, and statistical provision > 0
- Slowdown from year 3 onwards, with increase in specific provision, with statistical provision decreasing though still > 0
- Recession, around year 6, with many problem loans and strong increase in specific provisions, while statistical provision < 0 (which essentially means it is used up)
- Resumption of economic growth from year 8 onwards; in this case the statistical provision < 0 but eventually it will become > 0.

This simulation has shown that it is possible to keep a fairly steady level of reserves. Going through the downturn has not been geared on procyclicality, and this contrasts to the old approach which was procyclical. The simulation also demonstrated that on average the statistical provision takes roughly 10 percent of yearly profits out of the P&L and puts this money in the bank's own special fund. This provides a way of increasing the bank's economic capital without leveraging – while gearing is at the core of the Modigliani-Miller model discussed in Chapter 9.

Statistical reserves is a neat solution which is worth examining for implementation by all supervisors. Attention should, however, be paid to proper coordination with accounting rules and legislative issues.

One of the money center banks with important retail operations in Spain, pointed out that the statistical reserve is off-balance sheet; it is not part of B/S accounting records. This seems to create important problems for the accountants, which require appropriate solution. Let me add to this reference that the coordination between new regulations, legislative differences, and accounting principles is a global problem faced by banks, and other entities, all over the world.

Several senior executives who contributed to the research which led to this book brought up the issue of global accounting standards. The latest development has been phrased in October 2003 by Jos Wieleman, of ABN Amro in the following terms: 'A tripartite meeting has been scheduled with IASB (International Accounting Standards Board), Basel Committee and IIF (International Institute of Finance), to discuss coherence and consistency issues . . . the attitude of the accounting discipline seems to become much more constructive than it used to be. They need an incentive! Accounting should not – no longer – be an enemy of good risk management.'

Notes

1 D.N. Chorafas (1995). *Rocket Scientists in Banking*. Lafferty Publications.
2 See D.N. Chorafas (1994). *Advanced Financial Analysis*. Euromoney.
3 D.N. Chorafas (2003). *Stress Testing: Risk Management Strategies for Extreme Events*. Euromoney.
4 D.N. Chorafas (2003). *Alternative Investments and the Mismanagement of Risk*. Macmillan/Palgrave.
5 R. Cornwell (1983). *God's Banker*. Victor Gollanz.
6 D.N. Chorafas (2000). *Managing Credit Risk, Volume 1, Analyzing, Rating and Pricing the Probability of Default*. Euromoney.
7 W. Buffett (2003). Avoiding a megacatastrophe, *Fortune*, 17 March.

9 Strategies used by banks to increase their capital base

9.1 Introduction

A capital increase is important first and foremost to meet regulatory requirements. Then, economic capital must be increased as a bank targets a specific rating, such as AA or AA+, and aims to balance assumed risk(s) with financial resources. There are different strategies leading to capital increase. The most popular are based on: equity, debt, Tier 1 capital, Tier 2 capital, Tier 3 capital (see Chapter 3), asset sales, securitization, and special investment vehicles (SIVs).

As is to be expected, every one of these strategies has its strengths and weaknesses. There is no universal best method. For instance, the downside of equity-based approaches is that raising new equity depends on the markets' response, raising equity and equity buybacks bite each other, raising equity can be dilutive, particularly given fat executive options[1] and this may be an expensive solution contrasted, for instance, to securitization.

Debt financing is a strategy which derives a good deal of its strength from the Modigliani-Miller hypothesis (see section 9.2). As it often goes with different economic theories, assumptions underpinning them look good till they start 'taking-in water'. Eventually many of them sink, being replaced by others whose appeal is rising but may not last long.

Sometimes economic theories fade away because the hypothesis on which they rest cannot be proven, was unstable in the first place or has been deeply upset by subsequent economic facts and figures. Modigliani and Miller, for instance, should have been aware that leveraging (see Chapter 2) has limits – but they did not seem to have taken this into account (more on this issue in sections 9.2 and 9.3). Moreover, there is an enormous difference between:

- A process whose purpose is equilibrium of supply and demand, and
- One in which supply or demand has a selection and promotion function, rather than equilibrium.

Leverage underpins a promotion function, which is, after all, its reason for being. By contrast, the statistical reserves method developed by Banco de Espana (discussed in Chapter 8, as a means to combat procyclicality) aims at maintaining a certain equilibrium. The problem with high gearing is that, in the typical case, little if any thought has been given to its integration into the financial system and to its running – till the bubble bursts.

Growth of 'something' without limits, whatever this something may be, is the philosophy of the cancer cell. It is also the most fundamental force propelling financial bubbles like that of the late 1990s. Factors promoting bubbles have historically been (in order of importance):

- Increased use of leverage, through rapid growth of debt
- Excessive liquidity, with plenty of money searching for a home
- A growing turnover of assets, some of which are dubious
- New issuances which promise too much but deliver peanuts, yet initially they look credible, and
- Too many new investors with too little experience joining the market.

Each one of these references has its aftermath; the more so when two or three work in synergy. They also have a message. For instance, the last three points suggest that securitization, too, has its limits (see sections 9.6 and 9.7).

The most important of the original objectives of securitization has been to take credit risk out of the bank's books and into the portfolio of different investors. This has been only partly achieved, and in some cases has not been achieved at all. The most recent aim of securitization is that of providing a capital arbitrage. With reserves for securitization on the increase, Basel II sees to it that there will be less incentives for capital arbitrage, at least in the form it is done today.

These are the issues the present chapter examines. All of them have their impact on the ways and means used by credit institutions to increase their capital base, and on the results which they obtain for their effort. Let me add this in conclusion: contrary to what some bankers and investors think, there are no miracle solutions for capital increase. We will see the reasons for this statement.

9.2 The Modigliani-Miller hypothesis on equity *vs* debt

As opening salvo, let us start with the statement that growth of liabilities, in contrast to growth of assets, brings nearer the entity's default point. The European Central Bank defines the DP as that of equality of market value of assets and total liabilities. The proxy for the value of assets is capitalization. As equity price drops, total liabilities may exceed capitalization because:

- Debt-financing has inflated leveraging, and
- It has created financial instability in a downturn.

For instance, when in October 2002 the equity price of JP Morgan Chase fell to about $18.5, there was a certain panic at Wall Street, because the DP of that bank stood at $20. (Since then the stock has rebounded; it hovered somewhat above $20, then went above $30.) There are other challenges, as well, related to leveraging and its aftermath. Economists now point out that:

- Beyond a certain point in gearing, worried bondholders see to it that the cost of a firm's debt sharply rises.
- This pushes down the entity's rating, as independent rating agencies are (correctly) watching out for market signals.

Therefore, while the issuing of debt to support asset growth provides a cheaper source of capital, default point, probability of default and other metrics change the equation and they can turn the Modigliani-Miller hypothesis on its head (more on this later).

Not everything is against the Modigliani-Miller hypothesis, however. For instance, some banks say equity capital is the most expensive sort of capital that can be found. Others point out that equity capital is there to absorb risks on net asset value – and while it has to be present, it does not need to be exorbitant.

Should a company target more equity or more debt? This equity *vs* debt issue has been treated by Franco Modigliani and Merton Miller. Their hypothesis practically says that the value of a firm is *the same* whether it finances itself with equity or with debt. In their work, Dr Modigliani and Dr Miller saw debt as the best possible solution because:

- Dividends are taxed twice
- While interest is tax deductible.

This is true enough. Modigliani and Miller however forgot that, other things being equal, the higher a firm's debt-to-equity ratio, the greater the chances of it defaulting. Whether this has been simplification or absent-mindedness, the much revered Modigliani-Miller hypothesis seems to be another of the theories that come and go.

The statement made in the preceding paragraph is iconoclastic, but this does not change the facts. What it does is to bring attention to the risk of underweighting the effect of leverage – as well as bringing to mind one of the aphorisms by President Johnson.

The way I heard it in Washington, DC, one of Lyndon Johnson's immediate assistants tried to convince him to attend a lecture by a famous economist and university professor. Johnson rejected the invitation. The assistant insisted bringing up different arguments; this renowned economist, he said, was a major Democratic Party fund-raiser. Johnson still did not bite. 'But he has a hot economic theory,' said the assistant in a last ditch attempt to convince the US President. Johnson is said to have answered that hot economic theories are like someone making 'pipi' in his trousers. It is hot stuff. But only to him.

There is no evidence that Lyndon Johnson took a position in regard to the Modigliani-Miller hypothesis, but other economists contest the views of Dr Modigliani and Dr Miller in connection with equity and debt – and, by extension, with the hedging of a company's assets. These economists come to this conclusion after having taken a different path than the aforementioned hypothesis.

For instance, in their study of hedging, Peter DeMarzo and Darrell Duffie have shown that if a company has proprietary information concerning its own dividend stream that is not made available to its shareholders or to the market, it may be in the interest of both the firm and its shareholders to adopt a financial hedging policy.[2] Such a result, says Clara C. Raposo, is in contrast with Modigliani-Miller hypothesis on the irrelevance of hedging under symmetry of information. This, Raposo adds, is true, even if hedging is costly – because a risk premium has to be paid.[3]

Dr Fischer Black and Dr Myron Scholes, too, do not seem to be in accord with their colleagues Franco Modigliani and Merton Miller. In the 1970s, they argued that the stock of a firm is simply a call on the firm's assets. The Black-Scholes hypothesis has led to *contingent claim analysis*. On this basis Fischer Black, Myron Scholes and Robert Merton developed the option pricing model which has been widely used by analysts to study the claims on a firm by:

- Debtholders, and
- Shareholders.

Contrary to the equality of equity and debt taken by Modigliani and Miller – the option theory by Black, Scholes and Merton looks at debtholders' and shareholders' claims as being quite different from one another. Shareholders have the right but not the obligation to buy. After the upside may come the downside to the point of the firm going bankrupt.

The position of bondholders defined by Black, Scholes and Merton, is that of having sold a put option to shareholders. The bondholders' upside is the fee they receive for that option. This is essentially the interest on loans they make to the company. This option theory-based approach to contingent claims is helpful in analysing the market's view of a company's creditworthiness.

The more likely, bondholders think, a firm is to default – the default point of ECB – the greater the fee and therefore the interest they will charge. Hence the importance of knowing how much a firm owes, which reveals a great deal on how valuable the business is. This is often done by using equity price as indicator. Just as important is to know the volatility of that business; again using equity price as proxy. For any practical purpose, this is what the KMV model does (see Chapter 13).

9.3 Leveraging increases significantly the probability of default

Leveraging is a means for accomplishing a certain purpose. Leveraging comes at a price because the means it provides goes beyond the resources one has. Debt acts as a lever and the cost is not only the interest paid for borrowed capital. It is also, if not more so, the risk associated with gearing up. As it can easily be appreciated through the pattern in Figure 9.1, in the last four decades of the twentieth century there has been a significant increases in two ratios:

- Debt to profits, and
- Debt to gross domestic product (GDP).

The debt to profits ratio has moved about 40 percent faster than economic growth, creating an imbalance which led to the bubble of the 1990s, and to it bursting in 2000. One of the main reason companies prefer debt is because it has become easier to raise debt than equity. Another basic motivation is that, under current laws, interest payments on debt are deductible from income, while dividend payments on stock are not (which has been one of the foundations of the Modigliani-Miller hypothesis).

Many economists think that the preferential treatment of debt through tax deductibility explains why corporate debt soared in the 1990s, while net issuance of stock actually went the opposite way. From 1998 to 2000, companies bought back

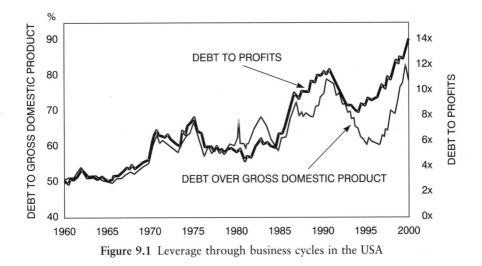

Figure 9.1 Leverage through business cycles in the USA

roughly $570 billion in stock, even taking into account all the shares issued by the proliferating technology companies and other initial public offerings (IPOs).

What essentially this means is that, in their way, tax laws encourage increasing leverage among companies. In turn, this makes the financial system more unstable. Tax laws also induce corporations into taking advantage of a variety of tax loopholes, including moving their headquarters to offshores to lower their tax bills. In this sense:

- The ease of raising economic capital through debt, and tax avoidance work in unison.
- This has very little to do with critical analysis, and a great deal with exploitation of loopholes.

The message contained in these two points seems not to have come to the attention of politicians and legislators. The aftermath is that it opens a window to illegal corporate tax dodging, because companies do not have to disclose when they undertake transactions simply to evade taxes, nor do they face stiffer penalties for tax-evasion maneuvers – as long as these have some semblance of legality. For instance, firms claim a headquarters overseas for tax purposes when their real decisions are made in their country of origin.

The synergy between the ease of raising capital through debt and tax evasion has seen to it that leverage has ballooned and capital markets have got accustomed to high leverage and low-quality paper. A good example of the after-effect is the development of the junk-bond market in the late 1980s and of credit derivatives in the late 1990s.

At the same time, other factors, too, have changed. Banks have had to compete with other intermediaries, many of whom have better ratings than the credit institutions themselves, and are therefore able to raise money more cheaply than the banking sector. As a result, banks have started to lend to much riskier borrowers to maintain their earnings; but their ratings have suffered as a result.

Another reason banks are disadvantaged in their competition with non-banks, in terms of borrowing through capital markets, is their cost structure, which is much higher than that of capital markets. It is inevitable that all these factors play a very important role in any equation that contrasts financing through equity *vs* debt. Notice that many of the factors raised in the preceding paragraphs are not new. They were around half a century ago, when Modigliani and Miller came up with their hypothesis.

This is not necessarily a critique of the work that has been done by Dr Modigliani and Dr Miller. Modeling always involves abstraction from real-life situation – and, therefore, simplification. To better appreciate this issue, we should briefly look back to the conditions prevailing in 1958, when Modigliani and Miller suggested that – given certain assumptions – the value of a firm is just the same whether:

- It finances itself with debt, or
- Its financing is based on equity.

Tax treatment may have altered the balances in the 1950s, but taking tax laws as a constant is an oversimplification. At the time, dividends were taxed while interest payments were not. Since then, interest payments are taxed in many countries and as of 2003 the EU is negotiating, among its members, a continent-wide interest tax – one which steeply rises over the years.

On the other hand, in the late 1970s in the USA, President Carter, wanted to end the double taxation of dividends. This did not happen but, to jump start the American economy, in 2003 President Bush returned to this theme. The point is that tax laws are a variable, not a constant.

In 1963, Modigliani and Miller returned to this argument on tax laws aftermath in company management decisions. On that occasion, they also stated that there was a mystery why firms did not finance themselves almost entirely with debt. There is evidently something wanting in such a logic because, in the most flagrant way, it disregards the sharply increasing likelihood of bankruptcy due to high leveraging. That is the worst advice an economist can ever give to banks on how to strengthen their economic capital.

In the manufacturing industry, too, corporations finance investment by borrowing rather than issuing new equity. Companies doing so say that this procedure lowers taxes because the interest payments are tax deductible at corporate level. As we have seen, however, such arguments forget that:

- Debt-financing inflates the debt-equity ratio, and
- It creates financial instability, especially in downturns.

Still another issue Modigliani, Miller and those economists following their path have failed to consider – but it is most important to financial institutions gearing up with debt – is the costs associated with debt financing. The greater the risk of bankruptcy the more the cost of money increases. As section 9.2 revealed, the higher a firm's debt-to-equity ratio,

- The greater the chances of it defaulting, and
- The higher the interest investors demand for entrusting it with their wealth.

The puzzle is not that two theoretical economists made such a mistake but, rather, that bankers around the world are forgetting about probability of default when invoking the Modigliani-Miller hypothesis. Once, in a conference in London, the lecturer remarked that the word 'dog' does not bite. Sometimes, however, the wrong hypotheses do just that.

Some years after they came up with their original idea, which earned them a Nobel prize, the two economists produced a modified version of their hypothesis which said something rather different than their first version. The second hypothesis allowed for the fact that the original assumptions, particularly on taxation, might not apply.

■ Profitable companies with stable cashflows and tangible assets can afford more debt.
■ Unprofitable and/or risky ones with largely intangible assets cannot afford the gamble, and the market knows it.

As an example, dotcoms should not have been carrying any debt at all. Even if for a couple of years they were able to fool the markets, real life caught up with them. Also, companies in highly cyclical industries should be wary of taking on too much debt. Moreover, a major shortcoming of the Modigliani-Miller hypothesis is that it does not imply limits to borrowings which are connected to markets, industries and individual companies.

It is therefore surprising that in 2003 there are economists who find it wise to suggest scrapping the prudential regulatory measures of Basel II, in favor of the high uncertainty of some Modigliani-Miller ideas and their leveraging aftermath. This is, for instance, what is practically suggested by the self-appointed Shadow Financial Regulatory Committee (SFRC), whose proposals are discussed in Chapter 16.

9.4 Economic capital increases should only be done in a responsible way

'Too much equity and not enough debt' is a highly theoretical hypothesis, at best, because it pays no attention to the fact that optimization requires a solid mix of debt and equity. The cost of money to a company will be much less if it maintains good credit rating – which is a basic reason why self-respecting banks now strive for at least AA rating. In plain terms:

■ The accumulation of debt benefits shareholders only up to a point.
■ That point is reached when bondholders get so worried about the company defaulting that the cost of its debt sharply rises.

These two points turn the Modigliani-Miller hypothesis on its head. Continuing to borrow beyond a certain limit, which can be established by taking into account all key market variables, drives bondholders away and it eventually leads to bankruptcy. It also raises the fact that there are other factors at play, which Modigliani and Miller do not seem to have considered.

While abstraction and modeling have become 'musts' in today's complex economic and financial environment, too much simplification is counterproductive. The increase in regulatory capital and economic capital is often a necessity, but it must be done in a responsible way. The blind following of the Modigliani-Miller hypothesis, or of any other 'theory' for that matter:

■ Serves the economy as a whole in a very negative way, and
■ It reduces most significantly management insight and foresight.

I am particularly emphasizing this issue because it has become a sort of policy that, if and when they get into trouble, companies increase their liabilities in the hope this will enable them to carry out their plans. That is what the telecom firms have done in a big way, to their detriment in the late 1990s and early twenty-first century. Only when they are close to default do geared companies panic and try to reduce their leverage. But then it is too late.

All this is very relevant to a discussion on strategies used by banks to increase their capital base because it helps to underline that there are limits to the amount of borrowed money to which credit institutions and other companies can help themselves. The break point can be reached very quickly. After that, leverage becomes more and more counterproductive, leading to disaster.

Invariably, once it starts on the downward slope an entity finds out that trying to rebalance its fortunes through more leverage is an illusion. As Jesús Saurina, Head of Financial Stability Unit, Banco de Espana, said in his lecture,[4] several studies have shown that the practice of rebalancing to fixed weights with leverage creates trading patterns that lead to forced liquidation of positions.

■ The impetus behind rebalancing with leverage is that total wealth drops faster than equity price(s), necessitating a decrease in risky positions.
■ Another factor that contributes to procyclicality is damage control: selling the asset to cut losses after a fall in its price.

The two events described above have nothing to do with margin calls related to leveraged positions, even if the latter have a similar effect. A sensible strategy in dealing with the financial cycle is to ensure that adequate defenses have been built up in upswings, and they can be relied upon when the rough times arrive (see section 8.7 in Chapter 8). A range of instruments would seem worthy of consideration. As Andrew Crockett, general manager of the Bank for International Settlements, once suggested, these could include variants of forward-looking provisioning for prudential purposes.

'Prudential' is a keyword in corporate governance. Increases in economic capital, or for that matter regulatory capital, at the last minute identify management which is not worth its salt. Rushing at last minute is done by credit institutions and insurance companies prone to fall into the trap of procyclicality, after strong credit (or underwriting) growth associated with:

■ Risk underpricing
■ Lower quality of counterparties
■ Lower level of loan loss provisions to total credit.

Part of the illusion that high leverage means salvation is due to timelag till adversity hits. Only the most experienced bankers realize that credit growth affects problem loans with a three-year lag, and it hits the hardest in a downturn. Many banks with a policy to grow rapidly and increase their market share, do so by lowering credit standards, which eventually leads to hefty capital requirements.

No matter in which domain it takes place, the fire brigade approach has never provided commendable results. Rather than based on theories which come and go, regulatory capital and economic capital increases should be undertaken in a carefully balanced, proactive way. This has been the basis of the Banco de Espana statistical provision discussed in Chapter 8. It is computed on a quarterly basis, and it is applied individually by credit institutions. Notice that this is not a national reserve, therefore it is not possible to compensate a positive provision of one bank with a negative in another bank in the same consolidated group.

Moreover, Banco de Espana has established rules which imply a significant level of transparency. Banks must disclose yearly the amount of statistical provision, apart from their specific and general provisions. Similarly, the method used to calculate it must be reported to the regulators. This policy is based on the fact that transparency and prudential regulation complement each other.

José Saurina, of Banco de Espana, also insisted on the fact that apart from the avoidance of procyclicality targeted by the statistical provision, the latter has the after-effect of making the banks' senior managers better aware of credit risk assumed by their institution. Favorable results show in:

■ Risk appraisal
■ Risk pricing, and
■ Internal management control policies.

Altogether, what has just been explained leads to sounder accounting practices, because it corrects excess volatility in connection to bank profits brought about by *ex post* acknowledgement of credit risk. This is not an approach expected to take care of all modern ills like lax management, superaggressive lending and huge trading losses. Rather, its goal is to work counterclockwise to the law of unintended consequences associated with expansion through gearing – which has seen to it that the private labels of so many formerly well-known banks are no longer around in today's financial world.

9.5 Diversification in the banking business is often wanting

The concept underpinning diversification is like that of motherhood and apple pie. You do not find people talking against diversification and the benefits it may bring in terms of risk control – but in a surprisingly large number of cases diversification is only an illusion. Some banks simply cannot diversify because of their charter. For instance, the business goal of S&Ls and building societies, is mortgages. Others cannot diversify because of their culture and the way they run their business.

As far as first principles are concerned, there is no question about the soundness of diversification as a policy. The better diversified one's portfolio, the lower the economic capital that needs to be allocated. But is this doable in practical terms in all cases? Many global banks which expanded internationally by following or leading their clients abroad, have a concentrated exposure to these clients.

A good number of the experts who participated in the research leading to this book brought up another impediment to real diversification. They commented that while diversification has merits, it also spreads thinly the bank's management. Others were of the opinion that banks do not really care enough to be diversified. In its own way, each institution is concentrated on:

- Countries
- Industries
- Clients.

As these experts saw it, one of the reasons why diversification in banking is often wanting is that the analysis necessary to pinpoint concentrations is frequently biased or incomplete. In other cases, a diversification plan turns sour because it substitutes one concentration for another. Here is a recent example.

After being appointed as the new CEO of Abbey National Bank, Lugman Arnold started steering away from the ill-fated diversification plan initiated by Ian Harley, his predecessor. Abbey National is Britain's sixth biggest bank. Historically, given its building society origins, it has been a specialist mortgage lender – and a successful one for that matter – but this is no longer true.

Going after higher returns during the 1990s, Abbey's then senior management had directed its wholesale banking division into investing heavily in junk bonds and in big company loans. That is the aggressive type lending to which reference was made in section 9.4. In the aftermath, Abbey National lost money on Enron and other former big companies. On 26 February 2003, the bank announced:

- A pre-tax loss of £984 million ($1.47 billion) for 2002, and
- A new strategy, which mainly consists of being friendlier to customers than other British banks are.

This was been Abbey's first full-year loss since it was demutualized in 1989. The market did not like what it saw. Abbey National's share price had fallen by two-thirds in 2001–02. 'It is deeply depressing to see how management wrecked the shareholders' investment,' said a money manager.[5] The blame, other analysts said, lies with the overgrown wholesale operations of the bank. The reason, they suggested, is not so much the total size of the positions that the bank had taken, as their high concentration.

- The foray into wholesale banking was done as means of diversifying away from heavy dependence on mortgages, the bank's traditional base.
- But when the economic and financial bubble burst, this strategy backfired. By 2003 only five names made up £1.9 billion-worth of the bank's exposure to BBB-rated assets.

Then, there is the issue of 'which goal' a diversification strategy is after. Many examples can be found which show that geographic diversification is higher grade

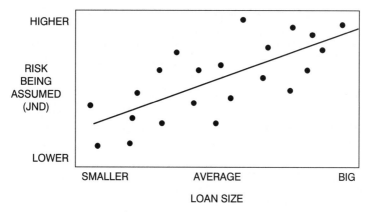

Figure 9.2 Risk associated with client concentration

than industry diversification in the same country. As for client diversification, a bank needs a large number of names to diversify, for instance, 100 000. Figure 9.2 shows the pattern of risk associated with client concentration. Yet, even the largest banks today have about 10 000 big names each – not enough for effective diversification.

Lars Hunsche of Moody's KMV pointed out that several things can go wrong with a diversification project. Consider the following example. The president of a bank gave to one of his senior traders the mission: 'Create me a portfolio with forty bonds of European banks.' This mission and the way it was executed, have a number of defects in terms of permitting diversification:

1 The sample is too small. A sample of 100 would have been better.
2 The portfolio is concentrated in one industry: financials. Therefore, it is highly dependent on that one industry.
3 The originators of the chosen forty bonds comprised only seventeen banks. This greatly increased the concentration in terms of credit risk.
4 These seventeen banks were chosen from only two neighbouring countries, which belong to the same economic community. This further increased concentration as these two economies move in unison.
5 The portfolio gave equal weights to the forty bonds. The weights should have been diverse, capitalizing on factors which reflect the attractiveness of each bond: its duration, its rate, callable or bullet, the issuer and other characteristics. Remember this example the next time you talk about portfolio diversification. Remember also that quite often client diversification follows a similar pattern, and the model to which it leads is not dependable.

9.6 Capital arbitrage through securitization

Securitization strategies come into focus as banks actively search to satisfy a dual objective: increase their capital base and reduce the amount of credit risk they have assumed. Whether these goals are attainable is something which is increasingly challenged by senior bankers. 'We don't believe securitization transfers any risk at all. The default stays with the bank,' said an executive at Barclays.

'Securitization is supposed to be risk mitigation – but not much risk is transferred,' suggested one of the managers at Standard & Poor's. 'Rather, securitization is a form of capital arbitrage.' This capital arbitrage is what Basel II may take away, as reserves for securitization are scheduled to increase. 'The likely outcome is that there will be less incentives for arbitrage,' said one of the experts at the Basel Committee.

Also in the City of London and on Wall Street many analysts stated that securitizations do not really transfer much risk. Some added that the banks themselves do not feel significant risk is being transferred. Others suggested a better approach to risk mitigation might be some form of insurance. However, insurance introduces its own type of credit risk – that of the underwriter. There is also the issue of risks that are insurable and those that are not. (More on the use of insurance, later on.)

One of the money-center banks noted that securitization is mainly a profit and loss issue. Much depends on what is securitized, as well as on how the assets are valued. With credit derivatives, the bank wants to transfer the risk, but the assets may be:

- Partly marked to market
- Partly on accruals accounting.

Such differences lead to destabilization of P&L. This and similar references suggest a sea change in the way bankers think about the role of securitization. In the 1980s and 1990s the process of securitization was looked at by many as a mechanism for risk transfer. Since then, however, practical experience has shown that very often this is an illusion because the issuer retains the first (worst) tranche, and keeps it in its balance sheet. This is particularly true with credit derivatives where:

- There is practically no risk transfer
- But there exists a significant reduction in transparency,
- And at the same time the balance sheet is shrinking.

Figure 9.3 (published with the permission of Walter Pompliano of S&P) brings this issue of risk transfer associated to tranches under perspective. Along with the risk of the tranches, come issues of supervisory weights. And apart from the need for regulatory capital in connection to securitization, there is an accounting problem which can be expressed as:

- It is not enough to look at face value of position.
- It is also necessary to examine possible mismatches.

Many bankers now say that though securitization has its merits, it is increasingly characterized by institutional imperfection. Some bankers have commented that because their institutions retain the first tranche with securitization, the risk actually

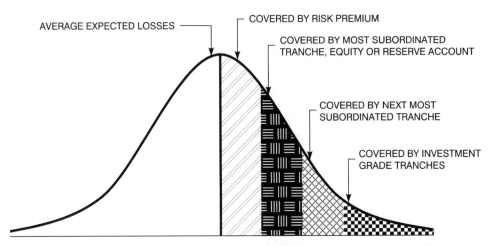

Figure 9.3 Credit losses associated with an asset securitization transaction, and parties absorbing credit risk (Reproduced by permission of Walter Pompliano, Standard & Poor's)

goes up. Whether it is possible to sell the first tranche is a matter of how much credit risk adverse the market is, and what will be the regulatory weights attached to some types of securitization deals and their tranches. The formula being developed by regulators for estimating risk from securitization promises to be fairly complex, with risk weights depending on:

- Type of instrument
- Credit rating
- Effective number of exposures, and
- Seniority position relative to size of pool.

The required capital reserve under IRB will be the ratio of capital requirement for the underlying exposures to the notional amount of the pool. As credit enhancement level (L) will be used the ratio of notional amount of exposures subordinate to tranching to the total notional amount, with thickness of exposure (T) being the ratio of the size of the tranche to the total.

$$\text{IRB Capital Charge} = (S(L+T) - S(L)) \bullet \text{Notional amount} \tag{9.1}$$

In regard to the treatment of securitized assets, the Basel Committee has established proposals which address two classes: one is where an interest has been retained; the other where the bank is the investor of securitized assets. The background rules differ from those under Basel I where first-loss positions were simply to be deducted from capital. While this will continue,

- It will also include first loss provided on securitizations originated by other banks, and
- Under certain circumstances, second-loss and other subordinated positions must also be deducted.

Banks using the standardized approach of Basel II will derive capital charges for securitization positions from external ratings, as they will do for other forms of credit risk. Two solutions are defined for IRB banks:

- Ratings-based approach (RBA), which is relatively standard, or
- Supervisory formula approach (SFA), based on K_{IRB}, but with qualifications.

Under the supervisory formula, a credit institution must assess the capital that would have been held against the underlying loans, using IRB. The charges are based on this. Under the ratings-based approach, banks holding rated securitized assets can use a table of set charges.

There is also the issue of choice between funded and synthetic securitization. *Funded securitization* exploits new sources of funding, requires assets transfer and gives a wholesale-type funding source. Some models are simple and quick to execute, but may lead to creative funding. Others can become rather complex.

Synthetic securitization can handle many instruments, for example, mortgages, business loans, corporates; helps in reducing risk profile and mismatch; provides portfolio guarantee which frees up core equity at reasonable cost; and uses single name credit default swaps which assist in discharging some asset concentrations. But while in general all this helps in arbitraging regulatory capital, it does not discharge associated risk.

Moreover, securitization using IRB requires deduction of deeply subordinated positions. Effectively these are any first-loss position. It also calls for definition of liquidity facilities, with the credit conversion factor depending on conditions of securitization, duration and other criteria. All this suggests that a lot of work will be necessary for securitization under IRB – particularly in connection with specialized lending and other facilities requiring capital commitments.

9.7 Statistics on securitized corporate debt and other instruments

Credit institutions must apply the Basel-defined securitization framework for determining regulatory capital requirements on exposures. Because securitizations may be structured in many different ways, their capital treatment is being determined on the basis of its economic substance rather than legal form.

- Banks should consult with their supervisors when there is uncertainty about whether a transaction can be considered as securitization.
- National supervisors will look at economic substance of a transaction to determine the rules to which it will be subject.

Statistics on past and present events are instrumental in helping to define the economic substance. This is particularly true as the current effort on securitization by G-10 regulators, and therefore by the Basel Committee, is an attempt better to measure the degree of risk transfer, thereby assigning appropriate capital weights.

This fits well with the goal of the revision of the 1988 Capital Accord, which aims to make the regulatory framework more risk sensitive. As the Basel Committee suggested, broadly speaking the result might be that regulatory capital is more aligned with economic capital – however this is defined.

The impact the changes outlined in section 9.6 and in this section will have on the economy and on financial institutions can be judged by looking at exposure statistics from asset-backed securities. Based on US securitizations at 1 January 2003, such statistics help to emphasize securitization's aftermath. As of 1 January 2003, there were more than $1.5 trillion in asset-backed securities outstanding in the USA alone:

- 28 percent were securities backed by credit-card payments
- 17 percent, backed by home equity payments
- 14 percent, backed by auto loan payments
- The other 41 percent were quite diverse, including factoring of receivables.

However, on 1 January 2003, ABS accounted for only about 7 percent of the over $20 trillion US bond market. Moreover, its $1.5 trillion is still a fraction of the $4.5 trillion in mortgage-backed securities – or the $4 trillion in corporate bonds. The other issue, however, is that there has been a significant increase in ABS as well as in collateralized debt obligation, in the US market in recent years.

In particular, ABS loans covered by mortgage loans, credit card debts and car purchase loans have experienced a boom in the twenty-first century. However, during the same period the risks of such an investment have also increased. In 2002:

- Twenty-one ABS issuers have gone bankrupt, and
- 409 individual ABS loans were downgraded by Standard & Poor's.

According to estimates by investment bankers, the volume of ABS secured by lower-ranking mortgage loans is steadily rising, which means decreasing quality. In addition, credit derivatives are being used in the current markets by various banks for the purpose of risk transfer, however ill-documented this may be (see section 9.6). All told, default risk has very significantly increased during the last six years, as shown in Figure 9.4.

Statistics on evolution of assumed credit risk are important because, as a buyer of credit derivatives, an investor is making a payment in exchange for a potential payoff. The system works both ways. Credit protection is provided by credit options. If the investor buys credit protection, then he or she gains if the underlying reference credit defaults.

- In this transaction, the investor shorts the credit and benefits if the credit deteriorates.
- The underwriter sells the credit protection, therefore he or she becomes long on credit risk and benefits if the credit improves.

Credit options are a special class of derivative instruments. They are applicable only to risky debt; therefore, they are speculative. When the credit deteriorates, as in Figure

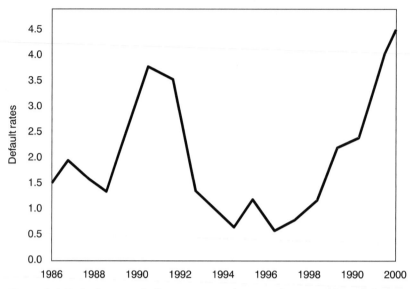

Figure 9.4 Default rates of all corporates: who pays the cost of loan defaults?

9.4, the price of credit options rises significantly to compensate for the added risk. This is not a win-win situation.

In the opinion of senior executives of Commission Bancaire, Banque de France, credit institutions should develop a rating system for corporates, with greater detail and precision, which corresponds to the real credit risk assumed by institutions and other investors in securitized instruments. The Banque de France has such a rating system based on three scales working in parallel. The highest grade is A37. 'A' denotes yearly turnover. On a four-threshold ADEF scale, 'A' stands for a turnover of FF5 billion ($850 million) or more. The second position indicates default history, and it also varies between four thresholds: 3, 4, 5 and 6. A grade of '3' means there has been no default.

The message conveyed by the third digit concerns the case of payments incident: '7' indicates delay or rescheduling of interest and principal; '8' is an average position, while '9' is the worst grade in terms of payment incidents. This three-way scale provides an important classification of credit risk. A rating of '3' (taken in conjunction with 'A' and '7') is necessary for repurchase agreements.

More sophisticated rating systems are necessary in view of the fact that the use of novel financial instruments is altering the way banks manage risk (and securitizations are at the heart of the game). Without appropriate measuring and monitoring standards, the sheer complexity of the positions often outruns the ability of credit institutions to track exposure in an effective way. This sees to it that several banks are disposed to take on more risk than they should.

The rules embedded in the new capital adequacy framework provide evidence, the Basel Committee recognizes, that while securitizations are helping in risk diversification, at the same time they involve transfer of ownership and/or risks to other parties. Therefore, they should be subject to robust treatment in order to avoid:

- Capital arbitrage, and
- The calculation of capital requirements non-commensurate to the risks being taken.[6]

For banks choosing the standardized approach of Basel II, the new rules involve a difference in treatment of lower quality and unrated securitizations than the one characterizing higher-quality securitizations. For IRB banks that originate securitizations, a crucial element of the calculation of needed capital is that the institution would have been required to hold on to the underlying pool had it not securitized the exposures.

Securitized corporates have re-emphasized the importance of collateral, guarantees and balance sheet structure. Procedural improvements can be obtained through real-time modeling. Several experts believe that expert systems, like those used by the Deutsche Bundesbank, and sophisticated credit-oriented eigenmodels will constitute the backbone of IRB methods, rather than a replay of VAR. However, many central national bankers and bankers' associations are worried that the majority of commercial banks and retail banks under their jurisdiction do not have the expertise to develop and apply advanced modeling techniques.

Finally, prior to closing this chapter, it is appropriate to bring to the reader's attention a method of capital increase through special investment vehicles (SIVs).[7] To improve their rating and attract trading partners, several banks and brokers set-up SIVs. They do so to gain for the new entity an AAA or AA+ rating, as the market believes SIVs can be:

- Better capitalized than their parent
- Protected from the parent's bankruptcy, and
- Able to ringfence their transactions.

This is often more imaginary than real. There is a number of SIVs which look like great stories, but suddenly 'drop off the radar screen'. Several SIVs have been too exposed to credit risk, market risk, or both – but they did not keep control of their risks. It is a characteristic of serious bankers that they avoid generalizations. Every case should be considered on its own merits.

Because the risks are so polyvalent, the basis of the framing of IRB rules is the ability to absorb losses. Basel II incorporates an explicit treatment of liquidity facilities provided by banks, dependent upon a number of factors including asset quality of the underlying pool and the degree to which credit enhancements are available. The conditions underpinning the approaches which will be followed with the new regulations are, however, in full evolution. Steering them is the mission of both the Capital Task Force (CTF) and Accord Implementation Group (AIG) of the Basel Committee.

Notes

1 D.N. Chorafas (2004). *Management Risk: The Bottleneck is at the Top of the Bottle*. Macmillan/Palgrave.

2 P. DeMarzo and D. Duffie (1991). Corporate financial hedging with proprietary information. *Journal of Economic Theory*, **53**.
3 C.C. Raposo (1998). Corporate risk management theory; a review of the theory. Thesis, London Business School.
4 'Basel II Masterclass', organized by IIR, London, 27–28 March 2003.
5 *The Economist*, 1 March 2003.
6 Basel Committee on Banking Supervision (2003). *Overview of the New Basel Capital Accord*. BIS, April.
7 See also Chapter 12 on special purpose vehicles (SPVs).

3

Defaults, internal ratings and technological solutions

10 Default defined

10.1 Introduction

Regulators and rating agencies define default as any of the following events: bankruptcy, write-down, 90 days past due loan or placement on internal non-accrual list. The obligor is considered defaulted as of the date of any of these accounting and financial failures. In general, however, if a company has its loans restructured, this is not considered to be a default – even when there is an adverse effect upon the lender.

Originally, the Basel Committee suggested that, to ensure consistent estimation of credit risk across the banking industry and provide for data sources concerning default statistics, a *default* be defined as involving one or more of four criteria:

- It is determined that the obligor is unlikely to pay its debt obligations (principal, interest, or fees) in full.
- There is a charge-off, specific provision or distressed restructuring involving the forgiveness or postponement of principal, interest, or fees.
- The obligor is overdue more than 90 days on any credit obligation.
- The obligor has filed for bankruptcy or similar protection from creditors.

Subsequently, these four criteria have been reduced to only two: more than 90 days overdue, and unlikely to pay in full – as we saw in Chapter 1. Credit rating agencies add some more flavour to this definition. For instance, Moody's RiskCalc looks at default connected to private debt through the following criteria: placement in internal non-accrual list, the credit is written down,[1] 90 days overdue, and declared bankruptcy

Any company can fail. This is part of the risk of being in business. But, because quite frequently the central bank provides a safety net for credit institutions, particularly the larger companies whose default can lead to systemic risk, Fitch Ratings makes an important distinction between bank failure and bank default. As defined by Fitch:

- A bank has *failed* if it is kept going only by state support, by being acquired by another entity, through injection of new funds from shareholders, *or* if it has defaulted.
- A bank has *defaulted* if it files for bankruptcy, or bankruptcy protection; fails to make timely payments of interest and principal; credit is written down, as 90 days overdue; *or* makes distressed restructuring, like offering diminished structural or economic terms.

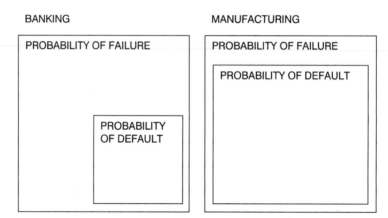

Figure 10.1 In the banking industry the probability of default is a subset of the probability of failure

This difference in practical terminology between entities in banking and, say, in manufacturing is shown in Figure 10.1. Because of the aforementioned distinction, Fitch Ratings suggests that a bank is about six times more likely to fail than to default. Such statistics contrast with the fact that a credit institution is twice as likely to fail as other companies which default because industrial corporations are not being rescued by the central bank.

The thesis advanced by Fitch Ratings is confirmed through statistics. In the 1989 to 2001 timeframe, for example, there were forty-eight bank failures in developed countries, of which only four were defaults. In other words, 8 percent of the credit institutions that failed defaulted. The other 92 percent got a suspended sentence either at taxpayers' expense or at the expense of shareholders of some other credit institution.

What is the reason behind bank failures? A survey of twenty-two British banks, carried out by the Bank of England, suggests that the most fundamental reason for bank failure is poor management. Next to this, comes poor asset quality, basically in the loans book. Only two cases among the failed banks involved severe dealing losses. The problem, however, is that much of market risk is hidden. Quite often:

- Financial instruments are mispriced
- Profits are overstated, and
- Risks can change very fast, at intraday pace.

Whether we talk about banking, manufacturing, merchandising or any other industry, the probability of default (PD) of every entity must be studied in the short, medium and longer term. Table 10.1 gives a bird's eye view of the average likelihood of failure of rated companies over one, five, ten and fifteen years. Notice that a 1 percent probability of default of BB rating in one year becomes nearly 20 percent over the fifteen years timeframe.

Moreover, default probabilities change as a function of time, because independent rating agencies watch out for weak credits. Typically, in terms of credit rating, there are more downgrades than upgrades. The average American company, says Tim Kasta

	1 year	2 years	10 years	15 years
AAA	0.00	0.24	1.40	1.40
AA	0.00	0.43	1.25	1.48
A	0.06	0.65	2.17	3.11
BBB	0.18	1.78	4.34	4.70
BB	1.06	10.97	17.73	19.91

Table 10.1 Likelihood of failure for rated companies

of Moody's KMV, now has a 4.4 percent chance of default, more than four times the average in the 1990s.[2] A major concern is that even as the market value of their businesses falls, companies continue to add debt which eventually pulls them down to oblivion (see Chapter 9 on the aftermath of leverage).

10.2 Default milestones

The introduction to this chapter underlined that a default occurs when the obligor is unlikely to pay its debt obligations in full: principal, interest, fees. Alternatively, the obligor may have filed for bankruptcy or for protection from creditors. When borrowers approach default conditions, lenders start calculating how many cents in the dollar they might recover. There is nothing like a 'guaranteed return'.

The aftermath of borrower defaults dampens profit expectations. It also influences in a significant way the lender's propensity to lend. This becomes a general trend when insolvencies rise, as shown in the graph in Figure 10.2.

With *default*, the lender places the loan in an internal non-accrual list, and the credit is written down. By contrast, *impaired loans* are those where losses are probable and estimable. A fast and dirty example is when the book value of the claim exceeds the book value of cash flows in future periods. Write-downs are accounting for interest, principal payments and collateral.

The reader will recall from Chapter 9, particularly the discussion on the Modigliani-Miller hypothesis, that a milestone in this process of estimating approaching default is the definition of *default point*. Default point identifies the asset value at which the company will default. As such, it must be dynamically recomputed because it changes over time (more on this in section 10.3).

Another important reference which helps in defining the default profile of borrower(s) is that of *default correlations* (not to be confused with asset correlation). These measure the degree to which are related default risks of various borrowers and other counterparties (such as trading partners) in the bank's portfolio.

Default points and default correlations are so important because they impact in a significant way on credit decisions and ratings. Credit decisions are all decisions on new loans, new securitizations, new participating interests, revisions of participating interests, restructuring, loan increases and extensions, overdrafts, changes in risk-relevant circumstances and the definition of borrower-specific limits.

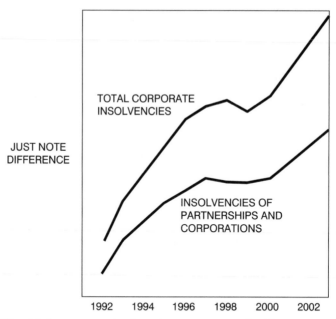

Figure 10.2 The risk in corporate insolvencies zooms upward with an economic downturn (Statistics from the German Federal Republic)

Probabilities of default change in view of the variables outlined in the preceding paragraph. The discipline of Basel II is so good because banks are required to derive a one-year probability of default for each of their counterparties graded in the scale shown in Table 10.2, or (preferably) finer thresholds. A good rule for credit risk control is that borrowers are regularly re-evaluated, with attention being paid to:

Ten-grade scale	Rating scale	Probability of default: 1 year	Probability of default: 5 years	Management quality[1]
1	AAA, AA+			
2	AA, AA–			
3	A+, A			
4	A–, BBB+			
5	BBB, BBB–			
6	BB+, BB			
7	BB–, B+			
8	B, B–			
9	C			
10	D			

Note: 1 This can be used only to decrease the grade scale classification, not to increase it.

Table 10.2 A ten-grade credit risk classification (rating buckets must be calibrated to default)

- Migration across grades
- Quantification of loss estimates per grade, and
- Comparison of realized default rates against expectations.

Part and parcel of these references is the fact that, as has already been brought to the reader's attention, there is no upside with liabilities. Unlike equities, debt has no upward potential in terms of profits. This means that damage control is king – and, therefore, the case for managing default risk in diversified portfolios is truly compelling.

Damage control is exercised so much more effectively when the board, the CEO and the senior management of the bank appreciate that credit risk exists from the moment the customer takes the loan, not just when the loan goes sour. Hence, in any loans book there is *latent risk*, even if this is not generally recognized. This leads to:

- An asymmetry in capital reserves, and
- Poorly balanced risk management procedures.

Jesus Saurina, of Banco de Espana, has aptly stated, during the Basel II Masterclass in London, that most mistakes on credit risk management are made in good times, by failing to account for exposure being assumed. Contrary to general opinion, they are not made at the time the loan becomes damaged goods.

This is tantamount to saying that well-managed banks follow a proactive approach. At Citigroup, for example, credit risk control is a steady ongoing process, and it is measured counterparty by counterparty. The institution's chief risk management officer wants to have credit risk allocated down to desk level in order to gain better visibility.

A focused, proactive credit risk control is a complex business and requires significant skills. Among other challenges, it poses a problem with large counterparties, as one desk may be short with a given counterparty while another desk may be long with the same business partner. This is particularly crucial for an institution like Citigroup which has more than thirty-six major counterparties doing over 100 transactions each per day – but it is doable.

It takes high technology to tackle the magnitude of such problems. Citigroup seems to have a timely tuned system in place – one which is available twenty-four hours per day, seven days in the week, anywhere in the world. During a research meeting at Citigroup's London headquarters, Dr David Lawrence mentioned a company in Australia which asked his bank for a $100 million loan on a Sunday.

This company was not a customer, but it was rated because Citigroup has a policy of keeping ratings up to date including PDs and LGDs (see Chapter 4), not only for clients but also for prospects. Hence, it was sufficient for the potential customer to call the relationship manager and get an offer, because the latter had all the necessary information interactively available. (This loan, incidentally, was approved.)

As I never tire of repeating in my seminars and in my books, the bank which wants to be ahead of the curve must not only use high technology, but also keep on updating its technology in a way that leaves its competition behind. This is as true of credit risk control as it is of trading and of investment management. In fact, there is a common background in analytics for loans, trading and investments. Typically we find as pillars of such common ground:

- Interactive datamining, which permits study of the past and detection of strengths, weaknesses, and trends
- Ability to project in the future, including discounted cash flows, cost structures, return on assets, assumed risks and their distribution
- Real-time experimentation, permitting to evaluate alternatives and to provide documentation prior to reaching capital decisions.

The concept behind default milestones essentially rests on these three pillars. Experimentation is vital, even if the way to bet is that, as suggested in Figure 10.3,

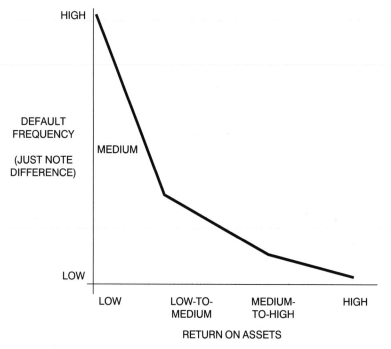

Figure 10.3 Default frequency decreases when return on assets is high

default frequency decreases when return on assets is high. I have also found it most interesting to monetize risk and compute the *misery index*. The latter includes:

- The bank's administrative cost (overhead), classified in three buckets: under 50 percent, 50–60 percent, over 60 percent
- Plus the monetization of risks embedded in the portfolio: derivatives, loans and other instruments.

In every one of these references the credit rating by the bank itself and by independent agencies comes into the picture. Purposely, I emphasize both sources of credit ratings, not just one of them. Experience teaches me that it is silly to reinvent the wheel all the time, and every time make the wheel a little less round. We must capitalize on reliable information everywhere it can be found. Independent rating agencies are one of the sources.

Many institutions, particularly big banks, say that they have their own credit rating system and do not need that of independent rating agencies. This argument, however, ignores the advantages provided by a global credit rating system within the globalized economy. To be meaningful, the probability of default should also be universally defined. However, the verdict is still out on questions such as:

- Should legal risk be associated to credit ratings and, if so, in which sense?
- Will universal credit rating improve or deteriorate the pattern of default likelihood?
- How far can default transition matrices improve the bank's ability to gauge counterparty risk in a global sense?

Beyond these queries lies the fact that credit rating is time-consuming and costly; hence, it raises another question: buy or build? Borrowers must be rerated at least once a year to capture their current risk situation – and, in some cases, much faster than that. There is also a dependability question. Internal and external auditors should audit both quality of ratings and adequacy of their use. Moreover, rating must be subject to internal stress tests.

10.3　Definition of default point

The DP maps the extent of the entity's liabilities compared with its assets. It is the level of market value of an entity's assets, below which it would fail to face up to its obligations, for instance, to make scheduled debt payments according to outstanding contracts.

Each DP is a time-specific function of the entity's liability structure. In developing its DP methodology, Moody's KMV did extensive research which looked at thousands of defaulting firms. Each DP was observed in relation to market value of its assets at the time of default. This and other DP calculations, for instance, the one by the ECB consider:

- Assets at market value
- Divided by book value of liabilities.

This is a measure of the entity's leverage. Book value of liabilities is the amount the firm must repay. The market value of its equity is the funds the company may have available. Theoretically, the entity will default when the market value of its assets is insufficient to repay its liabilities.

In the background of DP calculation lies the fact that capital markets anticipate the future prospects of a firm; debt markets do not necessarily do so. Moreover, equity markets are broader, deeper and more liquid than debt markets.

Part of the power of default probabilities comes from the fact that they are absolute measures of credit quality. For instance, *if* a company has a PD of 10 percent, *then* if we take a large enough pool of similar companies over a specific period of time, 10 percent of them will default. But having a high one-year, two-year or five-year PD is only one of the dimensions of a high-risk entity. Other indicators of credit quality deterioration that can lead to default are:

■ High volatility of PDs
■ Steep deterioration of PDs, and
■ Levels that are much higher or lower than the industry average.

The downside of the DP algorithm is that capital markets are not necessarily efficient; it takes time to digest all relevant financial information – provided that financial statements are reliable which, as the late 1990s scandals show, is not always the case. Neither are capital markets always rational. They may be carried away by trends and glamor, as documented by the 1995 to 2000 bubble.

The calculation of DPs is not an alternative but a complement to balance sheet analysis. Unlike balance sheets, a projected DP offers a forward-looking measure of:

■ Value
■ Volatility, and
■ Leverage.

This enables its prospects to be gaged through its debt and management. Practically, the DP tells us about the implied market value of a business by giving a signal as to changing fortunes which impact upon the entity's creditworthiness. There are also other criteria to account for.

'In forecasting a bank's default probability, we take into account the degree of support by the regulator,' said an executive of one of the rating agencies. 'There are many institutional and other factors deciding what the central bank is going to do.' Politics play a role; and systemic risk is an important factor. Credit Lyonnais was salvaged, but it was a big bank. The Banque de France let smaller credit institutions fail.

In the UK, Barings folded. If it was not Barings but Barclays, would the Bank of England have reached the same decision? Behind these queries lies the fact that, in regard to bank failure, the likelihood of support by regulators is very important – and it tends to be rather predictable. That is exactly where lies the difference between probability of failure and probability of default, of which we spoke in the Introduction.

State support in case of failure, however, has a high price. It wipes out the credit institution's equity. The CEO and board are aware of this; hence they favor *credit mitigation*. Credit mitigation techniques target the reduction or transfer of credit risk, but this has a downside, because it simultaneously increases legal risk, liquidity risk and market risk. Therefore, banks must employ robust procedures and processes to control these risks, carefully watching out for:

■ Legal enforceability
■ Liquidity constraints

- Ways and means to curb operational risks
- Objective market value of collateral
- Frequent revaluation done in documented and factual way.

Most necessary is ongoing monitoring of any permissible prior claims on collateral (Maxwell risk). If the collateral shrinks while the leveraging of the bank's client increases, this leads to another problem – that of an imbalance in current liabilities (CLs) and liquid funds (LFs), as compared to assets. Figure 10.4 brings to the reader's

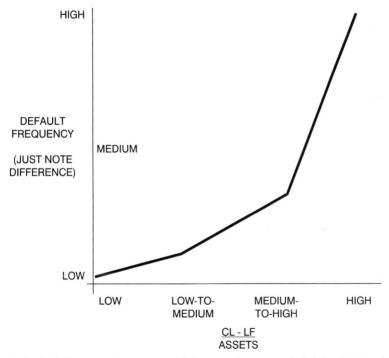

Figure 10.4 Default frequency increases with increase in current liabilities (CL) and decrease in liquid funds (LF)

attention the resulting pattern with axes of reference *default frequency* and CL minus LF, over assets. A typical balance sheet of commercial banks, like the one in Table 10.3, tells an interesting story:

- With shareholder equity at 5.5 percent, the leverage factor is nearly 20.
- But as this factor increases, the distance to default significantly shrinks.

The second of the above statements is documented by the model developed by the ECB in connection with *distance to default*. Its kernel is the default point. The ECB says its model has more predictive power for banks likely to fail but also those likely

Assets(%)		Liabilities (%)	
Cash and cash equivalents	0.8	Interbank borrowing (deposits)	10.1
Interbank lending	12.4	Customer deposits	60.4
Securities	8.5	Debt securities	10.9
Loans and advances to customers:		Other liabilities	4.6
Gross loan amounts	69.0		
Loan loss reserves	(0.8)		
Loans net of reserves	68.2		
Prepayments and accrued income	1.9	Accruals and deferred income	2.8
Tangible and intangible fixed assets	3.4	Loss reserves (provisions) for liabilities and charges	1.2
Other assets, including goodwill	4.8	Subordinated debt	4.5
		Total shareholder equity	5.5
Total assets	100	Total liabilities	100

Basel Committee on Banking Supervision (2001). *Risk Management Practices and Regulatory Capital: A Cross-Sectoral Comparison*. BIS, November.

Table 10.3 Typical balance sheet for a commercial bank

to benefit from government support. In this particular algorithm, the DP is the equality of:

- Market value of assets (MVA), and
- The bank's total liabilities (TLs).

As a proxy for MVA, ECB takes equity capitalization of the company, using the option pricing algorithm.[3] Volatility matters. The ECB's model uses moving average six-month volatility. The ECB puts current and long-term liabilities on the same footing. Its algorithm for option pricing starts with:

$$\frac{\text{Assets}}{\text{Liabilities}} \tag{10.1}$$

where, as stated, *liabilities* are taken at book value. This contrasts with the proxy for *assets* which is equity capitalization of the institution.

- *If* equity value drops,
- *Then* distance to default is shorter.

Therefore, volatility matters. Mapping the standard deviation as a moving average of six-month volatility, Figure 10.5 shows the pattern of monthly data on median distance to default of the fifty largest euroland banks. This is ECB statistics.

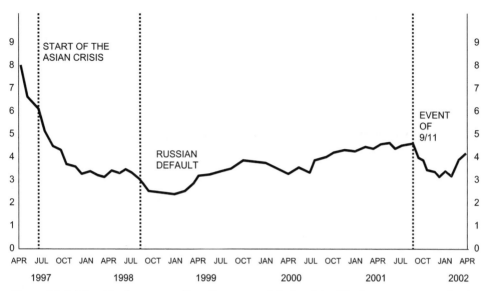

Figure 10.5 Monthly data on median distance to default of the fifty largest euro area banks (expressed in standard deviations away from assets = liabilities) (*Source*: statistics from ECB)

Moody's KMV computes the DP through a somewhat different algorithm, because the company's research has demonstrated that the most frequently encountered benchmark for solvency is at the crossroads of a company value roughly equal to the sum of current liabilities plus only part of its long-term liabilities (see also in section 10.6 the discussion of expected default frequency – EDF).

With the Moody's KMV model, the benchmark for solvency – hence default – is at the crossroads of a company's value equal to current liabilities, plus half the long-term liabilities. As with the ECB, KMV's *distance to default* represents the number of standard deviations an asset value must drop to reach the DP. In this case:

$$\text{Distance to default} = \frac{\text{EMVA} - \text{DP}}{\text{VA} \bullet \text{EMVA}} \tag{10.2}$$

where EMVA = expected market value of assets
      DP   = default point
      VA   = volatility of assets.

Because distance to default is normalized, it can also be used both for comparing one company to another and as a way of bond rating. The reader will take notice of this widening domain of applicability.

Reference must also be made to *default resolution*. Recently, the average time of default resolution is just under 1.5 years: traditional Chapter 11 cases are averaging 1.6 years, while pre-packaged Chapter 11 bankruptcy filings are averaging slightly over one year. Secured loans claims are settled faster than unsecured loans. It takes 1.3 years for secured loans and 1.7 years for unsecured loans.

In conclusion, the pattern developed by DPs has the potential to evolve into a good prognosticator for credit risk exposure. While the ECB and Moody's KMV models (see also Chapter 13) are somewhat different, they do share a common culture – which is much more important than algorithmic difference. Credit institutions will be well advised to use DP patterns, both for themselves and for their clients.

10.4   Contribution of default point to credit risk strategy

The definition of the pattern of movement of a DP, the way it has been explained in section 10.3, is a major breakthrough in the management of credit institutions. The best way to look at it is as a valuable tool in the formulation of a credit risk strategy, helping to define lending activities, over an adequate planning period, by:

- Providing a snapshot on the risks associated with the credit business, and
- Taking into account the credit institution's ability to bear risk, associated with the creditworthiness of its counterparties.

Once top management is aware that the counterparty's default point is not stable, but constitutes a moving target, it will be eager to find out at any moment *if* the DP is approaching. When it does, management knows that the institution is faced with urgent tasks, such as reviewing exposure individually and by correlation, between parties and channels – which requires assignment of competencies and monitoring.

Indeed, the DP is a dramatic reminder of the requirement for timely risk assessment of every type of exposure, and of any risk-provisioning measure that might be necessary. A prerequisite to doing a comprehensive job, however, is risk classification procedures for individually assessing:

- Counterparty risk
- Instrument risk, and
- Other exposures, like country risk.

Awareness of a DP affecting the institution and the bank's credit risk strategy correlate. Together, they make mandatory systems and procedures for the early identification, tracking and control of risks arising from credit business and all other product lines. They also bring senior management's attention to the need for closer supervision connected to:

- The introduction of new types of products, and
- The commencement of business activities on new markets.

To remain effective, framework conditions have to be reviewed at least annually, and amended as appropriate. They also have to be documented and tested for performance as well as for cost-effectiveness. The DP provides a common ground for all transactions; transcending the division of managerial responsibilities prevalent in commercial banking. All managers, regardless of the internal assignment of competencies, are collectively responsible for ensuring:

- The orderly organization of credit operations, and
- Proper monitoring and management of risks.

The default point also raises issues concerning sufficient qualification of the staff who perform credit screening and follow-up activities. This relates not only to the personnel active in lending, but also to all individuals involved in the various processes of the credit chain. It also has an effect on the human resources division – from careful selection of staff to employee training programs and credit risk supervision.

Moreover, the need for rigorous approaches to credit risk management, with the DP in perspective, goes beyond employees and managers, to the bank's policies as well as its systems and procedures. An example is the independent monitoring of rating systems under Basel II, and accountability associated study, development and quality inspection of risk classification procedures. This work must definitely be independent of the front office doing the lending. Policies should be focusing on:

- Credit risk strategies
- Identification and management of exposures
- Structure of the terms and conditions
- Examination of legal responsibilities
- Assignment of competencies, and
- Risk-provisioning strategies.

As all reputable bankers appreciate, sound credit policies are based on risk information provided by internal and external rating systems. The accurate computation of the DP supplements this information by bringing in evidence of the counterparties' survivability, and loss given default – and, therefore, the bank's own financial health.

This comes just in time as, according to available statistics, debt provisions of European and American banks are mounting. On 1 August 2002 – when the research which led to this book started – several European banks announced soaring bad debt provisions, leading investors to fear for the financial sector's exposure to failing companies and nations which might tilt Argentina's way in Latin America. Both corporate and sovereign risk had taken a turn for the worse.

It is not surprising that equity capitalization felt the after-effect of investors' reaction. Shares in all major banks fell after Barclays in the UK, Deutsche Bank in Germany, and BNP Paribas and Credit Lyonnais in France said bad debt provisions had to rise. This followed a profit warning from the Allianz insurance company, because of bad debts at its Dresdner Bank subsidiary.

At about the same time, also in Germany, HypoVereinsbank, the country's second largest bank, fell into a loss and said 2002 was the most difficult year in banking, since World War II. Bad debt provisions are always likely to rise in trying times, as corporate insolvencies, especially in the USA, Japan, Germany (and, to a lesser extent, the UK), have been coming thick and fast.

- At Barclays, net provisions rose 43 percent to £713 million ($1.08 billion), because of a major risk from Argentina.

- At Deutsche Bank, provisions climbed in the second quarter of 2002 to 588 million euros ($583 million, at the time), more than double the same period a year earlier.

Even worse news was that Deutsche Bank's provisions covered only 48 percent of its non-performing loans, against 52 percent at the start of 2002. Barclays' coverage ratio was much better – but that, too, dropped from 72 percent to 61 percent. From a lower coverage level it is always harder to conjure up releases of general provisions, as earnings get flatter and revenue growth is hard to come by. Deutsche's revenues in the first half of 2002 were down 12 percent, BNP's down 3 percent, but Barclays' were up 4 percent.

- The business debt carried by American and US-based banks skyrocketed from some $7 trillion in 1990 to over $16 trillion in 2002.

In 2002, the household debt alone has surged to $8.4 trillion, from less than half that amount in 1990. About three-quarters of that amount is mortgages, and there is a mortgage bubble in the USA, at the time of writing. Bubbles mean an inordinate amount of exposure, because they bring DP so much nearer.

Given Japan's woes during the last twelve years, it comes as no surprise that Japanese banks are still in bad shape. In Tokyo the government has been moving from one major bank reorganization program to the next, trying to cope with the fact that Japanese banks have more than $1 trillion in non-performing loans. (By mid-March 2003 the index at the Tokyo Stock Exchange fell to the 1983 level – twenty years wasted.) As the Governor of the Bank of Japan put it:

- The strength of Japanese banks has declined, and
- The market's trust has been damaged.

Meanwhile in Tokyo there was no relief from the bad news, as huge financial and industrial companies made public astonishing losses, as figures for the fiscal year ending 31 March 2003, rolled in. On 4 April 2003, Mitsui Financial Group – one of Japan's top five banks – announced it was $4 billion in the red.

Credit institutions should appreciate that it is to their advantage not only to calculate and steadily update their clients' DP – and their own – but also closely to monitor that of their competitors, at home and abroad, which contributes to market discipline. A basic requirement for doing so is public disclosure of DP information. Figure 10.6 presents some interesting statistics in regard to loans by German banks of more than 1.5 million euros. As the reader can appreciate,

- 59 percent of loans monitored by the Bundesbank go to domestic and foreign credit institutions, and
- Only 34 percent find their way into the treasury of domestic and foreign industrial companies and individuals.

Some experts suggest this pattern is also representative of derivatives deals. It is as if Volkswagen was selling to Daimler-Chrysler 59 percent of its cars – and vice versa.

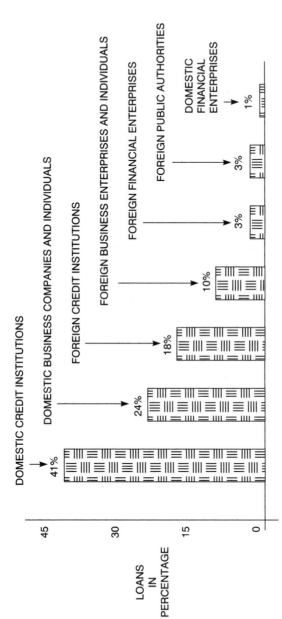

Figure 10.6 Loans of more than 1.5 million euros by major group of borrowers (*Source*: statistics from Deutsche Bundesbank)

Such huge interbank exposure in the financial sector increases the need for appropriate credit risk organization, and associated monitoring requirements, as well as for clear definition of management responsibilities.

In conclusion, the evidence provided by the DP should immediately be brought to the attention of the CEO and the board. It must also be incorporated in reviews by the internal and external auditors. All managers in the bank's chain of command must be familiar with DP, as well as with internally defined risk management methods. They should also have the necessary qualifications to take corrective action *before* counterparty risks get out of hand.

10.5   Credit risk information can be painful news

Caring about views of national regulators, underlying market conditions in different countries and specific issues raised by banks, the Basel Committee has taken plenty of time to fine-tune the new capital adequacy framework. The reader will recall from Chapter 1, the references to quantitative impact studies (QISs) and results that have been obtained.

These QISs enabled the pretesting of the aftermath of Basel II through simulation. At the same time, improvements made to the method raised the level of complexity of the new capital adequacy rules. Subsequently, the Basel Committee did its best to simplify the rules, while seeing to it that capital requirements were reflected fairly closely to actual risks in different areas of banking business.

An example is the treatment of residual exposure associated with credit risk mitigation techniques. This has been left to the discretion of the banks' national supervisors, most likely because it is very difficult to establish global standards which would be valid in all jurisdictions. Another example is the fact that banks will be able to set PDs for specialized loans, like project finance, under direct supervision by their regulators.

As these examples document, one of the ironies with global supervisory rules is that, to be meaningful they necessarily carry with them exceptions. In project financing, the exception regards highly volatile commercial real estate and associated compulsory treatment with higher risk weights. It is inevitable that national regulators are given the responsibility of calibrating capital requirements more accurately with risks involved in banking. On the other hand,

■ Exceptions add to complexity, and
■ This makes life so much more difficult for global banks.

The answer to this is streamlined internal organization, better monitoring policies, knowledge-enriched systems solutions and rigorous metrics. Rigorous metrics, like the DP, should be subject to public disclosure, as documented by the Basel Committee survey on credit risk.[4]

Credit institutions must make a great leap forward to fulfill such requirements. One of the findings of this survey is that disclosure rates generally decrease as the sophistication, complexity and degree of proprietary information increases. When this happens, other critical information, too, is not forthcoming. For instance, the aforementioned Basel survey indicates that:

■ About 20 percent of banks did not disclose how they determine *when* their credits are impaired or overdue,

■ While data about credit risk modeling, credit derivatives and securitization was disclosed by fewer than 50 percent of the banks.

As this Basel Committee surveyed further documents, only 11 percent of banks provided information on credit risk models, comparable to disclosure about market risk. And only 7 percent of credit institutions disclosed the replacement cost of non-performing derivatives – which talks volumes about some of the dark areas of finance, and the pain associated with credit risk and market risk information.

Moreover, while almost all banks disclosed their risk-based capital ratio, fewer than half provided information on credit and market risk against which capital acts as buffer. This contradicts the principle that well-managed credit institutions are supposed to have available *and* to communicate plenty of information, which would have been of significant interest to lenders and investors.

The reader will remember that, as Chapter 4 has emphasized, sound management, investor information and market discipline correlate. Bad news will in any case become public, and rumours act as magnifiers. On 25 October 2002, *Executive Intelligence Review* published an article on the troubled banking industry in the USA, Japan and Germany. An extract of the statistics is presented in Table 10.4.

Year	Total loan commitments ($)	Adversely rated loan commitments as % of total
1997	1435	2.9
1998	1759	2.6
1999	1829	3.7
2000	1951	5.1
2001	2050	9.4
2002	1871	12.9

Table 10.4 Sour loans commitments weighting on US banks. Extract of statistics from *Executive Intelligence Review*, 25 October 2002.

The numbers in Table 10.4 are stunning, providing plenty of food for thought. In the 1997 to 2002 timeframe classified loan commitments, which include different levels of non-performing loans, went from $22 billion to $157 billion, more than a sevenfold increase.

■ Loans in default skyrocketed from $0.9 billion in 1997, to $19.6 billion in 2002.

■ Special loans have gone from $22 billion to $79 billion, in that timeframe.

■ While adversely rated loans, as a percentage of total loan syndication commitments, increased 250 percent.

True enough, since April 2000 credit institutions had to absorb a series of shocks as one industry sector after another faced a severe downturn, leading several experts to suggest that over the horizon may be looming a debt disaster. First the dotcoms melted away, then came the turn of telecommunications companies, followed by the debacle of their formerly mighty suppliers of advanced technological gear.[5]

As formerly prosperous companies were going deeper into debt which they could no longer repay, in the first couple of years of the twenty-first century industry risk boomed 44 percent. One after the other, syndicated loans to the telecommunications sector were adversely rated. Other industry sectors also suffered, with the average company having debt 6.1 times its cash flow. This indeed makes it difficult to serve the rising mountain of liabilities, even if management wishes to perform.

As expected, the banking industry has been in the frontline of these woes. On 9 October 2002, Moody's Investors Service cut its rating on JP Morgan Chase's long-term debt, by one notch, down to 'A1' – a far cry from AA and AA+ banks are now targeting (see Chapters 5 and 6). This affected the rating on $42 billion of JP Morgan Chase's long-term debt.

- Beyond its problem loans, with $759 billion in assets JP Morgan Chase has been the world's leading derivatives bank.
- 'Leading' is no compliment because, at the end of 2002, its exposure amounted to $28.9 trillion in notional principal in highly leveraged bets.[6]

No wonder that from the start of 2001 to December 2002, Morgan Chase's market capitalization shrank from $106.5 billion to $33 billion. Neither is the composition of this huge derivatives portfolio providing any comfort. Included in the $28.9 trillion in derivatives exposure were $366 billion in credit derivatives. This is nearly twice the

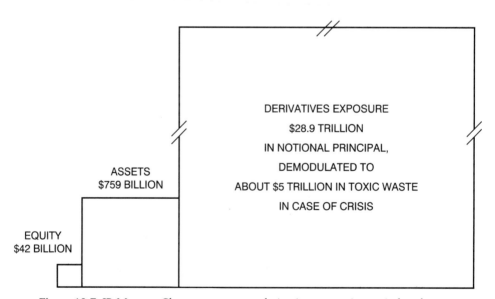

Figure 10.7 JP Morgan Chase: exposure to derivatives *vs* equity capital and assets

$186 billion the bank had in loans; yet loans are, after all, a commercial bank's main line of business. The scary ratio of derivatives exposure to equity capital and assets is shown in Figure 10.7.

Other financial services companies also faced a hard time with derivatives. In the third quarter of 2002, Fannie Mae, the US national mortgage corporation, had a loss of $1.38 billion in the derivatives markets. In the aftermath, its earnings for the quarter fell 19 percent. Profits were also down in spite of its ongoing refinancing activities. The more damaging news came right after the end of that same year. In early 2003 Fannie Mae announced that it had suffered a $4.54 billion loss in 2002.

Financial companies are not alone in terms of painful credit risk news. The early part of the twenty-first century has not been kind to industrial household names such as Pacific Gas & Electric (PG&E), Polaroid, Bethlehem Steel, Regal Cinemas, Enron, Global Crossing, Adelphia Communications and WorldCom. These have been formerly big names in America which failed. In Europe, Deutsche Telekom, France Telecom, Ericsson, Alcatel, Vivendi Universal, Suez and many more, also became overindebted.

Painful credit risk news accelerated as 2001 rolled into 2002. The number of bankruptcies became alarming, while the rate of default on junk bonds approached the all-time peak of 10.3 percent, set in 1991. Analysts did not fail to notice that at below 2 percent of outstanding issues, defaults were pretty stable between 1993 and 1998, weathering the storm of the late 1980s (Milken risk). What worried analysts about the reaccelerated credit risk was that:

■ The 2001–02 problems came from a more widespread base than in the late 1980s/early 1990s, and
■ They were not confined to particular firms that were known to have taken on too much debt.

Other events, too, added their weight to the balance. In the aftermath of the 11 September 2001 terrorist attacks, whole industry sectors like airlines, hotels, movie theatres, nursing homes, steel and other firms, were in major trouble. This happened in spite of the fact that interest rates were low. Banks tightened their lending standards because,

■ Credit risk increased, and
■ There was growing uncertainty about how to value a firm in the fast-changing economy.

Although exact figures are still missing, loan losses written off by the big investment banks in America and Europe are believed to total more than $130 billion in 2002. This is the highest level ever recorded, and it has made analysts and investors nervous, raising again worries of major credit risks hitting the banking industry and depleting its credit risk reserves.

Things got somewhat better by early 2003 as the bond market became increasingly liquid, and spreads between corporate bonds and risk-free Treasury issues were narrowing – a sign of better credit quality. Banks, however, remained picky, though fewer tightened their lending standards in 2003 in contrast to 2002. The reference to spread between corporate bonds and Treasuries is important because, in G-10 countries, the credit quality of a banking system is measured through such spread, as well as by calculating the spread between Treasury bills and time deposits in the banks of the system.

10.6 Expected default frequency and the database

As the examples of credit exposure described in sections 10.4 and 10.5 show, the financial industry needs an early warning system that makes possible prognostication, not just monitoring, of changes in credit quality. Alarms should trigger when a company's debt structure and associated credit exposure measures surpass a defined threshold, which can be customized for each major borrower.

To say that banks need policies, a methodology and models to properly control their credit risk, is to state the obvious. One of the tools available is the *expected default frequency* (EDF™) by Moody's KMV (see also Chapter 13 on the KMV model for economic capital allocation). EDF is a proprietary, market-based credit metric that measures the probability that an entity will default within a given horizon; typically one year.

The EDF value represents default information contained in a firm's equity price, combined with its latest financial statements. Hence, it provides a useful parameter which, in conjunction with a valuation model, can be used to provide an analytical approach to debt valuation. Note that EDF's range in value is from 0.02 per cent to 20 per cent (more on this in Chapter 13).

The objective of this computation is to help distinguish between default-prone and non-default-prone obligors, by means of an indicator which may flash warning signals ahead of rating agency upgrades and downgrades. The contribution of EDF is to estimate the number of standard deviations from the expected default point (see section 10.3). A basic premise of the structural model used to compute EDF is that if the market value of a company drops below a certain level, then:

- Exposure due to outstanding loans proportionally rises, and
- The entity's propensity to default significantly increases.

Regarding prognostication, in the course of the research meeting with Moody's KMV, it was brought to my attention that in early September 2001 this model was able to foretell the bankruptcy of Enron before it happened. The prognosticator seems to have been three months ahead of events. It did so by:

- Including information on the movement in the value of Enron's stock, and
- Looking at the company's balance sheet.

The model found discrepancies in these evaluations and, as one of the Moody's KMV executives said: 'When you can't figure it out, something bad is hidden.' EDF follows the market's view of the entity, determined by its equity value, equity volatility and liability structure. To do so, it employs a proprietary design, based on options theory, which treats the company's equity as a call option on its underlying book value.

The guiding principle is that the higher the market value's volatility, the greater the risk that the company's liabilities will fall below the default threshold. Key to this approach is the standard deviation of annual percentage change in market value of the company's assets. The default threshold is that below which the entity will fail to make scheduled payments satisfying its financial obligations. In the general case, this is a function of the company's liability structure.

Algorithms represent only 20 percent of the total credit risk control equation. Practically all independent ratings agencies are working to create a credit risk database. (This information is gathered primarily through the press, rather than through banks.) Also, for the time being, the majority of banks participating in such cooperative projects are in the USA. The model used in computation of EDFs assumes that:

- Distance to default of DD is a sufficient statistic for credit state, and
- Conditional on a particular DD, obligor location provides no additional information.

Credit risk information that is accurate and timely is a challenge. The problem with any effort of this kind outside the USA, Japan and major European countries, is that the building up of valid databases requires a statistically meaningful sample by country but also industry. Moreover,

- Because concentrations have well-known dangers, banks keep such statistics close to their chest, and
- Since such information is perishable, a credit database has to be steadily updated – or it becomes useless.

In other words, even if an institution's portfolio of financial instruments is diversified along industry, product and geographic lines, ongoing transactions as well as market changes may turn this diversification on its head. Both concentrations and diversification are based on management's best estimate. Some of the assumptions are based on past experience, which may not be common or valid.

Another one of the problems associated with hidden concentrations, is the lack of information that would permit tracking probability of default in real-time. Up to a point, this has to do with internal policies and management control action, as well as system solutions.

Typically, line management conducts the day-to-day credit process, which has many facets: origination, underwriting, risk management in accordance with policies guided by a vague definition of risk, return and portfolio targets. Line management initiates and approves all extensions of credit and is responsible for credit quality, only theoretically connected to a focused risk appetite which reflects top management decisions. (Note MKMV has a loan origination tool called Deal Analyzer.)

Because the board's and senior management's guidelines are usually too general, line managers should establish supplementary credit policies specific to each business line. Yet, even if they have the skills to do so, they don't necessarily have available real-time tools to:

- Monitor portfolio positions (see Chapter 6), and
- Process credit data quickly to avoid undue exposures.

This situation handicaps the performance of people whose job it is to identify problem credits, or to manage such problem credits. Delays in response prevent one from amending deficiencies in a timely manner, much less stopping them before they occur. The result is that models and their implementation often leave much to be desired (see also Chapter 11).

In conclusion, most banks say that their credit standards and credit programs are reviewed annually. Some add that this is done more frequently when necessary, but few have in place an integrated system that permits corrective action. This is a gap that tools like EDF do not close when used standalone. A basic prerequisite of able management is that not just one, but all crucial factors are present: board commitment, real-time solutions, powerful tools, rich credit-risk databases and the all-important internal control.[7]

Notes

1 In the USA this means placed in the regulatory classifications of substandard, doubtful or loss.
2 *The Economist*, 27 July 2002.
3 See D.N. Chorafas (1994). *Advanced Financial Analysis*. Euromoney.
4 Basel Committee on Banking Supervision (2002). *Public Disclosure by Banks: Results of the 2000 Disclosure Survey*. BIS, May.
5 D.N. Chorafas (2004). *Management Risk: The Bottleneck is at the Top of the Bottle*. Macmillan/Palgrave.
6 *Executive Intelligence Review*, 28 March 2003.
7 D.N. Chorafas (2001). *Implementing and Auditing the Internal Control System*. Macmillan.

11 IRB, technological infrastructure, models and correlations

11.1 Introduction

Well-managed banks appreciate that once the necessary restructuring of operations and of the balance sheet is put in motion, targeting the A-IRB solution may be the better option with Basel II. The regulators themselves believe that midway approaches like F-IRB for credit risk, and IMA for operational risk,[1] may not have so much mileage in the longer run – while they require nearly as much preparation as the advanced approaches.

How much restructuring, what kind of skills and what level of high technology are required, are three good questions. Reorganization and restructuring mean open, clearer lines of authority and responsibility than ever before, truly effective internal control and much better risk management. Also the ironing out of significant overlaps like those shown in Figure 11.1, to make sure that there exists full personal accountability.

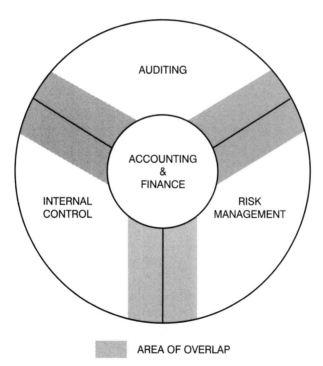

Figure 11.1 Auditing, internal control and risk management tend to overlap in functionality and deliverables

Another prerequisite, which goes beyond reorganization, is that IT is both subordinated to the bank's strategic objectives and, at the same time, is way ahead of that which is being used by competitors. Advanced IT and enterprise risk management correlate. Effective enterprise-wide risk management must be a disciplined approach, aligning:

- Policies
- Systems
- Processes, and
- People

with the goal of evaluating risk and return at any time, for any instrument and for every counterparty – everywhere in the world. This is far from being the case in the banking industry. As far as IT is concerned, many credit institutions have made the situation worse for themselves by:

- Spending an inordinate amount of money for obsolete technology, and
- Continuing to fall behind the state of the art in terms of the deliverables they get.

In contrast to such retrograde practices, the modern bank should be a high-technology implementer, as well as an integrator of financial services. Another interesting statistic to retain is that, today among top-tier credit institutions, between 60 and 80 percent of new technology implementation is in system integration because:

- Enterprise-wide integration is at the core of the bank's economic capital calculation, and
- It is the cornerstone to providing a platform for further product and account management functions.

Even the best, most wholesome default definition (see Chapter 10) will do nothing in keeping counterparty risk at bay, unless systems, procedures and high-technology IT are in place to make rigorous management planning and control possible. This is the reason behind the deliberate choice to follow immediately after a default definition with a definition of the right IT.

Moreover, because models have entered risk management in a big way, *model literacy* is another prerequisite. While mathematical models are currently a glamor subject, few banking executives really appreciate what their use means in terms of advantages, limitations and a horde of implementation challenges. To provide the reader with a snapshot of the background, Table 11.1 outlines the nine most important advantages associated with the development and use of models – along with a list of disadvantages.

In principle, the use of models in the banking industry is most rewarding when the internal culture is tuned to requirements connected to their effective use. This includes the accuracy of the models' input and output, the technology employed to handle them in real-time, rich databases available to back them up and an appreciation of limitations associated to model usage.

Advantages	Disadvantages
Provide a common visual language	True model skills are rare
Bring management attention	Several hypotheses are oracles
Pattern events in a distribution	There is model risk
Flash exceptions	Oversimplifications reduce accuracy
Spot trends	Curves may be wrongly guestimated
Track concentrations	Time horizons may be incompatible
Track instruments	Default theories may be heterogeneous
Help in risk-based pricing	Significant differences in α
Permit stress testing	Some factors and/or criteria are myths

Table 11.1 Advantages and disadvantages of models

Models do not only have advantages, and this must be understood by everybody. For instance, one of the problems with models, and quantitative methods at large, is that you can make the numbers show what you want to them to show. To avoid such high-level massaging, we need standards which provide a reliable common ground and establish a frame of reference. For instance, standards on:

- Admitted level of abstraction
- Time horizon, and other variables
- Level of confidence, and
- Accountability for accuracy of model output.

It is also most advisable to appreciate that numbers tell only half the story. For this reason, the late Dr J.P. Morgan worked on the principle: 'Only lend to someone, once you have looked him in the eye and shaken his hand.' We need both qualitative and quantitative information to reach a factual and documented decision.

There is one more issue to bring to the reader's attention in this introduction. It is particularly important for banks which go for the A-IRB method, and to lesser extent for F-IRB, to have somebody to talk to and collaborate with in pinpointing mistakes. The advice is do not take the road alone. Learn a lesson from Columbus – who sent small flotillas of vessels, capable of supporting one another in case of major problem(s) confronting anyone. The same ought to become policy with IRB and with the use of fast-evolving high technology in banking.

11.2 IRB and the technology needed by credit institutions

The fact that new regulations not just welcome but also promote the use of internal credit risk measures, is an important innovation in the banking industry; one that will have far-reaching ramifications. New supervisory policies not only want to cause a proactive solution to risk control, but also to make commercial banks partners in supervision through market discipline (see Chapter 4) to reduce the likelihood of the regulatory framework becoming fast outdated as a result of new developments in:

- Innovative financial products, and
- The technology supporting them.

The aftermath of what is outlined in the preceding paragraph sounds very positive, and it is. But well-managed banks also appreciate that there are many prerequisites which have to be met in order to be able to implement A-IRB. One of the most basic is the cultural change within the bank, followed by technological leadership. By placing responsibility for high technology clearly with senior management,

- IRB gives banks incentives to steadily update their internal risk control systems.
- It also obliges them to develop clear technological advantages and, by exploiting them properly, gain the upper ground in risk control.

The regulators, too, benefit from the fact that control, flexibility and technological leadership become learning tools promoting management's sensitivity. For instance, increasing the ability to recognize *credit portfolio diversification* through default risk correlations between borrowers (see sections 11.6 and 11.7). The lack of such sensitivity has often been identified as one of the weak points in modern banking with the result that capital charges are disconnected from actual risks.

The ability to predict frequency and impact of unexpected risks is another example along the foregoing frame of reference (see the theoretical background for UL in Chapter 7, through a Deutsche Bundesbank example, and more on UL modeling in Chapter 14). A pattern for stochastic calculation of unexpected risks is shown in Figure 11.2. The implementation of a solution along these lines requires:

- Clear management policies
- Effective real-time systems (see section 11.3)
- Analytical skills (see section 11.4), and
- Financial databases which are accurate and rich in content.

Meeting these objectives calls for projects able to bring *our* bank ahead of the curve in technological solutions. Therefore, Basel II should be seen as the catalyst for leadership in IT. This requires analysis, design, implementation and follow up at each individual bank's level. There are no one-size, readymade solutions banks can implement with closed eyes or minimal efforts.

A different way to making this statement is that Basel II's IRB should be seen as an intermediate step towards regulatory supervision of internal technological developments addressing credit risk, market risk and operational risk in a sophisticated way. Properly tested advanced solutions will put the credit institution in a position to *precommit* itself on capital needs through foresight and insight.

Nobody should underestimate the prerequisites. Take as a relatively simple example the enterprise-wide on-line evaluation of loans applicants. Tactical risk control requires on-line interactive assessments of whether margins get better or worse (gross, net), information regarding on-the-spot market volatility and liquidity,

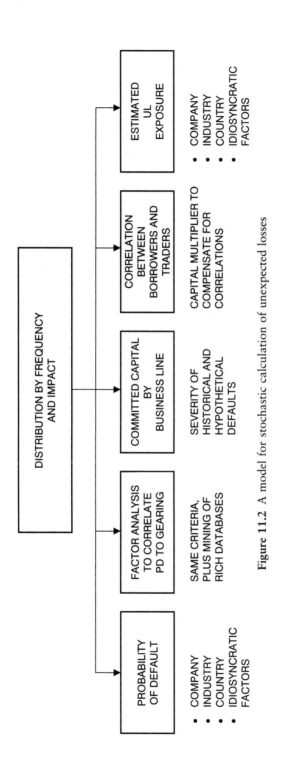

Figure 11.2 A model for stochastic calculation of unexpected losses

as well as peer data on business loans. Other critical information which should be fully updated is:

- Our bank's liquidity
- Diversification of our loans portfolio
- Leverage of the client
- Capital structure of the client, and
- Acid test of the client, by business unit and in whole.

This needs to be backed-up by information on sustainable growth of the client, cash flow of the client, depth of *our* service commitments to the client – leading to the ability to tell the client during negotiation of the loan: 'This is what you represent to the bank as credit risk . . .' Risk adjusted return on capital can play a crucial role as a background model (more on this later).

To perform such duties in an able manner, the technological infrastructure must span the credit institution from top to bottom, and vice versa, doing so in real-space (see section 11.3). Figure 11.3 gives an overview of required structure, for reasons ranging from loans approval to loans portfolio management, including consulting on major problem areas such as near misses – which have the potential to become bad loans. The bank's on-line interactive system must:

- Link CEO, chief operating officer (COO), CFO, chief credit officer, senior risk executives and chief auditor, to help them identify the origin of problems and their sequel
- Bring to all authorized parties the pattern of exposure, starting with the origins of the problem
- Have available on request solutions which have been considered, if, when and where they were tried and what have been the results
- Integrate partial results, identify where the gaps lie and suggest possible corrective action to top management.

To be of immediate assistance, the real-space system must provide basic information, statistics and profiles of clients with loans, particularly bad loans, integrate trading exposures, establish the pattern and size of misfortunes, look into other similar cases in the same market (and solutions by competitors at home and abroad) and make cross-market evaluations.

Nothing like that can be done manually. Real-time models are a 'must'. No valid solutions can be supported through paper, pencil and phone calls. Just as important is to use the real-space system to promote the bank's internal control, provide evidence of its effectiveness, demonstrate how it monitors events *and* non-events, and document how frequently, as well as accurately, internal control provides management with action-oriented information. Senior management must be enabled to:

- Examine what action has been taken after credit risk findings, and how this influenced the bad loans book
- Then study and analyze findings on financial staying power, developing a plan for future action to improve upon the current situation.

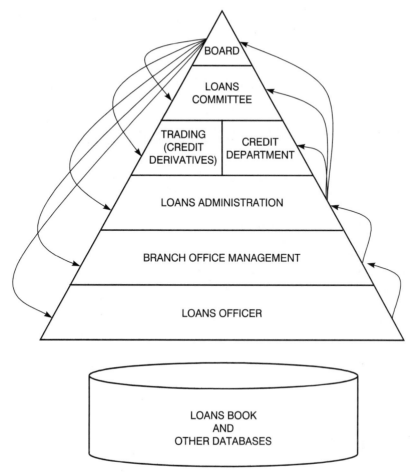

Figure 11.3 A top-down and bottom-up view of real-time system support for loans

The new corporate culture promoted by Basel II is worthy of support precisely because all of these steps point towards a more objective credit risk control which takes full advantage of high technology. A significant improvement would be the introduction of levels of confidence into the bank's culture – such as the 99 percent or, better still, 99.9 percent level – as well as the introduction of stress tests on the threat of a capital shortage in worsened economic conditions.

11.3 Twenty-first century real-time and real-space in the banking industry

The any-to-any, enterprise-wide real-time connection is one of the elements in differentiating a credit institution from its competitors. Real-time is not 'yesterday's' development, but one of the early to mid-1960s. It has taken several decades for it to be used effectively in banking for complex financial services, but many institutions still do not support it because they live in outdated computing times, based on an inordinate amount of:

- Cobol programs (legacy software),
- Mainframes and other technological obscenities.

Etymologically, the term *real-time* was coined to differentiate between batch operations, whose output took ages to reach the end-user, and the possibility of accessing on-line information stored in the machine with minimal delay. On-line access practically compressed to zero (or, at the most, to a few seconds) the time necessary to obtain and/or manipulate data in computer memory. The classical twenty-four hour cycle of information update is a disaster to the bank – even if it is still widely practiced.

It is appropriate to add that the now classical real-time terminology also refers to computer systems or programs that perform calculations during the actual time that a related physical process transpires. Real-time should not be confused with *timesharing* a central resource. The latter provides on-line service to many users by working on each one's task part of the time.

Definitions, however, evolve. With increasingly intelligent communicating work-stations and servers available today under every desk, the 1960s' image of real-time is no longer high technology. In order to survive in an increasingly competitive and sophisticated financial environment, the modern bank needs not just to compress time but also to compress space. This is the concept behind *real-space*, which high technology makes feasible. What this real-space includes is distributed:

- Information elements
- Intelligent artefacts, and
- Computing engines.

The information elements may be clients' accounts, balance sheet entries, exposure references and so on. The intelligent artefacts are interactive expert systems (agents, knowledge robots)[2] which two decades ago were peak technology but today are staple elements among top-tier banks.[3]

In their way, real-space solutions enriched with knowledge artefacts are the most versatile personal executive tool ever invented. Figure 11.4 presents, as an example, an interactive management report based on the bank's trading book and accessed in real-space. The object is position risk (see Chapter 6) at different levels of reference.

The reader can better appreciate the background, importance and competitive advantage of real-space solutions through a brief reference to the evolution of technology available to the banking industry during the past fifty years. From the 1950s till the late 1960s, classical data processing has been *batch*. It remains that way in a larger number of user organizations who look towards the future through the rear-view mirror.[4]

In the 1960s *timesharing* enabled the use of centralized resources by accessing and combining information on-line, but still addressed itself only to data – and databases updated through batch. By the mid-1970s, *electronic messaging* systems made feasible

TRANSACTION / INSTRUMENT	SPOT	FORWARDS	OPTIONS
INTEREST RATES			
CURRENCY EXCHANGE RATES			
EQUITIES			
SECURITIZED PRODUCTS			
OTHER DERIVATIVE INSTRUMENTS			

Figure 11.4 Exposure on instruments and transactions: a real-space report on position risk

the first significant computer support at management level; a parallel step, in the same decade, has been *decision support systems* (DSSs), *management information systems* (MISs) and the wider use of minicomputers as distributed resources.

Since the mid-1970s, parallel networks, with packet switching protocol, have linked these minicomputers among themselves and with central resources. This has been a significant improvement over the point-to-point links of timesharing, and multidrop lines of early real-time, in terms of:

■ System reliability, and
■ Cost-effectiveness.

But an advance of the 1970s is a backwater condition today. In the early 1980s, personal computers and local area networks came into wider use. Client-server solutions followed. By the late 1980s, communications-intense environments improved in sophistication and performance. They made feasible handling *multimedia* and shrinking the time and distance separating decision-makers.

Since the early 1990s, this is the mission given to real-space implementation. A money-center bank operates twenty-four hours a day. From New York to London, Zurich, Paris, Frankfurt and Tokyo, the sun never sets on the international bank. When the financial markets open in Europe they have not yet closed in Japan. When the exchanges open for New York, it is midday in Europe.

■ Dealers, traders, managers in different financial centers need to communicate among themselves as if they were in the same place.
■ They are after zero lag time, and current technology can offer it to them at an affordable price.

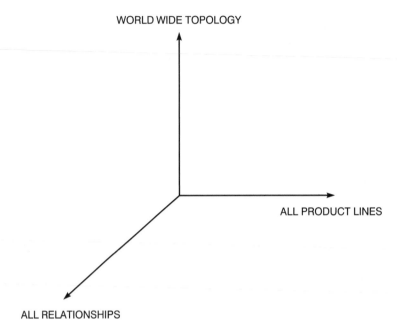

Figure 11.5 Real-space solutions for risk management should address a three-dimensional
perspective

As an example, Figure 11.5 shows a three-dimensional reporting framework
implemented by top-tier banks since the early 1990s for risk management reasons.
Another area of real-space applications is the balance sheet. The reader will recall that
State Street Bank is able to compute worldwide its virtual balance sheet – and,
therefore, its exposure – in less than thirty minutes.

Very few financial institutions are able to match this performance. Yet, for risk
management purposes this type of real-space implementation is crucial. It is also a
cornerstone of the A-IRB solution.

Notice that these are developments of the 1990s, even if still today the majority of
banks are not up to such standards. Can we say which will be the major IT trends, in
the coming years, and therefore the shape of advanced technological solutions by the
end of this decade? The answer is:

- We are moving away from a data-centric world. This has been part of the change
  which takes place over several years, but its effects are only now becoming evident.
  Fundamentally, data-centric approaches comprise a two-tier model with straightforward request-driven computer usage. The main theme in this environment has
  been accessing distributed relational or object databases in real-space.

- The new paradigm is a message-centered world. This means n-tier models, with complex operations that span or exist outside users' requests. The concept is one of self-organizing systems with significant machine intelligence. The challenges, too, are expanding n-fold both because of complexity and for the reason of addressing simultaneously many specific issues of one's work – and associated environmental interactions.

Is such evolution in IT the direct consequence of developments which during the last decade have taken place in the banking industry? Without doubt, the answer is 'yes'. Take liquidity as an example. As Figure 11.6 suggests, a bank's liquidity position changes intraday with the volume and type of transaction. Each of these transactions contributes to exposure, and it is better to forget about netting through model-based approaches. As Warren Buffett aptly suggests, quite often 'marking-to-model' turns out to be 'marking-to-myth'.

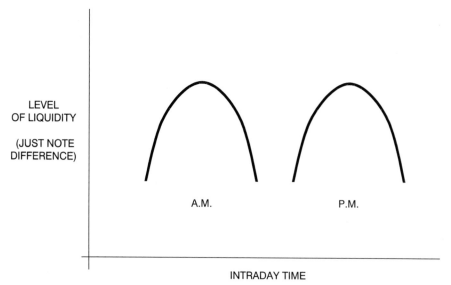

Figure 11.6 A bank's liquidity position changes intraday with the volume of transactions

As Buffett sees it,

> I can assure you that the marking errors in the derivatives business have not been symmetrical. Almost invariably, they have favored either the trader, who was eyeing a multimillion dollar loan, or the CEO who wanted to report impressive 'earnings' (or both) . . . only much later did shareholders learn that the reported earnings were a sham.[5]

A frequent aftermath of shams is to drain the bank's liquidity. But, to survive, the credit institution must at all times be in charge of its liquidity position – in real-space.

In the twenty-first century, systems supporting the most technologically advanced institutions will be communicating:

■ In asynchronous ways
■ With self-created in-flight data.

Among the IT tools necessary to handle such solutions are universal description, discovery and integration (UDDI) procedures; web services description language (WSDL); and simple object access protocol (SOAP). Because this is not a book on IT, I will not elaborate further on these issues, but bear mind that the twenty-first century has its own IT terminology, management supports and cost-effectiveness goals.

11.4   Requirements for efficient IRB modeling

The best description of financial modeling I ever heard comes from Tim Thompson of Barclays Bank, who said: 'All models are wrong. But some are useful.' This section and section 11.5 address the useful function of models and their associated system requirements. They also bring to the reader's attention some of the models' limitations, and the reasons why they may be wrong.

Let me start with a paradigm familiar to bankers, which helps to explain that the concept of models, and the models themselves, evolve over time. Credit rating is a model. In earlier times, credit rating used to represent only the probability of default, as shown in the two-dimensional pattern in Figure 11.7. More recently, however, credit rating has developed into a method of evaluating expected loss from credit risk.

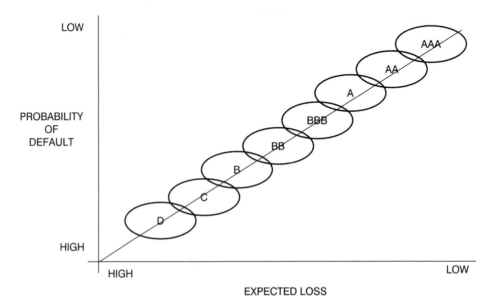

Figure 11.7 A two-dimensional approach to rating through expected loss

The information now being provided is richer, because the evolved credit rating model includes both the probability of default and the severity of loss in the event of default. The new algorithms are simple enough, but they provide investors with an indicator of credit quality versus contractual standing of the obligation:

Expected loss = probability of default × severity of loss upon default (11.1)

Expected credit loss rate = probability of default × (1-recovery rate) (11.2)

Typically, in their rating the independent agencies consider each entity's senior unsecured debt. If there is none, this yields an assessment credit risk relatively unaffected by considerations of collateral (see Chapter 12) or of position within the capital structure. A properly designed system:

■ Permits making rating distinctions among the different liabilities of a company, and
■ Is instrumental in considering a number of different classes of debt outstanding.

Credit risk modeling essentially exploits the concept behind these two points. To effectively use this method, credit institutions will be well advised to employ in their rating a granularity of 20, like independent rating agencies do. Used in an able manner, greater detail will be instrumental in helping commercial banks calibrate their exposure. The Basel Committee says that when statistical models are used in rating, management must ensure that the credit institution has a comprehensive methodology, which:

■ Provides a detailed statement and justification of the hypotheses being made
■ Outlines the data source(s) used to make the estimates on ratings and trends, and
■ Explains the mathematical and empirical basis of assignment of probability of default estimates to grades, for individual obligors.

Other requirements include establishing a rigorous statistical process, incorporating out-of-time and out-of-sample performance tests, and providing a sound basis for validating the selection of explanatory variables. I would add to this list that management need to be fully aware of the model's limitations. Not only models are imperfect. The same aphorism applies to human judgment – which, in the last analysis reflects itself into the model.

What has just been explained is part of the conceptual infrastructure required for effective risk modeling. This infrastructure includes issues such as correlations (see sections 11.6 and 11.7) and of weights (see Chapter 12). Risk migration, too, must be taken into account. There are, for example, some credit risks which migrate into operational risks.

The geographical pattern of credit risks is another variable which should be considered. The better known independent rating agencies carry out their work on a country-by-country basis, and then within each country on a bank-by-bank basis. S&P defines the probability of default universally, but while the statistics in its databases are very good for the USA, Canada, the UK and some continental European countries, for other countries credit information is not forthcoming, and the statistics are therefore not foolproof.

Topology is a major challenge in a universal credit modeling perspective, increased by the fact that factors characterizing creditworthiness are not the same all over. For G-10 countries there are fairly similar cross-country factors which, in many cases, permit an almost level field. When cross-country factors affecting credit rating are fairly consistent, the resulting pattern tends to be reliable.

Beyond the references being made which impact on the dependability of credit risk models, comes the fact that such models are used both for planning and for control. Therefore, they must be dynamic and forward-looking rather than simply relying on accounting data that is intrinsically historical and comes long after the facts. The answer to the query as to whether historical data could help in prognostication depends on:

- The length of time series, and
- The periodicity of patterns.

To properly analyze events characterizing the British economy, Dr Brandon Davies, of Barclays Bank, considered two centuries of data: from 1800 to 1997, when the study was done. When the breadth of the study is so rigorous, extrapolations are meaningful because hypotheses behind them can be tested, so to speak, by 'forecasting the past' – thereby controlling the assumptions being made.

The project's objectives evidently play a critical role. Current, ongoing probabilities of default are essential elements in modeling, but even more crucial in debt pricing and portfolio management at large is the ability to guestimate future default rates (see Chapter 10). Such probabilities are often based on a cause-and-effect model which:

- Is strong in evaluating likelihood of default events, and
- Provides a performance measure that, while consistent over time, also flashed out outliers.

Figure 11.8 gives an example on forecasting trends for two ratings: Ba3 and B1. The trend line spans sixty months before default and it provides a good basis for mean tendency – therefore at 50 percent probability level. The bank's analysts should bring this trend line at 99 percent level of confidence ($\alpha = 0.01$) using the credit institution's own, internal default data.

In procedural terms, a rating is assigned to an issuer's most important class of liabilities. Then, the issuer's other debt obligations are rated in regard to this initial step. Sometimes, qualitative modifications to the senior ratings procedure are necessary, to help the bank's own management (and investors) better judge the credit risks of debt issuers.

It is appropriate to add that an efficient credit rating requires a steady follow-up process. Entities, even those rated BB, seldom fail overnight. As shown in Figure 11.8 with Moody's Investors Service statistics, trends develop over many months before default. Moreover, credit risk scores for consecutive years are correlated (more on this in sections 11.6 and 11.7).

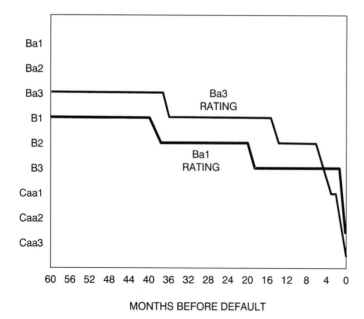

Figure 11.8 Moody's statistics on median rating decay before default

Trends and correlation provide an opportunity for designing appropriate tests for benchmarking credit risk ratings. Great care should be exercised, however, with models, data collection and databases. As already explained, rating agencies, banks and other entities using a model-based approach for expected loss from credit risk, must have firstclass databases. They should collect, store and interactively retrieve information not only on risk events but also on:

- Rating decisions
- Rating histories of borrowers
- Probabilities of default associated with rating grades, and
- Ratings migration which makes feasible predictive power.

For each borrower, a complete rating history must be retained, including methodology being used, type of data employed, person or model who assigned the rating, dates ratings were assigned and the trends in rating. All this is part of a support system whose consistency and accuracy can make or break the whole effort of being in charge of credit risk.

11.5   Management must be careful with models and statistics

Section 11.4 has explained the crucial role played in credit modeling by data and statistics. Sections 11.6 and 11.7 will bring to the reader's attention the issue of correlated risks. Between these references, *statistics* is an often recurring theme. It is therefore appropriate to emphasize the fact that one must be very careful with statistical information. Two of the most frequent reasons why figures and statistics stand out as being wrong are that:

- They seem to be surprisingly precise
- They are improbably pertinent, or wholesale.

Either and both reasons see to it that statements based on statistics may collapse after a second look. Also present in the interpretation of statistical evidence, which often filters into modeling, are two tendencies which do not necessarily balance each other out:

- To boast, and
- To understate.

Overstating and understating are asymmetric. Another element which is often at fault in modeling – whether the artefact concerns credit risk, market risk or operational risk – is the sampling method being used. Substandard sampling exists at the heart of many false statistics. Samples may be:

- Too small
- Biased, or
- Plainly irrelevant.

The users of statistical evidence will be well advised to bear in mind that the results of every statistical study are no better than the sample it is based on. Beyond this is the fact that while statistics provide a quantitative estimate, successful credit risk modeling is seldom (if ever) wholly quantitative. It is a combination of both quantitative and qualitative approaches.

It should indeed be remembered that the current internal risk-based modeling effort centres on Pillar 1, which follows a rather narrow, capital-based view. Management quality which is very important in creditworthiness comes under Pillar 2. Therefore, the IRB model should be constructed in a way that it can expand, with modules added for:

- Pillar 2, the regulator's responsibilities, and
- Pillar 3, transparency and market discipline.

A credit-oriented IRB model which incorporates credit ratings should integrate all reasons for expected losses. It should also target liquidity through a Monte Carlo simulation, and mismatch risk accounting for short-term deposits and medium/long-term loans. A sound approach is that of:

- Emulating the aftermath of all deposits withdrawn on short notice, in part and in full, and
- Stress testing through hypotheses of unexpected losses, as well as by evaluating probability of default over a number of years.

A more sophisticated approach will look for risk mitigation solutions such as securitization, insurance and novel capital markets instruments. These more complex and more demanding approaches see to it that old, tired models – as, for instance, CreditVAR – cannot fulfil current and future requirements.[6]

Though some banks find it convenient to use the different versions of this model, for a number of reasons, several supervisors do not currently recognize VAR as a measure of credit risk. Not only the model itself, but also the information it often uses is unreliable. Internal data on defaults and recovery rates are not always collected in a useful format, while external data, from ratings or to equity prices tend to be dominated by experience in some countries which may not be valid elsewhere.

Another major fault of the model itself, and its statistics, is that information on the influence of factors such as the economic cycle, geographic location, industry sector, loan maturity upon default and recovery rates, is rather poor. This is made worse by the incompleteness of data which affects the estimate of credit correlations. The latter are often based on proxies – a practice introducing more approximations.

A third reason that CreditVAR type models using normal distributions do not answer requirements, is that credit returns tend to be skewed and fat-tailed. Therefore, Monte Carlo simulation may be more appropriate for credit risk evaluation, but its computational burden poses a problem with large portfolios in the sense that, as discussed in sections 11.2 and 11.3, many credit institutions still use old-fashioned electronic data processing (EDP) technology.

The fourth reason for miscarriages in deliverables is that appropriate holding periods differ widely; they range from a comparatively short timeframe for marketable securities, to much longer ones for non-marketable loans held to maturity. This complicates the task of parameter setting, and is only slightly eased with credit derivatives.

Still another reason accounting for the fact that supervisors are reserved when considering the suitability of VAR models for simulation of credit risk, is their inability to handle the profile of an institution's counterparties. Yet this profile is very important in determining the appropriateness of marking-to-model credit risk. Estimations and correlations cannot be meaningfully done by basing them on a guestimated average profile.

- CreditVAR and other similar models require that companies are classified by industry type.
- This is a weak hypothesis, with the result that estimates are most often approximations which do not permit any accuracy in computing counterparty risk.

A sixth important reason is that, most often, institutions have a relatively limited number of big counterparties. This leads to credit risk concentration rather than diversification targeted by CreditVAR models. What is more, classification by type of exposure leads to very small samples where the chi-square distribution is applicable.

Many banks fail to realize that VAR-type models favor firms with a high diversity of credit exposures, therefore less correlated default probabilities (see sections 11.6 and 11.7). Neither do they pay attention to the fact that normal distribution hypotheses see to it that additional safeguards are necessary like rigorous exposure rules in terms of capital requirements. Such additional safeguards are anathema to most banks.

These six major reasons see to it that the contribution of CreditVAR and similar models is questionable. 'VAR gives incorrect assessment of the market,' said a senior executive of Merrill Lynch, adding: 'We see a lot more event risk in the market than is indicated by VAR.' To overcome some of the limitations, Barclays uses generalized autoregressive conditional heteroschedasticity (GARCH) distribution of VAR – an eigenmodel. The GARCH family of models is far more sophisticated than VAR. Barclays Bank also subjects the outcome to a series of stress tests.

In conclusion, because accuracy is so important, focused modeling solutions must see to it that both quantification and qualification of credit risk have a role in evaluating and testing regulatory capital requirements. How much of a role will depend on the ingenuity of rocket scientists in solving the aforementioned constraints, developing and testing eigenmodels as well as addressing issues related to the correlation of risks.[7]

11.6   The calculation and evaluation of correlation coefficients

Correlation is the mathematical measure of association in the way of change in values of two entities. As such, correlation is a commonly used statistical description. Expressed as ρ, it provides a mathematical relationship, or inverse relationship, between two sets of data. ρ varies between +1 and −1, with $\rho = 0$ indicating no correlation. Correlation and regression should not be confused with one another:

■ Regression considers the frequency distribution of one variable while another is fixed.
■ A correlation addresses the joint variation of two streams of measurements each related to the values of a given entity.

Figure 11.9 shows a correlation of about 0.7 between expected credit risk and rating by an independent agency. (More on this later.) A similar correlation exists between expected credit risk and needed regulatory capital. Many factors in finance are correlated, for instance, the behavior of G-10 stock markets.

Correlations are not cast in stone. They change over time. Financial history teaches that a crisis often causes seemingly independent factors to correlate in a manner unheard of under normal market conditions. In financial analysis, it is therefore wise to distinguish between:

■ Correlations existing under tranquil times, and
■ Correlations developing or happening under stress.

Two types of correlations characterize the latter conditions: daisy-chain and add-ons. Daisy-chain type risk happens when credit risk piles upon market risk, and market risk upon more credit risk. An add-on effect takes place, for example, with exposure to derivatives contracts which require that a company suffering a credit downgrade

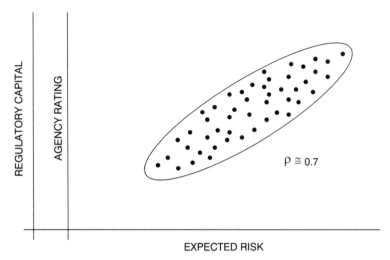

Figure 11.9 Regulatory capital, agency rating and expected risk correlate

immediately supplies collateral to counterparties. In this section, and in sections 11.7 and 11.8, we will not consider correlations under stress or market panics.

Another important dichotomy among financial correlations is between those characterizing defaults and those addressing assets. Default correlations are a vital tool in credit rating. With IRB, asset correlations will be embedded in risk weights (see Chapter 12). Basel will publish asset correlation tables. Under Basel II, there is no option under which banks can estimate their own asset correlations.

Moreover, in connection with asset correlations, KMV researchers have found that equity correlations are poor proxy for assets correlations.[8] Their research documents that asset values are firm specific. Therefore, EDF (see Chapter 10) computes asset values taken as equity capitalization plus book value of debt.

The reader should appreciate that today, to a very substantial extent, the effort of computing correlations among individual instruments, securities and risk factors, within a portfolio, is accomplished through quantitative approaches. Correlations, however, are about far more than quantitative guidelines and industry concentration limits, which may well be subjective.

Even *if* correlations were affected only by quantitative factors, *data insufficiency* would have seen to it that computed values could become notoriously unreliable. Subjective judgments further impact on correlation results, and there are differences in entity size and country which may lead to lower correlations than industry differences in the same country.

A good approach to dealing with the wealth of qualitative factors in connection to correlations is the *Delphi method*.[9] Delphi is an established methodology which can be instrumental in improving the accuracy of computed correlations, as well as in guestimating correlations when data is not readily available in a statistically valid sense. This method is based on iterative queries to known experts.

Also keep in mind the issue of the resulting correlations matrix which, in certain cases, may become unmanageable. During our meeting, a senior executive of A.M.

Best said that sometimes, to arrive at meaningful conclusions, the correlation matrix becomes so huge that it is no longer effective. Hence, it becomes necessary to work around correlations:

- Giving credit for diversification (merits), and
- Charging premiums for non-diversification (demerits).

Delphi and merits/demerits may be valid alternatives when the database is weak and, as such, it does not allow reliable data analysis to establish how far instruments and/or business lines are correlated. Remember that the database should run over a two-digit number of years, and the analysis should include covariance for buckets of risk.

11.7   Are correlation coefficients reliable and well understood?

With the background section 11.6 has provided, in the following paragraphs we will be concerned only with default correlations under more or less normal market conditions. Even so, there are plenty of themes which arise. One of these concerns the derivation and use of correlation coefficients. As advice to the reader, based on experience, when looking at statistics watch out for a switch somewhere between:

- The raw figure, and
- The author's conclusion.

Often what is missing in a presentation of correlation coefficients is the factor that caused a change to occur. In other cases, the correlation derived may be misleading, or plainly irrelevant. A major bank said that in one of its divisions it found:

- A correlation of 68 percent between credit risk and market risk.

Plenty of queries follow up a statement like this. For instance, what might have caused high correlation? Is there any industry norm to compare it to? Is this 68 percent 'too high' or 'too low'? Most importantly, is this 68 percent correlation 'good' or is it 'bad' for the bank to which it applies, and to its capital requirements?

I have asked this in a seminar on regulatory and economic capital allocation in London in June 2003, and only two people out of twenty raised their hand to say: 'It is high.' The others had no opinion about it. As this real-life example demonstrates, the question is not whether correlation coefficients are important to the banking industry. They are. The real queries are:

- Are they reliable?
- Are they understood in regard to their meaning?

An area of particular interest in connection with calculation and interpretation of correlation coefficients is that concerning counterparty default rates, and their evolution. Over time, one major bank found a distribution of coefficients in the range of $\rho = 0.70$ to $\rho = 0.80$, with $\rho = 0.75$ as mean, for areas as diverse as:

	Correlation coefficients
Wholesale lending and international lending	0.70
Interest rate spread and credit risk	0.50
Equity markets among themselves	0.50
International loans and domestic loans (personal, mortgages, SME)	0.50
Real estate/office building	0.50
Real estate	0.25

Table 11.2 Calculation of correlation coefficient ρ for credit risk, among a sample of banks

- Wholesale lending and international lending
- Interest rate spread and credit risk
- Equity markets among themselves
- International loans and domestic loans (personal, mortgages, SME).

Other banks to whom I have shown these figures contested them, because *their* experience with correlations has been quite different. The central tendency of their findings is shown in Table 11.2.

An interesting divergence of opinion concerned correlations in real estate. To start with, much depends on the type of asset: office building, apartment houses made by developers, individual homes. This is reflected in the correlation coefficients shown in Table 11.2. The executives of several banks said that correlation of real estate to all lending gravitates around $\rho = 0.25$. But there is no universal agreement on this figure. 'I disagree one hundred percent with $\rho = 0.25$ for real estate,' said Tim Thompson of Barclays.

In connection with international and domestic lending, Thompson said that Barclays Bank typically assumes 100 percent correlation. But if the market is really tranquil, then 70 percent can go. Notice, however, that these reflections on correlations are just a few examples stated by experts and reflecting individual banks' conditions. They are not universal standards.

So much for credit risk. For market risk, correlation coefficients are usually computed through historical simulation. Datamining aims to unearth correlations built into historical time series. A macrofund said its correlation in equity markets is only 0.2, but it also experiences mean reversion. Other institutions put that correlation much higher.

Stress testing is typically done through macroscenarios taking different sets of data, and studying which scenario makes worst case. Worst cases are studied by looking into crises and their after-effects:

- High correlations, like $\rho = 0.85$, are judged as being bad.
- Low correlations, like $\rho = 0.15$, show effects of diversification.

ρ	credit risk, market risk	=	60–70%
ρ	credit risk, business conditions	=	80–90%
ρ	market risk, market environment	=	85–90%
ρ	operational risk, credit/market risk	=	10–15%

Table 11.3 Correlation coefficients between risk types
and market conditions

Correlation coefficients also exist between different types of risks: credit, market and operational. Table 11.3 provides a reference to ranges among the three main types. Here are some examples of correlation between credit risk and operational risk:

- Balance sheet analysis which leaves fraudulent claims undetected
- Grading procedure which approves loans that should not be granted
- Account officer who does not detect early enough changes in client behavior
- Information on missed payments is skipped, due to an IT error.

These and more failures are everyday happenings. Operational risk management, after all, is about avoiding such nasty surprises which have become commonplace in a great number of cases.[10] For economic capital allocation purposes, conservative banks take higher ρ, because, in crisis, correlations move towards 1. Moreover, well-managed institutions have adopted a policy of at least annual correlation revision. If there is a substantial financial or political event between annual revisions, they look up ρ through:

- A sampling of expert opinions, and
- Datamining involving long-term (ten years) and short-term data series.

This policy has been established in appreciation of the fact that it is necessary not only to keep developing correlation coefficients but also to update them so that their accuracy is preserved. Even the more accurate calculations will be outdated in a couple of years, if not updated. It is also necessary to put correlations under stress to reveal possible weaknesses.

In conclusion the computation of prevailing correlations is typically based on measurement and data sets. However, for evaluation reasons, quite often expert opinion scenarios and database mining are made at least every year, and ad hoc if something big takes place. One of the major banks has a team devoted to stress analysis of correlations.

11.8 Beware of magnitude of risk with correlated exposures

Regulators have introduced correlations to make bankers aware that different risks and their characteristic factors may move the same way. The Basel Committee says that credit institutions must validate correlation assumptions through analysis, and the correlation coefficient they use must be proven. An easy role to recall is that:

- *If* risks are correlated
- *Then* change in one influences total exposure.
- *If* they are independent
- *Then* the influence of the larger one is diminished.

Misjudgment of correlations has been the problem with LTCM. Their investments had high correlations and they moved the same way on the downside. High correlations in market risk are particularly painful in market crisis. The damage they produce is much more than that of credit risk.

'Hardly anybody knows the true correlations,' said a senior executive of Merrill Lynch. 'It is a *time barrier* measure.' Another investment advisor added, correlation between assets sometimes comes as shock even to the experts. And there are cases where you cannot use correlations. For instance:

- *If* the change is rapid and/or
- It involves extreme values.

Indeed, one of the challenging problems associated with correlations is that of handling correlated risks, leading to aggravation of exposure. 'The relative impact of correlations' said a senior executive of S&P, 'is that the further we look in the tail, the greater is the impact of correlations.'

Because, unexpected financial shocks occur at the tail of risks distributions, it is most valuable to generate the whole tail of events. This is where the picture of losses is broader and more representative of reality; it is also part of the macrolevel whose analysis requires the proverbial long, hard look.

Warren Buffett distinguishes between the microlevel and the macrolevel. The latter concerns him the most. As he put it in an article mid-March 2003: 'The macro picture is dangerous and getting more so. Large amounts of risk, particularly credit risk, have become concentrated in the hands of relatively few derivatives dealers who in addition trade extensively with one another.'[11]

This speaks volumes about the lack of diversification. While fundamentally diversification helps to reduce default correlation by keeping low co-movement and dependence, more often than not diversification is just an illusion – a fact which should be given a great deal of attention in the computation of correlations.

Another thing to watch out for, in lightly reached conclusions, is whether a correlation has been inferred to continue beyond the data with which it has been demonstrated. This is important inasmuch as quite often a positive (or negative) default correlation holds up to a point – then it may become the inverse of what it used to be prior to that break point. Percentiles, too, can be deceptive. An odd thing about percentiles is that:

- While a 99 percent rating is definitely superior to one of 90 percent
- Those at 40 percent and 60 percent levels may be of almost equal achievements. Some 90 percent of correlations are within $2s$ of the mean, as shown in Figure 11.10.

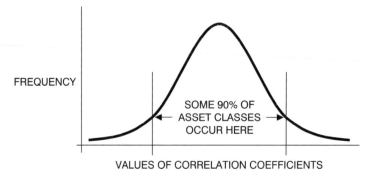

FREQUENCY

SOME 90% OF
← ASSET CLASSES →
OCCUR HERE

VALUES OF CORRELATION COEFFICIENTS

Figure 11.10 The values of correlation coefficients tend to cluster around the mean

Beyond this, correlation coefficients must be reasonable. A $\rho = 0.0$ or $\rho = 0.1$ is far too high (or too low) even for major (or very minor) events. Many characteristics of financial instruments cluster around their own average, forming the normal distribution curve, and in this case the frequency of a certain value is important. But there are also tail events. A good question to ask is what is the background reason for change in frequency. A recent study found the reason has been quality of assets.

Another area which needs a great deal of analysis, beyond what it has received so far, is that of uncorrelated risks. Theoretically at least, uncorrelated risks are typically found in different business lines, event types and geographic areas. But there are always exceptions. Beyond that, both correlated risks and uncorrelated risks must be studied through confidence levels, such as 99.9 percent.

In fact, some banks now believe *confidence intervals* are better than correlations we cannot document. They also emphasize that it is important to differentiate between frequency and impact of the risks whose correlation, or lack of it, we are analyzing.

- Frequency and impact should be associated to practically every risk factor we study.
- Their detection requires a high degree of granularity, and sensitivity to the effect of drift or other reasons for change.

We have also to keep in mind that globalization has changed not only the correlation between capital markets of the USA, Europe and Asia, but also their frequency and impact. Because of uncertainties associated with their measurement, many correlations come in fuzzy sets. For instance:

- $\rho = 0.15$ may mean $\rho = 0.10$ or $\rho = 0.20$.

Another issue which should be brought to the reader's attention is the correlation square rule. Moody's KMV *portfolio manager* (see Chapter 13) uses the square of correlation coefficients: ρ^2. This tells how much knowing one variable helps to understand the other. Big companies like Microsoft, ICI, Volkswagen and Fuji are high ρ names. There is even larger ρ with major, same country/same industry firms, like GM and Ford.

It has been the opinion of risk managers that the square of the correlation coefficient ρ^2 spreads better the correlation effects. It also helps to overcome one of the problems with correlations – their reversal from negative to positive, and vice versa.

These approaches are worth examining because one of the problems with Basel II is defining the right correlations. Practically, everybody tries to find the 'best solution', but concepts differ.

- Some banks stick to milestone values $\rho = 1$, 0.75, 0.50, 0.25, 0.0.
- Others, say, never use $\rho = 0$, because you don't know if there is a hidden correlation. Rather use $\rho = 0.15$ as proxy.
- Still others establish databases which permit to measure ρ more accurately.

To be prudent, when in doubt use 100 percent correlation, choose the upper range of ρ computed through analytics, and regularly revalidate the values of ρ. Rich databases which can be mined for correlations are evidently a 'must'.

One more question is in order before rounding up this subject. 'Is it possible to share risk correlations?' The answer to the query 'Will banks exchange correlation factors in the future?' is negative. The general opinion which I received from cognizant bankers is:

- These numbers are too close to the chest, and
- Correlation factors tend to be quite different from one bank to the other.

'There is no sharing of correlation coefficients,' said Eugen Buck of Rabobank, adding that: 'Correlation factors must be computed in conjunction to diversification and they are very specific to an institution.'

Other senior bankers, too, said every credit institution has its own portfolio pattern, and correlations. The general consensus was that, in regard to correlation coefficients, much depends on:

- The type of bank
- Its business, and
- The risks that it assumes.

Risk correlations are specific to market conditions, financial instruments and methods used to identify and measure them. Hence, we must be very careful when evaluating and using correlations.

- *If* regulators really want banks to use correlations in an able manner,
- *Then* they have to come up with guidelines and correlation estimates.

Among regulators, the Dutch Central Bank wants to know how banks under its jurisdiction look at correlations at present, and in the future, as steering mechanisms.

In conclusion, correlations are a subject that is still full of unknowns in the banking industry. While there is an *apparent* transmission mechanism between different types of losses, nobody has yet been dipping in deep enough to properly identify it. This gap in our knowledge – a gap widespread in the financial industry – can have serious consequences. When they suddenly surface, strong correlations could trigger major systemic problems.

Notes

1 D.N. Chorafas (2004). *Operational Risk Control with Basel II*. Butterworth-Heinemann.
2 D.N. Chorafas (1998). *Agent Technology Handbook*. McGraw-Hill.
3 D.N. Chorafas and Heinrich Steinmann (1991). *Expert Systems in Banking*. Macmillan.
4 This is the so-called 'electronic data processing' or EDP. The new American definition of EDP as 'emotionally disturbed persons' has its origin in this basically batch-oriented mentality.
5 Warren Buffett (2003). Avoiding a megacatastrophe. *Fortune*, 17 March.
6 D.N. Chorafas (2002). *Modelling the Survival of Financial and Industrial Enterprises: Advantages, Challenges, and Problems with the Internal Rating-Based (IRB) Method*. Palgrave/Macmillan.
7 Two mathematical economists, Clive Granger of the UK who is emeritus professor at the University of California in San Diego, and Robert F. Engle of the US, also an academic, have shared the 2003 Nobel Prize for Economics. Both worked in the use of sophisticated statistical techniques that aid understanding of market movements. Engle's method is commonly used to analyze prices in financial markets which go through periods of low variance followed by periods of much higher volatility. Traditional tools of analysis assumed that volatility was constant. By contrast, Engle focuses on autoregressive conditional hetero-schedasticity (ARCH) which predicts volatility would depend on its own behavior in the past.
8 Dr Morton's contribution is that of considering equity capitalization as proxy of assets.
9 D.N. Chorafas (2002). *Modelling the Survival of Financial and Industrial Enterprises: Advantages, Challenges, and Problems with the Internal Rating-Based (IRB) Method*. Palgrave/Macmillan.
10 D.N. Chorafas (2004). *Operational Risk Control with Basel II*. Butterworth-Heinemann.
11 Warren Buffett (2003). Avoiding a megacatastrophe. *Fortune*, 17 March.

12 Internal ratings, supervisory weights and collateral

12.1 Introduction

Chapters 10 and 11 have illustrated the evolutionary character of Basel II approaches to measuring credit risk, and brought to the reader's attention issues characterizing the supporting infrastructure. To be in control of exposure to default, a credit institution must achieve meaningful differentiation of risks within its loans book. Internal rating systems should be forward oriented providing warnings about risk drivers. To do so, they must analyze distinct but interconnected dimensions:

- Borrowers' creditworthiness
- Weights applicable to exposure (see sections 12.4, 12.5 and 12.6)
- Collateral associated to the loan (see sections 12.7 and 12.8).

In addition, internal rating systems should address all important credit risks, with both general and specific factors of exposure prescribed in detail – which may be specific to *our* bank. This requires significant advancements in methodology and analytics, as well as senior management policies adopted within Basel II guidelines.

To assure objectivity and independence of the processes of assigning credit ratings, as well as of monitoring the bank's rating system, the board should delegate authority and responsibility for credit rating to a unit independent of the loans operations. Beyond this, auditing must be accountable for reviewing the:

- Objectivity of the bank's rating system
- Way in which weights are applied, and
- Means for keeping collateral updated in value.

The implementation of a sound methodology would see to it that every borrower has a rating, and therefore a probability of default, which is used to compute the required amount of regulatory capital. These are basic premises put forward by Basel II, and they evidently impact on corporate governance and senior management's responsibility for:

- The adequacy of internal credit rating, and
- Its use in borrower evaluation and risk management.

All this contributes to the process of a sound economic capital allocation, along the frame of reference in Figure 12.1. The raw material is financial information subject to rigorous analysis. But financial information alone cannot be the complete answer. The

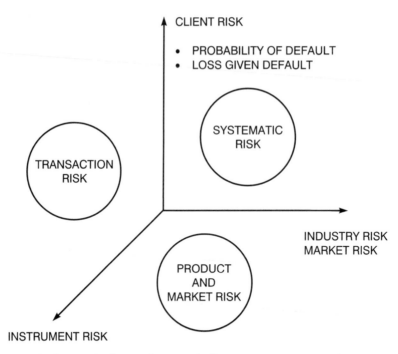

Figure 12.1 The frame of reference for capital allocation on an entity and instrument basis

solution adopted, or to be adopted, by a credit institution must form an integral part of its internal culture. Examples include:

■ Ratings-based lending decisions since the initiation of loans
■ Establishment of a dynamic system of limits for credit risk, and
■ Assignment of competencies, as well as remuneration systems which are credit risk-dependent.

Rating systems conceived merely to satisfy regulatory requirements, but not being used simultaneously for internal control and risk management, end up being counterproductive. The internal ratings-based approach is not just a regulatory exercise. Its most basic contribution is that of improving the bank's risk management policies and procedures, thereby promoting the stability of the banking industry in a global sense.

12.2 The volatility of capital reserves and Basel II

Credit institutions who chose to hold capital beyond the 8 percent adequacy requirements of Basel I, did so by analyzing and quantifying probability of default, as well as accounting for the effects of diversification and its opposite, concentration of credit risks. These banks have found that, as far as needed capital is concerned, required capital reserves over time tends to be a sinusoidal curve. An example is given

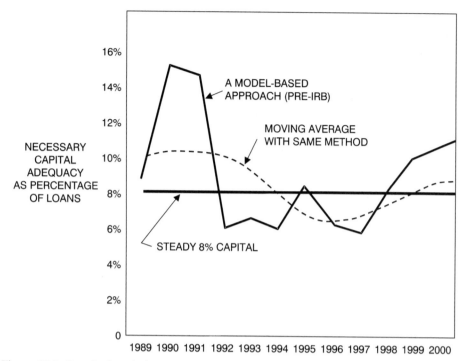

Figure 12.2 Required capital reserve over time, computed through an algorithmic approach (*Source*: extract from a study by the ECB)

in Figure 12.2, which has been computed through a method predecessor of the IRB approach.

The reader will appreciate that the results provided by this model greatly contrast with the straight 8 percent capital requirement, which does not change over time in spite of volatility in credit risk assumed by an institution. It needs no explaining that different portfolio compositions will give different sinusoidal curves, although all of them will tend to present over time a significant difference from the steady 8 percent of Basel I.

Indeed, the outcome of the quantitative impact studies presented in Chapter 1, documents what has just been stated. The difference is that QIS2, QIS2.5 and QIS3 have been snapshots, while the pattern in Figure 12.2 is dynamic and continues over twelve years. No two sinusoidal curves are equal because no two portfolio compositions are the same.

Based on similar findings, some regulators underline the prudential character of the minimum capital requirements in their jurisdiction, and the need to hold capital beyond this minimum. As the Deutsche Bundesbank aptly stated in its January 2003 *Monthly Report*, the relationship between the minimum requirements and IRB is in many respects similar to the relationship between the:

■ Minimum requirements for trading activities of credit institutions, and
■ The banks' internal models for calculating capital charges for market risk, in line with the 1996 Market Risk Amendment.

In that sense, the computation of both the minimum requirements for trading activities and minimum requirements for the credit business of commercial banks provide the necessary patterns against which to test internal models and procedures. The floor established through minima and maxima in capital reserves has played a crucial role in making senior management aware of capital needs, and in the longer run this assisted in reversing past trends. Capital ratios are not cast in stone. During the past century, average capital ratios have been declining:

■ From up to 36 percent in the 1860s
■ To 4 percent or less in the mid-1980s (see Chapter 1).

For each individual credit institution, the capital ratio was reset to 8 percent in 1988, of which 4 percent must be T-1, basically permanent equity (see Chapter 3). Such minimum regulatory capital requirements became generally applicable with Basel I and they proved to be a wise measure. A sound capital ratio:

■ Enables the bank to perform liquidity transformation services
■ Relieves different sorts of sequential service constraints
■ Gives confidence to the market in spite of asymmetric information
■ Acts as a buffer in case of adversity, and
■ Helps in executing payments and settlements.

Every one of these activities is critical to the correct functioning of the banking industry. In Europe, banks provide over 50 percent of capital needed for financing the non-financial sectors of the economy, as shown in Figure 12.3 which is based on

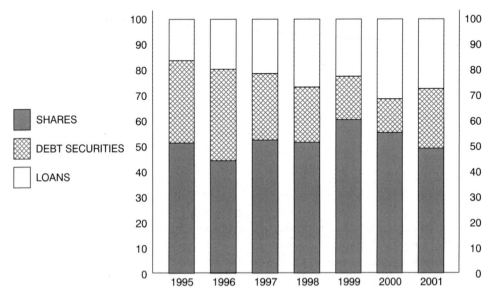

Figure 12.3 Financing of the non-financial sectors, excluding financial derivatives and other accounts payable (as a percentage of total financing) (*Source*: ECB)

	Bank deposits (% of GDP)	Bank loans (% of GDP)	Bank loans to non-financial corporations
Euro area	79.1	107.7	41.8
USA	37.7	50.8	38.2
Japan	110.7	103.8	72.8

Sources: The ECB, the Federal Reserve and the Bank of Japan.

Table 12.1 Bank deposits and loans in Euroland, the USA and Japan at the end of 2000, as a percentage of GDP

statistics from the ECB. Other interesting statistics are shown in Table 12.1, suggesting that only in Japan is there a rough equivalence between deposits and loans, with the former being slightly ahead of the latter.

As a percentage of GDP, loans are well ahead of deposits in Europe and in the USA. This contributes to systemic instability. Moreover, given the credit risks involved in financing, particularly in the negative economic climate of the early twenty-first century, many analysts – including rating agency agents – believe that loan loss reserves are now below the right level. The 8 percent capital adequacy is not a magic number, as the QIS tests and Figure 12.2 have shown.

A growing number of experts debit this mismatch between needed and available capital, not so much to management unwillingness but, rather, to the classical way credit institutions deal with the possibility of bad loans. With adverse economic conditions, how much more money banks set aside for bad loans reserves depends on:

■ How bad they expect the downturn to be, and
■ How many debtors may have difficulty repaying their loans.

The trouble is that without a rigorous and controllable methodology like IRB, quite often credit institutions underestimate their requirements, and they pay dearly such is the underestimating of risks they take. A study of thirty-eight large banks by UBS Warburg suggests that with the 2000–01 recession many among them have been too optimistic, setting aside too few reserves to deal with the likely prospect of:

■ Slow payments, and
■ Soaring defaults.

For instance, in spite of deteriorating conditions, in 2001 most credit institutions have kept reserves at 2000 levels. As 2001 rolled through, however, a worsening economy and rising rates of charge-offs upset their estimates. One of the experts participating in this research pointed out that even before 11 September 2001, charge-offs of bad loans had risen by 40 percent from the second quarter of 2001, while growing unemployment further increased the stress.

On Wall Street, analysts have estimated that, worldwide, seven of the larger banks needed to boost their reserves by a combined 40 percent to deal with the likelihood of a sharp deterioration in their loan portfolios. A UBS Warburg estimate has been that, given their outstanding loans totalled more than $800 billion, this 40 percent increase would knock out $6.4 billion from pre-tax earnings.[1]

Seen in this light, it is not surprising that QIS2, QIS2.5 and QIS3 pointed to the need faced by a long list of banks to increase their capital reserves, given the level of exposure they have assumed. In spite of the fact regulators bend the capital requirements curves (more on this later), through the QIS simulations many credit institutions found that they were short of capital. This is a good example of sensitivity to risk promoted by Basel II (see Chapter 1 on the QIS results).

Moreover, in connection with timely and accurate evaluation of credit risk, many credit institutions started to appreciate that credit volatility increases with the reduction of credit rating. Indeed, as Figure 12.4 shows, this is one of the weaknesses of fixed levels of reserves – and of current internal rating systems – which do not account for the volatility of different grades.

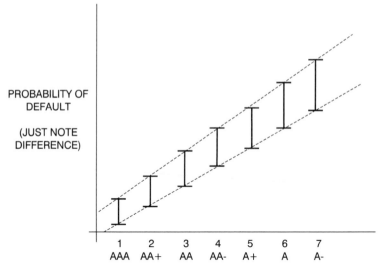

Figure 12.4 With lower grades the amplitude of probability of default increases

The fact that credit volatility ranges between a higher and lower value at the same threshold leads to the outcome that three different ratings can at some time have the same probability of default, but their ranges are diverse Regulators are currently looking into this issue. Another subject which by all accounts needs fixing is the effect of company size to probability of default. Big companies do not default at the same rate small companies do. Other things being equal, small companies have a higher likelihood of default, particularly in their early life.

Finally, it is appropriate to consider the issue of disclosure to the regulators and for market discipline reasons. Under Basel II, credit institutions seeking to qualify for one of the two IRB approaches must disclose in their annual accounts aggregated risk information, such as forecast and actual PD, LGD and EAD per rating class. This data can be used by market participants to obtain a clearer picture of the institution's risk structure.

12.3 Meeting the prerequisites of layers of supervision

The Basel Committee has advanced eight basic requirements for banks to be eligible for the IRB approaches. The first is having a meaningful differentiation of credit risks in internal ratings; the second concerns completeness and integrity of rating responsibilities; the third addresses criteria and the orientation of a rating system.

A fourth prerequisite sets minimum requirements for estimation of probability of default; a fifth regards the oversight of rating system and of evaluation processes; the sixth, calls for a solid IT solution (see Chapter 11), dependable data collection and reliable technology systems. Two more prerequisites are factual and documented internal validation of IRB results; and dependable disclosure procedures for the supervisors and for market discipline.

Still under discussion is a question of balance regarding data which would make it possible to infer information about individual borrowers. Associated with this, however, are issues which make data collection and analysis problematic in terms of data protection. Some information is not published, but the screening between publishable and non-publishable data is still one of the rough edges of the new regulation, which will be smoothed out in time.

A similar statement is valid about some of the other prerequisites, briefly outlined in the opening paragraphs of this section. Take, as an example, the first basic requirement – that of having a meaningful differentiation of credit risks. Credit risk quantification by means of a dependable estimation of PD, LGD and EAD means that:

- Each legal entity to which a loan is made must first be rated, and
- Cumulative failures associated with risk factors will be databased and datamined in search of patterns, as in Figure 12.5.

Aware of the impact of cumulative default patterns, Basel II has introduced the concept of cumulative default rates (CDR). To assure that a given risk weight is appropriate for a particular credit risk assessment, the Basel Committee recommends that regulators evaluate the cumulative default rate associated with all issues assigned to the same credit rating.

To provide a sense of a longer-term default experience, supervisors should evaluate the ten-year average of the three-year CDR, provided this depth of data is available. They should also consider the most recent three-year CDR associated with each risk assessment.

Patterning is part of the IRB approaches, because it greatly assists in handling loans and problem loans. Patterns are shaped by rules concerning the management of credit business. The appropriate preparatory work requires finer-grain risk identification and classification of risks. A good internal rating system would be:

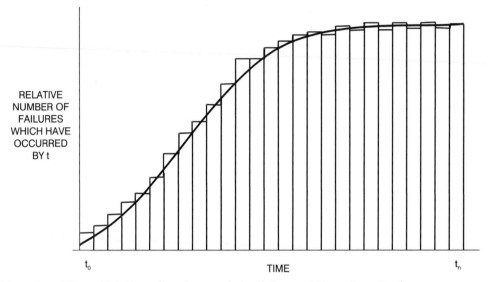

Figure 12.5 Recording the cumulative failures within a given timeframe

- Transparent
- Predictive, and
- Documented.

When these prerequisites are fulfilled, the IRB solution can help in several ways with credit risk control, capital allocation and risk-based pricing. A good deal can be learned through the research work that has been undertaken by the regulators.

In an article published in *Latin Finance*,[2] Howard Davies, the CEO of the UK's Financial Services Authority, suggested that his organization has done a preliminary assessment of the 10 000 or so firms it currently regulates. The goal of this assessment was to identify the level of risk they pose, and to help in shaping ongoing analysis and monitoring of each firm under the FSA's authority.

Risk classification in the regulatory domain is necessary because, where firms pose substantial risks, the regulators have to monitor them more proactively. Where the level of risk is lower, the relationship will be more at arm's length, although such credit institutions and other financial companies will have to:

- Meet standards set out by supervisors, as in the FSA's *Handbook of Rules and Guidance*, and
- Submit regular reports to the supervisory authority so that it is possible to monitor the business of these institutions.

Classification, for instance, has been found necessary for sampling purposes. Under a newly established stratified sampling system, all firms under the FSA's authority are allocated to one of four categories described as A, B, C and D. At one end of the spectrum, with category A, the regulators maintain close and continuous relationships, and at the other end is a rather routine oversight. This is true of institutions in category D, based mainly on:

- Remote monitoring
- Cross-sectoral thematic work, and
- Sampling of particular lines of business.

The FSA is a good example because it supervises not only credit institutions, but also other financial companies like brokers/dealers. In the USA, too, brokers/dealers are subject to regulations covering all aspects of the securities business but they are supervised by the SEC, not by the Fed, OCC and FDIC which regulate the commercial banking sector. The SEC has established requirements to be reflected in a model for prudential control. These include:

- Capital structure
- Sales methods
- Trade practices among brokers/dealers
- Use and safekeeping of customers' funds
- Financing of customers' purchases
- Reliable record-keeping
- Conduct of directors, officers and employees.

Besides the SEC, American brokers are regulated by other organizations including the National Association of Securities Dealers (NASD). Depending on their specific nature, they may also be regulated by the Commodities Futures Trading Commission (CFTC), the municipal department of the treasury, and exchanges of which they may be a member, such as the New York Stock Exchange (NYSE).

The message the reader should retain from these references is that while the centerpiece of our discussion is Basel II, IRB and economic capital allocation, it is equally important to pay attention to non-Basel Committee authorities, and to their layers of supervision whose requirements have to be satisfied. Whether the entities subject to regulation are credit institutions, brokers/dealers, insurance companies, pension funds, mutual funds or hedge funds, in a globalized economy the standards should be universal, including:

- Definition of relevant credit factors
- Calculation of risk-weighted exposures, and
- Minimum capital requirements to qualify for a license.

Beyond such minimum regulatory requirements come the add-ons of each regulatory agency, which expand the universe of supervisory rules – particularly in a cross-border sense. The reader will remember that Citigroup has to report to more than 100 regulators, in the long list of countries where it operates.

To face this expanding universe of jurisdictions and supervisory authorities in an able manner, a financial institution needs a *unified methodology*. Short of this, it will be buried under the many layers of supervisory requests and their jurisdictional differences. Technology provides the answer *if*, and only *if*, it is employed in a sophisticated way, making sure that:

- Economic capital is calculated and allocated in a focused manner, and
- The financial standing of each counterparty is carefully assessed.

To keep risks under control, each counterparty's assets and liabilities, as well as the bank's own, must be most carefully valued. As Warren Buffett suggests:

> The valuation problem is far from academic. In recent years some huge-scale frauds and near-frauds have been facilitated by derivatives trades. In the energy and electric utility sectors, for example, companies used derivatives and trading activities to report great 'earnings' – until the roof fell in when they actually tried to convert the derivatives-related receivables on their balance sheets into cash. 'Mark-to-market' then turned out to be truly 'mark-to-myth'.[3]

Marking-to-myth has been generally promoted by two forces: the urge felt by managers, traders, loans officers and investment specialists to find a justification for their actions, where such justification simply does not exist; and the great shortage of rocket scientists with a deep knowledge of both finance and mathematics, to develop, implement and upkeep pragmatic mathematical models.

Neither is market discipline enhanced when quantitative and qualitative financial reporting is esoteric and obscure. 'When (we) finish reading the long footnotes detailing the derivatives activities of major banks, the only thing we understand is that we *don't* understand how much risk the institution is running,' Buffett suggests. It is a realistic expectation that, after the credit risk control parameters are settled, regulators will be looking in the most diligent manner at the development of a unified methodology promoting management control in all areas of exposure.

12.4 Problems and opportunities associated with risk weights

Correlations is one of the metrics which enters, as a parameter, into a unified methodology for credit risk management. The challenges presented with correlations have been discussed, in a fair degree of detail, in sections 11.6 and 11.7 of Chapter 11. The theme of this section, as well as of sections 12.5 and 12.6 is *weights*, another of the crucial parameters for the calculation of capital adequacy in a risk-sensitive manner.

Risk-weight functions translate a bank's exposure into a specific capital requirement. In their background can be found modern risk management approaches that involve statistical assessment of exposure. In principle, the corporate IRB risk-weight function produces a specific capital requirement for exposure assumed with the targeted transaction.

Risk-weighted assumptions are part of commercial banking, and of all other financial services. Typically, risk weights are computed in different ways by different banks, for many reasons – among them differences in jurisdictions, cutting of corners, and differences in interpretation. Risk-weighted differentiation is still too crude between various exposures, whether these concern:

- Credit risk
- Market risk, or
- Operational risk.

In general, prior to Basel II, risk weights were relatively static. The fact that this issue is dynamic was not given the attention it deserved. The after-effect of such failure carried all the way into modeling, because assumptions underpinning development and use of models impact on risk weights. For instance, as already stated, market risk is underestimated by VAR.

Dynamics aside, another reason making global agreements on risk weights fairly complex is the particularities of different markets. Moreover, the treatment of risk mitigation techniques like insurance and securitization is still in its infancy. Concentrations and correlations of risks are often ignored, and compromises affect risk weights and their use. For example, in the aftermath of QIS2, since January 2001 risk weights:

- For residential mortgages were reduced from 50 percent to 40 percent.

As Patricia Jackson, Head, Financial Industry and Regulation Division, Bank of England, points out:

> Banks tend to make sizeable losses on mortgage books only when higher unemployment coincides with a downturn in house prices. This correlation delivers, for a given LGD, a relatively high basic risk-weight curve, but when taken together with actual LGD numbers, which are very low (25 percent or so), it produces low overall capital requirements.[4]

- For other retail banking, risk weights were reduced from 100 percent to 75 percent – but were kept at 150 percent for defaulted loans.

The setting of risk weights by regulators, and changes made in an effort to find global ground, give lots of work to analysts who try to look at risk-weighted approaches and what they mean to the bank's bottom line.

It needs no explaining that a great deal of the success of an international level playing field concerns the correct level of own capital to be maintained by credit institutions – and this requires appropriate weighting of individual risks. Like any other standard established by or for an industry, weights must not only be computed but also calibrated. This is important in safeguarding the suitability and stability of controls applied to the financial system.

Risk weights can change the capital allocation framework. The Basel Committee on Banking Supervision believes that the average level of provisioning with own funds for capital adequacy reasons in the G-10 countries should essentially remain stable with a mean of 8 percent. However, each bank's individual risk situation impacts on economic capital. Risk-based capital requirements inevitably lead to:

- Raising the level of capital needed by some banks, and
- Lowering it in the case of other credit institutions facing lesser risks.

Therefore, when calibrating risk weights under the IRB approach, banks should account for the fact that the new capital adequacy framework provides explicit capital charges which were hitherto implicitly covered by other chapters. An example is operational risk. In general, minimum requirements associated with the use of IRB approaches include, among other issues:

- Integrity, completeness and accuracy of rating assignments
- Minimum requirements for the assessment of guarantors and sellers of credit derivatives and other instruments
- A rigorous method for internal data collection, and access to external data sources
- Appropriate allocation of weights for operational risks, including IT systems.

While each credit institution should do its own analytical studies, in an industry-wide sense the computation of a *representative portfolio* by supervisors can play an important role in calibrating risk weights. A representative portfolio should be designed to reflect:

- The weighting of various risks by asset class under the IRB approach, and
- The way in which risk assets are distributed among the various credit rating thresholds.

For instance, if credit risk capital reserves of, say, 8 percent relate to the weighted mean of all portfolio groups recognized by IRB, in some groups, such as corporates, higher weighting may be required because of credit risk concentration. In other groups, such as retail banking, risk-based approaches may lead to lower weighting.

There are, however, limits on how high risk weights can go. Take trade finance as an example. Regulators are confronted with two conflicting goals in trade finance. On the one hand, there should be available prudential reserves. On the other, a high level of reserves might have serious consequences on world trade, because it will act as a dampening factor at a time when the world economy depends on transborder trade.

Commercial bankers who promote lower weights for trade finance suggest that, historically, documentary credit does not have high risk. Even in the case of Russia and Argentina, countries do not default in trade finance because:

- This immediately stops their credit, and
- Their foreign trade risks close down.

Even without state guarantees, which are quite common, banks maintain that they rarely lose money with trade finance, hence the reserve level for issuers at 20 percent seems just right. But Basel does not wholly buy this argument. Its position is that confirming to another bank is equal to lending to that bank, hence the reserve should be more than 20 percent of the trade.

Similar arguments exist in other domains, affecting the level at which weights are set. It is no less true that, in weight calibration, account has also to be taken of greater recognition given to the effects of credit risk mitigation approaches. This requires a method of determining benchmark risk weights, particularly for corporates, as a function of the borrower's probability of default.

Notice also that, with Basel II, the *supervisory review process* (SRP) of Pillar 2 has practically equal status with minimum capital requirements, with particular emphasis placed on the need for qualitative banking supervision. Its main aim is to renew and restructure the supervisory review culture, as well as to provide a greater transparency in financial reporting.

With SRP, all credit institutions, and especially the bigger banks, are encouraged to make continuous improvements to their internal systems and procedures – including their technology and their internal control. A factual and documented computation of correlations and weights falls in this domain, because it is a cornerstone in assessing institution-specific:

- Risk profile, and
- Capital adequacy.

The supervisory review process also aims to capture external factors, like the influence of the business cycle, and risk areas which have not yet been completely taken into consideration when computing minimum capital requirements. For example:

- Interest rate risk in the banking book, and
- Uncertainties connected to measuring operational risk.

Supervisory review promoted by the Basel Committee enhances the dialogue between central banks and credit institutions, since the bank's own procedures become the yardstick of supervisory assessment to a much greater degree than in the past. Central bankers also aim to evaluate the commercial banks' and retail banks' ability to identify, monitor, measure and manage their exposure.

12.5   A case study with small and medium enterprises

One way of looking at banking needs of different industry sectors is that of a dichotomy between capital requirements for wholesale banking *vs* small and medium enterprises (or business loans). This distinction is particularly important in some countries. In Germany, for instance, the Mittelstand are a vital industrial employment factor.

In other countries, too, SMEs contribute a great deal to employment and, therefore, their financial needs deserve special attention. This attention should be commensurate with credit risks being incurred – but without unduly penalizing the SMEs.

Statistics on the weight on the economy, and on employment, by different types and sizes of firms, vary considerably from one country to the other. Therefore, generalizations do not mean much. A 2003 study by Forrester Research divided the whole industrial sector into five broad classes of firms:

- Very large
- Medium-large
- Small-large
- Small and medium
- Micro, or the smallest firms.

Forrester Research suggests that in the SME class come companies employing 10–249 people. This is a wide range, and the employment distribution is skewed at the lower end. Though such a range is by no means a universal standard, it constitutes a good frame of reference in defining who are the SMEs.

In order to give a helping hand in loans to SMEs and assist them to survive and grow, the Basel Committee made a significant adjustment to capital weights for companies with an annual turnover of less than 50 million euros ($50 million) – which will include part of the aforementioned range. On average the weight is:

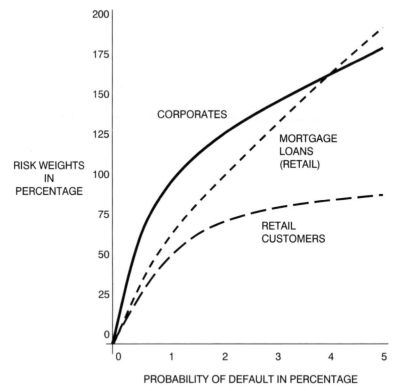

Figure 12.6 Bundesbank: risk-weight functions under the IRB approach (*Source*: Deutsche Bundesbank, *Monthly Report*, January 2002)

- 10 percent lower for small to medium firms
- 20 percent lower for the smallest companies.

Also, small businesses may now be included in the bank's retail portfolio, where there is less capital charge because, at least in Europe, personal bankruptcies are not common and this impacts on retail risk weights. Figure 12.6 provides a snapshot of risk weights for corporates and retail, as of January 2002. But is the relief for SMEs factual or is the issue of lending to them too political?

Lending to SMEs is both a political and a technical problem. It is technical because of the difference in issues characterizing SMEs and dividing them from big business. It is political because SMEs underpin employment in an economy and, therefore, stand high on the political agenda.

Given the fact of political patronage, the trend is towards more flexibility in SME lending. Basel addressed this issue by throwing at least part of the problem out of Pillar 1 and into Pillar 2, this means to the local regulator. Critics said that such an approach is not a long-term solution.

Typically, corporate (or wholesale) customers are few. They are primarily listed companies, and data on their financial conditions is relatively easy to obtain. By contrast, there are many SMEs, a good deal of whom are private companies, and therefore financial data is difficult to obtain. Yet, for a factual and documented decision on loans it is important to know:

- Past failures
- Past defaults, and
- Their ratings history.

There is also a critical question to be answered with a wider portfolio impact: 'What exactly is a portfolio of small business lending?' Fundamentally, many banks think that lending to a small business is very risky, but they also believe that the level of riskiness varies by:

- Country, and
- History of the SME.

There is statistical evidence that after it has survived its first ten years, the life expectancy of an SME improves significantly, and this should be reflected in risk weights. The downside is that such developments in terms of survival are not necessarily universal, neither do they constitute an unbreakable rule. Particularly in a downturn, statistics do not give much comfort.

More than 37 500 companies failed in 2002 in Germany alone, according to official figures. This represents an increase of 16.4 percent in number of bankruptcies over 2001. Some 274 000 people were employed by these companies, which suggests that on average they were of smaller size. Moreover, the resulting unemployment is bigger than the direct employment of failed companies themselves, because bankruptcies also adversley affect the outsourcers.

Indeed, including professionals who failed, as well as other entities, the total number of German bankruptcies in 2002 reached an alarming 84 428 cases, nearly 70 percent higher than the 49 324 cases in 2001. Statistics make depressing reading as seven out of ten of the bigger family companies in the EU in 2002 were in Germany.[5]

What these numbers suggest is that the survival of SMEs and family companies is by no means a sure thing when adversity hits, even if lending terms are more lenient. Many of them are undercapitalized. But at the same time these firms are pillars of employment in an economy. Regulators are therefore aware that something has to be done which allows banks to continue lending to SMEs. This can be seen in the fact that in the consecutive consultative papers of Basel II, weights for SMEs have been lowered. An example is given in Figure 12.7. This evolution in risk weights sees to it that lending to SMEs benefits from:

■ Lower correlations for high PD corporate loans
■ A reduction in requirements for smaller firms, and
■ The inclusion of very small companies in the even lower retail curves.

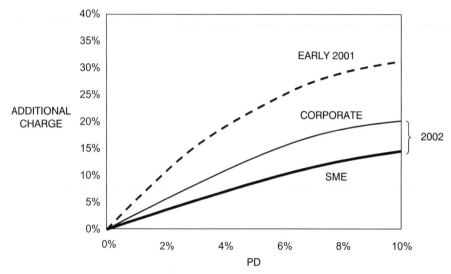

Figure 12.7 Capital charges for corporate and SME exposures (assumed LGD, 45 percent)

For instance, loans of up to 1 million euros to SMEs can be included in the retail portfolios as long as they are managed as retail credits, and meet certain other basic criteria. With the standardized approach in case a bank's total exposure to a small business amounts to 1 million euros or less, it can be counted as a retail exposure, which is favorable in terms of loss given default treatment.

The good news is that at least some evidence suggests that correlation among losses is less for smaller companies than for large companies – in spite of the fact SMEs tend to dominate the higher probability of the default bracket. The explanation of this most likely is that, as far as SMEs are concerned, defaults seem to be less concentrated in economic downturns than is the case with large firms. To reflect this fact, Basel has changed the correlations and the weights.

12.6 Risk weights with standardized and IRB methods

With the *standardized approach* to Basel II, risk weights are specified for certain types of claims. In addition to the familiar weights 0 percent, 20 percent, 50 percent and 100 percent, a new weighting factor of 150 percent has been introduced. This 150 percent factor is applicable to borrowers with a poor rating. There is also a class of asset backed securities. Table 12.2 gives the standard percentage risk weights.

	AAA to AA–	A+ to A–	BBB+ to BBB–	BB+ to BB–	B+ to B–	Below B– and defaulted	Unrated
Sovereigns	0	20	50	100	100	150	100
Banks 1	20	50	100	100	100	150	100
Banks 2							
<Three months	20	20	20	50	50	150	20
>Three months	20	50	50	100	100	150	50
Corporates	20	50	100	100	150	150	100
Asset-backed securities	20	50	100	150	1250	1250	1250

Note: The Basel Committee has also changed the treatment of defaulted assets, and flattened the curves, because the originals were too steep.

Table 12.2 Standard percentage risk weights, January 2003

The standardized approach sees to it that risk weighting in individual risk groups, mainly *banks*, *non-banks* and *sovereigns*, substantially depends on assessments by independent credit rating agencies for companies, and the export credit authority of the Organization for Economic Co-operation and Development (OECD) for sovereigns. Claims on sovereigns are weighted between 0 percent and 150 percent, depending on their rating.

The use of weights helps in making the computation of capital charge for a loan fairly straightforward. Say, for instance, that a bank has a loan of $10 million with an AA-rated enterprise. The capital charge is:

$$\$10\,000\,000 \times \text{risk weight } 20\% \times \text{capital ratio } 8\% = \$160\,000 \qquad (12.1)$$

This capital charge would have been zero if the same loan was with an AA-rated sovereign. By contrast, if the loan was with a BB or B-rated sovereign, the capital charge would have been $800 000 (the full 8 percent level). And if the loan was given to a B-rated enterprise (non-bank), the capital charge would have been $1 200 000, because the risk weight is 150 percent. This method is a refinement over the flat 8 percent capital adequacy requirement by the 1988 Capital Accord.

The pattern in Figure 12.8 compares risk weights of the IRB method with the 100 percent line of the standardized approach. Internal ratings-based solutions favor a portfolio of high quality. Low quality is penalized. As shown in Table 12.3, the top

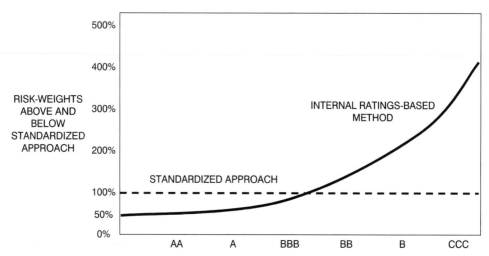

Figure 12.8 With IRB risk-weights are much lower for high ratings but rise exponentially with low ratings

risk weight under the standard solution is 150; with IRB it can go up to 625. Also, an 'unrated' class is not permitted under IRB.

Basel II provides two options for claims on banks, leaving it to the national supervisors to decide which one will be applied to banks in their jurisdiction. Under the first option, banks are assigned a risk weight one category less favorable than that given to claims on sovereigns. According to the second option, a bank's risk weighting is based on the maturity of the loan.

External rating grade	Probability of default (%)[2]	Risk weights	
		Standardized approach	IRB approach[3]
Floor	0.03	20	14
AAA to AA−	0.03 to 0.05	20	14 to 19
A+ to A−	0.06 to 0.11	50	21 to 31
BBB+ to BB−	0.12 to 1.33	100	33 to 149
B+ to B−	1.34 to 20.00	150	150 to 625
Cap	20.00	150	625
Unrated		100	

Notes:
1 ECB (2001). *Monthly Bulletin*, May.
2 According to KMV Corporation data.
3 Based on maturity assumption of three years, loss given default of 50 percent and exposure at default of 100 percent.

Table 12.3 Standardized and IRB approaches for corporate credits[1]

- Lower risk weights apply to lending and refinancing in domestic currency, if the original maturity is three months or less.
- Within certain limits, short-term claims, with a maturity of three months or less, are assigned a preferential risk weight.

Claims on investment banks and securities firms are treated using the same rules as those envisaged for credit institutions, provided that the brokerages are subject to comparable supervisory and regulatory rules, characterized by the same capital requirements.

Claims on non-central government public sector entities are weighted in the same way as claims on banks. However, subject to national discretion, claims on domestic public sector entities may also be treated as claims on sovereigns in whose jurisdictions these entities are established. Other classes of claims are of a retail banking nature. Basel II divides retail exposures into three main classes:

- Secured by residential mortgages
- Qualifying revolving retail exposures (QRRE)
- Other non-mortgage exposures (other retail).

Specialized lending addresses individual projects where repayment is highly dependent on the performance of an underlying pool of collateral. A class of specialized lending is that of high volatility commercial real estate (HVCRE). Banks that do not meet the requirements for estimation of PD, or whose supervisor has chosen not to implement F-IRB or A-IRB in regard to HVCRE, must map their internal grades to five supervisory classes. To each class is allocated a specific risk weight.

Claims secured by mortgages on residential property that is rented, and is (or will be) occupied by the borrower, are risk weighted at 50 percent. Claims secured on commercial real estate are subject to a cautious 100 percent weighting. However, a reduced weighting of 50 percent is also possible under certain conditions. These include providing evidence over a period of at least ten years that, on a national average,

- Losses stemming from commercial real estate lending does not exceed 0.3 percent of the outstanding loans in any given year, and
- Overall losses stemming from commercial real estate lending does not exceed 0.5 percent of the outstanding loans in any given year.

A new 150 percent risk weight category has been introduced for claims with a poor internal rating, and claims for which delays in payment have occurred. In particular, the unsecured portion of claims on any asset, net of specific provisions, that is overdue for more than 90 days is to be risk weighted at 150 percent.

One of the terms pertinent to risk weights is that of *granularity*. It denotes a unit of measurement for the number and size of the individual claims in relation to the overall volume of the portfolio. For instance, retail loans have higher granularity, hence risk weight exposures are lower.

The decision on whether an independent rating agency is recognized as being suitable to assign regulatory risk weights is taken by the national supervisors. To be recognized, the rating agency must satisfy several criteria, beyond that of having sufficient resources to carry out high-quality credit assessments, with ongoing contact with senior and operational levels of the entities being assessed. These criteria include:

- Its credit assessments should be regarded as credible by credit institutions, regulators and the market.
- Its assessment procedures should adhere to objective criteria based on historical experience.
- Its risk assessment procedures should be subject to ongoing review.
- Its rating should be independent of political or economic influences.

Also, the independent rating agency's methodology must be publicly accessible, and documentation on individual assessments should be available to domestic and foreign institutions. The best independent credit rating agencies, such as Standard & Poor's, Moody's Investors Service, Fitch Ratings and A.M. Best satisfy these criteria. In the USA, independent rating agencies are supervised by the Securities and Exchange Commission.

A similar list to that characterizing the dependability of the work done by independent rating agencies should apply to IRB approaches. Many money-center banks and other institutions have a good rating system, but this does not mean that they cannot benefit from the methodology, tools and rating thresholds established by independent rating agencies.

One of the problems with internal ratings as contrasted to those of independent agencies is that, with the exception of money-center banks, globalization makes it difficult to rate all counterparties in a homogeneous manner no matter where they are operating around the world. Therefore, outsourcing some of the credit rating to specialized independent agencies makes sense, and it also provides a more uniform methodology for credit evaluation reasons.

12.7   The handling of collateral

In order to gain perspective, let us start with the origin of collateral. The ancient Egyptian king, Asychis, is credited as being its inventor.[6] It seems that under his reign the Egyptians got short of money. To create liquidity, he published a law which allowed the citizen to borrow, using as collateral the mummy of their father or grandfather.

By all evidence, many Egyptians found no difficulty in separating themselves from their father's mummy in exchange for money, and several kept the loan, leaving the collateral with the lender. Therefore, a second law from king Asychis extended the guarantees offered by collateral by making the lender the owner of the borrower's graveyard.

- *If* the borrower could not repay his debt
- *Then* he could no longer use his graveyard for himself or his family. His *hyperperan* home was gone.

Apart from the interesting historical reference, this case is illustrative for another reason: it shows that collateral can be misused and, in some cases, abused. Therefore, regulators see to it that collateral has to meet standards, such as:

- Legal certainty: clear rights, ability to take legal possession
- Accurate, robust procedures for timely liquidation, and
- Negative correlation between credit quality and value of collateral.

The concept and the nature of collateral have evolved over time. An important feature of Basel II is the expanded range of collateral that can be recognized by banks using the standardized approach. The new regulation refers to such instruments as credit risk *mitigants*. For IRB banks, the different supervisory LGD values reflect the presence of a range of types of collateral, guided by common rules:

- Senior exposures must be divided into fully collateralized and uncollateralized parts.
- Fully collateralized exposures receive the LGD associated to the corresponding type of collateral.
- The remaining part of exposure is considered unsecured and receives an LGD of 45 percent.

Critical to this secured/unsecured distribution is the ratio C_E/C^*, where C_E is current value of exposure, and C^* is the required minimum collateralization level for this specific type of exposure. All this is a welcome level of detail because, in a modern economy, the proper handling of collateral plays a key role; it is, therefore, not surprising that the IRB solutions pay attention to this issue. Simulations have nevertheless shown gaps between the F-IRB method and A-IRB method in collateral handling. Because banks use lower LGD ratios than those expected by Basel,

- F-IRB imposes limits as to what sort of collateral is needed.
- By contrast, A-IRB makes it possible to use nearly everything as collateral.

Compared with the levels indicated with the first consultation paper, the Basel Committee has lowered supervisory LGDs in the F-IRB approach by 10 percent of the parameter – which means 10 percent less in capital requirements. For example, a senior loan unsecured is lowered from 50 percent to 45 percent. Also, more forms of collateral are recognized:

- Receivables
- Plant
- Machinery, and so on.

Time will tell if this change will present capital adequacy problems and, therefore, whether or not it will be maintained. A special case requiring a great deal of attention is that of asset-backed securities, as Basel II introduces a homogeneous international regulation on supervisory treatment of ABS. This, however, is not doing away with the fact that the computed credit risk is not necessarily equal to actual credit risk – a case especially present when taking portfolio effects into account.

A discrepancy between projected and actual credit risk is in a way unavoidable, and its existence has led market analysts and other players to develop ways and means for discharging credit risk. For instance, as Chapter 9 has explained, securitization has been widely used as a method of optimizing internal capital management. Securitized instruments are bought by investors who may:

- Keep them to maturity
- Trade them again in secondary market, or
- Use them as collateral for other transactions.

Banks using any element of A-IRB are required to measure effective maturity for each facility. Effective maturity is 2.5 years for banks using F-IRB for corporates – the exception being repo-type transactions where it is six months.

As far as derivative financial instruments are concerned, the effective maturity of the underlying exposure should be estimated as the longest possible remaining time before the counterparty is scheduled to fulfill its obligation. The maturity of both underlying exposure and of the hedge must be defined conservatively. Hedges of less than a one-year residual maturity, which do not have matching maturities with underlying exposures, will not be recognized.

Basel II provides standards for credit assessment and risk weights specifically addressed to ABSs. These are based on ratings by recognized independent agencies. In a nutshell, they are shown in Table 12.4 with ratings from AAA to BB–. Thereafter, from B+ to below B– and unrated ABSs the risk weight becomes 1250 percent.

Moreover, as sections 12.4 to 12.6 emphasized, the allocation of risk weights has an after-effect on credit risk mitigation approaches. Conservative risk weights make mitigation solutions more reliable, because they enable the credit risk factor to be quantified– thereby establishing a basis for recognition of collateral.

The good news for the finance industry at large is that the principle developed by the Basel Committee to guide the hand of credit institutions in risk mitigation techniques are now available to all investors. The methodology is intended to recognize collateral at a fair value for its usage.

- This fair value can be a market value, thereby requiring marking-to-market.
- Alternatively, it may be a computed value, whose algorithm has been defined and universally accepted.

Rating	Risk weight (%)
AAA to AA–	20
A+ to A–	50
BBB+ to BBB–	100
BB+ to BB–	150

Table 12.4 Risk weights for asset-backed securities

The computed value will be typically based on current market value of collateral received, plus some other factors influencing its value over time. The algorithm advanced by the Basel Committee on Banking Supervision in connection with the new capital adequacy framework, is known as an *adjusted value*, C_A, computed through the following algorithm:

$$C_A = \frac{C_C}{1 + H_C + H_E + H_{FX}} \qquad (12.2)$$

where C_A = adjusted value
        C_C = current market value of collateral received
        H_C = haircut appropriate to collateral received
        H_E = haircut to protect against volatility of the loan
        H_{FX} = haircut to protect against foreign exchange risk.

Risk weights provided to incorporate mitigation of risk by the collateral reflect the uncollateralized exposure and the secured portion of the transaction. All haircuts are applied to the current market value C_C, of the received collateral.

While these are supervisory rules and, as such, they must be fully observed, banks can improve the handling of collateral by using fuzzy engineering.[7] There are two advantages of fuzzy sets over deterministic and classical probabilistic approaches: they enable uncertainty (and there is plenty of it in evaluating collateral) to be handled, and they make it feasible to incorporate subjective judgment. Subjective judgment is unavoidable when evaluating what a given collateral is worth.

12.8   Remargining of collateral, credit derivatives and special vehicles

Standard supervisory *haircuts* assuming daily marking-to-market and remargining are shown in Table 12.5. It does not need particular explaining that daily marking-to-market requires a considerable amount of work, and it is under the constraint that there is a market for that product. This is not evident with ABS. Furthermore, with large loan portfolios, remargining can only be effectively served through high technology.

The formula for computing risk exposure for a collateralized transaction, after risk mitigation is:

$$C_E^* = \max\left\{0, \left[C_E \bullet (1 + H_E) - C_C \bullet (1 - H_C - H_{FX})\right]\right\} \qquad (12.3)$$

where C_E^* = the exposure value after risk mitigation
        C_E = current value of the exposure
        H_E = haircut appropriate to the exposure
        C_C = current value of the collateral received
        H_C = haircut appropriate to the collateral
        H_{FX} = haircut appropriate for currency mismatch between the collateral and exposure.

Collateral	Sovereigns	Banks/corporates
Issue rating for debt securities, by residual maturity		
AAA/AA ≤ 1 year	0.5	1.0
> 1 year, ≤ 5 years	2.0	4.0
> 5 years	4.0	8.0
A/BBB ≤ 1 year	1.0	2.0
> 1 year, ≤ 5 years	3.0	6.0
> 5 years	6.0	12.0
BB ≤ 1 year	20.0	
> 1 year, ≤ 5 years	20.0	
> 5 years	20.0	
Main index equities	20.0	
Other equities listed on a recognized exchange	30.0	
Cash	0.0	
Gold	15.0	
Surcharge for foreign exchange risk	8.0	

Table 12.5 Standard supervisory haircuts assuming daily marking-to-market and remargining (percentage)

To obtain the risk-weighted asset amount for the collateralized transaction, the exposure amount after risk mitigation must be multiplied by the risk weight of the counterparty.

This and other references made in the preceding paragraph should be kept in mind when planning risk mitigation strategies. Credit institutions need to rethink not only how they recognize the instruments they use for securing loans including guarantees, but also what they will be doing afterwards with these loans – from credit derivatives to on-balance sheet netting. A main difference between:

- The classical collateral, and
- Post-mortem processes like credit derivatives

is that, in the case of classical collateral of the Asychis type, the lending bank receives an asset that it can use in the event of the borrower defaulting. Under Basel II, eligible collateral consists of cash on deposit with the lending bank, securities issued by sovereigns and other public entities, banks, securities firms and corporates, as well as investment fund certificates and gold. (However, restrictions do apply to some of the above collateral instruments.)

With Basel II, banks are permitted to recognize, for capital reasons, credit derivatives that do not involve restructuring. This provision is valid as long as they have complete control over the decision of whether or not there will be restructuring of underlying obligation. In the case of *credit derivatives* and some types of guarantees, risk reduction is based on the promise to pay off the guarantor or the protection provider. Such a promise evidently involves considerable credit risk while, at the same time, there is a market risk associated with the financial instrument itself.

Moreover, a credit derivative guarantee must represent direct claims on the protection provider. It must also explicitly refer to specific exposures so that the extent of the cover is clearly defined and incontrovertible.[8] The minimum requirement for guarantees are relevant also for single name credit derivatives. However, additional considerations arise in regard to asset mismatches.

Behind these provisions is the likelihood of market risk. Because the markets are dynamic, the value of collateral changes over time. *Haircuts* to the value of the posted collateral are designed to protect against price volatility. In section 12.7 I have suggested that a dynamic application of fuzzy engineering provides better results than static haircuts. It is well worth always taking into account:

- The frequency with which the collateral is valued, and
- The possibility of demanding variation margins which affect the collateral's value.

Apart from the likelihood of a decrease in the value of the collateral, credit risk is always present because of probability of default of the issuer or guarantor, or plain weaknesses in contractual terms. Basel II sees to it that the factor applied to the collateralized portion of the exposure is 15 percent of the risk weight of the original borrower; this is known as the *weight* (w) factor, and it may be dispensed with for certain types of collateral.

- With short-term repo, securities lending and securities borrowing, and transactions with domestic government securities, a 100 percent collateralization is recognized if such transactions are subject to certain conditions, including daily remargining.
- But with guarantees and credit derivatives, the risk weight of the protection provider is assigned to the collateralized exposure. The application of the w factor is a new element in valuation.

Also with Basel II, collateralization techniques are enhanced through a risk mitigation approach which is applied even if there is a maturity mismatch between the loan and hedging instrument. The extent to which the mitigation of risk is recognized, however, depends on the length of the collateralized period in relation to residual maturity.

The reader will notice that the handling of collateral and of ABSs correlate. Not only can ABS instruments be used as collateral, but also collateralized obligations may be liabilities based, rather than assets based. Practically all ABSs are liabilities of somebody else.

Credit institutions securitizing their clients' liabilities try to hit two birds with one well-aimed stone. Through ABS transactions, they recover money they lend out and at the same time lower their own regulatory capital requirements without a corresponding reduction in the bank's credit risk. This process is known as regulatory *capital arbitrage* and, as we have seen, supervisory authorities try to stamp it out. New regulations require that a fundamental distinction is made between two types of ABS transactions:

- A *traditional* ABS involves a given asset of a credit institution, as the originator, being sold to a third party which has been set up solely for this purpose. This third party is known as a *special purpose vehicle* (SPV). The SPV refinances itself by issuing securities, the redemption of which is linked to the servicing of the acquired asset. Figure 12.9 shows, left to right, the way this solution works. Notice the existence of a credit default swap in the left half of the figure. Payments arising from the credit default swap are made only *if* a credit event occurs. In the right half, issue proceeds are used for hedging the credit default swap.

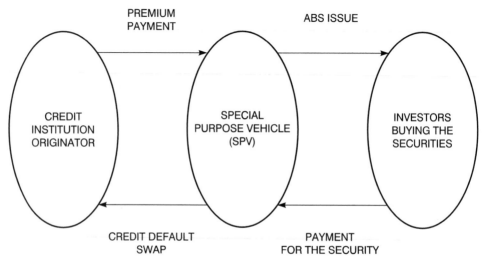

Figure 12.9 Asset-backed securities transactions using a special purpose vehicle

- Alternatively, with *synthetic structures*, the asset is not sold by the originator, but an effort is made to transfer the credit risk contained in the asset through the use of credit derivatives – by constituting a hedge.

In the case of the originating bank, critical for the minimum capital requirements is whether – and to what extent – the credit risk has been transferred as a result of securitization. The reader's attention has been drawn to the fact that this transfer is not self-evident. Therefore, regulators require that the explicit exposure is taken into account and weighted as a risk asset the bank assumes,

- By providing lines of liquidity, or
- By retaining individual tranches of ABS (see Chapter 9).

There may as well be implicit risks for the bank after securitization, in the form of non-contractual recourse. For instance, to protect its reputation, which is a business risk, a bank may counter a deterioration of the underlying assets by exchanging the claims that are subject to payment difficulties for more valuable assets.

In the case of collateral, the counterpart to this sort of market discipline-induced transaction is marking-to-market. If, for whatever reasons, the haircut no longer offers market risk protection, the borrower will be asked to provide assets considered to be more valuable. If my understanding is correct, explicit rules by regulators on the extent to which capital requirements should be tuned to fully account for implicit risks have not yet been concluded, but they are under consideration.

An article by Edward I. Altman, Brooks Brady, Andrea Resti, and Andrea Sironi, to be published in *The Journal of Business*, analyzes and measures the association between aggregate default and recovery rates on corporate bonds – seeking to empirically explain this critical relationship. After considering how credit risk models explicitly or implicitly treat the recovery rate variable, the researchers examine recovery rates by specifying rather straightforward linear, logarithmic and logistic regression models.[10]

This is a valuable input to bankers for their loans, and to investors: for corporate bonds, securitized instruments and credit derivatives. An aggregate default recovery rate analysis is a most timely effort, helping to explain background reasons for variance in bond recovery rates aggregated across:

■ Seniority, and
■ Collateral levels.

The core theme is that, fundamentally, aggregate recovery rates are a function of *supply* and *demand* for the securities in reference, with a pivotal role played by default rates. As Professor Altman pointed out, the issue of *recoveries* is associated to expected and unexpected losses. Moreover, it also affects procyclicality.

Notes

1 *BusinessWeek*, 26 November 2001.
2 *Latin Finance*, November 2001.
3 W. Buffett (2003). Avoiding a megacatastrophe. *Fortune*, 17 March.
4 P. Jackson (2002). Bank capital: Basel II developments. *Financial Stability Review*, Bank of England, December.
5 *Le Figaro Economique*, 23 March 2003.
6 J. Lacarriere (1981). *En Cheminement Avec Herodote*. Saghers.
7 D.N. Chorafas (2003). *Chaos Theory in the Financial Markets*. Probus.
8 Basel Committee on Banking Supervision (2003). *Overview of the New Basel Capital Accord*. BIS, April,
9 See also, in Chapter 9, the discussion on special investment vehicles (SIV). It has been a deliberate choice to maintain the SIV–SVP distinction.
10 E.I. Altman, B. Brady, A. Resti, A. Sironi (in press). The link between default and recovery rates: theory, empirical evidence and implications. *The Journal of Business*.

13 Software which can help in IRB implementation

13.1 Introduction

Chapter 11 has introduced the important role of a modern, advanced technological infrastructure and of fairly accurate models. The opportunities and risks presented by IT, and challenges posed by model risk, are pertinent to the implementation of Basel II. The computation, testing, application and updating of correlation coefficients was taken as an example of what can be done through mathematics and statistics.

The theme of Chapter 12 was the expanding role of internal ratings in credit risk management; the volatility of capital reserves and, therefore, weaknesses in the cushion being provided; and how supervisory weights assist in taking care of some visible and latent exposures. The same chapter also covered challenges associated with collateral, remargining procedures, the impact of credit derivatives and the role of special vehicles.

The present chapter is building upon all the above issues. Most particularly, it demonstrates how models can be put to work in mapping a real-life situation onto the computer, and what sort of benefits may be obtained from off-the-shelf software. In this particular connection it has been a deliberate choice to take as an example models offered by Moody's KMV – and their implementation in economic capital allocation (see sections 13.4 and 13.5).

Another pillar in economic capital allocation procedures is risk-adjusted return on capital (RAROC). The original RAROC was designed by Bankers Trust in the mid-1980s. Since then a whole family of models has developed around this concept. One of them is discussed in section 13.3.

The third important component of a rigorous economic capital allocation approach is capital measurement per se. One of the models I have found in my research and like most of all others, is Best Capital Adequacy Ratio (BCAR) by A.M. Best, the rating agency. This is covered in section 13.7.

The making of mathematical artefacts, but also the testing and control of eigenmodels, is the new business area of independent rating agencies. 'Today we spend much of our time on market risk and credit risk systems,' said Clifford Griep of Standard & Poor's in a research meeting. 'This gives us a relatively good information on account quality, even if the latter greatly depends on:

- Country-by-country accounting regulations, and
- Interpretation of these regulations by individual companies.'

In rating a financial institution, Standard & Poor's increasingly relies not only on external auditor statements, but also on the risk management models the bank has. 'We particularly focus on risk management models, value at risk and others,' Griep added. Because the now aging VAR is not that reliable, neither does it cover all instruments in terms of exposure, some banks and consultancies are advancing different derivatives of VAR, like return on VAR (RoVAR) – which is supposed to guide one's hand in economic capital allocation (see Chapter 5).

New, more meaningful and more accurate models are in great demand. Top-tier banks are now complaining that they are constrained to use slow-moving VAR estimators which can be beaten by a simple GARCH model[1] applied to P&L history. Like VAR, GARCH is also *ex ante* but more sophisticated. Banks which still depend on VAR answer that the purpose of VAR models is to produce a smooth capital requirement, and not necessarily to measure next day's risk with accuracy.

I do not agree with this argument. Neither should one forget that rocket science could be a two-edged knife. Models assist in timely risk management. But experience also demonstrates that those banks which are model-dependent are more active in derivatives because they have available real-time systems, algorithms and heuristics to measure their exposure. The irony is that this exposure increases rapidly and the complexity of new financial instruments sees to it that many of the available models become obsolete.

13.2   Mapping the analysis of bankruptcy patterns

An example of credit modeling is the mapping onto the computer of bankruptcy patterns. A mapping process which is accurate and documented can be an important contribution in credit risk control. Up to a point, credit rating assigned by independent agencies and default/bankruptcy patterns tend to correlate. However, there is also a downside. A critical issue with ratings-driven models is that the ratings may either:

- Not measure so well what they target, or
- Not measure it in the manner it is required by the models.

For instance, the way they are currently performed most internal ratings rarely track changes in default risk in a timely fashion. As a result, each ratings bucket includes companies whose actual default risk should put them in a completely different category. It serves precious little to process at high speed obsolete data (or models). This is what is known as 'garbage-in, garbage-out'.

Moreover, a properly maintained model would account for rating transitions and the probability of other changes which can reflect current conditions in a dynamic market. For this purpose, as Chapter 12 brought to the reader's attention, possible fuzzy engineering models provide a much more accurate service to their user than the two-valued system of classical probabilities.[2]

Still another problem with risk management models is that of underestimating exposure in economic booms, because of the tendency to implicitly extrapolate present conditions into the future. For instance, quite often the method for measuring counterparty risk relies on equity prices and it tends to show a lower risk of corporate defaults in booms, as equity prices are rising.

Another common flaw is that IRB systems used by banks to measure exposure tend to indicate a decline in credit risk when current default rates are low. This is an aftermath of reflecting the short horizon, over which risk is most frequently measured. At the same time, external credit ratings are often adjusted only after the materialization of some adverse events – while a better approach is to account also for credit risk building up.

With both internal and external models, hypotheses made about counterparty risk should reflect the principle that the rise in defaults in a downturn is better thought of as the materialization of risk accumulated, often unconsciously, during a boom. While from a practical perspective it is difficult to be precise when credit risk actually begins to increase during 'good times', evidence of:

■ Rapid credit growth
■ Strong gains in asset prices
■ Narrow lending spreads, and
■ High levels of investment

tend to have a negative longer-term aftermath. They are followed by stresses in the financial system, characterized by higher than average levels of counterparty risk, even if current economic conditions are strong. Failure to appreciate this type of exposure can play an important role in amplifying the upswing of a financial cycle, subsequently leading to a deeper downturn – like the one experienced in the early years of the twenty-first century.

All these are reasons why models and their hypotheses must be regularly and rigorously tested, over and above the testing of the algorithms per se. Both certified public accountants (CPAs, chartered accountants) and independent rating agencies have taken upon themselves this model-testing role. For instance, Standard & Poor's analysts are doing stress testing of portfolios to see if capital requirements are met. Time-wise,

■ They spend about one week per major derivatives line per company.
■ This may be one person-week or two person-week depending on the project, plus timesharing of the PhDs at headquarters.

As is the case with many rigorous tests, the analysts at Standard & Poor's are looking into model behavior under different scenarios, including extreme values (see Chapter 6 on stress testing). They also consider different types of model risk which may exist. Among model imperfections found through this type of research, by S&P's and other entities, are:

■ Failure to account for liquidity risk
■ Assumptions of orderly exits from the market
■ Lack of accounting for transaction costs, and
■ Absence of updates to accommodate the characteristics of new products and new markets.

Each shortcoming has its after-effect. The modeling of a given product may look great, but this particular instrument may not have a liquid market; or, it has a liquid market but transaction costs are too high, wiping out the margins. And there is always a need to understand the bank's liability structure which underpins every good treasury function.

One of the major tasks in model testing, which I encountered in my professional experience, is to understand the top management's tolerance for risk. After all, decisions targeting the avoidance of bad surprises like illiquidity, insolvency and bankruptcy, rest on the shoulders of the board and the CEO. Risk tolerance cannot be detected through written pronouncements. Instead, it requires:

- A look at trading results
- Flashing out exceptions, and
- Conducting frequent person-to-person meetings with board members and senior executives.

One of the strategies I have used in finding out the culture built into a given model is to ask the developers to explain why this artefact did not capture extreme events and outliers. While there is always the possibility that this may be due to model failure, sometimes the answers one gets reveal a great deal of the model's cultural background.

In all likelihood, in the coming years, value differentiation will be provided through the three-dimensional frame of reference shown in Figure 13.1. One of the dimensions, classical analysis, will continue with past practices – but it will be joined

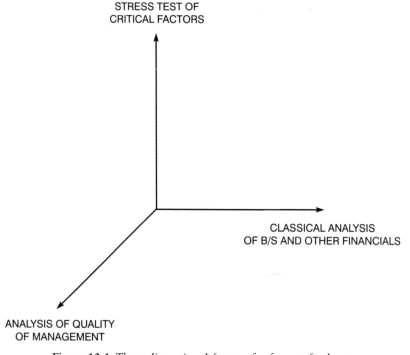

Figure 13.1 Three-dimensional frame of reference for loans

by the analysis of quality of management of the institution. Management quality provides both insight and foresight. The third dimension is that of stress tests,[3] which are a pivot element in both

- Model accuracy, and
- Risk-sensitivity in management decisions.

Another characteristic of expected evolution in loan valuation and management models is compliance with Basel II. This, too, is understandable. It is also a major benefit for credit institutions adopting the IRB methodologies, though even the standard approach is a step forward from regulatory rules and management control practices which have prevailed so far.

The eigenmodels background which I outlined, plus the fact that the development and testing of models requires considerable skill, and it can be costly, see to it that there is a market for modeling software. Provided this is of high quality, it may be worth the money it costs. It also makes feasible a common ground for different analytical approaches to portfolios positions. Sometimes it also helps to calibrate the banks' eigenmodels.

'A lot of our structure rating is model-based,' said Clifford Griep. 'Our work predominantly depends on fault analysis. For instance, in connection with loans we will interpret the behaviour of a portfolio versus fifteen-year ratings, examining the:

- Frequency, and
- Severity of defaults'.

Typically, the result of this and similar approaches which have become popular with the use of models are subject to Monte Carlo simulation and to recovery analysis. Another big chunk of model-testing is cash flow oriented stressing, including such issues as prepayment, spread and market risk exposure.

Standard & Poor's executives have also underlined the fact that, with practice, the risk management systems currently in use will become more sophisticated, leading towards a fairly accurate off-balance sheet modeling of exposure. Indeed, this is one of the potential benefits of adopting the A-IRB method. Banks that do so, sharpen their tools to eventually attack market risk – which, as stated in the introduction to this chapter, is currently served through VAR in a poor way.

13.3 Marking-to-model the loans portfolio: RAROC and LAS

Algorithmic solutions developed for the purpose of credit risk analysis are based on a number of selected critical factors, like the prevailing market value, characteristics of the loan, dependability of the counterparty, and certain chosen probabilities. Examples of such factors are:

- An overall default probability of the creditor, and
- The likelihood a loan would not default in the first year.

The loan is usually valued on expectation of cash flows, with the intrinsic value discounted at the appropriate interest rate. A risk premium is added to cover potential surprises. The best way to think about this added risk premium is as a sort of reinsurance which is not a single payment, but comes in stages, as credit risk exposure passes predetermined thresholds. This is the basic notion of practically all RAROC-type models (more on this later).

Sophisticated approaches to modeling pay attention to the time horizon. Accounting for the time horizon is important but there is no unique definition of it, as time horizons are different for credit risk, market risk and operational risk. For reasons of accuracy, the concept underpinning a time horizon must be examined instrument by instrument in connection with:

- Risk management
- Treasury and global capital needs
- Economic capital allocation
- Sales and trading, and
- Risk-based pricing of products and services.

For pricing and trading, for example, the whole projected life of the product or service must be accounted for in terms of risk and return. This requires a solid forecasting methodology as well as the use of confidence intervals. As shown in Figure 13.2, the curve of risk and return could turn at a moment's notice even amid a growing amount of effort to capitalize on market opportunities.

Inflexion points in a curve supposed to run smoothly, are a major challenge with all models. The aftermath can be severe because not only for loans, but also for all other instruments in which a bank trades or has positions, accuracy through marking-to-model is an integral part of implementing an advanced capital adequacy framework.

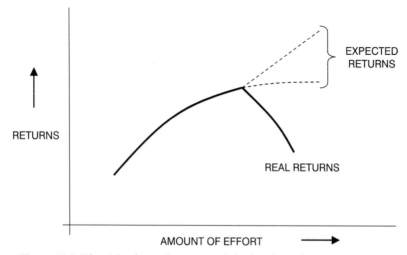

Figure 13.2 The risk of overshooting and the bending of the returns curve

- On the one hand, without a connection between the portfolio's market value and regulatory capital, Basel II will not work.
- But on the other hand, marking-to-market is not feasible for many of the inventoried instruments, because they do not have a market.

The reader has been exposed on several occasions to the fact that it is not easy to mark-to-market everything. With over-the-counter (OTC) derivatives, liquidity is lower than with other instruments, and market prices often lack meaning. Hence the emphasis placed by the Statement of Financial Accounting Standards 133 on *management intent*:

- Using accruals for maturity holding, and
- Marking-to-market the trading book.

Even so, the fact remains that outside the accruals method we need mathematical artefacts to help in the valuation process. But are we sure about their dependability? These are human-made solutions and, as such, they are prone to failure. Do we really know how good the models are that we buy or develop, and therefore how sound are:

- The hypotheses behind them?
- Their algorithms and heuristics?
- The data on which they are based?
- The tests which have been made?

It is unavoidable that there is *model risk*.[4] This has been dramatized in Chapters 11 and 12 through reference to Warren Buffett's dictum that, quite often, marking-to-model is 'marking-to-myth'. Indeed, one of the reasons why it is so important that members of the board, the CEO and the senior executives of a financial institution are both computer literate and model literate is that in the alternative case myth would carry the day.

Admitting, then, that marking-to-model is unavoidable, though it should be exercised with caution, and the models we use must be regularly tested and calibrated, let us look to one of the publicly available software packages for marking the loans portfolio. The example I chose is the Loan Analysis System (LAS) by KPMG.

The LAS addresses valuation issues originating in the optionality of loan instruments. In its design, it applies RAROC principles. In its mechanics, it accounts for differences between *internal* and *external* valuation criteria regarding loans. As far as loans are concerned such differences can be significant because of:

- Poor portfolio management
- Lack of market liquidity
- Securitization of corporate and other loans
- Failure to account for prepayment options
- Scarcity of information on rating of loans, and
- Lack of sensitivity to transition in borrower's rating.

In terms of organization and functionality the LAS rests on two pillars: cash flow and elements of structure. Cash flows are examined for their positive and negative effects on the portfolio's valuation. This method is no different than that used for intrinsic value calculations. Therefore, its accuracy is acceptable.

Structural elements include loan type (term, revolver, line of credit; fixed or floating rate); interest rate caps, floors and collars; fees (upfront and periodic payments); principal repayment; and grid pricing. Other LAS elements are call protection, collateral, debt seniority, financial covenants and exercise of options. All these elements assist in initial credit decisions by:

- Identifying portfolio credit exposures
- Providing credit migration paths
- Projecting future credit exposure(s) scenarios
- Assessing the value of loan structures, and
- Evaluating expected and unexpected losses.

As a model, LAS evaluates credit, uses transition probabilities in connection with rating, incorporates market-based credit risk premium and includes embedded options. Other publicly available software offers a fairly similar functionality, but KPMG stresses the added value such as attention to covenants and to security features attached to individual loans – in contrast to dependence only on the borrower's rating as a counterparty.

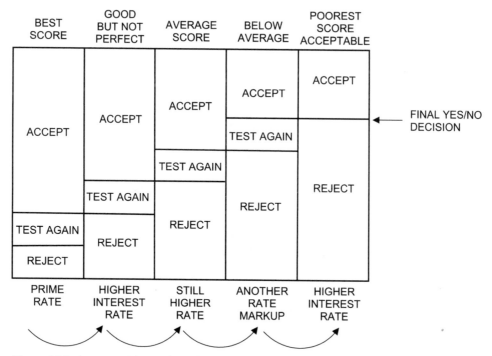

Figure 13.3 A sequential sampling plan avoids inflexible yes/no decisions taking reinsurance for higher risk

Both the basic and the value-added features contribute to the accuracy of the model's response with regard to valuation of the loans portfolio. This is where the mathematical tools underpinning the RAROC approach come into play, as well as other models widely used by the banking industry.

The concept underpinning a RAROC-type model is shown in Figure 13.3. The model is based on a calculation of risk and return. Through sequential sampling, the model is upping the interest rate of a loan, *as if* to provide a reinsurance scheme which offers protection for higher credit risk. This protection is paid through the interest rate differential.

The reader will recall that in Chapter 2 RAROC has been characterized as the first publicly available software for risk-sensitive pricing. While classically a loans officer accepts or rejects a loan application, RAROC follows an operations characteristics (OC) curve which allows it to capitalize on confidence levels and to price the loan by tranche of credit risk. This has been a major improvement on past practices, and it offers credit institutions the ability to value-differentiate their services from those of their competitors.

13.4   Moody's KMV family of models

Like virtually all independent rating agencies, Moody's Investors Service offers a suite of models which assist in credit risk management. To build up the skills necessary to offer such products at a time of growing competition and of demands for greater sophistication in credit risk analysis, Moody's has acquired three independent companies specializing in credit risk modeling. The most well-known among them was formerly called KMV, and the collective entity is now referred to as Moody's KMV or MKMV.

As demonstrated in this and the subsequent section, the concept underpinning MKMV's models is different from that of RAROC. As its basic credit risk model, MKMV employs Expected Default Frequency (EDF™) (reviewed in Chapter 10). There is an expanding poplation of default frequency models designed for credit risk evaluation and portfolio management in use.

Contrary to concepts underpinning RAROC, MKMV-type models treat correlations arising from variations in the default-risk credit state. They also model expected returns in excess of default-free rate. In this sense, they adapt the more classical risk *vs* return analysis to a dynamic frame of reference: *corporate debt vs equities* (see also in Chapter 9 the discussion on the Modigliani-Miller hypothesis).

Basic default-type models aim to provide a documented answer to the question: 'Given a portfolio, what is the incremental impact of the exposure I may be buying or selling on my positions?' One of the frames of reference in answering this query is the expected *return per unit of risk*, or the so-called Sharpe ratio (see section 13.6), within a particular time horizon. Note that one key incremental measure provided by MKMV in its Portfolio Manager™ tool is risk contribution, which is the incremental standard deviation in the portfolio return distribution at horizon due to changes in position of a particular exposure.

Two examples on critical statistics produced by MKMV are shown in Table 13.1. They concern market value of equity, market value of assets (MVA, an MKMV term),

	Anheuser-Busch	Compaq Computer
Market value of equity in $ billion	33.8	30.1
Market value of assets in $ billion	44.1	42.3
Asset volatility[1]	21%	39%
EDF (in a year)	0.03%	1.97%
Default point[2]	5.3	12.2

1 Standard deviation of annual percentage change in asset value. It is related to, but different from, equity volatility.
2 Default point is the asset value at which the company will default.

Table 13.1 Two examples of crucial statistics computed by KMV

asset volatility, one-year probability of default (termed the expectd default frequency, or EDF, by MKV), and default point. The metrics concern two well-known companies: Anheuser-Busch and Compaq Computer (since the computation, the default point of Compaq significantly deteriorated and, subsequently, the company merged with Hewlett-Packard).

In the KMV model, the computation of the market value of assets involves a proprietary algorithm which expresses the market's view of the value of the firm, using such variables as:

- Equity market capitalization
- Equity volatility, and
- Liability structure.

Since the market value of assets is not directly observable, it must be computed in conjunction with some algorithm. MKMV uses a variant on the Merton structural model (particularly the Vasicek-Kealhofer model) which treats equity value as a call option on the firm's underlying assets. MVA, then, is an estimate of the market value of the firm's assets, computed using the Vasicek-Kealhofer model and the following parameters:

- Market characteristics of the firm's equity, and
- The book value of the entity's liabilities.

If equity is a call option on the value of the firm, then the value of the assets exceeds the value of the equity, unless the strike price is negative.

Market value of assets, asset volatility and default probabilities correlate. Moody's KMV offers default probabilities from one year to five years. In so doing, it capitalizes on a database containing about 26 000 active public companies and about 110 000 active private companies worldwide. The output from this database helps banks in making lending decisions, as well as in pricing their loans.

A much more complex task is that of pricing tranched credit derivatives instruments such as collateralized debt obligations (CDOs). To price such instruments one needs to know the complete probability distribution of potential losses in the underlying portfolio. The distribution of potential losses in the underlying portfolio must be computed *before* structuring, or writing, either a collateralized bond obligation (CBO) – or collateralized debt obligations – which speaks volumes for the sophistication necessary on behalf of:

- The model,
- Its developers, and
- Its users.

Moody's KMV achieves this goal of a modeling complex processes using transparent economic models and a family of software products, as shown in Figure 13.4. Expected default frequency (EDF) has been discussed in Chapter 10 as it relates to current definitions of default. In practice, EDF tracks three different quantitative estimates:

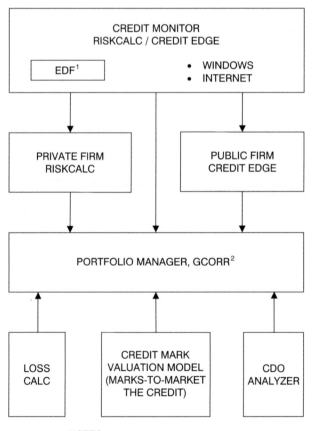

NOTES:
1 EXPECTED DEFAULT FREQUENCY
2 GLOBAL CORRELATION MODEL

Figure 13.4 Moody's KMV models

- Current market value of the company
- Level of the firm's obligations, and
- Vulnerability of the market value to large changes.

Probability of default is computed in basis points. Even a PD of 2 percent (200 basis points) puts a company in BB-rated territory. This can have dire consequences for stakeholders. Taking business statistics on the ABC company (a real entity) as an example of the model's output, the tool has shown that over one year:

- Total liabilities increased 46 percent, and
- Asset volatility went up 12 percent.

The five main modules shown in Figure 13.4 have diverse origins, but work together in the MKMV system. In addition, products are in development that target issues of Basel II compliance. In terms of their origin, the modules addressing public firms come from the former KMV, as do Portfolio Manager and CreditMark™ while RiskCalc™ for private firms originated from the former Moody's Risk Management Services (MRMS). (Both firms are now combined into the present-day Moody's KMV.)

A good example of the system's effectiveness occurred in 1998, when MKMV showed a sharp rise in WR Grace's probability of default. Within four months, the company went from good standing (an EDF of around 0.5 percent) to an EDF of 1.5 percent. Then came a steep EDF rise to 20 percent, which is the maximum quoted EDF level. Grace filed for bankruptcy in early April 2001.

The tool is an analytical approach that measures probability of default in a range from 0.02–20 percent. The careful reader will remember the reference made in Chapter 10 that the value derived from EDF represents default information contained in a firm's equity price, combined with its latest financial statements.

Changes are measured in one basis-point increments. Historical references are found in Moody's KMV databases. When computing EDF by industry sector, country or region, Moody's KMV splits the results into four classes:

1 The best, or E75, separates the upper 25 percent of companies from others in that sector.
2 The next, E50, represents the median value.
3 E25 marks the worst 25 percent, and
4 E10 marks the worst 10 percent.

The notion of the median value is that 50 percent of all firms have a lower than average risk of default and 50 percent have a higher than average risk. Figure 13.5 shows, as an example, the probability of default of US companies from 1997, as computed by MKMV.[5] This same figure shows the 25th and 10th percentile trend lines (items 3 and 4 above).

Moody's KMV associates the above four percentiles of EDF levels to each of Moody's and S&P's ratings classes at any point in time. (Note that these percentile bounds on each ratings class are dynamic in general.) For example, Table 13.2 gives the EDF percentiles on S&P ratings from AAA to D. Table 13.3 presents the model's

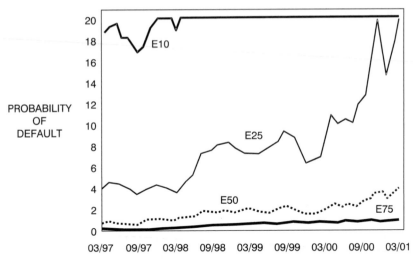

Figure 13.5 Probability of default of US companies in the 1997/2001 timeframe by KMV

results specific to nine different companies. The model encapsulated in EDF can be extremely valuable to portfolio managers because it tracks default risk of each entity through time.

EDF, used in conjunction with MKMV's Portfolio Manager (PM) can permit one to analytically evaluate credit risks associated with economic capital allocation (more on this later). Note that capital allocation in PM is based on risk contribution or tail risk contribution, and that standalone risk and portfolio risk are different quantities.

Information contained in expected default frequency serves senior management because it assists in determining decision-making factors closely correlated to a firm's credit metrics, including:

- Aftermath of changes in the company's current market value
- The level of a company's ongoing obligations
- Vulnerability of this market value to volatility and other variables.

Percentile	EDF	Equity rating
Min	0.02%	AAA
25%	0.11%	AA
50%	0.23%	A
75%	0.40%	BBB
90%	0.57%	BBB–
Max	20.00%	D

Table 13.2 EDF distribution and corresponding company ratings

Company	EDF (%)	Credit class
Nortel Networks	20.00	D
Xerox	11.61	CCC+
Computer Associates	5.63	B
El Paso	4.00	B+
Best Buy	3.03	BB–
Broadcom	2.94	BB–
AOL Time Warner	2.91	BB–
AT&T	0.68	BBB–
Federated Dept Stores	0.68	BBB–

Table 13.3 Computed EDF values and corresponding company credit class

It would be superfluous to point out that this information is dynamic – which is one of the reasons why it is so valuable. Credit outlook changes. As an example, in February 1998 median default probability for all US corporates was 1.2 percent. By the end of March 1998, it was 4 percent.

Models like MKMV's can act as prognosticators because volatility in equity prices and probability of default correlate. A company's equity market value is equal to its stock price multiplied by the number of shares outstanding. Equity prices contain everything known to markets. A basic hypothesis in this model is that the more an equity's value fluctuates, the higher the risk of default.

If investors collectively bid the price up and down, it could indicate general confusion about the firm's prospects. Eventually, stockholders may conclude that the company is troubled and sell their shares. For some of them, however, that decision will come too late.

Should one use actual book value of a company's assets, rather than market value? Investors who know how book value is computed, appreciate that it does not really mean much. In the end, market value may be the only 'intrinsic' value. By incorporating market value in its model, Moody's KMV offers an important advance in credit risk measurement.

13.5 Economic capital allocation by Moody's KMV portfolio manager

The general opinion of many experts involved in this book is that the first prerequisite for answering the question 'What should *our* capital be?' is to *decide on risk appetite and target rating*, for instance, AA, as Barclays does (see Chapter 2). This is instrumental in determining how much economic capital is necessary.

As Chapters 5 to 8 have demonstrated, the next major challenge is how to allocate the institution's financial resources. Capital allocation is a portfolio problem. Therefore, the answer to 'how much capital?' must be portfolio specific. A dynamic capital allocation approach can be sustained by using Moody's KMV Portfolio Manager.

Fundamentally, in capital allocation a portfolio manager must answer the query: 'When is a good deal no longer good?' Practically, what the bank does is to put credits and debits together and try to diversify exposure so as to reach its target rating.

To do so in a factual and documented manner, management should consider both expected and unexpected losses. MKMV has only one UL measure, and this is taken to be standard deviation of portfolio returns at the decision horizon. The estimation of unexpected losses has been discussed in Chapter 7, section 7.7, using the Deutsche Bundesbank's methodology and algorithms, as well as in Chapter 8, section 4 using a modified Basel Committee approach. UL measurements are treated also in Chapter 14 in conjunction with the necessary management skills and foresight.

One of the advantages of Moody's KMV model is that it is doing away with specific correlations substituting them with a global correlation model (GCORR), which is part of the Portfolio Manager (see page 300).

The problems faced with correlations have been discussed in Chapter 11, sections 11.6 and 11.7. According to some learned opinions, these problems are one of the major reasons behind the October 11, 2003 changes by the Basel Committee in the way the internal ratings-based (IRB) method should be applied (see Warning at the beginning of the book).

Both risk and return must be kept in perspective within the framework established by the preceding paragraphs. To reach this goal, Moody's KMV supplements its modeling approach with correlations based on historical data. This information is used to forecast future asset correlations (MKMV does not model correlations of default probabilities rather it models asset correlations.)

The model pays attention to portfolio liquidity, since it provides the flexibility necessary to reallocate capital and other assets. This is crucial to optimization. The problem is that, in the majority of financial institutions, more than 50 percent of the portfolio is not liquid. When this happens, it poses severe constraints to optimization.

The process of optimization is handicapped because it is not easy to move out of commitments which are not very liquid. Neither can there be perfect information available for management decisions regarding the fair value of non-liquid instruments.

Moreover, optimization is a process subject to model constraints. Different models use different optimization algorithms and therefore tend to lead to quite diverse results. The careful reader will notice that negatives discussed in the preceding paragraphs primarily come from gaps and failures in methodology.

People and companies using models must pay attention as well to the hypotheses and definitions underpinning them. Because many economic capital allocation decisions suffer from a certain confusion with regard to asset volatility, proper definitions associated with model usage are very important.

13.6   Sharpe ratio: its usage and misusage

As section 13.5 has explained, the model used by Moody's KMV measures the correlation between default risk of borrowers and counterparties. In this section we are particularly concerned with correlations between default risk of different corporate bonds separated from interest rate risk and probability that the issue will be called before maturity (see also Chapter 11 on correlations). Another focal point is measurement of expected returns in excess of default-free rate.

Given a portfolio, what is the incremental impact of exposure I may buy or sell on that portfolio? The frame of reference within a particular time horizon is the expected return per unit of risk. One of the algorithms is known as the *Sharpe ratio* (SR); more precisely the marginal Sharpe ratio, and Sharpe index, of buying or selling bonds for or from a portfolio of investments.

Not everybody is of the opinion that the Sharpe ratio is a valid indicator of what it is supposed to measure. Frank Reilly, professor of business and former dean of the College of Business Administration at the University of Notre Dame, suggests it is possible to apply equity analytics to bonds and arrive at a Sharpe ratio. But Reilly adds: 'I'm not sure how useful or meaningful it will be.'[6]

Neither am I. However, to better follow the argument for and against the use of Sharpe ratio, it is important to clarify what this is – and what it is not. In a nutshell, in 1965, W. Sharpe, then a young doctorate student, proposed a simple measure of relative performance. This became known as the Sharpe index (SI). The algorithm is:

$$SI = \frac{R}{s_R} \tag{13.1}$$

where   SI = Sharpe index
        R = average, or benchmark, return
        s_R = standard deviation of the return.

It is:

$$s_R = \sqrt{\frac{n}{n-1}(R^2 - R^2)} \tag{13.2}$$

where   n = number of returns on which the computation is based, over a given time
             horizon T
        R^2 = average of squared returns
        R^2 = square of average returns.

In 1994, Dr Sharpe revised formula 13.1, and this revision became known as the Sharpe ratio (SR). The newer algorithm is:

$$SR = \frac{(E - R)}{s_R} \tag{13.3}$$

where   E = expected return over a time horizon T
        R = benchmark return over same T
        s_R = standard deviation of return over T.

The benchmark represents a risk-free investment alternative, *or* the rate at which an investor sources its funding. The so-called Sharpe ratio rule has been used for the evaluation of alternative investment.[7] Here is an example. Say that X and Y are two mutually exclusive investments. An investor should invest in a mixture of X, therefore not in Y, if and only if, $SR_X \geq 0$, and $SR_X > SR_Y$.

The justification for this hypothesis is based on the assumptions that returns on X and Y are similarly distributed, and investors prefer higher returns for the same risk level, or lower risk levels for the same return. This is an oversimplification which is too close to the saying about motherhood and apple pie to be of practical use in business.

In theory, but only in theory, in both cases of the mutually exclusive investments X and Y, the Sharpe ratio in formula 13.3 could be applied. If so, the standard deviation s_R will be that of excess return over time horizon T. There are, however, two problems connected with this approach, not necessarily appreciated by those who use it.

- There are no confidence intervals associated with SR, yet the use of confidence intervals not only becomes widespread but is also a cornerstone of credit ratings and economic capital allocation.
- The SR formula uses the standard deviation s_R in the denominator, and this makes the metric unstable when s_R is near zero because there is really no excess return to talk about.

Besides the shortcomings identified by these two bullets, the relatively unsophisticated SR is unable to consider clustering of profit trades (or investments) and loss trades (or investments). At the same time, while it might measure realized losses it neglects unrealized losses – which is a serious handicap in risk and return analytics.[8]

All the points made in the preceding paragraphs are major gaps in the SI and SR models, particularly under present-day conditions for real-time computation and reporting of gains of both *recognized* and *realized* losses connected to financial instruments. Frequent calculations, for instance hourly or ad hoc based on intraday data streams, might be thought to remedy this deficiency – particularly in connection with a portfolio's performance. However,

- Some of the frequent, intraday calculations are bound to show very small s, and
- The lack of confidence intervals as well as the model's instability remain major problems.

It is surprising that not too many financial institutions see the limitations of this and other models which they use. Supposing that the limitations to which I make reference do not really exist, which is indeed a far-fetched assumption; the SR algorithm might work on the hypothesis that the values of the assets we analyze are normally distributed. However, in this case, too, it should be noted that:

- *If* we compare the performance of different businesses leading to very different return distributions
- *Then* a Sharpe-like rule, index or ratio, may mislead the investor's mindset in terms of asset choices.

In conclusion, as with all models, one has to be very careful with the hypotheses made, the algorithms underpinning them, the limits to which these artefacts can perform, the accuracy of available data, the conditions which characterize the data being used and the pitfalls which exist on the way. The Sharpe ratio/index is just an example of model risk. There are hundreds of models in banking today whose employment often defies good sense – because they are seen as a 'novelty' and 'sophisticated', whatever these words may mean.

13.7 Implementing the Best Capital Adequacy Ratio

Much can be learned in terms of economic capital allocation in banking from policies, procedures and algorithms that have been already been used with some success in other financial industries. This is the case of the Insurance Capital Adequacy Ratio (ICAR) which provides an estimate of:

- Capital plus reserves,
- Divided by an actuarial assessment of capital required.

This capital model has been developed by the American National Association of Insurance Commissioners (NAIC). Capital factors for the ICAR are worst-case scenarios. Independent rating agencies have also projected standards to judge the capital adequacy of insurance companies. An example is A.M. Best, which uses BCAR, on which this section concentrates.

Best's Capital Adequacy Ratio (BCAR) has been designed for property/casualty insurers. Its goal is to help them identify appropriate levels of risk-adjusted capital for their A&L structure. In my judgment, with some modification this model could be used by the banking industry in connection with:

- A focused approach to risk control which incorporates all pertinent elements.
- A documented estimate of capital adequacy based on risk factors.

Over the years, the use of BCAR has proved to be of help in indicating where there is excess capital that can be better used by the entity. It has also enabled A.M. Best's analysts to judge a company's financial strength. The algorithm is:

$$\text{BCAR} = \frac{\text{Adjusted surplus}}{\text{Net required capital}} \qquad (13.4)$$

Adjusted surplus is an American financial term, in the insurance industry. Its Basel II counterpart is *total economic equity*. The reader will remember that total economic equity has been defined in Part 1 as the sum of regulatory capital and economic capital – the latter taken in its wider interpretation to include capital for tail events.

In the USA, A.M. Best uses insurance data which cover at least 100 years. In Europe, the rating agency is currently converting its algorithm to current conditions and terminology, always focusing on the insurance industry. One of the important improvements being built into the model is that of tax implications under the different jurisdictions characterizing the European financial landscape. Notice that in equation 13.4 the denominator, net required capital (NRC), is computed through the following function:

$$\text{NRC} = \sqrt{\text{B1}^2 + \text{B2}^2 + \text{B3}^2 + 0.5\text{B4}^2 + (0.5\text{B4} + \text{B5})^2 + \text{B6}^2} + \text{B7} \qquad (13.5)$$

where NRC = net required capital
       B1   = bonds default risk
       B2   = equities risk
       B3   = bonds interest rate risk
       B4   = credit risk
       B5   = loss reserves
       B6   = net written premium
       B7   = off-balance sheet.

For fixed income securities, B1 addresses default risk. This contrasts with B3 which identifies the risk of having to sell the fixed income securities when their value declines due to a rise in interest rates. The credit risk class B4 applies capital charges to different receivable balances to reflect third-party default risk.

For instance, higher capital charges are ascribed to unaffiliated reinsurance recoverables, as well as recoverables from foreign affiliates. Required capital for credit risk may be modified after taking into account collateral offsets for reinsurance balances. A similar statement is valid in banking, in connection to the loans book.

There are haircuts applied with BCAR, which reflect the volatility of assets. Under B1, bonds are taken at book value. The haircuts are: for G-10 government 0 percent, AAA and AA rated firms 1 percent, A rated 3 percent, BBB 5 percent, BB and B 30 percent, mortgage-backed securities 10 percent, mutual funds 15 percent, non-rated securities 50 percent and affiliated entities 100 percent.

For B2, equities, the haircuts are[9] for non-affiliated, public firms 15 percent; non-affiliated, private firms 100 percent; mutual funds 15 percent; affiliated, public firms 15 percent; and affiliated, private firms 100 percent. Alternatively, B2 can be adjusted to market value by discounting book value to present value. There are also haircuts for B4, loans: for performing loans 10 percent, and non-performing 100 percent.

The loss reserve B5 relates to risk of adverse developments which use up loss reserves, put aside for that reason. The company is required to hold capital to cover such events – which is the reason why this factor is a component of net required capital. To account for statistical independence of the different components, a covariance adjustment serves to reduce a company's overall required capital by about 35 percent to 45 percent.

Notice that, correctly, special attention is paid by A.M. Best to off-balance sheet reserves: the derivatives component B7 is kept on its own, outside the square root. This special treatment contrasts to the more classical equity risk, B2. Off-balance sheet assets are associated with risk factors at 100 percent. Several of these elements are rated by A.M. Best. Among them are:

■ Non-controlled assets[10]
■ Guarantees for affiliates

- Contingent liabilities[11]
- Bank liabilities[12]
- Collateralized assets
- Letters of credit
- Long-term leases[13]
- Derivative exposure.[14]

A.M. Best did *not* say so, but in my opinion it should be possible to adapt BCAR to the requirement of the banking industry, in order derive a capital adequacy ratio which satisfies the analysts' worries with regard to the exposure of a credit institution. A straightforward approach is:

$$\text{Capital adequacy ratio} = \frac{\text{total economic equity}}{\text{net required capital}} \tag{13.6}$$

where

$$\text{NRC} = \sqrt{B1^2 + B2^2 + B3^2 + B4^2 + B5^2 + B6^2 + B7^2 + B8^2 + B9^2 + B10^2 + B11^2} \\ + B12 + \lambda B13 \tag{13.7}$$

In this algorithm, the on-balance sheet items are:

B1 = loans wholesale
B2 = loans SME
B3 = loans retail
B4 = mortgages
B5 = personal loans
B6 = auto loans
B7 = exchange-traded equities
B8 = direct investments and similar instruments
B9 = FOREX
B10 = interest rates
B11 = commodities.

The off-balance sheet items are:

B12 = exchanged traded derivatives
B13 = OTC derivatives.

In the bank-oriented NRC formula suggested in the preceding paragraphs, λ is a weight reflecting the fact that OTC derivative financial instruments have a greater risk embedded in them than exchanged-traded derivatives because they are illiquid. Equation 13.6 can become more sophisticated by incorporating factors addressing tail events in a distribution of expected and unexpected losses.

13.8 Using BCAR as a step towards a comprehensive solution

Basically, what both the BCAR formula and equation 13.6 are saying is that by holding undiscounted reserves in a non-risk adjusted manner, a company is estimating its economic capital, let alone its surplus. This is true both of insurance companies (in BCAR's case) and of banks. According to A.M. Best, in the case of US insurers, surplus adjustments are:

- Equity adjustments
- Debt adjustments
- Potential catastrophe losses, and
- Future operating losses.

The reader will recall from Chapter 7 the discussion on first-order risks and second-order risks, as well as the algorithm developed by the Deutsche Bundesbank for calculation of unexpected losses. He or she will also remember that Chapter 8 has presented a formula for UL_{AA}, which stands for unexpected losses to be computed with a view to capital requirements satisfying at least an AA credit rating by independent agencies. Both these references can be used in connection to a more sophisticated structuring of equation 13.6.

To develop a comprehensive solution for UL, I would advise employing a system which integrates all of the foregoing references, plus RAROC. This includes the UL in Chapters 7 and 8, Moody's KMV and the banking version of BCAR discussed in this chapter. To avoid one of the formulas stepping on the toes of the other, selection should not be indiscriminate, but based on rational choices which respect the risk profile of the bank putting together the planning and control system for economic capital management.

A question I have asked José Sanchez-Crespo, general manager of European operations A.M. Best, during our meeting is how the BCAR capital formula compares to the National Association of Insurance Commissioner's risk-based capital equation. With ICAR, required capital is computed to support three broad risk categories:

- Investment risk
- Credit risk, and
- Underwriting risk.

José Sanchez-Crespo said that BCAR is a further evolution of ICAR. The A.M. Best model was originally based on the NAIC model, but its practical use has shown the need for improvements. Best Capital Adequacy Ratio itself had a bifurcation in BCAR between:

- A US domestic version which uses development triangles to adjust the baseline factors, and
- An international version which relies on analysts' judgment and inputs such as inflation, legal environment, profitability and reserve stability.

Like the NAIC model, the Best approach contains an adjustment for covariance, reflecting the statistical independence of different individual components. To determine the BCAR ratio, a company's adjusted surplus is divided by its net required capital, after the covariance adjustment.

Among the differences between the two models, ICAR and BCAR, the latter uses 1 percent expected policy deficit. This is a concept which can be nicely adjusted and applied to the estimation of unexpected losses (see Chapter 14). Also BCAR lowers the credit risk charges in connection to credit risk upgrades, when they happen. The criteria A.M. Best uses for credit rating are shown in Table 13.4.

As an example, in Table 13.5 is a distribution of gross required capital generated by applying the BCAR capital model to the property/casualty industry in 2000. A significantly greater proportion of capital is needed with BCAR to support the premium component, than with the ICAR model. This is reflecting A.M. Best's more stringent risk factors.

The reader's attention is also brought to the correspondence between implied capital strength rating and absolute BCAR results, shown in Table 13.6. A.M. Best's absolute capital adequacy ratio indicates whether a rated company's capital strength aligns with *secure-vulnerable* rating. This addresses the specific risk of a firm's operation.

■ An absolute ratio below 100 percent would be considered to be *vulnerable*.
■ This means its indicated expected policyholder deficit is greater than 1 percent.

---

1 Business profile

Market position and competition analysis
Product mix
Distribution channels

2 Management and strategy

Overall corporate strategy
Management experience
Financial strategy
Acquisition or divestment strategy

3 Operating performance

Total: analysis of bottom line results
Technical profitability (underwriting)

4 Investment portfolio

5 Capitalization

Liquidity
Reinsurance protection
Reserves

All of the above, are always viewed and analyzed within a given:

Industry
Market risk, and
Regulatory framework

Table 13.4 Rating criteria for insurance companies by A.M. Best

Investments	36%
Written premiums	31%
Loss reserves	25%
Credit	8%
	100%

The details of investments chapter are as follows:

Investment in affiliates	15%
Non-affiliated stocks	9%
Interest rate	2%
All other	10%

Table 13.5 Industry aggregates in composition of gross required capital (2000, data by A.M. Best)

In determining a company's capital strength, the rating agency evaluates this company's capital based on the absolute BCAR relative to the secure/vulnerable cut-off, as indicated by the figures in Table 13.6. A few more words are necessary in respect of the calculation of covariance. A.M. Best recognizes the distortions caused by its square root rule covariance adjustment, whereby:

- The more capital-intensive underwriting risk components are disproportionately accentuated,
- While the less capital-intensive asset risk components are diminished in their relative contribution to net required capital.

However, tests made by the independent rating agency have shown that it is possible to counterbalance this apparent shortcoming. For instance, A.M. Best makes a number of adjustments to a company's reported surplus to provide a more economic

Implied capital strength rating	BCAR results
A++	>175
A+	160–175
A	145–160
A–	130–145
B++	115–130
B+	100–115
B–/B	80–100
C+/C++	60–80
C–/C	40–60

Table 13.6 Implied capital strength rating and BCAR results

and comparable basis for evaluating capital adequacy. These adjustments are largely related to equity, or economic values, imbedded in unearned premium reserves, loss and loss adjustment and expense reserves, and fixed-income securities. It needs no explaining that similar adjustments have also to be made when a model like BCAR is implemented in the banking industry.

Notes

1 D.N. Chorafas (1995). *How to Understand and Use Mathematics for Derivatives, Volume 2, Advanced Modelling Methods*. Euromoney.
2 D.N. Chorafas (1994). *Chaos Theory in the Financial Markets*. Probus/Irwin.
3 D.N. Chorafas (2003). *Stress Testing: Risk Management Strategies for Extreme Events*. Euromoney.
4 D.N. Chorafas (2002). *Modelling the Survival of Financial and Industrial Enterprises. Advantages, Challenges, and Problems with the Internal Rating-Based (IRB) Method*. Palgrave/Macmillan.
5 *Risk*, January 2002.
6 *Pensions & Investments*, 18 September 2000.
7 D.N. Chorafas (2003). *Alternative Investments and the Mismanagement of Risk*. Macmillan/Palgrave.
8 D.N. Chorafas (1998). *The 1996 Market Risk Amendment: Understanding the Marking-to-Model and Value-at-Risk*. McGraw-Hill.
9 The FSA has been asking insurance companies to take 30 percent as the stress test.
10 Amount of assets not exclusively under the control of the company, including assets sold or transferred subject to a put-option contract being in force.
11 A.M. Best requires thorough definition of contingencies included in disclosed value.
12 Banking liabilities held within consolidated operations.
13 Exposure is the total future minimum lease obligations through year 3, and beyond.
14 Exposure is the negative marking to market amount for derivative contracts outstanding at year-end. If exposure is positive, there is still counterparty risk that should start with a 1 percent charge and be varied from there depending upon number, type, and size of contracts.

14 How to be in charge of IRB

14.1 Introduction

What is meant by being in charge of the IRB method, or for that matter of any method which assists in prudent financial management, is that the credit institution is ahead of the curve in connection to its *solvency* and its *liquidity*. Failure to do so leads to catastrophic risks, from which banks traditionally suffer. By definition,

- A financial institution is *solvent* when its assets exceed its liabilities.
- *Liquidity* crises happen when counterparties ask for their money and such demands cannot be met even if the bank is solvent.

Depositors may ask to withdraw their savings which they entrusted to the credit institution, but the bank's treasury runs out of cash. When this happens, there is a run on deposits. Also, corresponding banks and other lenders may want to repatriate their capital, but this is not possible because the credit institution faces a liquidity crunch.

Corresponding banks, retail depositors and other parties may be induced to withdraw their money, fearing that the bank they dealt with might be in trouble. A vicious cycle ensures that once the fear starts it becomes self-fulfilling. Deposit insurance has aimed to break that sort of retail depositor panic, by providing a safety net. The downside is that without it, credit institutions would be obliged to follow much more cautious policies.

Liquidity crises can be met, if a bank can realize enough of its readiest assets to cover withdrawals. Sometimes insolvency can be masked if, through some artefact, confidence of depositors and lenders is maintained. Banks, however, deal in confidence, and when they start to run into trouble confidence runs out.

In blunt terms, the role of capital reserves is to see to it that this thinning of confidence does not happen. An internal ratings-based approach is an important tool in the process of assuring that the bank is well capitalized. Therefore, being in charge of IRB essentially means being in charge of one's own capital reserves – both regulatory and economic – at a significant level of confidence. That is what Basel II is all about.

As Chapter 13 explained, model literacy by the board, the CEO and senior management can be instrumental in reaching Basel II goals, and beyond. Figure 14.1 presents, in a nutshell, the hexagon which dominates economic capital reserves, a strategic approach aimed to ensure that the thinning of market confidence does not happen.

Practically every one of the items in Figure 14.1 has been discussed in the preceding thirteen chapters. It has also been brought to the reader's attention that paying lip

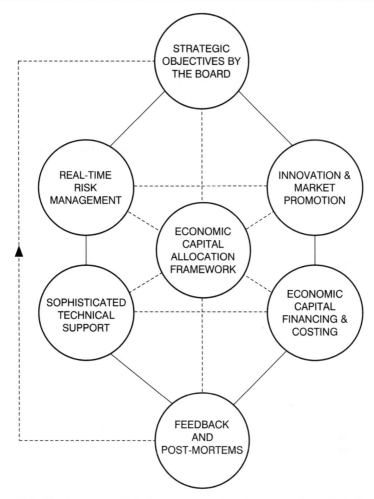

Figure 14.1 The hexagon which dominates an effective economic capital allocation

service to Basel II goals will not do any good. Being totally in charge of the IRB method requires both a policy and a system to manage risk through time. Beyond the real-time solutions we have to:

- Create the database
- Calibrate and update the models we use, and
- Benchmark and steadily stress test these models.

Everybody in the organization, at every management position, must understand the different levels of credit risk, market risk and operational risk assumed by the institution, as well as their change over time. Statistics show that in credit risk, for instance, the hazard rate of default starts low, rising rapidly to a peak at about four years. Then it decreases almost as rapidly at about ten years. Business plans made by surviving issuers begin to generate sufficient revenues to pay the debt.

This change in credit risk intensity and volatility is part and parcel of process dynamics which must be captured, reflected and reported through A-IRB and F-IRB methods. The opportunity to be in charge of one's destiny comes often. It knocks as frequently as one has an ear trained to hear it, an eye trained to see it, a hand trained to grasp it and a head trained to use it. That is what a bank should aim to accomplish through the methods and tools advanced by Basel II.

14.2   The risk of misinterpretation of financial information

Back to basics is the best way to look at financial information, its usage and misusage. One thing all management information systems have in common is the need to guard against the misinterpretation of financial data. There are a number of reasons why this happens. One is the limited imagination of managers, analysts and risk controllers – which is a human characteristic.

Typically, when we see a new phenomenon we try to fit it into the framework we already have. Few people truly realize where this leads. Only individuals trained in scientific research appreciate that until they have made enough experiments, *they don't know* whether there is really a difference in the data streams they get, let alone how important or how big that difference might be.

The second reason that leads to errors in perception and appreciation of the real situation conveyed by financial data, is the opposite of the first. While we think or believe that what we perceive is different, it may be something we already know. Sometimes, the same thing is repeated over and over again in a different form. This happens because:

- The markets have more than one way of doing or conveying similar things
- Markets tend to repeat their story over time but in a different format, which makes us think something has changed.

The third reason for misperception and misconception related to financial data streams, and MIS at large, is that data relates only to a small part of the problem; it does not map the bigger picture. This is precisely the background to Figure 14.2. There is often a larger picture underneath, from which things can be broken into parts that look different – like legs of the same animal or fingers on the same hand. The message conveyed in Figure 14.2 is that:

- To understand and appreciate complex situations we need a macroscope.
- Basel II provides the incentives to build such a macroscope over time, in connection to capital adequacy.

Given the complexity of the financial business, its globalization and sophistication, as well as the novelty of financial instruments, building a macroscope will not be easy, nor will it be fast. First, we have to establish the notions which underpin its background in the environment in which we operate. Then, we have to establish the way in which the five fingers will be put together with other elements to make a hand.

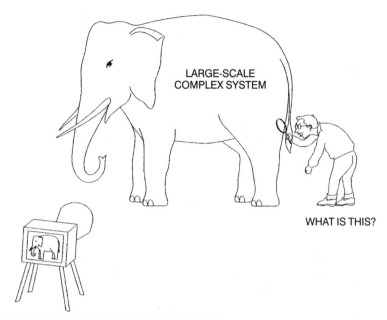

LARGE-SCALE
COMPLEX SYSTEM

WHAT IS THIS?

YOU CAN'T SEE ANYTHING WITHOUT A *MACROSCOPE*.

Figure 14.2 Many outsourcing agreements are large scale, complex systems, leading to loss of control by the bank's management

For instance, following this line of reasoning, financial institutions follow a policy which makes sure that exposure can be individualized by major counterparty – particularly other banks, large corporations, hedge funds and some high net worth individuals which are known to take big-risk positions. Then, the risk embedded in these exposures is integrated through rigorous solutions which call for a significant amount of management skill (see section 14.3).

In terms of financial analysis and risk control, two of the crucial elements are *relative capital* and *relative risk*; both constitute new concepts in banking supervision. Changes brought by Basel II to the rules regarding capital adequacy, practically align relative capital requirements quite closely with relative risk. This strategy significantly:

■ Lessens some of the distortions that have arisen under the 1988 Capital Accord, and
■ Strengthens the soundness of financial institutions in connection to their real capital needs.

By entering supervisory review and financial disclosure the concept of relative capital and relative risk have contributed to earlier recognition of problems by markets, banks and regulators. Leading to earlier corrective action by the bank's senior management is the fact that regulatory capital and economic capital requirement change through time, in line with the evolution of *measured risk*. Theoretically,

- This increases the banks' soundness, and
- It is reducing systemic risk in financial aggregates.

In practice, however, the degree to which such potential is realized, depends on how closely the risk being measured tracks underlying risk. One of the options under discussion is to design regulatory solutions that can act as a *built-in stabilizer*, limiting the procyclical nature of the financial system, which has haunted banking since its early days.

As an example of doable solutions to the procyclicality problem, Chapter 8 presented the policy established by Banco de Espana, the Spanish central bank. Behind this approach lies the fact that because capital and provisions provide a bank's main protection against expected losses and adverse events connected to unexpected losses, it is better to keep some statistical reserves for the rainy day subtracted from hefty profits made when everything goes well.

Within this notion of synchronization between relative capital and relative risk, provisioning rules can be designed to act as a flywheel of a credit institution – and, in the aggregate, of the financial system. This is why in Spain banks are required to create a provision against future losses at the time a loan is originated, with the size of reserves determined by the long-term historical loss experience for the particular type of loan.

Several regulators and financial analysts think this and similar approaches are likely to reduce the cyclical nature of bank profitability, by increasing provisioning expense in good times. Additional reserves would provide a cushion against loan defaults in bad times tuned to the general economic climate, not only to an institution's own exposures. The downside is that the creation of dynamic provisioning can lead to a write-down of the net assets of a credit institution.

- From an accounting viewpoint such writedown, at origination, is generally considered inappropriate because the fair value of a correctly priced loan should not be less than its face value.
- But supervisors take comfort from the additional cushion that the writedown provides, and ways may be found so that rule-based provisioning does not distort the financial health of a balance sheet.

In the credit risk domain, an alternative to relative capital matching relative risk is to require a provision to be created whenever the interest margin on a loan does not cover the expected losses arising from possible default. This can be based on the rating of a client firm and it can be assisted through RAROC. While provisions might generally not be required at origination, they may subsequently become necessary if the borrower's credit quality deteriorates.

This approach could be extended to full fair value accounting for all financial assets and liabilities along the model shown in Figure 14.3. This, too, has its challenges. The problem with fair value accounting is that, with the exception of credit derivatives, loans typically do not trade in markets, and their valuation is inevitably subjective, depending on:

- The bank's own assessment of the likelihood of repayment, or
- Valuation based on models which, as we saw in Chapter 11, in Warren Buffett's learned opinion may be marking-to-myth.

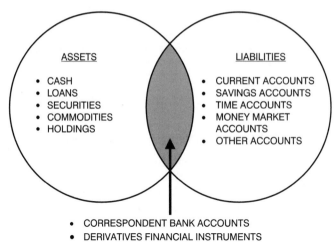

Figure 14.3 A framework for present value accounting of assets and liabilities

Indeed, some accounting standards boards worry that subjectivity and myth in fair value estimates opens up the possibility for bank management to use creative accounting methods – which is systematic misinterpretation of financial information. Therefore, the impact of fair value accounting on financial reporting depends very much on whether:

- Risk is assessed correctly through time, and
- Its mapping onto an entity's financial statement(s) is highly reliable.

It is interesting to note that a fair value approach evaluated at least daily through models and real-time execution may be instrumental in solving another current problem. This problem is the difficulty in forecasting *distant events* and unexpected risks (more about this, and what it involves in terms of management skills and technology, in section 14.3).

In conclusion, not only must the message embedded in financial information be properly read, but also a global view of exposure is instrumental in providing enterprise-wide management information. The latter helps to avoid the aftermath of extreme events. Extreme events, unexpected losses and senior management's action in their encounter are themes which correlate with management quality and the impact of being in charge of the institution's fortunes.

14.3 Management quality rating system by Goldman Sachs

The implementation of the IRB method of Basel II faces two key challenges. One of these is *completeness*. It should cover all exposures, both on-balance sheet and off-balance sheet. The other is *accuracy*, and with it materiality. An increase in accuracy requires a thorough revamping of the bank's accounting and technology, to permit data reconciliation in real-time. Both problems relate to detail.

- Many banks have few balance sheet lines, which is making reconciliation difficult.
- Very few banks have developed a method that is able to reconcile risk management with their general ledger.

Yet, risk management activities cut across general ledger information. This requires very significant detail in order to provide the institution with the ability to anticipate change, identify new opportunities and be ahead of the curve in pinpointing and assessing the size of sources of exposure.

These qualities and the means needed to support them have been important in every epoch. They are even more so today because, since the early 1970s, the long period of continuity of economic history came to an end and, since the late 1990s, we have entered an era of turbulence. Such macroeconomic turbulence, and its microeconomic aftermath on financial products, markets and companies require both:

- Management skill, and
- Human ingenuity to make intuitive judgments, under severe stress.

Therefore, it is not surprising that investment banks like Goldman Sachs put senior executives of companies they follow to the test. As a fund manager, Goldman Sachs estimates that nearly one-quarter of Britain's top 100 companies are run by managers who are either poor or very poor. The investment bank has also rated one in six of the best known cross-border European companies as poorly managed.[1]

It is not only corporate scandals, CEO malfeasance and outright bankruptcies that lead to growing unease about the worth of chief executives, prompting their scrutiny by investors. Senior management's overall performance, too, is being questioned. The rankings to which I refer have required Goldman Sachs to rate a company's leadership on:

- Competence
- Integrity
- Board structure, and
- Commitment to shareholders.

The rating system Goldman Sachs has developed uses a management quality score (MQS) in conjunction with a business quality score (BQS). This dual approach enables an overall judgment about a company to be reached. The investment bank's analysts award points on a scale of 1 to 5, with '1' representing a superior mark and '5' an inferior mark. The lowest rating means that:

- Managers may be placing their own interests above those of their shareholders, and
- They have a record of making bad deals, which could have been driven by factors other than those preserving shareholders interest.

Here is a practical example on conclusions reached by Goldman Sachs through MQS and BQS. About a quarter of companies in the FTSE 100 scored either '4' or '5', while in continental Europe thirty-six known companies received a score of '4' or '5'. These results are far from brilliant in management quality terms and they have raised questions about top executives' spiralling pay.

Among well-managed companies, pay should be commensurate with performance. But at FTSE 100 companies, for example, the investment bank's 2002 research demonstrated that executives enjoyed an average salary rise of 9.7 percent during 2001. With other cash elements, their earnings rose by an average of nearly 11 percent while:

- Management quality, and
- Company performance were dismal.

I bring up these facts in a book on economic capital allocation and compliance with Basel II because it is evident that under such conditions any talk of optimization in capital allocation, risk control and shareholder value is nothing more than fantasy. To reach its target in fulfilling the requirement of sound corporate governance, senior management has to have:

- Vision
- Clear thinking, and
- The ability to do the job well.

Vision, management skill, performance and high technology are four conditions for success in any enterprise – the more so when many unknowns come into play as, for instance, in the case of estimating extreme events and unexpected losses. Unexpected losses happen because of one or several of the following reasons:

- Bank management has misjudged the quality of its borrowers.
- Economic circumstances, or mismanagement, caused the downturn of once sound borrowers.
- The bank assumed a large amount of derivatives and other trading risks.
- The board, CEO and senior executives failed to diversify the bank's exposure.

Other negative factors have already been brought to the reader's attention: depositors withdraw funds faster and/or earlier than expected, the economic capital has been eroded and should have been significantly augmented, the bank's portfolio has been severely weakened, because of mismanagement or external factors, and extreme events have occurred which were not accounted for in economic capital.

This is by no means an exclusive list, but still it provides an appreciation of background factors which have a great deal to do with management quality. While what has been outlined are common elements to be found in many cases, other more specific reasons behind poor management may as well be present. Specific risks vary from one institution to the other, but a frequent occurrence is that senior management is too careless about the job with which it has been entrusted. When this is the case, the institution cannot be in charge of IRB, because IRB is a demanding enterprise.

14.4 Management's appreciation of unexpected losses

One proof of higher management quality is its ability to foresee and estimate unexpected losses. By means of practical examples on UL prognostication tools, we have gone through algorithmic approaches developed by different entities, and their associated methodology. Chapters 7, 8 and 13 have demonstrated that estimating UL is a challenging task.

Predicting UL is a mission falling not only to the credit institution's rocket scientists, but also – if not primarily – to its senior management and its professionals in all branches of activity. Management's appreciation of unlikely but plausible future events whose risk may have a high impact, is the foremost ingredient to being in control of the bank's destiny. Next to this comes availability of accurate models and of advanced information technology able to provide senior management with:

■ Exposure predictions, and
■ Other quantitative and qualitative input.

Chapter 7, section 7.7, provided the reader with the Deutsche Bundesbank's first-class example on algorithms and the method for computation of ULs. This has been expanded in Chapter 8 with reference to the Basel Committee's equation for ELs and Uls, as well as, through the examples which have been given in Chapter 13 including the distinction of three classes of UL made by Moody's KMV.

An issue whose consideration has been left to this chapter is how management establishes effective policies in order to be in charge of UL. Several qualitative factors are involved in this effort, including management's role in setting policies and procedures, making difficult decisions on risk and return, evaluating results obtained by keeping exposure under lock and key, and so on.

Alan Brown, who was for several years Barclays' Director of Group Risk, used to say that his credit institution calculates for each risk, and for all exposures, what they amount to when compared to the bank's whole portfolio. This computation is done steadily, it is accurate and it is made at 99 percent level of confidence. Still something may not go according to the projections – and therefore in line with the institution's exposure forecasts.

'You try to put volatility data at the middle of the curve, to predict what can happen in the tail,' Brown stated. 'This leaves you better off than having no calculation, but there is a danger that you might not quite believe in your estimates.' Even so, models addressing tail events help in getting a shot at *what if* scenarios, in case an extreme event occurs which, though low frequency, may have high financial impact.

Another senior banker suggested that, in his experience, when it comes to computing ULs, the simpler approach is scenario analysis. His credit institution uses the existing risk control framework for estimating:

■ Unexpected events, and
■ Deviations from expected developments.

This approach, the executive said, requires information elements stored in several databases including: rating history, collateral history, risks which occurred in the past, extreme events and their impact (both in his institution and among competitors), defaults, and losses due to other reasons.

While more or less the same reference to databases is used for ELs, stress tests help in investigating outliers. This is assisted by results obtained through the Delphi method,[2] which helps in mapping expert opinions about future unexpected events. A solution practiced by certain banks is to use complexity theory to obtain a better approximation to the likelihood of UL. Its upside is that of providing a form of distribution which can be statistically studied.[3]

A dual qualitative and quantitative investigation of ULs is so important because supervisors need banks to calculate regulatory capital requirement as the sum of ELs and ULs. Banks must demonstrate that they are adequately capturing EL and UL at different levels of likelihood, and that their estimates reflect their internal business practices. Moreover, they must demonstrate that tail events of the institution's exposure are adequately reflected in its:

- Reserves
- Pricing, and
- Expensing practices.

The problem evidently is that extreme values hidden in a distribution's long tail are not that easy to detect. Indeed, this has been a relatively recent preoccupation of financial analysts and regulators. Because outliers may have a high impact, rocket scientists are now paying significant attention to the shape of the underlying distribution, particularly under extreme market conditions.

The director of risk management of one of the better known money-center banks said that a policy adopted by his institution is to try to reshape the density function of loss events in a way that would thin out the frequency of the distribution's tail. The graph in Figure 14.4 provides an example of this approach. The transformation is accomplished by:

- Getting the loss history under control, and
- Using high technology to permit more timely and effective corrective action.

Another credit institution suggested that its method is based on experimental testing of whether (and which) previously observed extreme moves are likely to be repeated. This is done in conjunction with extreme value theory (EVT) which provides a way of estimating the potential for extreme market moves.

Instead of considering the entire distribution, the application of EVT focuses only on the parts that contribute information about extreme behavior – essentially the tails of the distribution. As such, it enables a useful framework for assessing the adequacy of financial resources to be put in place. The downside is that, at least in principle, extreme value theory calls for distributions of a large number of positions and there are constraints regarding diverse origins.

At the very least, EVT can contribute a source of information for assessing overall levels of protection provided by different types of default estimates. Results can be double-checked through other strategies. For instance, considerable help in the investigation of ULs can be assured by means of classification studies.[4]

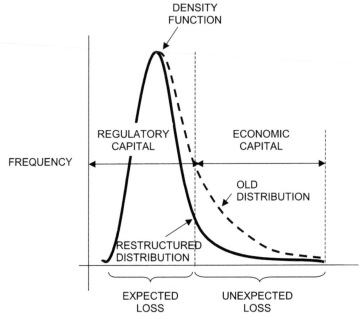

Figure 14.4 Restructuring the probability distribution of future losses of a loan portfolio, to thin out the tail

- Choices have to be made and these should be conditioned by Pareto's law.
- It would be hopeless to run after, at the same time, all reasons which might be found in the background of UL.

For starters, Pareto's law says that a small amount of a factor 'A' accounts for a great deal of another factor 'B'. This can be found in the background of power curves used by EDF (see Chapter 10). A good example of how to apply Pareto's law to a practical situation, is what Dr Robert McNamara, the former president of the World Bank, did when he was US Secretary of Defense.

McNamara's use of Pareto's law was to single out those items on which the US military should focus its attention. First a critical list was made classifying all items in cost terms. This way it was found out that about 4 percent of items represented 80 percent of costs. Then a second list was produced with the criterion being criticality in terms of military readiness. Here, a different 4 percent of items represented 80 percent of all items in the inventory of the US military, but the two lists did overlap up to a point.

Subsequently, these two lists were combined and, because they had common elements, the result has been that roughly 6 percent of all items amounted to 90 percent of a combined criterion which accounted for both readiness and costs. All items in this 6 percent were those to which the Secretary of Defense and his immediate assistants addressed their full attention. The three patterns are shown in Figure 14.5. That is the way to attack unexpected risks and extreme events. The method consists of:

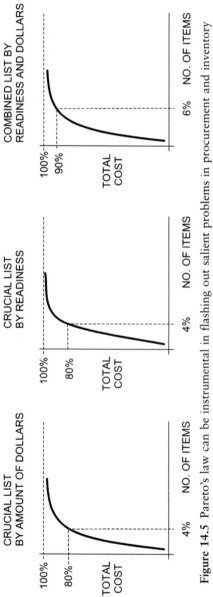

Figure 14.5 Pareto's law can be instrumental in flashing out salient problems in procurement and inventory management

- Sorting out all risks faced by the bank in terms of frequency and impact, and
- Addressing in the most rigorous manner those of low frequency but high impact;[5] the latter roughly corresponding to McNamara's decision-making criterion.

Compliance and legal risk can well be seen as counterparts of McNamara's readiness factor. Within this perspective, I would strongly advise to place the identification, qualification and quantification of unexpected losses in the top list of the credit institution's governance issues, putting such projects under close supervision by senior management.

A good example within this frame of reference is the attention paid to the control of operational risk by TIAA/CREF, and its evaluation of factors influencing investment decisions. TIAA/CREF is America's largest pension fund, the owner of more than 1 percent of stock exchange value. To help itself manage its assets, TIAA/CREF monitors twenty-five governance issues:

- From board independence and diversity,
- To the age of directors and their potential conflicts of interest.

Some 1500 companies make up its more than $100 billion equity investment. All these entities undergo regularly the aforementioned test. Those falling short under a point system devised by the fund, are subject to inspection visits regardless of market value or performance.

One does not need to spend a fortune to be in charge of quality. The budget behind the TIAA/CREF effort is about $1 million a year. The benefit is good governance by monitoring and encouragement of other companies' management to look after shareholder value. When assets are over $100 billion, $1 million a year is tiny in comparison to the benefits being obtained. According to TIAA/CREF this policy has provided first-class results.

14.5   Legal risk in a global economy and bankruptcy laws

Legal risk has been one of the reasons for ULs. With Basel II legal risk is a major part of the operational risk domain, which often finds its way into credit risk and market risk. Globalization accentuated the legal risk's aftermath. No two countries have the same laws, jurisprudence or legal system; but all three are determinants in defining legal risk at home and in the transnational economy.

For instance, the US legal system admits class actions and favors judgment by jury. It also accepts unlimited liability as well as high environmental liability. By contrast, in the UK there are no class actions (to date), the judges pronounce the verdict, there is a liability cap and environmental liability is not that high.

Legal risk is an operational risk that comes above the better known and, therefore, appreciated credit risk and market risk. Yet, in spite of its importance, the impact of legal risk has received scant attention in international financial dealing. Experts say that, if tested in court, many of the current transnational agreements will not stand up to scrutiny.

- This will have disastrous effects on business confidence, and
- It may even disrupt global trade because confidence is at the heart of the financial system.

The answer to the question 'Can I seize the borrower's assets?' is not that simple, and it brings under scrutiny the *legal risk* associated with the total entity *vs* single transaction and single entity concept. In case of bankruptcy, Swiss law considers the assets of the New York branch of a Swiss bank as part of the mass of its assets. In American law, it is the opposite: the NYC branch is a separate entity. Hence two different jurisdictions will make different judgments on the same bankruptcy case. With the separate entity approach, assets and liabilities will be sorted out at local level, and local lenders will have priority over its assets.

Indeed, as far as legal risk in global markets is concerned, the single biggest mess in international law is bankruptcy. Country by country, the bankruptcy laws may not be terribly different from one another, but they leave gaping holes when looked at as a system which defines the A&L of a transnational credit institution. Companies with experience in transborder court decisions suggest that such decisions tend to conflict.

The Basel Committee can recommend and approve capital requirements, but it cannot change the laws of the different jurisdictions. This has led plenty of bankers and other business people to suggest that bankruptcy laws are the Achilles heel of globalization. They also point out that legal risk, and other operational risks, are augmented by the fact that in a globalized economy credit institutions (and other companies) often engage in transactions that are:

- Initiated in one jurisdiction
- Recorded in a different jurisdiction, and
- Managed in yet another jurisdiction.

The globalization of business magnified differences in legislation, which have always existed, between countries. Legal risk problems get more complex because of differences in standards regarding:

- The courts, and
- The law enforcement industry.

Yet, despite the fact that legal differences play a king-size role, the likelihood of a transborder court fight are rarely considered by investors. This is tantamount to ignoring a major operational exposure and ULs associated with it. Because of transborder legal risk, investors should not lend to borrowers who can get into a global legal mess. The basic question a bank should ask itself, prior to commitment, is:

- Can we seize the borrower's assets?

The last thing one needs in bankruptcy of a global company, or in an international banking crisis, is courts fighting one another. Regulators can get together and agree much faster among themselves than can judges. Hence the wisdom of playing the devil's advocate. Country risk is a case in point. There are two most important issues with longer-term effects on country risk:

- Counterparty default resulting from multiple insolvencies, which borders systemic risk, and
- General prevention of payments by authorities, known as transfer risk.

In its internal measurement of country risk, an institution must also consider the probable financial impact of market disruptions because of country risk effects. With globalization, special attention has to be paid to the differences existing between insolvency laws. Insolvency laws in G-10 countries are by no means the same. In the UK, two parties, one of whom fails,

- Can net their exposure, and
- Only the resulting difference is brought to court.

This is the English *set-off* law. By contrast, in continental Europe not only does the set-off not apply, but also each country has different legislation on the underlying issues. Moreover:

- In the UK, insolvency starts at *noon*. This means that morning deals are covered.
- In continental Europe, Napoleonic laws specify *zero hour* insolvency. This means midnight.

In all likelihood, it will take ages for insolvency laws to change and to become homogeneous within the EU. Legal differences in a globalized business environment are so many that they cannot be solved on the run. A sound system has to be built which involves not only laws, regulations, counterparties and their management – but also the best legal skills available, information system support, feedbacks and post-mortems.

As these examples document, legal risk may well be the origin of ULs. It may also be an impediment to a solution to banking crises. In the case of bankruptcy, any solution requires legal certainty as to the owner of the claim(s) to future cash flows, or, a global insolvency regime. Legal certainty does not exist if there is doubt as to the jurisdiction in which assets are located, as

- Banks seek cross-border funds outsourcing
- Competitive pressure drives transborder aggregation of institutions, and
- More countries play host to foreign banks, which become economically important.

Cross-border funds outsourcing is a great idea *but* disclosure regimes differ markedly between countries, the location of the bank's assets is often uncertain, and the difference between banking failures and defaults (see Chapter 10) is to a large measure influenced by local laws and local politics.

All these reasons contribute to legal risk and, vice versa, legal risk has an impact upon them. They also see to it that claims fail to materialize as expected. One of the interesting aftermaths of legal risk is that not all depositors have equal rights – yet we read that in law all citizens are equal.

14.6 Longer-term liability and legal risk

One of the criteria for being in charge of IRB is that of appreciating the aftermath of an important development which occurred during the 1980s and 1990s and it has an impact both on finance and on legal risk. This is the issue of *liability* or, more precisely, of *who* is liable. Products and services which do not perform as expected are subject to a growing rate of:

- Liability procedures, and
- Demands for damages, loaded with ULs.

Both financial experts and legal counsels look at this liability development as one of the most important indicators of change in the customer–supplier relationship. The value of a product or service is no longer defined exclusively through its material characteristics, but increasingly depends on how the product or service performs and its after-effects. The asbestos case is an example.[6]

While Basel II correctly pays great attention to operational risk, and as we have seen legal risk is an important part of it, there is plenty that still needs to be done to answer the 'who is liable' question. The evolving legal perspective is that the buyer, an individual, company or community, reflects on the expected performance of a product not only prior to acquisition but also *after* the transaction. Therefore,

- The liability of designers, producers and vendors is not necessarily limited in time.
- The new perspective of liability might have a long life, well after the transaction's expiration.

The driving force behind the rich settlement Procter & Gamble gained in the 1990s against Bankers Trust rested precisely on these two points. Procter & Gamble's complaint had been that, some years earlier, Bankers Trust had sold it hedging instruments which were derivatives comprising a large amount of toxic waste. Essentially the buyer received in its books a great deal of risk rather than 'protection'.

An integral part of the development in the way supervisory authorities, and the market at large, look at liability issues, is that the very concept underpinning *due diligence* has changed. A disregard of the lifecycle of liability towards business partners can become a complex situation of unexpected losses. Take the Wall Street settlement of 28 April 2003, as an example. It included findings of fraud with associated penalties and disgorgements to the tune of nearly $1.4 billion as shown in Table 14.1.

Announcing the settlement in Washington, DC, William Donaldson, chairman of the Securities and Exchange Commission said: 'I am profoundly saddened – and angry – about the conduct that's alleged in our complaints. There is absolutely no place for

	Penalty	Disgorgement	Independent research	Inventor education	Total
Citigroup	150.0	150.0	75.0	25.0	400.0
Crédit Suisse First Boston	75.0	75.0	50.0	0.0	200.0
Merrill Lynch	100.0[1]	0.0	75.0	25.0	200.0
Morgan Stanley	25.0	25.0	75.0	0.0	125.0
Goldman Sachs	25.0	25.0	50.0	10.0	110.0
Bear Stearns	25.0	25.0	25.0	5.0	80.0
JP Morgan	25.0	25.0	25.0	5.0	80.0
Lehman Brothers	25.0	25.0	25.0	5.0	80.0
UBS Warburg	25.0	25.0	25.0	5.0	80.0
Piper Jaffray	12.5	12.5	7.5	0.0	32.5
Total	487.5	387.5	432.5	80.0	1387.5

Note: 1 Payment made prior to April 2003 settlement.

Table 14.1 The 28 April 2003 settlement with Wall Street firms
($ millions, in order of importance)

it in our markets, and it cannot be tolerated.'[7] But it had been tolerated during the boom years of the late 1990s and beyond:

- Were all these banks unaware of legal risk involved in their activities?
- Or were they after a fast buck, disregarding the longer-term aftermath?

Moreover, if market discipline did not work *then*, how and why is it expected to work *now*? Some of the experts to whom I have been talking in the course of my research left me in no doubt that, to their way of thinking, the prolonged stock market doldrums – worldwide, in the early years of the twenty-first century – has a great deal to do with the fact that CEO malfeasance has killed business confidence.[8]

One opinion I heard time and again during the research meetings is that penalties, 'disgorgement' of ill-gotten profits, payments to support independent research and investor education, have many characteristics of ULs – at least from the point of view of the timeframe during which the background acts took place. More ULs may still be to come as, having settled with the attorney-general and the regulators, Wall Street firms can now expect plaintiff lawyers to start filing civil suits, including class actions.

Eliot Spitzer, the attorney-general of New York State, who brought the charges, remarked during the settlement that malfeasance went well up the corporate food chain.[9] While the CEOs of the financial institutions which reached the settlement have been spared personal indictment, in the years to come legal documentation may well cover aspects of malfeasance and penalties associated with them. Banks and their counterparties should be seriously thinking about legal risk connected to management actions.

When it comes to dealing with counterparties, legal documentation should not only define the transaction itself and the obligations of all business partners, but also ensure that the customer can *really* understand the product and its risks – whether this product is a derivative instrument, or equity investment advice as in the case of Merrill Lynch and Citigroup. The importance of understanding what one is 'buying', is documented through a great deal of litigation over the past ten years.

According to this evolving view of business partnership between buyer and seller – or the investor and his or her bank – the notion of performance and of liability development are linked through a concept of legal vulnerability. In the coming years it is likely that this will be found at the core of the design of new risk-management systems.

There is still another view of this intersection between business risk (see Chapter 1), legal risk and documentation risk. With globalization, all three come in multiple forms, and all three are expected to increase. Legal experts, whose opinion I asked from perspective of legal risk connected to certain aspects of the implementation of Basel II, said that, while in some countries the rapid growth in number of conflicts and liabilities claims can be attributed to specific circumstances, in general:

- This phenomenon is fundamentally connected to the evolving way of doing business, and
- Moreover, it is here to stay; it is not simply a transient phenomenon or a current fashion.

One of the experts brought up as a precedent the case of the Year 2000 problem. He mentioned that in the UK, the Institute of Chartered Accountants warned that auditors may qualify accounts if there is no adequate record of preparations to adapt computers and their software for Y2K. While small, privately owned companies did not see this as a threat, they were bound to face problems obtaining loan approvals without an:

- Unqualified audit, and
- A Y2K compliance plan.

Had Standard & Poor's, Moody's Investors Service, Fitch Ratings, A.M. Best and the other independent rating agencies taken account of the Y2K problem in companies rating? 'We have attempted to factor it in,' said Clifford Griep of S&P in a meeting we held in New York, 'but this is difficult for an outside observer, beyond questioning management,

- The Y2K is an opaque risk,
- Therefore, we encourage disclosure.'

This is even more true of CEO malfeasance. To get as much information on Y2K as it could, S&P sent out a questionnaire. An interesting finding was that in many cases management did not even know where the company stood on Y2K compliance. Another legal expert mentioned the aftermath of Y2K litigation on the insurance industry, as defendants sought to force their insurers to cover:

- Their legal fees, and
- Damages awarded by courts.

Insurers acted proactively in that case. They moved quickly to prevent lawsuits by revising their policies to exclude Y2K claims. The grounds were that Y2K perils were not known to exist when policies were written. As a result,

- Premiums were not collected for such coverage, and
- The coverage itself did not exist.

How high can the cost of litigation go? Here is an example. In the early 1990s two banks, one operating in London the other in New York, were ordered by one of their clients to transfer $5 million from one institution to another. This was done by cable, and there was fraud. The case went to court. In the end, the case cost $6 million in legal fees, and there was no solution to the legal issue.

In conclusion, from product design to money transfers, product and service liability has basically to do with what is expected of the counterparty and of the system as a value, and how the user, conditioned by practice and real problems, reacts to it. The concept behind this evolution in legal risk is deeply rooted in the service economy.

We increasingly buy and consume 'performance' rather than just material products. *If* quality and performance become the basic criteria, *then* there should be measurement metrics and methods enabling them to be estimated in an objective manner, as well as to advise what can be expected in terms of results. Credit risk is essentially performance risk. This, practically, is where *rating* by independent agencies, including its accuracy and update, comes into the picture, as we will see in section 14.7.

14.7   Rating agencies, legal risk and other risks

Legal risk exists at different levels in connection with the work done by rating agencies, including the issue of credit rating itself and that of being rated. Since credit rating is a performance issue, the reasons underpinning legal risk are evident if we keep in mind the factors coming under *rating*, which include:

- Bond's structure
- Issuer
- Bankruptcy law
- Covenants, and
- Country.

The independent rating agencies and the users of rating results should bear in mind that there are caveats. For instance, in some countries security due to covenants is worthless in a bankruptcy court. An example is France where the judge can override covenants and put all lenders, secured and unsecured, on the same level. In other countries the court may be corrupt.

There are also transactions where *ex ante* legal opinion is overruled. An example is that of the Hammersmith judgment in the UK, and a power utility in Washington State, in the USA. Therefore, in their work, credit rating agencies have to look not only at legal risk per se, but also into what a regulator can and cannot do – or will not do. This is particularly important in structured finance.

Legal risk is more pronounced in countries where there exists a greater tendency to sue. In the USA, for example, rating agencies must be very careful when giving their opinion, for this very reason. There has been a critique of the rating of Enron debt, in the sense that nobody reacted in a timely way to inform bondholders. But so far such failure of information has not lead to court action.

In the course of my research, some rating agencies commented that the above type of legal risk cannot be deadly, because in court one has to prove negligence. One of the independent rating agencies said that, at least in the USA, ratings are protected by the First Amendment, which covers free speech and opinions. Somebody tried to sue S&P, and the answer was: 'This was our opinion.' But is this approach unassailable?

A precedent is the fact that rating agencies necessarily rely on the company's financial statements. This is, however, an argument that Andersen, the certified public accountant, used and it was not acceptable. With the regulators, the reliability of financial statements is part of accounting risk, which incorporates the likelihood of fraud.

- *If* there is no fraud,
- *Then* it is management risk.

Evidence provided during the research meetings suggests that, following Enron, there is greater focus on legal risk on the rating agencies' part. For instance, more stringent procedures are followed by their credit policy group, which confirms the ratings and oversees all matters from legal and other standpoints. A crucial question management now asks itself is 'how should it act as a rating agency?', because of the evolution which is taking place.

- The concept of rating by reliable independent agencies became popularized with bonds after World War II.
- But over the past three decades it expanded to financial institutions, sovereigns and subnationals – and it is now entering new domains.

One of these domains is management quality which is, in principle, an intangible, but as we saw in section 14.3 with the Goldman Sachs example, it could be quantified. This requires a system which rates quality, hence expected failure rate. The same can be said of investor education on the meaning of ratings. Beyond the understanding of advantages and limitations of a ratings system this education should include an understanding of:

- Control environments
- Risk assessments
- Monitoring duties
- Control activities, and
- Information responsibilities.

Independent rating agencies would be well advised to account for how well the management of companies they rate takes care to preserve the entity's assets. The SEC is right to insist on this last issue. A similar statement is valid for internal controls policies, systems, procedures and personal accountability connected to the:

- Survival of the institution, and
- Dependability of its financial statements.

This requires a framework whose construction necessitates three steps. The first is identifying and understanding the factors that can lead to fraudulent financial reporting, including those unique to the company, its culture and the quality of its internal control.[10] The second, is that of assessing the risk of fraudulent financial reporting created within the company, anywhere it operates. The third, is redesigning and restructuring the internal control to provide assurance that fraudulent financial reporting will be prevented or at least detected and corrected in timely manner.

In parallel to this, some issues which can potentially damage the firm must be most carefully avoided. For instance, senior management should take great care not to deplete the bank's economic capital through left and right acquisitions and exposures that are irrational, even if both events have become a trend. Another example of a bad trend is share buybacks; still another, lavish executive options.

Standard & Poor's looks at share buybacks as a decision which decreases the entity's available economic capital. One of the main reasons why in recent years companies have been buying back their own shares in large quantities is to support their equity's price and make executive options more valuable. The irony is that many of these purchases are financed not with retained profits, but with debt, thereby:

- Increasing a company's leverage, and
- Reducing its creditworthiness in the market's eyes.

Companies, including financial institutions, go for share buybacks on the false assumption (or excuse) that this improves shareholder value, while in reality it justifies more options to top management at shareholders' expense. Several recent examples revolve around the so-called 10 percent rule in stock buybacks, which is, by any account, most counterproductive.

Share buybacks have also been used as a way of turning a company's treasury into a gambling outfit. Many companies got into the habit of trading put options on their own shares. Others established a 'rule' that use of inventory limit is set at a maximum 10 percent of shares outstanding, using a corporate plan to reconcile sales of industrial holdings with buybacks. None of the excuses given for these trades is convincing.

One of the auditors with whom I spoke about the issues discussed in the preceding paragraphs pointed out that there is a loophole in accounting rules, and several companies are keen to exploit it. The effect of share buybacks does not enter group P&L, but is shown directly in the capital account. This leaves many investors unaware of the buybacks' aftermath. At the same time, though not illegal, such action increases the company's exposure.

Economic and financial history shows that, if left unchecked, weaknesses increase over time. Credit institutions should not weaken themselves through policies or acts which seek short-term profit but bring longer-term damages. Many of the examples included in the last three sections of this chapter have been deliberately chosen to demonstrate that, to be in charge of IRB, credit institutions have to go outside the Basel II confines to confront issues which contribute indirectly to unexpected losses, because they obey the law of unexpected consequences.

In conclusion, in qualifying and quantifying credit risk, and all other risks, an institution positions itself against market forces if, and only *if*, it is able to make an objective calculation of capital requirements associated with its exposure – in any form this is assumed, anywhere in the world. While the use of the notion of relative capital and relative risk has merits, the downside is that risk assessment might arguably become too short-sighted, while a long-term horizon is needed to raise capital and restructure the balance sheet, to estimate unexpected losses, including their origin, frequency and impact, and to be in charge of legal risk.

Notes

1 *Financial Times*, 18 November 2002.
2 D.N. Chorafas (2002). *Modelling the Survival of Financial and Industrial Enterprises: Advantages, Challenges, and Problems with the Internal Rating-Based (IRB) Method*. Palgrave/Macmillan.
3 D.N. Chorafas (1994). *Chaos Theory in the Financial Markets*. Probus.
4 D.N. Chorafas (2001). *Integrating ERP, CRM, Supply Chain Management and Smart Materials*. Auerbach.
5 D.N. Chorafas (2004). *Operational Risk Control with Basel II*. Butterworth-Heinemann.
6 Ibid.
7 *Financial Times*, 29 April 2003.
8 D.N. Chorafas (2004). *Management Risk: The Bottleneck Is at the Top of the Bottle*. Macmillan/Palgrave.
9 *The Economist*, 3 May 2003.
10 D.N. Chorafas (2001). *Implementing and Auditing the Internal Control System*. Macmillan.

4

Regulatory and political issues tend to be indivisible

15 Supervisory authorities and their regulatory policies

15.1 Introduction

One of the common goals of all regulators is financial stability. In the global market this is accomplished through close collaboration among supervisory authorities, and assurance of capital adequacy by banks and other financial institutions. If capital adequacy fails, then the strategy of G-10 regulators is that of using *least cost* and *payoff* as criteria, with varying degree of belief in the results of a salvage operation.

To a substantial degree this strategy of least cost and payoff to the taxpayer, and the economy as a whole, is consistent with the mission established by the central banks' (and other regulatory bodies) charter. This mission prescribes several duties, like serving as the bank of the government, but the three main functions are:

- Monetary policy
- Lender of last resort, and
- Supervisor of the banking sector.

The third bullet is not the general case. For instance, the Bank of England (since 1998) and the Swiss National Bank are not doing bank supervision. In the UK, this is the function of the Financial Services Authority and in Switzerland it is the responsibility of the Swiss Federal Banking Commission (SFBC) – not of the central bank.

Both the Bank of England and the Swiss National Bank, however, participate in the Basel Committee on Banking Supervision whose origin and objectives are presented in the Appendix. The UK and Switzerland are both G-10 countries, but there are also other groupings of central bankers and supervisors, as this chapter documents.

Within G-10, as well as in the global landscape, there exist significant differences in the way bank supervision is implemented. The Federal Reserve, Office of the Controller of the Currency and Federal Deposit Insurance Corporation (FDIC) have their own bank examiners. The FSA depends on the results of the audit of chartered accountants (independent auditors). So does the SFBC, but it gets involved in direct inspection if it is not happy with the auditor's report – and its Big Banks department has its own examiners, like the Fed.

A worry in the mind of all regulators, whether central banks or independent supervisory authorities, is the moral hazard of automatic support to banks in trouble. However, also weighing on the regulators' decision is the exit threat of big financial players and the systemic risk associated with carrying it out.

Still another worry of regulators is that politicians sometimes hinder bank supervision (see Chapter 16). Indeed, politics has much to do with regulatory policies. In 2002, in one of the emerging markets the boss of the local regulatory authority

	Have aggressive risk appetite	Understand credit risk taken	Understand market risk taken	Believe risks are effectively controlled
Senior management	75	80	65	55
Middle management	50	60	40	35
Lower management	25	35	20	22
All respondents	58	63	47	42

Table 15.1 Sensitivity to risk by the bank at different management levels, based on a small sample of institutions (percentage)

wanted to implement Basel's 1996 Market Risk Amendment. This did not please the local bankers, who complained to the government, and the politicians removed the regulator.

Neither is it self-evident that the banks, which, in the final analysis, benefit from regulatory activities, always appreciate the limits put on their gearing and on the risks which they take. In the majority of cases, this is due to low sensitivity to risk by different levels of management in the credit institution. Table 15.1 shows statistics which make sad reading in terms of risk sensitivity. The figures are based on a sample of commercial banks.

The Basel Committee on Banking Supervision tries to increase senior management's sensitivity to risk by making commercial banks partners in the setting of new standards, particularly in regard to risk weights and correlations. This is achieved by means of consultative papers and quantitative studies, as we saw in Chapter 1. The other side of the challenge, however, lies in the fact that there are overlapping supervisory structures and associated regulations, as shown in Figure 15.1. This can be confusing. It also makes it much more difficult minutely to adjust new prudential standards which must at the same time address:

- Maintenance of target debt rating
- Correlations and concentrations
- Time horizon brackets
- Objective analysis of all risks
- Volatility smiles
- Fair estimates of capital costs
- Lack of data for accurate modeling
- Ways to materialize risk transfer
- Incentive-based compensation structure
- Stress testing for outliers, and
- Factual execution of critical post-mortems.

This brings yet another challenge into the picture, that of *asymmetric skills*. Not all regulators, or commercial bankers, have the same level of tools and know-how – and in some cases regulators may have a lower level than commercial bankers employing rocket scientists. This is particularly true in developing countries.

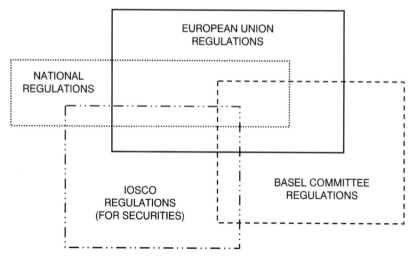

Figure 15.1 Partly overlapping regulations do not provide a crisp reporting structure

The Basel Committee is well aware of this deficiency and it has put in place a global program for educating the world of regulators. This is vital to the success of Basel II, because there is a big gap in educating emerging market central bankers. For this reason, the Financial Stability Institute (FSI) of the Bank for International Settlement is now conducting seminars to bring regulators up to speed.

15.2   Broader context of Basel II and its implementation

This section focuses on the goals of G-10 supervisors with Basel II. These fall mainly within the broader objectives of international co-operation among central bankers, and comprehensive evaluation of capital adequacy. The implementation of Basel II rules is left to every regulatory authority, which maintains its independence of action vis-à-vis the other regulators.

In America, for example, in March 2003 the Federal Reserve decided that the top twelve banks have to implement A-IRB of Basel II, the next ten US banks by assets (shown in Table 15.2) may do so, and the balance can stay with the fixed 8 percent ratio of Basel I. This is not the case in Europe where, as Chapter 16 documents, this has not yet been decided.

Compared with this list of the largest US credit institutions, with 370 billion euros in assets Holland's Rabobank stands in fourth position. In our meeting, Rabo left no doubt it will implement A-IRB. With 40 billion euros in assets, Austria's Erste Bank is in twenty-second position in the US banking list, on a par with the Union Bank of California. Yet, the Erste is already implementing A-IRB, starting with its retail banking operations (more on this later), while the Union Bank of California may well stay with Basel I.

Among analysts and other market experts, differences in terms of Basel II implementation, from one jurisdiction to the next, have got mixed reactions.

	US banks	$ billions
1	Citigroup	1100
2	JP Morgan Chase	759
3	Bank of America	660
4	Wells Fargo	349
5	Wachovia	342
6	Bank One	277
7	FleetBoston Financial	190
8	U.S. Bancorp	180
9	National City	118
10	Suntrust Banks	117
11	State Street	86
12	KeyCorp	85
13	Fifth Third Bancorp	81
14	BB&T	80
15	Bank of New York	77
16	PNC Financial Services Group	66
17	Comercia	53
18	SouthTrust	51
19	Regions Financial	48
20	Charter One Financial	42
21	Amsouth Bancorporation	41
22	UnionBanCal	40
23	Northern Trust	39
24	Mellon Financial	36
25	Union Planters	34
26	Popular	34
27	M & T Bank	33
28	Marshall & Ilsley	33
29	Huntington Bancsgares	28
30	Zions Bancorporation	27

Table 15.2 The top thirty US banks by assets, March 2003

Practically everybody recognizes that the two IRB methodologies, particularly A-IRB, are fairly complex. Small banks of up to, say, $500 million in assets, do not have the culture, know-how, technology and money to implement them. The standard approach is an option, but staying with Basel I might be another option.

An approach of choosing capital adequacy methodology by level of assets, would answer the objections of contrarians who say that thousands of banks, do not feel secure enough of themselves to graduate from a fixed capital ratio to more complex approaches, with heavy demands on skills, time and IT resources. One should, however, recall that with the 1996 Market Risk Amendment a large number of banks have management to enable them to be ahead of the curve.

Bigger banks in the $0.5 to $5.0 billion assets bracket could be given the signal to move to Basel II within a reasonable timeframe; and they should do so if they operate cross-border or engage in risky financial instruments. Basel II should be a 'must' for banks with over $5 billion in assets, given the fact that it represents a cultural change. Under the new framework, the quantitative and qualitative evaluation includes not only capital adequacy, as such, but also:

- Risk management
- Modeling procedures
- Financial reporting practices, and
- Disclosure requirements.

Another crucial element is the implementation of new, more rigorous accounting standards. Neither should the reader forget that with the new capital adequacy framework, bank supervisors aim to accomplish three main goals. They want to develop comprehensive formulas that bring capital charges closer to the banks' own measures of risk, establish a means which permits continuous review of banks' management, especially of their risk control, and create incentives for:

- Applying dependable methods for greater public disclosure of banks' risk exposures, and
- Allowing the market to take on more of a supervisory role, as explained in Chapter 4.

These objectives are not alien to the fact that over the years, particularly in the 1990 to 2000 period, there has been a sharp drop in the quality of bank ratings, more or less across the board. The three curves in Figure 15.2, based on statistics by Standard & Poor's, are relatively self-explanatory so that they do not need long discussion. Ratings of credit institutions are rapidly moving towards a non-investment grade. Basel II represents a way to reverse such a trend, as documented in Chapters 2 and 4.

There is, however, an important point, in terms of difference among jurisdictions, not yet generally appreciated in all quarters. What the Basel Committee establishes as the way for computing capital charges for credit institutions, will in the EU also be applied to all investment firms, including brokers and asset managers. This represents a great challenge to establish a level playing field, and it comes from the fact that the regulators would like to see practically all financial institutions become:

- More sophisticated, and
- Better able to promote an advanced applications environment.

Another central objective with Basel II, to my mind, is the generalization of supervision of financial institutions under a more or less homogeneous set of rules. Though the following references vary from one jurisdiction to the next, as a rule, retail banks, other commercial banks and universal banks are under central bank authority. Under either central bank or some other authority/authorities are investment banks, merchant banks, savings banks, agricultural banks and popular banks. Insurance companies are supervised by other regulators – very different from country to country – while under ill-defined supervision there are:

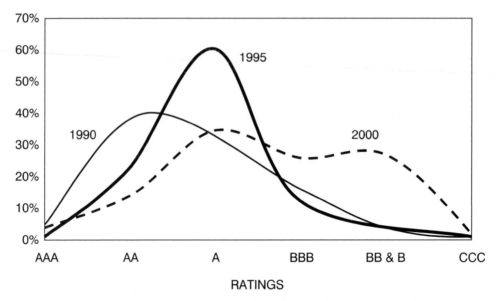

Figure 15.2 Ratings distribution of global banks according to Standard & Poor's
(Reproduced by permission of Walter Pompliano, Standard & Poor's)

- Postal banks
- Credit card companies
- Department stores with debit accounts
- Co-operative unions
- Mutual funds
- Pension funds
- Hedge funds.

The above statement needs qualifying. Several of the entities named in the list, particularly those quoted, are in some way supervised by stock exchange regulators, but only for part of their acts. Take the SEC as an example. By law the SEC is charged with reviewing the financial filings of 17000 US companies. Through this, it is overseeing:

- A universe of mutual funds, an industry that has grown more than fourfold in assets in the 1990s; and
- All brokerage firms as far as this concerns the effect of their activities on proper operation of the exchanges, insider trading, and so on.

The SEC watches over accounting transgressions, and investigates whenever anything goes wrong. On Wall Street, however, experts say the SEC has not been given enough resources even to read annual reports. In a speech in 2001, one of the agency's chief accountants admitted that only one in fifteen annual statements by supervised firms was reviewed in 2000.[1] This is an operational risk on the SEC's part. After Enron, the

Bush administration tried to correct it by significantly increasing the SEC's budget. But is a budgetary allocation the only thing that matters in prudential supervision of the financial industry?

15.3   The need to expand the supervisors' power of action

Let me take the supervisory solution adopted in the UK as an example which some countries, for instance Germany, consider as pattern-setter. Since 1 December 2001, following the implementation of the Financial Services and Markets Act 2000, all sorts of financial services and associated operations in the UK have been regulated by the FSA, as the FSA assumed the responsibilities of previous UK regulators:

- The Bank of England
- Securities and Futures Authority
- Investment Management Regulatory Organization, and so on.

The Bank of England's responsibilities for regulation of banking activities were transferred to the FSA by the Bank of England Act 1998. The FSA has established a risk-based approach to supervision with big banks, regulated by the Major Financial Groups section of the Deposit Takers and Markets Directorate.

Today, the FSA has a wide variety of supervisory tools available to it, including on-site inspections by supervisors, which may relate to a risk-based industry-wide theme, or they may be firm-specific. The FSA also has an extremely wide set of sanctions which it may impose under the Act, similar to those available to US regulators. And its responsibilities are expanding after successive evaluations of risks affecting market discipline.

For instance, after an eight-month consultation, in March 2003 the FSA has concluded that there should be no relaxation in the rules governing the sale of hedge funds to retail investors. Managers of hedge funds, the controversial entities that are frequently accused of causing market instability,[2] will be denied greater freedom to promote their products and services to small savers.

The way the FSA saw it, there was neither 'a great desire' to sell alternative investments and other products peddled by hedge funds and funds of funds to private investors, nor any significant demand from these savers for such services. The FSA received forty submissions on the subject, including feedback from its own consumer panel. Subsequent to this, the supervisory authority decided to:

- Keep the regulatory status of hedge funds under review, and
- Continue discussion with investment houses about the possibility of bringing more hedge funds within its regulatory regime for retail funds.

The caveat is that because hedge funds are usually domiciled offshore, they fall outside the scope of national regulators. However, hedge fund managers based in London must meet FSA standards of conduct and controls. Their teams must also have suitable qualifications, and these requirements see to it that even if hedge funds continue with the status of an unregulated industry, at least their contact with consumers and investors is supervised.

Such flexibility does not exist in the USA because only the different product lines of commercial banking are under supervision by the Fed, OCC and FDIC. As explained, investment banking falls under the SEC's authority. Let me add that investment services subject to oversight by UK regulators are regulated in accordance with EU directives requiring, among other things, compliance with:

- Capital adequacy standards
- Customer protection requirements, and
- Business conduct rules.

Such standards, requirements and rules are supposed to be similarly implemented, under the same directives, throughout the EU. At least in principle they are broadly comparable in scope and purpose to regulatory capital and customer protection requirements imposed under applicable US law – but, in principle, a single supervisory authority makes available to itself more degrees of freedom than when supervisory responsibilities are diffused among several entities.

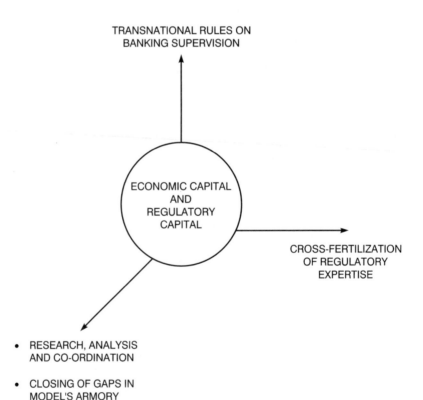

Figure 15.3 The role played by international collaboration of central bankers can be expressed in a three-dimensional frame of reference

All this demonstrates that the aftermath of Basel II will be widely felt in the banking and investment landscape as rules and regulators become rather uniform along the frame of reference shown in Figure 15.3, but also as the supervisory authorities are given a greater power of action. The positive side of the equation is that global uniformity among G-10 countries, and several others, is welcome – and the new rules come just in time because weaknesses in the banking system of one country can threaten financial stability both within that country and internationally.

15.4 Core Principles, the Financial Stability Forum and the Committee on the Global Financial System

The reader will wish to know that Basel II had a predecessor. This was the 1997 Basel Committee on Banking Supervision document on 'Core Principles for Effective Banking Supervision', which was endorsed by more than G-10 countries, including (in alphabetic order) Chile, China, Czech Republic, Hong Kong, Mexico, Russia, Thailand, and so on.

These Core Principles of 1997 comprise twenty-five milestones which have to be in place for a supervisory system to be effective. Cast within a general frame of reference, the principles relate to:

■ Legal and institutional preconditions for effective banking supervision (Principle 1)
■ Licensing and structure of banks (Principles 2 to 5)
■ Prudential regulations and its requirements (Principles 6 to 15)
■ Methods of ongoing banking supervision (Principles 16 to 20)
■ Formal powers of supervisors (Principle 22), and
■ Cross-border banking (Principles 23 to 25).

The Basel Committee's Core Principles of 1997 were supplemented by a methodology of assessing compliance with each one of them, published in October 1999. There have also been further measures designed to address certain circumstances and risks in the financial system of individual countries, and other international standards such as those on combating money laundering.

Moreover, upon a proposal by the Basel Committee, in May 1999, the IMF, in a joint effort with the World Bank, introduced a Financial Sector Assessment Program (FSAP). This program monitors compliance not only with the Core Principles but also with the minimum requirements established by IOSCO and IAIS – respectively for the supervision of securities trading and insurance business.

Because yet another goal of Basel II and of FSAP is to identify weaknesses in the two-way interaction between macroeconomic environment and the structure and development of the financial sector, macroprudential indicators of economic and financial stability have also been established. In many cases, these are thoroughly analyzed and subjected to a stress test by the parties concerned.

With the consent of countries being monitored, a Report on Observance of Standards and Codes (ROSC) has been published for a number of countries. In 2001, in co-operation with the World Bank, the IMF completed an FSAP for thirty-two countries: five advanced economies, ten transition countries and seventeen developing countries. Another twenty-two programs were done in 2002.

The Core Principles by the Basel Committee and the FSAP by the IMF should be examined in conjunction with the Financial Stability Forum (FSF), established in February 1999 at the Bank for International Settlements. The FSF was organized by the G-7 finance ministers and central bank governors to assess vulnerabilities affecting the international financial system, and to identify action to promote international financial stability. It accomplishes this mission through:

■ Enhanced information exchange
■ International co-operation in financial supervision, and
■ Support by a secretariat located at the BIS.

Since its establishment, the FSF has published recommendations on highly leveraged institutions (HLIs), volatile capital flows, and offshore financial centers (see also section 15.5). It has also reviewed developments in the insurance industry relevant to financial stability. The FSF is working on international guidance principles regarding deposit insurance schemes and is analyzing the implications of electronics-based finance for:

■ Surveillance
■ Regulation, and
■ Market functioning.

Moreover, the FSF is encouraging work to foster the implementation of international standards and codes – particularly a group of twelve key elements most relevant to sound and well-functioning financial systems. Within this broader perspective the FSF goal has been to promote international financial stability by bringing together, on a regular basis, senior representatives from international financial institutions, regulators, supervisors, central bank experts and national authorities responsible for financial stability in international financial centers.

This type of exchange helps not only in generating ideas but also in deeper examination of present and latent risks. While in the 1995 to 2000 period major financial markets and institutions had absorbed the existing strains fairly well, the interaction between the cyclical slowdown in the first years of the twenty-first century, and pre-existing financial imbalances, made mandatory increased vigilance and enhanced co-operation at supervisory level. By doing a reassessment of vulnerabilities, FSF has identified risk transfer mechanisms as potential element of significant exposure in financial markets. It has also considered the role of:

■ Novel financial instruments, and
■ New financial technology.

Both positive and negative aspects have been examined, like the role of new instruments and of IT in propagating herd behavior in the global banking industry – thereby creating a potential source of major risk in the world's financial system. The FSF also acts as a feedback channel, by regularly reviewing progress made in implementing earlier recommendations on:

- Capital flows
- Offshore financial centers, and
- Highly leveraged institutions.

Moreover, FSF is following up on the implementation of international standards for sound financial behavior, including calls for concrete actions by national authorities and the private sector. As a result of its research, the FSF identified gaps in the development of international guidance on dealing with weak banks, as well as with systematic banking problems. It also:

- Reviewed progress in developing international guidance on deposit insurance schemes
- Examined the implications of electronic banking for supervision and market functioning, and
- Analyzed a number of other international financial issues, including accounting and provisioning for financial institutions.

What the careful reader will retain from this discussion is that Basel II is not just a set of rules and regulations to do with regulatory capital (see Part 1), and the wisdom of economic capital allocation between business units and channels (which has been the theme of Part 2). It is supported by a system of nodes and links. Another node, beyond those referred to so far, is the BIS Committee on the Global Financial System (CGFS).

In parallel to the work done by the Basel Committee, the CGFS of the Bank for International Settlements, focuses on regular monitoring of international financial markets and the functioning of the financial system on a global scale, as a whole. Its prime areas of interest are the assessment and analysis of factors which:

- Could constitute vulnerabilities for financial aggregates, both domestic and international, and
- Pose a threat to the functioning of major industrial and emerging market economies.

An example is the many aspects of stress testing on which CGFS conducted a study. The setting of these aims followed up on work previously carried out in the area of market liquidity, as well as different types of stress tests.[3] A meeting between a number of CGFS members and private sector representatives explored the extent to which changes made by credit institutions in risk management policies and practices might affect market liquidity.

The survey on stress testing practices has been interesting. Forty-three banks from ten different countries participated in the census, which was initiated by CGFS to gain insights into the role of stress testing in risk management, and to identify which exceptional events were considered to be significant risks.

Another CGFS working group focused on risk management and market dynamics in wholesale markets. The aim was to assess trends and changes in the usage and availability of collateral, including how these changes might alter market dynamics, particularly at times of financial stress due to low liquidity, high volatility, an inordinate amount of bankruptcies, high leverage and other factors.

The reader will appreciate that what has been described in this section is a much broader approach to the global financial market which requires a structure that cannot be deviated from or subverted. One has to look at this whole environment to appreciate that, even if it still has some gaps in its armory, Basel II is:

■ A good deal
■ At the right time, and
■ For the right reasons.

Any evaluation of, or even reference to, Basel II should be done within this broader perspective which in ten to twelve years' time will lead to a well-knit global regulatory system – a Basel III, just as Basel I gave way to Basel II. In conclusion, the best way for banks to adapt to this most significant transition in regulatory perspectives and capital requirements is to take the needed changes to heart. Half-baked measures will not do, and they may be counterproductive.

15.5 Group of Seven, Group of Ten and Group of Twenty

The Group of Seven (G-7) was created in the mid-1970s to permit heads of state, prime ministers, finance ministers and central bankers to meet at least annually and exchange opinions, ideas and solutions to problems concerning all of them. Member countries of the G-7 are the USA, the UK, Japan, Germany, France, Italy and Canada. In recent years the chief of state of the Russian Federation also participates in the G-7 meetings.

Within the broader framework of co-operation in the G-7, finance ministers and central bank governors have met regularly to discuss key economic and financial issues of an international nature. Their meetings are mainly concerned with:

■ Economic and financial developments
■ Interest rates
■ Exchanges rates
■ Market panics
■ Risks being assumed, and
■ Evolution of the global economy, including international monetary and financial policy.

Informal exchanges of views within the G-7 help the participants to achieve a greater understanding of the different issues involved, while formal exchanges often lead to a 'sense of the meeting'. These discussions also provide the basis for a decision-making process which co-involves organizations such as the IMF, the World Bank and the OECD.

Following the launch of Stage Three of the European Monetary Union (EMU), the president of the European Central Bank participates in meetings of G-7 finance ministers and central bank governors, particularly those parts of meetings that deal with macroeconomic surveillance and exchange rate issues. As far as monetary policy of the euro area is concerned, the president of the ECB presents the views of the eurosystem, while the president of the eurogroup (a subset of the finance ministers) participates in discussions on other economic developments and policies in euroland.

The activities of the IMF and of G-10 finance ministers and central bank governors have been closely linked since the creation, in 1962, of the General Arrangement to Borrow (GAB). The GAB's resources complement the IMF's ordinary resources; issues discussed at meetings of G-10 ministers and governors are closely related to IMF policy matters. In recent years, their main focus has been:

- Prevention and management international financial crises
- Different types of involvement of the private sector, and
- The consolidation taking place in the financial industry.

As shown in Figure 15.4, G-10 has a broader base than G-7. Its members are the G-7 nations plus the Netherlands, Sweden, Switzerland, Spain and Belgium – with Luxembourg as observer, and Spain a recent addition. The G-10 is the club of central bankers who collaborate on the Basel Committee on Banking Supervision (see the Appendix) as well as other committees which are connected with transnational financial organizations.

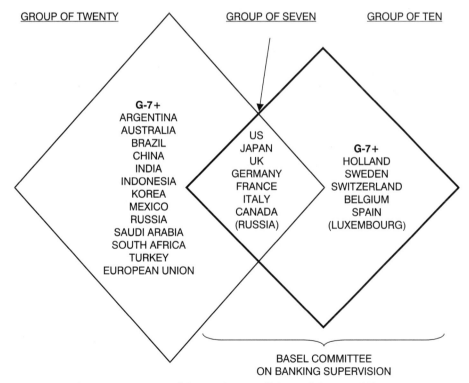

Figure 15.4 Group of Seven, Group of Ten and Group of Twenty

Another group, known as the Group of Twenty (G-20), was created on September 1999. It is an informal forum of finance ministers and central bank governors which includes the G-7 countries plus Argentina, Australia, Brazil, China, India, Indonesia, Korea, Mexico, Russia, Saudi Arabia, South Africa, Turkey and the EU as a body.

The concept behind the G-20 has been to co-involve key emerging countries in economic and financial decisions of global importance. This broadens the dialogue on international economic and financial policies. By facilitating an open exchange of views, it promotes consensus-building. The ECB and the EU presidency are members of the G-20. Issues addressed by the G-20 range:

- From means to reduce the vulnerability of countries to financial crises,
- To opportunities and challenges posed by globalization and international trade.

The G-20 keeps under review the adoption of exchange rate regimes by emerging economies, seeing to it that such policies are consistent with their specific macroeconomic and financial conditions. It also monitors prudent liability management, and has established a dialogue with private sector representatives on the involvement of private creditors in crisis prevention and resolution.

The Bank for International Settlements was organized in the 1920s. After World War II it became the central bank of central bankers. (See also the discussion on the Basel Committee in the Appendix.) Today, a key objective of the BIS is to promote co-operation of central banks through its active committees, and host the meetings of G-10 governors which usually take place at BIS headquarters, in Basel, on a bimonthly basis. This forum discusses:

- Economic trends in industrial countries and emerging market economies
- Potential threats to global financial stability, and
- Longer-term monetary and financial developments.

An important development which has taken place over the years is that these meetings are increasingly being opened to the central banks of those emerging market economies which are of systemic importance. The G-10 governors also act as a hub for a number of permanent committees and ad hoc working groups. Four permanent committees at BIS are:

- Basel Committee on Banking Supervision
- Committee on Payment and Settlement Systems
- Committee on the Global Financial System
- Gold and Foreign Exchange Committee.

Co-operation with other supervisory authorities, including IOSCO, takes place regularly in order to deal with issues of common concern. In recent years, BIS has also developed a close relationship with the international organization of insurance industry supervisors which is now located on BIS premises in Basel. Another important issue in connection with collaboration between central bank governors is the Memorandum of Understanding (MOU) discussed in section 15.6.

15.6 Memoranda of Understanding concerning the offshores and bankruptcies

One of the weakest spots in the armory of global prudential supervision has been the offshores. Two documents should be brought under perspective in this connection. The MOU between banking supervisors, and the so-called 'Basel Concordat' which preceded it, defining the obligations of central banks in case of bankruptcy of financial institutions under their regulatory authority.

Indeed, the first evidence of G-10 central bankers acting in unison is a 1975 agreement reached at the BIS, between central bankers, which became known as the Basel Concordat. In practical terms, it obliged a central bank to come to the aid of a credit institution in the territory of its jurisdiction. The central bank, however, is not obliged to act as lender of last resort for subsidiary holding companies established in other central bank's jurisdictions – much less so in offshores.

In May 1983, after the Ambrosiano scandal, and the collapse of the bank of the same name, the major central banks produced a revision to their Concordat of eight years earlier. Still, there is no formal agreement to financially support an entity outside a central bank's jurisdiction. Major events are being handled case by case on the basis that:

- Every circumstance and every subsidiary can be legally different,
- But at the same time large defaults can have a knock-on effect to other banks, as well as involve systemic risk.

This has been the case with Barings and, even more so, of Long-Term Capital Management with its huge exposure to market-led positions and astronomical gearing at the level of 350 percent[4] – and the ogre of systemic risk and reputational risk it brought to life.

The objective of the MOU for the offshores was different. The MOU was prepared by the working group on cross-border banking from the Basel Committee. This working group includes selected members of the Offshore Group of Banking Supervisors. The MOU's goal is to:

- Establish a basis of mutual co-operation between supervisors in connection with handling problems of financial institutions registered offshore, and
- Provide a framework for a rather general agreement, while leaving sufficient discretion to national supervisors to add details and specify additional responsibilities.

The basis of the MOU document is the need to share information among bank supervisors on a global basis. Working against this need is the fact that national laws, designed to protect the confidentiality of credit institutions and/or the interests of bank customers, tend to limit the transmission of information between supervisory authorities. Hence, the requirement that each supervisor should inform the others of the existence of legislative or administrative restrictions on information exchange.

Following this line of reference, the longer-term objective is to eliminate as much as possible impediments to the flow of information from a cross-border institution to its parent, for risk management purposes. This must be achieved on a global basis and make it possible to compile consolidated reports for the home supervisor. The counterside of information privacy is that significant impediments in data transmission essentially mean that the parent company is not able to conduct effective oversight of its own operations abroad.

Establishment of cross-border effective information sharing is defined as being able to access and analyze all information from an institution at any time, on any subject, anywhere in the world – including a branch, subsidiary or any other business unit within jurisdiction(s) other than that of the home country. Consolidated supervision cannot be done otherwise. According to the Core Principles laid down by the Basel Committee (see also section 15.4), each supervisory authority should be able to:

- Assess the nature and extent of supervision conducted by the other party, and
- Determine the extent of reliance that can be placed upon it.

Another provision is that the host supervisor should notify, without delay, the home supervisor, of applications for approval to establish offices or make acquisitions in the host jurisdiction; while, upon request, the home supervisor should inform the host supervisor whether the applicant bank is in substantial compliance with banking laws and regulations in its home country. Other critical information is whether the bank is expected to manage the cross-border establishment in an orderly manner, given its administrative structure and internal controls.

Using the same frame of reference, the home supervisor should inform the host supervisor about the nature of its regulatory system and the extent to which it will conduct consolidated supervision over the applicant bank. He or she should indicate the scope of its supervision, and outline any specific features that might give rise to the need for special arrangements.

Moreover, to the extent permitted by law, supervisors involved in cross-border arrangements should provide relevant information to their counterparty regarding material developments, or concerns, in respect of operational and other risks. They should also respond to requests for information about their respective national regulatory systems and inform each other about major changes affecting cross-border establishments.

Seen in this light, while protection of personal and confidential information continues to be all important, cross-border collaboration is necessary to develop mutual trust between supervisory authorities. This can only be achieved if exchanges of information are frank and open – as they should be in any internal control system – while all parties in this exchange are given assurance that:

- Every possible step is taken to preserve the confidentiality of the information received, and
- This information is used exclusively for lawful supervisory purposes.

These guidelines reflect the highlights of ongoing discussions under the auspices of the Financial Stability Forum at the BIS, where a number of countries have suggested that there is a need for a statement setting out the essential elements of a new, more rigorous MOU. As the preceding paragraphs demonstrate, the concept is that such a document can be used as a reference for establishing bilateral relationships:

- Between banking supervisory authorities in different countries, and
- Between banking supervisors and other financial regulators.

These notions have been reflected in the second version of MOU's high-level principles of co-operation in crisis-management situations, which specifies principles and procedures for cross-border co-operation to ensure the stability of the financial system during emergencies. The ECB says that the MOU is not a public document, adding that:

- The diversification of financial activities
- The growing number of large and complex financial institutions, and
- The integration of financial markets and market infrastructures in the EU,

have increased the likelihood of systemic disturbances affecting more than one member state. Several central bankers and financial analysts are of the opinion that the same reasons have also increased the scope and possible magnitude of cross-border contagion. These reasons are behind the MOU document signed on 10 March 2002 by central banks and financial supervisory agencies of Western and Eastern European countries.[5]

While the ECB did not explicitly say so, some experts suggest that information exchange rules and procedures should be extended to cover all hedge funds. The lack of supervisory control over hedge funds is indeed one of the sore points of global, national and local supervision. It is a huge loophole exploited by all parties who choose to work on the borderline of legality.

The expression of the need to regulate hedge funds is not new, but steps for prudential control have been resisted by the hedge funds inventory. The difference is that by mid-2003 this issue had been firmly raised. In Washington, William Donaldson, the recently appointed chairman of SEC, promised to take a long, hard look at hedge funds – for several reasons, including:

- The high profile scandals involving hedge funds, and
- The huge growth of the hedge funds industry, which went from $50 billion in 1990 to $600 billion in 2003.

In connection with the first point, in 2002 SEC brought twelve cases of fraud against hedge funds, more than twice as many as in each of the previous four years.[6] Moreover, hedge funds are increasingly selling their highly risky wares to consumers through funds of funds and new retail products marketed by banks – thereby exploiting a clientele which can hardly understand, if at all, the danger involved in alternative investments.[7]

15.7. Globalization, the wealth of nations and the finance industry

Basel II should not be studied independently of globalization of financial markets. Its capital requirements as well as its rules and clauses have been necessary precisely because of globalization of financial services. It is for this reason that, to better appreciate Basel II, we should look not only at globalization but also at transborder financial flows.

People who are dead set against globalization claim that, because of it, less developed countries are the losers. This is a near-sighted view which neither accounts for the fact of cross-border wealth transfer, nor for the findings of a late 2001 study by the World Bank which demolished that negative claim. If one divides poor countries into those that are *more* and less *globalized* we find that during the 1990s:

- The more globalized among the less developed countries have grown faster than rich countries.
- This contrasts markedly with less globalized countries which have seen income per person fall.[8]

The difference I am talking about reflects GDP, measured in personal purchasing power (PPP), which is shown in Figure 15.5. The World Bank suggests that in the first post-World War II decades, between 1945 and 1980, economic integration was concentrated among the highly industrialized countries. But in the 1980s and 1990s, this has changed, in favor of globalized countries in the process of development.

Manufactured goods, for example, rose from 25 percent of less developed country exports in 1980 to more than 80 percent in 1998. Notice that this integration was concentrated in twenty-four countries, including China, India and Mexico. These countries are home to 3 billion people – or half the world's population – and it is good

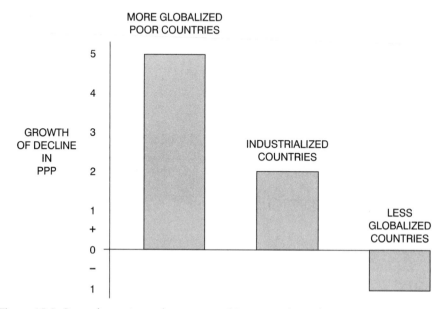

Figure 15.5 Gross domestic product measured in personal purchasing power (PPP) in the 1990s (*Source*: based on statistics from the World Bank)

news that over the last two decades of the twentieth century these same countries have doubled their ratio of trade to national income.

The result of the development described in the preceding paragraph is demonsrated by the fact that in the 1990s the GDP per head of the countries referred to above grew by an annual average of 5 percent.

International financial institutions have gained considerable advantages from this growth in personal purchasing power in China, India, Mexico, and other globalized less developed countries. Notice, however, that for the other 2 billion people who live in the rest of the less developed world, the statistics are quite different. During the 1990s:

- In these non-globalized economies including much of Africa, the ratio of trade to national output has fallen.
- In several countries which failed to globalize, income per head has shrunk and the number of people in poverty has risen.

This most interesting study casts new insight on the globalization story. As World Bank statistics suggest, the choice is between globalization and marginalization – and to a significant extent, the fault is that of the less globalized countries own doing. The world, as a whole, does not accept hostility and finger-pointing as a means to solve the problems one is faced with.

Hosni Mubarak, Egypt's president, says: 'In the emerging world there is a bitter sentiment of injustice. There is a sense that there must be something wrong with a system that wipes out years of hard-won development because of changes in market sentiments.'[9] Market sentiments change when the market is assaulted through bubbles (like that of late 1990s), CEO malfeasance, or criminal acts through a small but violent minority. Also Mubarak's complaint forgets some basic facts about globalization and money flows:

- Contrary to the post-World War II financial assistance programs, put up mainly by the USA, private money is not government handouts in disguise. It goes where it can make good profits, and it rushes out of the door when the perceived risks – financial or physical – exceed returns, and when the country benefiting from capital inflows is not able to put them to productive use, for whatever reason.
- Without this private money flow, the so-called emerging markets would never have emerged, and there would have been no 'years of hard-won development'. The best way to explain this is through a joke which was popular at the time the wave of globalization started in the 1980s. To the question: 'What's worse than being exploited by a multinational?', the answer was: 'Not being exploited by one or several of them.' That is where the issue of transborder capital flows connected to globalization comes in.

As George Soros suggests, the defining characteristic of globalization is the freedom of capital to move around – which is not matched by the freedom of people – therefore giving financial capital a privileged position.[10] A direct effect of this freedom of capital flows is that it undermines the ability of sovereign states to exercise control over capital flows. Hence the need for prudential regulation of the banking system, as envisaged by Basel II, to avoid overleveraging.

Whether at national or global level, overleveraging leads to bubbles and a sharp drop in market confidence. In turn, lack of business confidence has an adverse effect on transborder money flows, and this hurts the less developed countries the most.

The drop in business confidence which characterized the first years of the twenty-first century provides an example. According to the Washington-based Institute of International Finance, flows of private capital to emerging markets plunged by nearly a third in 2001, to $115 billion, the lowest level in a decade – but the distribution has been uneven.

Because of its huge domestic market, China sucks in lots of direct investment. Its companies raised $20 billion in offshore stock offerings in 2000 alone. Blind investments in 'emerging markets' are no longer favored by macroinvestors. The majority of these countries are not nurturing the political and corporate systems needed to sustain growth and eventually become modern financial entities. Critical factors such as fair labour practices, a free press and impartial courts are also very important, as a 2001/02 study by CalPers, the giant California pension fund, documents.

Moreover, global markets do not have the social cohesiveness which sometimes, though by no means always, characterizes national and local markets. They lack rigorous government supervision, shared values and social responsibility. Kofi Anan, the secretary general of the United Nations suggested that national markets are held together by shared values and confidence in certain minimum standards. But in the new global market, people do not yet have that confidence.

The national markets, too, are changing. Precisely because the old concept of sovereign states able to raise walls at their borders can no longer be supported, effective globalization requires supranational institutions capable of regulating and supervising the global market. These supranational institutions should be empowered to plan and to act both directly and through the intermediary of existing national institutions. This is not exactly the way the Basel Committee on Banking Supervision operates. Rather, its power comes through inverse delegation, as shown in Figure 15.6.

Direct authority is needed because transnational regulatory and supervisory institutions must not only plan effectively to avoid future systemic crises, but they also have to do so in a *symmetric* way. This would be a great step forward from current *asymmetries* which exist between crisis prevention and crisis intervention – the fire brigade approach which still characterizes the resolution of many financial crises.

Eventually, some sort of transnational regulatory and supervisory institutions will have to extend their realm beyond financial and economic matters into social issues, such as an even playing field regarding health care, a social safety net and taxation. Taxation of income and wealth used to be computed on a national scale, but globalization:

- Has rendered high tax rates counterproductive, and
- Has led companies to tax evasion through incorporation offshore.

For instance, under Internal Revenue Service (IRS) rules, American companies must pay taxes on their worldwide profits. But by incorporating abroad, firms can exclude foreign-earned profits from their US tax returns – which makes it much more attractive to incorporate in such lightly taxed places as Bermuda.

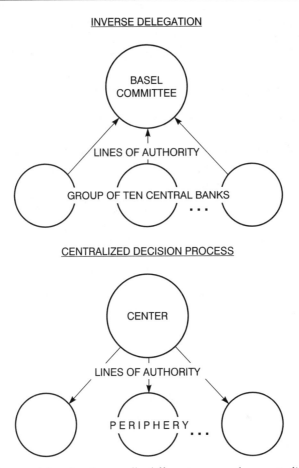

Figure 15.6 Inverse delegation is a totally different process than centralized authority

There are also other major challenges with globalization. A good example is the lack of cross-border infrastructural rules for prudential regulation. For instance, who regulates Citigroup, Deutsche Bank, BNP Paribas, Nomura or JP Morgan Chase? With operations in 100 countries or so, global financial conglomerates are, in theory, looked after by nobody.

In conclusion, there are many global firms in a fragmented world of national and sectoral watchdogs. Basel II is not necessarily targeting this huge regulatory loophole, but by providing a homogeneous risk-sensitive frame of reference, in capital adequacy terms, it brings with it a sense of a more transparent pattern of control. This is in itself a major achievement, which should be appreciated by everybody.

Notes

1 *Fortune*, 24 June 2002.
2 D.N. Chorafas (2003). *Alternative Investments and the Mismanagement of Risk.* Macmillan/Palgrave.

3 D.N. Chorafas (2003). *Stress Testing: Risk Management Strategies for Extreme Events*. Euromoney.

4 D.N. Chorafas (2001). *Managing Risk in the New Economy*. New York Institute of Finance.

5 *Executive Intelligence Review*, 21 March 2003.

6 *The Economist*, 17 May 2003.

7 D.N. Chorafas (2003). *Alternative Investments and the Mismanagement of Risk*. Macmillan/Palgrave.

8 World Bank Policy Research Report (2001). *Globalization, Growth and Poverty*. World Bank, December.

9 *Herald Tribune*, 22 February 1999.

10 George Soros (2001). *Draft Report on Globalization*. Public Affairs.

16 Contrarians to Basel II, CAD 3 and 2010 challenges

16.1 Introduction

By March 2003 it became evident that the implementation of Basel II would be variable by jurisdiction. The Dutch regulators, for example, informed all the big banks: ABN Amro, ING, Rabobank, and Fortis, the financial holdings company, that they had to use the A-IRB method for credit risk, and also implement all other requirements of the new capital adequacy framework.

Theoretically, this is no different than what the Federal Reserve said in the USA. The Fed of New York left no doubt that at least the ten to twelve largest American banks *must* use A-IRB. Practically, however, there exists a wide gap between the Dutch (and other European) regulators and the US regulators, because the top ten, twelve or twenty US banks are a very small proportion of a population of over 6500 American credit institutions. The difference is caused by politics.

The resistance by the American banking industry to Basel II came to the fore during the 27 February 2003, and subsequent hearings on Basel II, by the US House of Representatives and US Senate. More hearings are expected in late 2003, at which critics of the new capital accord will have plenty of opportunity to win the support of lawmakers.[1] A good deal of the focus of this opposition is on the operational risk capital charge. But Basel II is also attacked for having raised several concerns among the medium and smaller US banks about:

- Its complexity, and
- Its indirect impact on average size institutions.

Through the case study on the German savings banks, Chapter 2 provided the evidence that both arguments are fake. Theoretical economists, too, have tried to make a name for themselves by attacking Basel II. Several did so through the self-appointed Shadow Financial Regulatory Committee. Out of the blue, they offered an 'evidently better' alternative plan for bank regulation (discussed in section 16.4) where:

- Leverage would have a ball, and
- Equity will be sent to oblivion, while debt will be king (see also Chapter 9 on the Modigliani-Miller hypothesis).

Other late-in-the-day critics have found different flaws with Basel II. For instance, some are suggesting that one of its problems is that banks will design assets to fit particular classes of risk. To continue with capital arbitrage, these critics say, credit institutions will be bending whatever connection there might previously have been between:

- A rating applied after the fact, and
- The level of risk being assumed.

Because companies are made of people, and many people specialize in how to bend or break the rules, this is not at all unlikely. A better way of approaching this issue, however, is not by outright criticism of the new capital adequacy framework, but by bringing attention to the fact that there should be a steady watch for violations and bypasses. This is what Pillar 2 and Pillar 3 are supposed to do. Let us not forget that:

- Capital arbitrage has been the banks' twist of Basel I, and
- Basel II tries to stamp it out through better focused regulations.

Other critics target the independent rating agencies, which have a major role to play with Basel II's standardized method. They say that the rating agencies are faced with a possible conflict of interest, if not outright moral hazard, by being tempted to debase their ratings in order to acquire business from banks, and because rating agencies engage in risk management consulting and in training.

For these reasons, these critics suggest that credit risk rating standards are likely to deteriorate. They also point out that this has happened with certified public accountants who have been faced with similar conflicts of interest in their external auditing of financial and industrial entities, because they have been earning more money from consulting than from auditing.

What this argument points out is that relying on independent rating agencies seems questionable, even if in principle it may be desirable to draw on wider sources of credit risk information. The same critics are also using academic research which suggests that rating agencies change their opinion too slowly, and their record in the East Asian financial crisis, Enron, Global Crossing, WorldCom and so on, was hardly impressive. But has anybody done any better?

The fact of the matter is that criticism is always welcome, as long as it is constructive – pointing out weaknesses and presenting alternatives in a factual and documented manner. This is not the case with theoretical economists, politicians and others behind them who came out at the eleventh hour – nearly four years after the first consultative paper of Basel II was released – to hinder rather than to help in improving the new capital accord.

16.2 Dissent is an integral part of sound governance: the good news

The introduction to this chapter has left no doubt that the new capital adequacy framework by the Basel Committee has its critics. The argument is not against being critical and having a contrarian opinion but, rather, about doing so out of time and place, just to make a name for oneself at the expense of the others, or to stop sound prudential rules from taking hold because they are contrary to one's interests.

As a matter of principle in sound governance, criticism should be *welcome* and *constructive*. What the Basel Committee did with successive consultative papers and quantitative impact studies (see Chapter 1) was intended to invite constructive criticism, which has helped to improve the regulatory system and its capital adequacy rules.

Practically all standards bodies follow this policy, even if classically financial, industrial and government organizations – in their inner workings – tend to weed out the non-conformist elements. This weeding out of contrarian opinion is one of the reasons they respond slowly to change. Only more enlightened management appreciates that eliminating dissent creates a monolithic group aligned behind one approach, which finds it difficult to predict a sound path, let alone the best one.

By contrast, a credit institution or any other organization that tolerates dissent is able to respond to market shifts in a flexible and effective way. It can change more easily the allocation of its resources if the market moves in a different direction than originally expected or projected. Moreover, business life teaches that:

- Perfectly aligned organizations tend to reduce creativity.
- By contrast, dissent forces a company to face constraints and produce better rounded solutions.

Rubber-stamping and intolerance of dissent cause the board and senior management to consider few alternatives, exaggerate one's prospects of success and underestimate possible exposure. There are major risks embedded in too much alignment, the greatest peril being that of moving blind-folded to the precipice. Basel II is not addressing these issues, because it does not enter into corporate governance per se.

Clear-thinking CEOs appreciate the benefits that can be gained from dissent, and they take whatever measures they judge necessary to realize them. Alfred P. Sloan Jr, the legendary General Motor's chairman and CEO, once said at a board meeting: 'Gentlemen, I take it we are all in complete agreement on the decision here.' When the assembled senior executives all nodded their assent, Sloan proposed delaying further discussion on this matter until the next meeting to:

- Give the board members time to develop disagreement, and
- Gain some understanding of what the decision was all about.

In a way, through successive consultative papers, QIS and emphasis on market discipline (see Chapter 4), this is what the Basel Committee has done with its own members, the regulators and with hundreds of commercial banks around the globe – over a four-year period.

Individually, following Sloan's principle, in every credit institution CEOs will be well advised to provide for themselves and their immediate assistants a mechanism that brings constantly across everybody's desk the query, 'Which are *my* alternatives?', along with a reminder of three crucial questions which confront every manager, whether or not he or she likes it:

- What should we do?
- Are we doing it?
- Is the last policy working?

Principles of sound management dictate that to be able to drive the company in an effective manner, the chief executive should listen to dissent, then convey his or her decision through a few simple ideas – which outline the direction, and set the pace for action. The CEO should listen to dissent, but should not elaborate, and surely not excuse himself for having a different opinion.

Complexities belong to the middle levels of the organization. If they reach the top, they paralyze. The CEO cannot be exposed to a hundred sides, and then mark time like a centipede. Neither should he feel he has solved a problem if all his immediate assistants accept a decision which may be expressed in a way which is either meaningless or ambiguous. The CEO's decision must be:

- Clear
- Unambiguous
- Able to give a sense of duty.

If a decision can be misunderstood, it will be. *If* a decision is misunderstood, *then* the CEO will get the most of what he or she wants the least, his or her people will be overcome by trivialities and the company will lack direction. But making a clear decision requires: skill, practice and, most important, daring. Basically, that's what the Basel Committee attempted to do with Basel II.

Daring decisions are necessary to provide the organization's *future vision* and to face coming business challenges. In their way, daring decisions shape the culture of an organization, as well as of a regulatory environment. Indeed, one of the after-effects of Basel II is that the culture it brings with it will base the financial industry of the future on five pillars as shown in Figure 16.1, and by so doing will affect every individual credit institution – whether or not it implements Basel II.

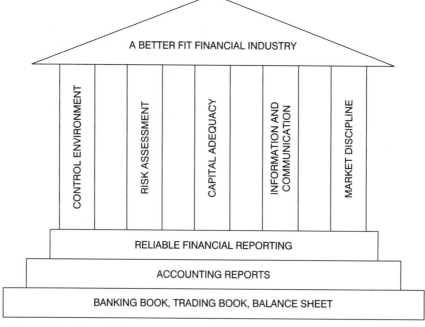

Figure 16.1 The reliable reporting structure created in the longer run by Basel II

The structure in Figure 16.1 points to the most significant aftermath of cultural change in the banking industry, which has been underestimated by practically all the adverse reactions to Basel II. While nobody failed to notice the difficulties associated with its implementation, few entities (and people) have paid due attention to:

- The significant benefits which it provides
- The fact these benefits are cultural, managerial and technical
- The need for stratification in Basel II adoption, which is part of its optimization.

'Almost everybody is in favor of Basel II on balance,' said Dr Edward I. Altman, of the Leonard N. Stern School of Business, New York, in his testimony at the Senate Banking Committee hearings (see Sections 16.5–16.7). Professor Altman stated that the Basel Committee has made 'great strides' in improving the accord, and he criticized the decision that only ten American banks should be obliged to comply with Basel II and meet the most advanced credit measurement approaches as 'unfortunate and should be reconsidered'.

Correctly, Altman pointed out that the possible exemption from Basel II compliance of some of the largest banks ranked eleventh to thirtieth, and the very likely exemption of significant banks ranked thirty-first to fiftieth, 'seems arbitrary and belittles the possible sophistication and motivation of these banks, which would be substantial institutions in most other countries of the world'.

For instance, the fiftieth largest bank in the US in terms of assets (Compass Bank with $24.3 billion), or in terms of deposits (Mellon Bank, with $15.2 billion), would be huge institutions in most countries, Dr Altman noted. He is as well concerned that many countries might follow the US example and impose bifurcated capital adequacy systems in banking which will diminish the accord's stimulus to better risk management globally.

As far as I can see, there is as well another danger with half-baked approaches to Basel II implementation. While in a way it makes sense for *very small* banks which are not involved in risky trades, like derivatives, to live with Basel I compliance there is the risk that such small banks may be used by big banks as proxies, in an effort to bypass Basel II requirements.

Let me repeat this statement. One of the risks in making exceptions to a universal Basel II implementation is that big banks might use small banks, still on Basel I, for capital arbitrage and other reasons. Moreover, this could happen within the same holding because big banks hold small banks, particularly abroad.

It is wise to keep in mind that Basel II's implementation timetable has been specified in a way allowing banks using IRB solutions to delay introducing them for their overseas subsidiaries, where market data may be:

- Less accessible, or
- Less satisfactory than IRB requires.

Stated in a different way: one has to be very careful about the 'small banks' argument. The risk is that a political dimension introduced into Basel II may lead to loopholes, make a policy out of hard bargaining or twist the path of implementation by means of technical arguments. For instance, some experts say European banks would have an easier time in handling complexity, because they hire graduates with engineering degrees.

16.3   Reservations about Basel II expressed by professional bodies

Regulatory capital requirements promoted by Basel II, and the way to compute them, have been criticized for several reasons. One of these criticisms is the 'small banks' argument discussed in section 16.2. But there is also a critique regarding holding companies.

Some people feel that the application of Basel II to holding groups that predominantly engage in banking activities, will create competitive disadvantages for banking organizations compared with other financial services firms. The answer to this is that quite often the 'holding groups' themselves are 'Trojan horses'.

True enough, there exist differences in national treatment of banking entities, and even more differences prevail across national borders regarding holding companies. For this and for other reasons, it is the opinion of the American Bankers Association that Basel II should not apply on a fully consolidated basis to holding companies of predominantly banking groups. Experts who disagree with this argument point out that, if this happens, it will be tantamount to dismantling all prudential regulation.

Correctly (in my opinion), Basel II applies on a subconsolidated basis to all internationally active banks, at every tier below the top banking group level. A blanket coverage is the best way to prevent loopholes, preserve the integrity of capital adequacy and eliminate double gearing in a banking group.

Where the different national bankers associations opposing Basel II implementation by bank holding groups have a point, is that because local regulators of the G-10 retain their authority, within their jurisdiction, the new capital accord would allow differences in national treatment of some financial subsidiaries. This is not a flaw of Basel II but, rather, the aftermath of the way in which the Basel Committee works, with its authority based on inverse delegation by its members (see Chapter 15).

The reader will recall that the Basel Committee's authority flows from the periphery to the center, not vice versa. This has evidently led to compromises – both in a cross-border sense and across financial industry sectors. For instance, Basel II would not consolidate insurance subsidiaries, requiring instead the deduction of bank investments in such entities. Further, it would deduct from banks' capital any significant investments in commercial entities that exceed established thresholds.

What has been stated in the preceding paragraph is of concern to American banks because, in 1999, a wider range of financial activities for new financial holding companies (FHCs) through the Gramm-Leach-Bliley Act (GLBA) was authorized. In the US financial landscape, the GLBA made it possible for financial conglomerates incorporating commercial banking, insurance, securities and merchant banking to benefit from various aspects of deregulation.

For instance, under the new law, the Federal Reserve may assess capital adequacy of the FHC, but it is prohibited from setting capital adequacy standards for non-bank financial subsidiaries. Neither is the GLBA permitting the Fed to set capital requirements for commercial firms with large non-bank financial services operations, which are barred from becoming new FHCs.

On a totally different issue, which has been brought up by national banking associations, while increasing the number of risk categories improves the current basis of handling risk, many banks do not have the experience to do so. The answer, of course, is that they should do their best to fill this gap in their skills armory. If anything, to serve the objective of improved management, the control of risk should be further increased. This will also better the granularity of risk weightings against which have moved the economists in SFRC (see section 16.4). All risks should be:

■ Subject to a thorough classification and identification, with appropriately defined thresholds, and
■ Handled in a sophisticated way, including knowledge artefacts which enable risks and their patterns to be tracked at any time, anywhere in the world.

Critics of Basel II say that today the majority of credit institutions are simply not equipped to do what the foregoing points suggest. Such failure, however, reflects the quality and depth of each bank's governance. That is where criticisms and corrections should be directed.

For reasons outlined in the preceding paragraphs, and some others, as far back as April 2000 the Institute of International Finance had outlined broad concerns with the Basel Committee on Banking Supervision. In its response to the reform of the 1998 Basel Accord, the IIF raised a number of questions but, contrary to latter-day critics:

■ It brought forward its points early enough, so that they could be openly discussed, and
■ It collaborated in a significant way through the QIS test, most particularly in connection with QIS3.

In the objections to Basel II, which it formulated in April 2000, the IIF said that the proposed new capital adequacy framework could substantially impair banks' ability to compete with other financial services providers, while simultaneously establishing a framework that does not measurably increase the relationship between true risk and regulatory capital. The way Jan Klaff, chairman of ABN-Amro and head of the IIF's steering committee on Basel proposals, put it:

> We live in an era of technological change, globalization and growing competitive pressures. Banks today are active in many parts of the world, they undertake transactions that involve a vast range of different types of risks and they compete against many non-banking institutions. The eight percent rule implies that all corporate risks are equal. Naturally, this is not the case.[2]

Reading between the lines, Klaff's statement is not a critique of Basel II, but of the 1988 Capital Accord. What IIF practically said is that a blanket capital requirement does not adequately represent individual banks' exposure to risk. This is essentially a positive comment on Basel II, because the latter makes possible tailoring capital requirements to each bank's exposure (see Chapter 2 on risk-based pricing).

The IIF criticized Basel II's reliance on external rating agencies for credit risk evaluation and capital assessments. Instead, it suggested banks be permitted to use their internal risk rating systems as a basis for assessing capital requirements, subject to regulatory approval. That is practically what has been done. Note should, however, be taken of the fact that:

- Most banks have a coarse grading scale, not the one of twenty thresholds of the independent rating agencies, and
- Internal and external ratings are not necessarily opposed to one another. Rather, they are complementary.

In fact, the banks themselves use independent rating agencies to rate their bonds and securitized products. Why should they be against using the agencies' other ratings? Moreover, the Basel Committee never said banks cannot use, or should not use, their own credit rating systems. On the contrary, the new capital adequacy framework promotes internal rating models. But at a time of globalization of financial services,

- Credit scores thoroughly researched by independent rating agencies offer a common level ground.
- By contrast, ratings by individual banks can differ greatly from one another; neither are they publicly available.

The IIF had also complained about what it considered to be insufficient differentiation between the different types of risk banks undertake. It pressed the need for more thorough consideration of benefits from collateral and other risk mitigation tools (see Chapter 12 on collateral). This is an argument that should be handled with care.

As Robert Maxwell, and so many others, have thoroughly demonstrated through malfeasance, collateral may turn out to be of questionable value. In a number of cases, with the assistance of dematerialization, the same collateral is pledged to more than one party. As for the 'risk mitigation tools' (for which read, derivative financial instruments) they may bring to the bank more risk than they supposedly waive.[3]

Last, but not least, as far as technical expertise, capital requirements and supervisory duties are concerned, the proposed creation of a bifurcated banking system: of Basel II versus Basel I, is generating increasingly strong opposition among credit institutions. Several start to feel that their capital requirements will be higher than those of the big banks that are able to use the A-IRB method.

Moreover, as we will see in section 16.5 a reason for the uncertain trumpet in the US jurisdiction is the discord which exists among US regulators in regard to Basel II. To placate critics, the regulators have promised that they will consider all comments made in response to their Advance Notice of Proposed Rulemaking (ANPR) – jointly issued mid-July 2003 by four regulatory agencies: Federal Reserve, Office of the Comptroller of the Currency, Office of Thrift Supervision and Federal Deposit Insurance Corporation.

At the same time, the unveiling of ANPR seems to bring under spotlight the splits between US regulators after their attempt to close ranks in front of the Senate and

House committees. Classically, disagreements between regulatory agencies have been resolved by the time notices of advanced rule making are issued. But questions posed by this ANPR tend to reveal a split in opinions in regard to Basel II and its rules.

Such last minute discords are counterproductive because as far as its technical aspects are concerned, Basel II has been on the right track, though with practice its clauses can, and will, be improved. New regulations must enhance competitiveness by bringing individual banks' capital requirements more in line with actual risks. The problem is that 'actual risk' is a highly dynamic concept and its computation is an art, not a science.

Effective regulation, therefore, must induce banks to foresee *risk volatility* as well as the likelihood of future developments which may adversely affect the credit institutions' position. Beyond this, effective regulation finds hurdles in its way because of clashing political interests, which is the theme of sections 16.5 to 16.8. Political risk is much greater than technical risk when applying effective bank supervision.

16.4   The Shadow Financial Regulatory Committee and its 'debt is king' proposal

The introduction to this chapter made reference to the self-appointed SFRC. This is an independent outfit, mainly manned by theoretical economists in academia, which lobbies for reform in the banking industry. Shadow Financial Regulatory Committee economists argue that while Basel II is an improved capital accord over Basel I, it still has defects which can be corrected through some debt magic.

It is appropriate to state at the outset that this Shadow Financial Regulatory Committee is not an official body, and it has no authority to set capital adequacy or any other rules. Its economists suggest a method different to that of the Basel Committee, drawing heavily on concepts from the highly leveraged late 1990s which led to the 2000–03 market blues. They also look at the way Federal Deposit Insurance Corporation works – coupled with an 'early intervention', whatever this might mean. The SFRC's alternative capital adequacy has five components:[4]

1 Measure each bank's capital in a way that reflects market (not book) values, and regularly disclose this to the markets.
2 Require credit institutions to maintain a level of capital capable of absorbing almost all losses that would be incurred by prudent management.
3 Allow banks to meet this capital requirement by issuing subordinated debt, like uninsured certificates of deposit.
4 Require large banks to issue and regularly reissue a particular form of subordinated debt, to replenish their coffers.
5 Furnish the financial markets with both information and incentives they need to monitor the banks and their exposure.

That is typical talk by theorists, that is by people who lack real practical experience. Setting aside the fact that points 1 and 5 in the list overlap to a large extent, one should not fail to notice that they say nothing different to Pillar 3 of Basel II. As the reader will recall, Pillar 3 underpins the importance of market discipline, from both a national and a global perspective (see Chapter 4).

Specifically regarding the SFRC's first point, the reader will recall the many references made in this book to the advantages of marking-to-market over book value – but also to the risks involved in marking-to-market because:

- Many instruments particularly in the bank's trading book have no market, and
- This obliges marking-to-model which, as Warren Buffett aptly suggests, often amounts to marking-to-myth.

Regarding the second point of the SFRC's list, this is nothing 'new'. Indeed, it is what Basel II is all about. It requires credit institutions to maintain a capital that would permit banks to absorb all losses under prudent management – essentially, the expected losses. It is interesting that the SFRC carefully avoids any reference to unexpected losses. Yet, as we have seen throughout this book, UL is a much more difficult proposition than EL, to judge and provide for.

The SFRC's points 3 and 4 are merely a version of one another. They are also crazy because they try to promote more debt rather than more equity – which is precisely the opposite of what should be done (see Chapter 9 on the Modigliani-Miller hypothesis and its flaws).

Who other than an economist would ever have suggested that buying large amounts of the banks' subordinate debt will be a popular investment in the capital market? Most likely, what will happen is quite the opposite. After all, this is money at a knife edge, because the debt the investor will supposedly buy will not be recovered if a bank fails – as the SFRC proposal has it. Such debt:

- Has the worst characteristics of equity,
- But contrary to equity, which has a potential upside, it does not have any benefits of that sort.

Among the advantages the SFRC suggests for its scheme is that there would be no risk-weighting as with Basel II. Weights, the SFRC argues, distort lending decisions and fail to convey the information they are meant to. The theoretical economists behind the SFRC's proposals forget to notice that subordinated debt, too, requires weights. Their argument is incomplete for two reasons:

- Though they are by no means perfect, and their accuracy is average, risk-weights (see Chapter 12) are not as bad as they are said to be, and
- Risk-weights have somehow integrated themselves into banking practices. To get them out of the system, one has to provide better alternatives, and the SFRC offers none.

Neither does the arbitrary 10 percent capital requirement the SFRC suggests – in a way decoupled from assumed exposure, which varies widely by institution – make any sense. It simply changes the flat 8 percent Basel I into a flat10 percent. Big deal! Indeed, the great merit of Basel II is that:

- It closely aligns capital adequacy to risk management, and that
- It leads to risk-based pricing of financial instruments.

This is a major improvement over the past. Implying a 10 percent flat capital adequacy rate, without close linkage to assumed exposure, is tantamount to driving at 100 mph on a road but looking through the rear-view mirror. This makes the SFRC's proposal worse than a non-starter. It is a dangerous suggestion, even if it includes the adjunct notion of an FDIC-type intervention. The five points we have examined:

- Are not a 'solution' to regulatory capital needs,
- Or a road map on how to avoid systemic risk.

Moreover, for the information of the SFRC's economists, the FDIC has statutory rights, which the Basel Committee lacks, because it works through inverse delegation. Notice also that the statutory rights of the FDIC are limited in the USA, and they can be changed by act of Congress, as with the recent FDICIA legislation documents. No regulator or supervisory agency has *global* statutory rights in connection with the banking industry.

It is also appropriate to keep in mind that, to accomplish its work in an able manner, the FDIC has a body of well-trained, tough examiners who can shred the balance sheet of institutions under their authority to pieces, if they need to. There is no such body with its own examiners working on a global scale. Unlike the Fed, the OCC and the FDIC in the USA, in other countries most national regulators do not even have their own examiners. They depend on CPAs – that is, on independent firms – to do that job. The case of Arthur Andersen carries a message about where this has led in terms of conflicts of interest.

So much for the technical hurdles confronting the implementation of Basel II. Those promoting Basel II, however, are not only theoretical technicians; they are also politicians – to whose activities are dedicated the following sections.

16.5 The 27 February 2003 Testimony to the US Congress Subcommittee

The introduction to this chapter referred to the 27 February 2003 hearings on Basel II, called by the Domestic and International Monetary Policy, Trade and Technology Subcommittee on Financial Services of the House of Representatives, US Congress. In the course of these hearings, Roger Ferguson, Federal Reserve Board vice chairman and Basel Committee member, faced tough and relentless questioning during a three-hour session.

The attack against Basel II came from a relatively small, vocal minority of the subcommittee. For political reasons, some Congressmen felt it necessary to demonstrate that they were paying due attention to the concerns of their constituencies in bypassing Basel II rules. Analysts noted that the constituency of Barney Frank, the ranking Democrat on the House Financial Services Committee was in Boston, where the State Street Bank is headquartered. State Street is:

- One of the world's largest asset managers
- A major global custodian, and
- A fierce opponent of operational risk charges.

As the reader will appreciate between the lines of these three bullets, opposition to parts of Basel II has been building among specialized banks – like custodians – who feel that they will be penalized by the new operational risk charge. These vocal critics have managed to activate the political process in the USA, but banks which are in charge of their operational risks, and other exposures, have come out in favor of Basel II.

For instance, in his July 2003 testimony to the US Senate Banking Committee, Kevin Blakely, KeyCorporation, gave strong backing for the new capital adequacy accord: 'We simply believe that it is good banking practice to develop the risk management tools that are the foundation of Basel II.' Blakely was a bank regulator until 1990 when he became a private sector banker.

Although much has been said about the cost of building the models necessary to comply with Basel II, 'at KeyCorporation we wonder how anyone can afford not to build them' Blakely stated. Cleveland-based KeyCorporation is the twelfth largest banking company in the US, so it is not included in the top ten most internationally active institutions. While it will not be obliged by the Fed to comply with Basel II accord when it comes into effect at the end of 2006, the bank intends to opt for inclusion in the wider list of banks electing to comply.

It should be noted that some of the regulators, too, expressed concerns about Basel II clauses. John Hawke, Comptroller of the Currency, and Donald Powell, chairman of the FDIC registered reservations about Basel II while backing it in principle. Notice that all three US regulatory agencies, the Federal Reserve Board, including the New York Fed, the FDIC and the OCC, are represented on the Basel Committee and have approved its decisions.

In his territory, John Hawke pointed out some of the accord's negative aspects, and he expressed his concern that competitive equality between banks might not be maintained under the Basel II regime. Roger Ferguson, however, rejected such criticisms; most particularly those concerning the new capital accord's 'excessive complexity'.

The Federal Reserve's vice chairman used his testimony to disclose important elements of Fed policy towards Basel II. He was more precise than hitherto about how many US banks would be obliged to comply with the accord, and made the revelation that US supervisors intend to apply only the A-IRB method. Ferguson said that:

- The Fed will not be adopting the two other variants – the standardized and foundation IRB approaches, developed by the Basel Committee, and
- The Fed intended to require about ten large US banks to adopt A-IRB, but it also anticipated that a small number of other large US banking entities will choose to adopt it as well.

Understandably, this statement greatly surprised European bank supervisors who had contributed to Basel II, and project its implementation by all credit institutions under their jurisdiction. After having underlined that only internationally active banks will be required to adopt A-IRB, Ferguson added that all other banks in the USA will remain on Basel I capital standard when the new accord is implemented – because the shortfall in current rules is not sufficiently large to warrant a mandatory shift to Basel II.

Roger Ferguson stated in his testimony that any of the American credit institutions will have the option to adopt A-IRB, after making the necessary investment to support their participation. This means that they will have to meet the same high standards of internal infrastructure and controls that will be required of the big banks in the core group. This has significant potential ramifications on the Basel II debate in Europe.

The vice chairman of the Fed also made it clear that the banks to which the new Basel regime applies would have to adopt the most advanced operational risk measurement approach, along with A-IRB for credit risk measurement. But the Basel I exception that the Fed unilaterally granted was interpreted in Europe as soft-pedalling and it has been a major hindrance for regulators who see Basel II as a global standard to be applied to all credit institutions, at least in G-10 countries.

Some analysts noted that even the reference to internationally active banks may be watered down when the Fed talks about only ten to twelve US institutions. To European regulators, this reference meant that banks as big as State Street, Bank of New York, Mellon Financial Corporation, PNC Financial Services, and Northern Trust, which all have large international payments and securities operations, might escape the new rules. Indeed, State Street and Mellon have been lobbying hard in this direction, arguing that the Basel II charge for operational risk is improper.

The State Street's argument that operational risk is impossible to quantify does not really make sense.[5] Based on such shaky ground, the bank suggests that it would therefore be better if supervisors monitored the institutions' efforts to mitigate these risks and then set a 'subjective' capital charge. (More on State Street's testimony in section 16.6.)

Neither American nor European regulators accept this type of argument. In Europe, reaction has been particularly negative because a version of Basel II is to be incorporated into EU law and applied to all commercial banks and investment firms, not just internationally active institutions. But at the same time, European regulators are concerned that members of the European Parliament might also try to reshape Basel II's rules. Alexander Radwan, who will report to the European Parliament on Basel II, has already expressed several concerns. Among these are that:

- Capital charges that are more sensitive to credit risk could curb lending to small companies, a fear previously expressed also by the German government, and
- The fact of bank-supervision rules being drawn up and amended by unelected experts, like the Basel Committee, practically brings financial legislation outside the purview of politicians.

The Europeans, however, are not deprived of bargaining tools. American banks cannot operate in Europe under capital adequacy and rules of supervision not approved by the EU, unless these are judged to be of 'equivalent' standard. American banks may soon find that Basel I will not be deemed equivalent within the EU after 2006, when CAD 3 is due to take effect (see section 16.8).

Furthermore, some US investment banks may be caught by another EU directive on financial conglomerates, which comes into force in 2005. To continue operating in European countries, they may have to seek out a consolidated supervisor with stronger oversight than their current one, the Securities and Exchange Commission. We shall see what happens in a year or two.

16.6   The eleventh hour is no time for constructive criticisms

In his February 2003 testimony, John Hawke said that the OCC was concerned about maintaining an appropriate competitive balance in the USA between the large, internationally active banks and the thousands of smaller banks and S&Ls (thrifts, building societies). Thrifts, however, are not concerned by Basel II, neither are they under OCC jurisdiction – while the statement that Basel II 'would discourage innovation in market practices and advances in risk management' is clearly wrong.[6]

John Hawke also expressed concerns about the impact of the Basel II accord on the competitive balance in the banking industry, namely, between banks and non-banks. In this, the Controller of the Currency is right. The lack of regulation of non-banks – including hedge funds and other financials (see Chapter 15) – is a huge loophole exploited also by banks when they channel money through hedge funds and their vehicles. The puzzle is that John Hawke, who is a member of the Basel Committee, did not bring this matter up in 1999 but treated it only in 2003.

A few months later, John Hawke's July 2003 testimony to both the House and the Senate committees was widely viewed as closer to the Fed's position than some of his previous statements. His most important reservation regarded the Basel Committee's third study of the quantificative impact (QIS3, see Chapter 1) of the new accord on the world's banking system. Hawke said the resulting data still do not 'provide a sufficiently reliable estimate of the likely regulatory requirements for banks subject to Basel II.' This is not the sort of statement one would expect from senior persons.

Also, in July 2003, James Gilleran, Director, Office of Thrift Supervision (OTS), stressed the need to maintain the competitive equality of community banks which play a significant role in small business lending. He said the OTS was attempting to take a more active role in small business lending internationally 'because of the impact of Basel on the institutions we regulate'.

During the first Congress hearings, of late Feburary 2003, more constructive than the testimony of other regulators was that by Donald Powell, chairman of the FDIC. In his testimony, he brought up three issues which, he said, need to be addressed before the Basel II regime is implemented in the USA:

■ The accord must assure that appropriate minimum capital requirements are maintained, regardless of what models say. This has already been done by maintaining the 8 percent capital adequacy as a floor, as documented by the Basel Committee's consultative document, *Overview of the New Basel Capital Accord*, issued April 2003. On page 2/17 of that document it explicitly states: 'The resulting capital ratio may be no less than 8 percent'.
■ The accord must ensure that internal risk estimates used as inputs to the new capital formulas are made in a sound way. Powell added that such estimates must be conservative, and evaluated consistently going forward, using a uniform interagency process for doing so. That is correct, and it is mainly a Pillar 2 issue.
■ The competitive impact of Basel II must be fully accessed, so that it does not result in lower capital charges for the biggest US banks.

Donald Powell also set down criteria for his approval of Basel II rules, including supervisory consistency when judging the soundness of banks' internal risk models.

This is fully supported by Warren Buffett in his article in the 17 March 2003 *Fortune Magazine* where he stated that sometimes marking-to-model is marking-to-myth (several references have been already made to Buffett's dictum).

Most of the concerns US regulators expressed in their testimony were valid, though they came late in the day. By contrast, the deposition of other critics, mainly commercial or investment bankers and consultants whose work saw to it that there might well have been a conflict of interest in the background, to the congressional subcommittee has been rather curious.

One of the bankers was David Spina, CEO of State Street Corporation. Another was Wilson Ervin, head of strategic risk management at Crédit Suisse First Boston. Analysts viewed Ervin as among the most antagonistic to Basel II. This puzzled them, given that the CSFB has been one of the banks indicted on 28 April 2003 for underwriting and recommending bad stocks during the bubble years of the late 1980s – paying a penalty and disgorgement of ill-gotten profits to the tune of $200 million[7](see Chapter 14).

Where is the moral standing to criticize the agreement reached by regulators?[8] To my mind, there is a striking resemblance between the attack on Basel II by Spina and Ervin and what Gerhard Schroeder and Jacques Chirac did to the Atlantic Alliance and the United Nations in connection with the Iraqi affair. Both the two bankers and the two politicians were members of exclusive clubs:

- The politicians through debates which took place in the North Atlantic Treaty Organization, the United Nations and, no doubt, person-to-person meetings.
- The bankers of the big banks intimately involved in shaping Basel II through consultative papers and quantitative impact tests.

In both cases, those who have not carried the day have tried their hand at political maneuvers for short-term benefit: financial in one case, political in the other (but here, too, with financial impact). With this, the longer term has been sacrificed for the short term, which is not precisely the most clear-sighted managerial approach.

To better appreciate this issue, let us look more closely into the background of each of the aforementioned contrarian testimonies by commercial and investment bankers. As of 2003, State Street had total assets of $85.8 billion, making it the eleventh largest American banking company. The institution is the tops in technology, which makes it difficult to see why it would be opposed to operational risk reserves, if it were not for the fact that:

- Being the world's second largest custodian, State Street management is aware of the extent of its operational risks, and
- Large operational risks need hefty capital reserves to face the challenges, which will evidently be quite costly.

In his prepared testimony to the House Subcommittee, David Spina argued strongly against the proposed imposition of an operational risk capital charge for banks, saying that this charge 'is misguided and creates a competitive disadvantage for US banks'. This argument is nonsense because all banks have to comply with Basel II, at least all important banks like his own.

Spina also maintained that quantitative methodologies for assessing such risks are underdeveloped and untested. Such argument forgets that operational risk control methodologies will never become rigorous, unless banks take appropriate measures to comply with the new rules. State Street's CEO also added that operational risks should be dealt with through supervision and incentives to build controls, not additional regulatory capital. This argument is self-contradictory.

David Spina said he believes that US regulators should insist that the Basel Committee abandon its current proposed Pillar I regulatory capital regime for operational risk, adopting in its place, a rigorous, effective Pillar 2 supervisory treatment. And why not adopt Pillar 3 of market discipline, with other banks refusing to deal with an institution which does not abide by the rules of Basel II in operational risk control and capital provisions?

State Street's CEO also testified he was against the use of gross income as the denominator for calculating operational risk, as proposed under the standardized and basic approaches for setting the capital charge. He said that: 'Our experience at State Street suggests that the two factors are not related.' He was right in this claim, except that a big bank like his own should not go for the basic approach and for GI. It should engage in detailed data gathering for operational risk losses – like the ORX Consortium is doing (a group of a dozen banks including American, German, Dutch and French institutions).[9]

More curious has been the deposition by Wilson Ervin, a managing director of CSFB, who lashed out at several aspects of Basel II in his February 2003 testimony to the House Subcommittee. One of the puzzles here is that the CSFB is an integral part of Crédit Suisse, and the parent company is actively working on Basel II's implementation, as documented by my research, and, above all, as required by Swiss regulators.

The Basel proposal 'is too complex, too costly and too inflexible to provide a robust, durable framework for bank supervision going forward,' said Ervin. Somewhat complex may be, but to the contrary it is flexible. The inflexibility argument is wholly wrong; and as for complexity, if a big bank does not have the rocket scientists to deal with it, then pity the bank!

Moreover, as every senior banker should know, flexibility can only be judged through applications over a period of time – not through the miracle of a 'one-off'. Equally unsubstantiated has been Ervin's claim that 'Implementing the proposed accord may have the effect of freezing the development required to hold capital for operational risk, using a procedure to develop the size of that charge known as the advanced measurement approaches (AMA).' Apart from the fact that Spina and Ervin contradicted one another in their respective testimonies the latter's statement is:

- Totally confused, and
- Highly inaccurate.[10]

That Ervin's statement is inaccurate has also been the opinion of Roger Ferguson. Rebutting the arguments of operational risk critics in the USA, the Fed's vice chairman said: 'I have not found the arguments of the operational risk sceptics to be convincing.' Ferguson also added that US supervisors are 'convinced that the explicit Pillar 1 capital charge creates incentives for (banks) to reduce (operational) risks, while ensuring that minimum capital is allocated to absorbing the remaining risk'.

16.7   If one does not want to be taken for fool, one should not say foolish things

Wilson Ervin included in his testimony another area of concern to him and, perhaps, to his institution: the level of disclosure required under Pillar 3 of the new accord. He said such disclosure was likely to add twenty to thirty pages of highly technical disclosures to the bank's annual reports – more than doubling the current amount, adding to costs while providing little or no information of value to the reader.

This reference to information of no value to the reader simply cannot be a statement coming from a highly paid banker. It is ridiculous and void of any substance. Just as improper was the fact that the managing director of CSFB stated in his congressional testimony that he was talking not only on behalf of his bank, but also on behalf of the Financial Services Roundtable. In this, he was rebutted by:

- Citigroup which confirmed that it remains positive about the new capital accord, and 'it supports the objectives of Basel II', and
- JP Morgan Chase which said that while the accord would 'benefit from certain revisions', the bank 'believes it contains many positive elements'.

While CSFB has been making no public comment, there has been an acknowledgement that Ervin was not talking on behalf of the Roundtable's 100 or so financial firms. A group of ten or fifteen banks are said to have been active in formulating the Roundtable's policy on Basel II, and there has been no evidence that all of them were on the same wavelength.

The third banker who gave a deposition to the House Subcommittee came from Colonial BancGroup, a $15.8 billion asset institution, headquartered in Montgomery, Alabama. The February 2003 testimony of Sarah Moore could be considered as representative of the US regional banks, and the challenges which they face in connection to cultural changes necessary to implement Basel II in a successful manner.

According to Sarah Moore, the most problematic issue in the Basel II capital accord has been the proposed treatment of commercial real estate, and the impact it would have on banks and their customers. She said in her testimony that commercial real estate lending is identified in the accord as a volatile, high-risk type of lending – more so than any other type of lending.

According to this opinion, the treatment of real estate lending with high risk-weights will discourage participation by banks in the real estate sector. Moore saw this as negative, because, for regional and community banks, commercial real estate lending accounts for a much larger slice of total lending than it does for big American banks.

At face value, such a statement is not wrong. It should, however, be recalled that these higher risk-weights have been adopted precisely because in the USA and the UK real estate lending is a risky business, particularly so in the case of commercial real estate. Swiss, Dutch and German banks face a much lower real estate risk, and for this reason they have complained about the higher weights cut to the size of riskiness in America and in Britain.

For the record, quite often in Switzerland and in the Netherlands house mortgages are never really repaid. The banks see to it that their valuation of collateral is conservative and they roll over their loans – while having mortgages brings tax benefit to their clients. Notice, however, that this is true only of residential mortgages, not of big commercial real estate developments.

Sarah Moore also claimed that asset correlation of commercial real estate loans was no higher than that for loans to other sectors, such as technology, telecommunications and airlines. While the 2002–03 market blues confirm this statement, it should not be forgotten that:

- The US real estate crisis of the early 1980s sank big banks like Continental Illinois and Seattle First,
- The late 1980s interest rate mismatch in the mortgage business hit the savings and loans like a hammer, creating a hole of $800 billion, and
- In 1991 the Bank of New England failed because of its overexposure in real estate and in derivatives.

Karen Shaw Petrou, who manages Federal Financial Analytics, an advisory service, was another February 2003 witness who gave a deposition to the House Subcommittee. Her statement that each of the proposed options to operational risk based capital charges, including the advanced measurements approaches, would result in regulatory capital considerably higher than economic capital, is either wrong or her meaning of what is economic capital is twisted beyond easy recognition (see Chapter 5).

Petrou justified her statement on grounds of reliance on gross income as the basis for calculating the charge, failure to scale the charge and lack of recognition of 'proven' forms of operational risk mitigation. However, like David Spina, she failed to identify a better alternative to gross income – and also failed to document in a dependable way the 'proven' forms. For starters, what is incorrectly called 'proven' operational risk mitigation, is largely done through insurance, and insurance involves its own risks. There is no 'free lunch' in risk management.

Further in her testimony – like Spina – Karen Petrou emphasized that, in developing international regulatory standards, a much bigger role should be given to Pillar 2, the section concerned with supervision. She said that 'recent experience in the US, EU and Japan points to the critical importance of supervision, backed up by meaningful enforcement, as well as to the irrelevance of international risk-based capital standards when domestic regulators choose to fudge the capital books'.

That regulators should not fudge the capital adequacy books is self-evident. But the witness should not first state that this happens, then put so much weight on Pillar 2 – that is, regulatory action. Indeed, Pillar 2 is weak in some countries because bank supervisors, just like the judiciary, and the law enforcement industry may be subject to criminal interests and their pressures. Precisely because the financial police may be corrupt,

- Pillar 1 is most important, and
- Capital adequacy for credit risk, market risk and operational risk should be higher rather than lower.

Another concern expressed by Petrou in her testimony has been that Basel II will put some large US banks at a disadvantage, especially where their financial services rivals are not chartered as banks. In this Karen Petrou is wholly right, except that the most mighty non-banks are US-based. Not only the proposed capital adequacy regime, but also Basel I puts banks at a disadvantage as compared with hedge funds for which:

- There exists no capital adequacy, and
- Where they are not supervised by any regulator (see Chapter 15).

There have been, as well, other testimonies I will describe as inconclusive. For instance, in July 2003, Karen Thomas, Director of Regulatory Affairs, Independent Community Banks of America (ICBA), testified that she was pleased that US regulators had concluded that the costs of applying Basel II to the entire population of US banks would greatly outweigh any benefit. As the experience of Sparkasse Lüneburg and many other small-to-medium German savings banks demonstrates, this settlement is utterly undocumented.

Also in July 2003, Steven Elliott, Senior Vice-Chairman of Mellon Financial Corporation, asked the Congress committee for the complete elimination of capital charge for operational risk under Pillar 1. As in the case of State Street, this borders on conflict of interest. Elliott's Pittsburg-based bank, which has about $2.9 trillion under management administration or custody, expects to require significant capital reserves for operational risk.

Mellon is concerned that operational risk capital charge will reduce its competitiveness in relation to non-bank rivals, but its top management probably forgets that non-banks don't have custody operations. Elliott argued that the goal of promoting internal controls and capital allocation can be far better achieved by Pillar 2. Who is going to pay the supervisors' examiners for doing the job a commercial banker should have done?

There have also been other testimonies whose content showed bias, which should not be the case of professional people when they deposit in congressional hearing. For instance, Micah Green, President of the Bond Market Association expressed general support for the objectives of the Basel Committee in aligning regulatory requirements with actual risk, but then he expressed concern on two key issues:

- Securitization, and
- Securities lending.

In both areas, Green said, the proposed regulations would meet the Basel Committee's goal of aligning capital requirements with risk levels, because institutions would be required to maintain a higher level of capital than is warranted by the practical risk of their positions. I would have like to hear Green answering just one question: Is his organization, and its members, using models? If yes, is the exposure being computed as a practical risk or a theoretical risk?

We all aim at practical approaches but the solution should not be to reduce the capital adequacy of banks, leading the world's financial system to bankruptcy. A better policy, assuring a level playing field, is to apply capital adequacy requirements to hedge funds, also putting them under rigorous supervision and subjecting them to market discipline. Doing the opposite, as some of the testimonies to the Congress suggest, is similar to what communism did in its heyday: it improved the lot of those financially weak by making everybody poor.

16.8.   Basel II and the EU's third Capital Adequacy Directive

In the EU, it is not Basel II as such, but the third release of the Commission's Capital Adequacy Directive (CAD 3) that will be the law of the land. Basel II is the underpinning to CAD 3. Indeed, European directives will now be called European *laws*. As a draft, CAD 3 became available in mid-2003, but this is a consultative paper and discussion on its clauses will go on until the end of the year. Then, in early 2004 a formal proposal will be made by Brussels to be debated by the European Parliament. The target dates are shown in Table 16.1.

Dates	Actions
November 2003	Impact study
March 2004	EU commission proposal
June 2004	European Parliament elections
Mid-2004	New EU Commission
End 2004	EU enlargement
September 2005 (perhaps)	CAD 3 approval
January 2006	Start of parallel testing
January 2007	Basel II implementation

Table 16.1 Target dates of the European Union's third Capital Adequacy Directive (CAD 3)

We have to wait and see exactly what will be included in the formal proposal by the EU, but there are already known to be some technical problems. For instance, to make it feasible for more banks to use F-IRB, the draft CAD 3 assigns probabilities of default to several asset classes and calls this IRB. Moreover,

■ Credit institutions are encouraged to use PDs derived from rating agency ratings, and
■ They are instructed to map them onto their own internal ratings, to arrive at individual bank's PDs.

Such a procedure is suggested wherever banks lack data to comply with IRB. On this issue, Annex D5 of the draft CAD 3 states: 'An external rating can be the primary factor determining an internal rating assignment; however, the institution shall ensure that it considers other relevant information.'

There is, indeed, nothing wrong with using external ratings. This is a good idea, since we should not try to reinvent the wheel. But to effectively integrate external and internal ratings, banks have to thoroughly restructure their rating system – from between five and eight thresholds most credit institutions now have, to twenty as S&P's, Moody's, and Fitch do. Also, CAD 3 should explicitly state that credit ratings are the bank's own responsibility, no matter if they bought them. Hence, banks:

■ Should use independent agencies ratings as background information.
■ But they should calibrate them with their own credit data.

A much bigger problem than this, connected with the belated EU initiative in capital adequacy matters, is that of political interference. Politicians have no business to mess with the bank regulators' efforts, though sometimes they try to do so. In early March 2002, for example, Andrew Crockett, head of the BIS, answered criticism of plans for new global banking standards from Gerhard Schröder, the beleaguered German chancellor, by warning politicians not to interfere.

The way Crockett sees it, and rightly so, is that the new Basel capital accord should not become a political football. It is because of different pressures that the implementation of Basel II, originally scheduled for January 2004, has been delayed to the end of 2006. Andrew Crockett acknowledged concerns that the new provisions could make economic cycles more pronounced by:

- Encouraging more lending during economic expansion
- Causing banks to cut back sharply in downturns, and
- Probably facing certain procyclical events.[11]

But the chief executive of BIS also pointed out that business cycles should not deter financial regulators from protecting the financial system. Neither should risks be discounted. An example of discounting is the very important family of operational risks, which so far has been given scant attention by banks and whose capital provisions have been attacked – as we saw in sections 16.5 and 16.6, in the course of Congressional testimonies.

Of critical importance, as well, is the much greater range of disclosure initiatives advanced by Basel II, which have been designed to make both capital positions and risks assumed by a bank more transparent. Greater disclosure could also involve the release of sensitive information, with a significant impact on financial reporting practices. A further point Crockett made is that a rigorous approach to capital planning and risk control would positively affect all banks, provided that:

- They fully understand and embrace the new regulatory rules, and
- They appreciate the impact of these reforms on their own growth and survival.

Beyond the damage to be suffered by the financial industry through political interference in its regulation and supervision, come the implementation's timetable conflicts. The current European Parliament is to be dissolved in April 2004, and it is generally expected that one-third or so of its deputies will not return. After the elections, scheduled to take place in August or September 2004, the Parliament's committees will re-form.

Experts say that, at this point in time, it is impossible to have any idea of who will be in these committees and what might become the committees' political complexion. Will there be significant support for loans to SMEs, and for other issues which impact on the parliamentary committee's reaction to Basel II? Nobody can answer such queries at this time. What is more or less sure is that, barring major delays, the final EU text on CAD 3 will be available *circa* September 2005. That is the target – and this date is too close for comfort because the timetable foresees:

- 1 January 2006, start of parallel testing, and
- 1 January 2007, Basel II implementation.

Some of the experts I talked to believe that the Basel Committee and national regulators will position themselves to move speedily, as circumstances dictate. However, legislative bodies, evidently including the European Parliament, do not work that way. In a democracy, one cannot influence legislation until:

- Deputies can halfway understand what this legislation is actually going to do to their constituency, and
- They are able to identify what can be traded to get an agreement, and what cannot be bought or sold.

This is tantamount to saying that the legislative process is definitely neither fast nor predictable. But this also means that the detail of CAD 3 will not be settled until some later date, which may well lie outside the target dates in Table 16.1. Delayed training and hundreds of needed procedural papers made in a rush may jam the parallel running between Basel I and Basel II, in 2006.

Neither is it only the European Parliament who will be looking into Basel II and CAD3. The European Commission also has a say. The directorate general (DG) for internal markets will look into Basel II clauses in consultation with the other DGs of Brussels. This will be done, more or less, in parallel with the work of the European Parliament committee. Then, it will be submitted to the Council of the EU finance ministers for final approval.

With all these discussions and delays, experts suggest, it seems that lots of compromises are on the way, until CAD3 is submitted to the Parliament in Strasbourg for the final vote. What will happen then is anyone's guess. The vote could split along:

- Party lines
- National lines, or
- Interest group lines.

Each DG, each parliamentary committee president and each of the finance and economy ministers, can bring along his or her priorities. Also, let us not forget that by 2004 there is going to be a new European Commission – and something may happen in the very last minute. An example is the interminable debate on the EU tax on savings.

- Moving towards common agreement took years.
- Then, this 'agreement' collapsed, because the Italian government traded its accord for milk quotas.

As if all these hurdles were not enough, there is something else beyond them. Brussels, too, works through inverse delegation. To become law, every country must pass CAD 3 through its own parliament. Nobody would dare to say that CAD 3 will sail through twenty-five parliaments without hitting problems, because by 2004 there is as well EU's enlargement bringing new players into the bargaining arena (see section 16.9).

Renewal of the EU Commission coupled with enlargement practically means the EU will get a whole new cast, with no experience of what has taken place so far in terms of bank regulation among its current fifteen EU members. To understand what is going to hold the attention of the EU's new members, look no further than the negotiations which have taken place so far on agricultural subsidies.

Moreover, beyond the Basel II clauses which focus on commercial banks, there is in the EU a simultaneous development of new regulatory guidelines for investment banks. This is known as the Lamfalussy process on securities, and it is currently being introduced into the EU. Beyond all that comes the challenge of regulating globalized markets.

So far, investment banks were kept out of Basel II because their regulators are not members of the Basel Committee on Banking Supervision, but of Montreal-based IOSCO. It is clear that risk-adjusted capital requirements will bring much needed upgrading of the industry's risk management practices. It will also require investment banks and asset managers to hold significantly more capital, prompting industry shakeouts.

In conclusion, the European Commission wants to apply CAD 3 not only to all credit institutions in what, by the end of 2006, will be an expanded, twenty-five nation EU, but also to all investment firms. This is a wider scope than Basel II, since the latter is confined only to banks.

The reason why the Commission has taken a broader perspective is that it wants to make the EU's financial system safer by getting banks and investment companies to align their capital more accurately to the risks they face. At the same time, this extension will disable some companies from gaming the system.

16.9 The challenge of regulating globalized markets

An integral part of the total picture regarding Basel II and CAD 3, as well as their common background, is the need for global financial regulation. At a time when the markets themselves have become global, it is no longer possible – or wise – to have significant differences in supervision from one country to another. Yet this is what is currently happening, in spite of the new rules brought forward via Basel II.

Several reasons can be found to be at the root of this problem. One is that globalization or not, national markets still differ in their basic characteristics. The same is true of implementation. For instance, Basel II rollout is a national issue. A second reason is that with systems which work through inverse delegation (the case of Basel and of Brussels) there must be a consensus, particularly so since:

■ In the banking industry, the national regulators keep their prerogatives.
■ In the EU, the different governments are sovereign; there is no political union.

No political union means that economic, social and other differences remain. These might be hidden when one traces only general guidelines, but they become evident when one gets into details. The devil is in the details, often hiding behind the lack of proper preparation for:

■ Reaching consensus, and
■ Stepping up into more sophisticated solutions.

In all likelihood, the aftermath of poor preparation for the implementation of Basel II/CAD 3 will be particularly critical in Eastern Europe, because of what has been called the 'EU steamroller'. It looks as though CAD 3 will oblige even the smaller banks to comply with the new capital adequacy rules.

A similar statement, though for opposite reasons, can be made about the US rejection of wider Basel II implementation. If obliging the smaller banks to comply with Basel II rules is not wise, keeping 99.9 percent of banks under Basel I does not make much sense either.

Experts also point out the existence of certain assumptions which have not been backed up by the facts, and which stand a good chance of being proven false. For instance, when Basel II was first mooted many people thought the cost of its implementation would consolidate the banking industry. This has not happened, and it is unlikely that it will happen in the future – just because Basel II or CAD 3 is implemented.

Another challenge is known as the *home-host* issue and has to do with the internationalization of finance (see the Warning). Global credit institutions will, in principle, be under supervisory control at home, but they also have to follow the regulations of each country in which they operate. National regulatory discretion sees to it that, unavoidably, there will be differences.

- Theoretically, these are taken care of by the first and second Memorandum of Understanding (see Chapter 15).
- Practically, existing differences are not likely to be ironed out, even if there are regular meetings between banks and supervisors.

Moreover, among possible hurdles are materiality issues, often interpreted differently in the home country and in the host countries. There is also the fact that in most emerging markets local regulators are unprepared for Basel II – though the BIS does its best to train emerging markets' regulators. The way Barbara Ridpath of S&P's put it: 'We don't believe regulatory bodies are prepared to deal with the complexity of Basel II.'[12]

Quite independently of Basel II, in a globalized economy, regulatory unpreparedness to which are added accounting system differences can have disastrous effects. One of the major victims is the consolidation of balance sheets, which becomes difficult because of incompatibilities in different legislations and regulations. And as far as Basel II is concerned, differences characterizing the jurisdictions certainly impact on pillar 3, with adverse effects on:

- Market discipline, and
- Transparency of financial statements.

Behind these issues is a horde of factors, some of them historical, which have not been addressed either by Basel II or by CAD 3. Every internationally active bank has to worry about dozens of regulators. Only consistency of application of Basel II by all regulators and jurisdictions can solve this huge problem.

It is only fair to add that the challenge to which I refer has come in the aftermath of globalization of banking and of financial markets – not of Basel II. The new capital adequacy requirements raised the matter because it stressed on metrics like probability of default, loss given default and exposure at default.

■ Theoretically, PD, LGD and EAD have been uniquely defined.
■ Practically, there exist differences in their interpretation and implementation, mainly by jurisdiction.

The detail varies between countries, and the EU's idea to try to standardize some of the metrics for all banks, without other prerequisites – like a common accounting system – being met, might well lead to distortions, even irrelevancy. The calculation of a credit institution's exposure must rest on firm ground, not on uncertainties. (Note that these 'other prerequisites' start and end with the EU's lack of political union, not with Basel II.)

In conclusion, the challenge now facing the G-10 and EU's regulators and commercial bankers is not only to get ready for Basel II and pass the legislative hurdles associated with the final confirmation of Basel II and CAD 3 by governments and parliaments, it is also to plan for Basel III. The next major challenge is what Basel III should target, by 2010. This should include a global homogeneous consolidation of balance sheets and P&L statements in the financial landscape – and, most particularly, it should target the regulation and prudential supervision of hedge funds, pension funds and financial conglomerates.

Notes

1 The hearings, on 'The new Basel accord: sound regulation or crushing complexity,' were called by the Domestic and International Monetary Policy, Trade and Technology Subcommittee on Financial Services of the House of Representatives, US Congress.
2 *Financial Times*, 12 April 2000.
3 D.N. Chorafas (2003). *Alternative Investments and the Mismanagement of Risk*. Macmillan/Palgrave.
4 *The Economist*, 3 May 2003.
5 D.N. Chorafas (2004). *Operational Risk Control with Basel II*. Butterworth-Heinemann.
6 Statements made by different executives, and quoted in this section as well as in section 16.7, are from *Global Risk Regulator* and *Retail & Private Banking Systems*, March 2003 issues, IBC Publishing.
7 *The Economist*, 3 May 2003.
8 Let us neither forget that on 12 April 2003, CSFB's former star performer, Frank Quattrone, was formally charged by the American authorities with a list of malpractices. This case is in court.
9 D.N. Chorafas (2004). *Operational Risk Control with Basel II*. Butterworth-Heinemann.
10 In fact, in his July 2003 testimony to the US Congress Ervin seems to have changed opinion saying that he is 55–45 percent in favor of Basel II.
11 See in Chapters 8 and 9 the way Banco de Espana deals with procyclicality.
12 'Basel II masterclass', organized by IIR, London, 27–28 March 2003.

Appendix: the Basel Committee on Banking Supervision and Basel II

The Basel Committee on Banking Supervision was established by the central bank governors of the Group of Ten (G-10) countries in 1975. It consists of senior representatives of central banks and bank supervisory authorities from Belgium, Canada, France, Germany, Italy, Japan, the Netherlands, Sweden, Switzerland, the UK and the USA – with Spain and Luxembourg as observers.

The Basel Committee usually meets every three months at the Bank for International Settlements in Basel, where are located its permanent secretarial services. One of the first acts of global importance by the Basel Committee has been the International Convergence of Capital Measurement and Capital Standards, agreed upon by the G-10 bank supervisors in July 1988. Then, in January 1996, came the Market Risk Amendment to the Capital Accord, aiming to incorporate market risks.

Because the standards on which capital requirements are based change over time, in June 1999 the Basel Committee presented a proposal for a revised version of the 1988 Basel Capital Accord. This proposal became known as the New Capital Adequacy Framework,[1] its objective being that of making the capital requirements for banks:

- More strongly dependent than hitherto on the economic risk, and
- Paying full attention to recent developments in financial markets and in the institutions' risk management.

One of the major contributions of Basel II is that it outlined requirements for qualitative supervision. These involve regulatory authorities having intensive contacts with the banks, credit institutions using modeling and experimentation to compute capital standards, and more extensive disclosure obligations through supplementary elements. Credit risk rating by independent agencies is an example.

While the original Capital Accord was initially directed only at internationally operating credit institutions, over the years it became a globally recognized capital standard for banks, applied in over 100 countries. This recognition also applied to the Market Risk Amendment, and can be expected to prevail with Basel II.

New regulations, more dynamic than ever before, are necessary because of the growing importance of trading activities and associated market price risks, including price risks in the trading book, foreign exchange risks, commodities risks and other exposures by credit institutions. Indeed, one of the interesting aftermaths of the Market Risk Amendment is the model culture.

■ Banks are increasingly able to use their internal models to manage market risk, because a model-based calculation of capital adequacy can work in their favor, and
■ Once the model culture has been acquired, it can also be used for credit risk, even for new financial instruments like credit derivatives.[2]

At the same time, experience with the 1988 Capital Accord has shown that the leveraging of a bank's capital, through greater credit risk and market risk, alters the actual risk profile of a bank. By revising the Capital Accord, the Basel Committee set itself the goal of eliminating past shortcomings, bringing the measurement of exposure more closely into line with the banks' risk control procedures.

It is important to note that the old, simple *rule-based* methodology of 1988 failed to prevent banks from assuming more and more risks without increasing the required capital. This sort of gearing is especially prevalent for corporate loans, because all loans to private sector firms were grouped together – by the 1988 Capital Accord – in a single risk bucket, irrespective of the underlying exposure.

Regulators have also been concerned by the fact that steady financial innovation has rendered the focus on traditional on-balance sheet credit risks inadequate. Asset securitization and other transactions have helped to reduce the regulatory capital burden, but have also affected negatively, in many cases, the banks' asset quality. As a result, the New Capital Adequacy Framework entails substantial innovations in prudential supervision to remedy the aforementioned distortions. In turn, this:

■ Increases the efficiency of financial intermediation through greater risk recognition, and
■ Enhances the stability of the banking system by reducing systemic risk.

Finally, Basel II has been established after extensive interaction with banks and industry groups, which led to successive comprehensive consultative packages and their test by the banking sector. This enabled the Basel Committee to receive significant feedback on its proposals and to produce a comprehensive framework that will be implemented by 2006 or shortly thereafter.

Notes

1 D.N. Chorafas (2000). *New Regulation of the Financial Industry.* Macmillan.
2 D.N. Chorafas (2000). *Credit Derivatives and the Management of Risk.* New York Institute of Finance.

Acknowledgments

The following organizations, through their senior executives and system specialists, participated in the recent research projects that led to the contents of this book and its documentation. (Countries are listed in alphabetical order.)

Austria

National Bank of Austria
Dr Martin Ohms
Finance Market Analysis Department
3, Otto Wagner Platz
Postfach 61
A-1011 Vienna

**Association of Austrian Banks and
    Bankers**
Dr Fritz Diwok
Secretary General
11, Boersengasse
1013 Vienna

Bank Austria
Dr Peter Fischer
Senior General Manager, Treasury
    Division
Peter Gabriel
Deputy General Manager, Trading
2, Am Hof
1010 Vienna

Die Erste (First Austrian Bank)
Franz Reif
Head of Group Risk Control
Neutorgasse 8
A-1010 Vienna

Creditanstalt
Dr Wolfgang Lichtl
Market Risk Management
Julius Tandler Platz 3
A-1090 Vienna

**Wiener Betriebs- and Baugesellschaft
    mbH**
Dr Josef Fritz
General Manager
1, Anschützstrasse
1153 Vienna

France

Banque de France
Pierre Jaillet
Director, Monetary Studies and
    Statistics
Yvan Oronnal
Manager, Monetary Analyses and
    Statistics
G. Tournemire, Analyst, Monetary
    Studies
39, rue Croix des Petits Champs
75001 Paris

**Secretariat Général de la Commission
Bancaire – Banque de France**
Didier Peny
Director, Control of Big Banks and
  International Banks
73, rue de Richelieu
75002 Paris
F. Visnowsky
Manager of International Affairs
Supervisory Policy and Research
  Division
Benjamin Sahel
Market Risk Control
115, Rue Réaumur
75049 Paris Cedex 01

**Ministry of Finance and the Economy,
Conseil National de la Comptabilité**
Alain Le Bars
Director International Relations and
  Cooperation
6, rue Louise Weiss
75703 Paris Cedex 13

Germany

Deutsche Bundesbank
Hans-Dietrich Peters
Director
Hans Werner Voth
Director
Dr Frank Heid
Banking and Financial Supervision
  Department
Wilhelm-Epstein Strasse 14
60431 Frankfurt am Main

Federal Banking Supervisory Office
Hans-Joachim Dohr
Director Dept. I
Jochen Kayser
Risk Model Examination
Ludger Hanenberg
Internal Controls
71–101, Gardeschützenweg
12203 Berlin

European Central Bank
Mauro Grande
Director
29, Kaiserstrasse
29th Floor
60216 Frankfurt am Main

Deutsches Aktieninstitut
Dr Rüdiger Von Rosen
President
Biebergasse 6 bis 10
60313 Frankfurt-am-Main

Commerzbank
Peter Bürger
Senior Vice President, Strategy and
  Controlling
Markus Rumpel
Senior Vice President, Credit Risk
  Management
Kaiserplatz
60261 Frankfurt am Main

Deutsche Bank
Professor Manfred Timmermann
Head of Controlling
Rainer Rauleder
Global Head, Capital Management
Hans Voit
Head of Process Management,
  Controlling Department
12, Taunusanlage
60325 Frankfurt

Dresdner Bank
Oliver Ewald
Head of Strategic Risk and Treasury
  Control
Dr Marita Balks
Investment Bank, Risk Control
Dr Hermann Haaf
Mathematical Models for Risk Control
Claas Carsten Kohl
Financial Engineer
1, Jürgen Ponto Platz
60301 Frankfurt

Volkswagen Foundation
Katja Ebeling
Office of the General Secretary
35, Kastanienallee
30519 Hanover

Herbert Quandt Foundation
Dr Kai Schellhorn
Member of the Board
Hanauer Strasse 46
D-80788 Munich

GMD First – Research Institute for Computer Architecture, Software Technology and Graphics
Prof. Dr Ing. Wolfgang K. Giloi
General Manager
5, Rudower Chaussee
D-1199 Berlin

Hungary

Hungarian Banking and Capital Market Supervision
Dr Janos Kun
Head, Department of Regulation and Analyses
Dr Erika Vörös
Senior Economist, Department of Regulation and Analyses
Dr Géza Nyiry
Head, Section of Information Audit
Csalogany u. 9–11
H-1027 Budapest

Hungarian Academy of Sciences
Prof. Dr Tibor Vamos
Chairman, Computer and Automation Research Institute
Nador U. 7
1051 Budapest

Iceland

The National Bank of Iceland Ltd
Gunnar T. Andersen
Managing Director
International Banking & Treasury
Laugavegur 77
155 Reykjavik

India

i-flex
H. S. Rajashekar
Principal Consultant, Risk Management
i-flex Center
146 Infantry Road
Bangalore 560 001

Italy

Banca d'Italia
Eugene Gaiotti
Research Department, Monetary and Financial Division
Ing. Dario Focarelli
Research Department
91, via Nazionale
00184 Rome

Istituto Bancario San Paolo di Torino
Dr Paolo Chiulenti
Director of Budgeting
Roberto Costa
Director of Private Banking
Pino Ravelli
Director Bergamo Region
27, via G. Camozzi
24121 Bergamo

Luxembourg

Banque Générale de Luxembourg
Prof. Dr Yves Wagner
Director of Asset and Risk
  Management
Hans Jörg Paris, International Risk
  Manager
27, avenue Monterey
L-2951 Luxembourg

Clearstream
André Lussi
President and CEO
3–5, Place Winston Churchill
L-2964 Luxembourg

The Netherlands

ABN-AMRO
Jos Wieleman
Senior VP Group Risk Management
PO Box 283
HQ 2031
1000 EA Amsterdam

Poland

Securities and Exchange Commission
Beata Stelmach
Secretary of the Commission
1, Pl Powstancow Warszawy
00–950 Warsaw

Sweden

**The Royal Swedish Academy of
  Sciences**
Dr Solgerd Björn-Rasmussen
Head Information Department
Dr Olof Tanberg
Foreign Secretary
10405 Stockholm

Skandinaviska Enskilda Banken
Bernt Gyllenswärd
Head of Group Audit
Box 16067
10322 Stockholm

Irdem AB
Gian Medri
Former Director of Research at
  Nordbanken
19, Flintlasvagen
S-19154 Sollentuna

Switzerland

Swiss National Bank
Dr Werner Hermann
Head of International Monetary
  Relations
Dr Bertrand Rime
Vice President, Representative to the
  Basle Committee
Prof. Urs Birchler
Director, Advisor on Systemic Stability
Robert Fluri
Assistant Director, Statistics Section
15 Börsenstrasse
8022 Zurich

Federal Banking Commission
Dr Susanne Brandenberger
Risk Management
Renate Lischer
Representative to Risk Management
  Subgroup, Basle Committee
Marktgasse 37
3001 Bern

Bank for International Settlements
Mr Claude Sivy
Head of Internal Audit
Stephen Senior
Member of the Secretariat, Basle
  Committee on Banking Supervision

Hirotaka Hideshima
Member of the Secretariat, Basle
    Committee on Banking Supervision
Herbie Poenisch
Senior Economist, Monetary and
    Economic Department
Ingo Fender
Committee on the Global Financial
    System
2, Centralplatz
4002 Basle

Crédit Suisse
Dr Harry Stordel
Director, Group Risk Management
Christian A. Walter
Vice President, Risk Management
Paradeplatz 8
8070 Zurich
Ahmad Abu El-Ata
Managing Director, Head of IT Office
Dr Burkhard P. Varnholt
Managing Director, Global Research
12/14 Bahnhofstrasse
CH-8070 Zurich

Bank Leu AG
Dr Urs Morgenthaler
Member of Management
Director of Risk Control
32, Bahnhofstrasse
Zurich

**Bank J. Vontobel and Vontobel
    Holding**
Heinz Frauchiger
Chief, Internal Audit Department
Tödistrasse 23
CH-8022 Zurich

United Bank of Switzerland
Dr Heinrich Steinmann
Member of the Executive Board
    (Retired)
Claridenstrasse
8021 Zurich

UBS Financial Services Group
Dr Per-Göran Persson
Executive Director, Group Strategic
    Analysis
George Pastrana
Executive, Economic Capital Allocation
Stockerstrasse 64
8098 Zurich

University of Fribourg
Prof. Dr Jürgen Kohlas
Prof. Dr Andreas Meier
Department of Informatics
2, rue Faucigny
CH-1700 Fribourg

Swiss Re
Dr Thomas Hess
Head of Economic Research &
    Consulting
Mythenquai 50/60
PO Box
CH-8022 Zürich

United Kingdom

Bank of England
Richard Britton
Director, Complex Groups Division,
    CGD Policy Department
Ian M. Michael
Senior Manager, Financial Industry and
    Regulation Division
Threadneedle Street
London EC2R 8AH

Financial Services Authority (FSA)
Lieselotte Burgdorf-Cook
International Relations
7th Floor
25 The North Colonnade
Canary Wharf
London E14 5HS

British Bankers Association
Paul Chisnall
Assistant Director
Pinners Hall
105–108 Old Broad Street
London EC2N 1EX

Accounting Standards Board
A.V.C. Cook
Technical Director
Sandra Thompson
Project Director
Holborn Hall
100 Gray's Inn Road
London WC1X 8AL

Barclays Bank Plc
Brandon Davies
Treasurer, Global Corporate Banking
Tim Thompson
Head of Economic Capital
Julian Knight
Manager, Group Risk Analysis and
    Policy
Alan Brown
Director, Group Risk
54 Lombard Street
London EC3P 3AH

Citigroup
Dr David Lawrence
European Head of Risk Methodologies
    and Analytics
33 Canada Square
Canary Wharf
London E14 5LB

Rabobank Nederland
Eugen Buck
Managing Director
Senior Project Manager Economic
    Capital
Thames Court
One Queenhithe
London EC4V 3RL

Abbey National Treasury Services plc
John Hasson
Director of Information Technology &
    Treasury Operations
Abbey National House
2 Triton Square
Regent's Place
London NW1 3AN

ABN-AMRO Investment Bank N.V.
David Woods
Chief Operations Officer, Global
    Equity Directorate
Annette C. Austin
Head of Operational Risk Management
    Wholesale Client
250 Bishopsgate
London EC2M 4AA

Bankgesellschaft Berlin
Stephen F. Myers
Head of Market Risk
1 Crown Court
Cheapside, London

Standard & Poor's
David T. Beers
Managing Director, Sovereign &
    International Public Finance Ratings
Barbara Ridpath
Managing Director, Chief Credit
    Officer, Europe
Walter Pompliano
Director, Financial Institutions Group,
    Financial Services Ratings
Broadgate West
9 Appold Street
London EC2A 2AP

Moody's Investor Services
Samuel S. Theodore
Managing Director, European Banks
David Frohriep
Communications Manager, Europe
2 Minster Court
Mincing Lane
London EC3R 7XB

Moody's K.M.V.
Alastair Graham
Senior Vice President, Director of
    Global Training
Lynn Valkenaar
Project Manager, KMV
Lars Hunsche
Manager
Well Court House
8–9 Well Court
London EC4M 9DN

Fitch Ratings
Charles Prescott
Group Managing Director
David Andrews
Managing Director, Financial
    Institutions
Travor Pitman
Managing Director, Corporations
Richard Fox
Director, International Public Finance
Eldon House
2 Eldon Street
London EC2M 7UA

A.M. BEST Europe
Jose Sanchez-Crespo
General Manager
Mark Coleman
Financial Analyst
1 Minster Court
Mincing Lane
London EC3R 7AA

Merrill Lynch International
Bart Dowling
Director, Global Asset Allocation
Elena Dimova
Vice President, Equity Sales
Erik Banks
Managing Director of Risk
    Management
Merrill Lynch Financial Center
2 King Edward Street
London EC1A 1HQ

The Auditing Practices Board
Jonathan E.C. Grant
Technical Director
Steve Leonard
Internal Controls Project Manager
P.O.Box 433
Moorgate Place
London EC2P 2BJ

International Accounting Standards
    Committee
Ms Liesel Knorr
Technical Director
166 Fleet Street
London EC4A 2DY

MeesPierson ICS
Arjan P. Verkerk
Director, Market Risk
Camomile Court
23 Camomile Street
London EC3A 7PP

Charles Schwab
Dan Hattrup
International Investment Specialist
Crosby Court
38 Bishopsgate
London EC2N 4AJ

Charity Commission
Susan Polak
Mike McKillop
J. Chauhan
13–15 Bouverie Street
London EC4Y 8DP

The Wellcome Trust
Clare Matterson
Member of the Eexecutive Board and
    Head of Policy
210 Euston Road
London NW1 2BE

Association of Charitable Foundations
Nigel Siederer
Chief Executive
2 Plough Yard
Shoreditch High Street
London EC2A 3LP

IBM United Kingdom
Derek Duerden
Technical Strategy, EMEA Banking
  Finance & Securities Business
76 Upper Ground
London SE1 9PZ

City University Business School
Professor Elias Dinenis
Head, Department of Investment
Risk Management & Insurance
Prof. Dr John Hagnioannides
Department of Finance
Frobisher Crescent
Barbican Centre
London EC2Y 8BH

TT International
Timothy A. Tacchi
Co-Chief Executive Officer
Henry Bedford
Co-Chief Executive Officer
Robin A.E. Hunt
Martin House
5 Martin Lane
London EC4R 0DP

**Alternative Investment Management
  Association (AIMA)**
Emma Mugridge
Director
10 Stanhope Gate
Mayfair
London W1K 1AL

Ernst & Young
Pierre-Yves Maurois
Senior Manager, Risk Management and
  Regulatory Services

Rolls House
7 Rolls Buildings
Fetter Lane
London E4A 1NH

Brit Syndicates Limited at Lloyd's
Peter Christmas
Hull Underwriter
Anthony Forsyth
Marine Underwriter
Marine, Aviation, Transport & Space
  Division
Box 035
Lloyd's
1 Lime Street
London EC3M 7DQ

Trema UK Ltd
Dr Vincent Kilcoyne
Business Architecture
75 Cannon Street
London EC2N 5BN

STP Information Systems
Graeme Austin
Managing Director
16 Hewett Street
London EC2A 3NN

United States

**Federal Reserve System, Board of
  Governors**
David L. Robinson
Deputy Director, Chief Federal Reserve
  Examiner
Alan H. Osterholm, CIA, CISA
Manager, Financial Examinations
  Section
Paul W. Bettge
Assistant Director, Division of Reserve
  Bank Operations
Gregory E. Eller
Supervisory Financial Analyst, Banking
Gregory L. Evans
Manager, Financial Accounting

Martha Stallard
Financial Accounting, Reserve Bank
  Operations
20th and Constitution, NW
Washington, DC 20551

Federal Reserve Bank of Boston
William McDonough
Executive Vice President
James T. Nolan
Assistant Vice President
P.O.Box 2076
600 Atlantic Avenue
Boston, MA

Federal Reserve Bank of San Francisco
Nigel R. Ogilvie, CFA
Supervising Financial Analyst
Emerging Issues
101 Market Street
San Francisco, CA

**Seattle Branch, Federal Reserve Bank
  of San Francisco**
Jimmy F. Kamada
Assistant Vice President
Gale P. Ansell
Assistant Vice President, Business
  Development
1015 2nd Avenue
Seattle, WA 98122–3567

**Office of the Comptroller of the
  Currency (OCC)**
Bill Morris
National Bank Examiner/Policy
  Analyst,
Core Policy Development Division
Gene Green
Deputy Chief Accountant
Office of the Chief Accountant
250 E Street, SW
7th Floor
Washington, DC

**Federal Deposit Insurance Corporation
  (FDIC)**
Curtis Wong
Capital Markets, Examination Support
Tanya Smith
Examination Specialist, International
  Branch
Doris L. Marsh
Examination Specialist, Policy Branch
550 17th Street, N.W.
Washington, DC

Office of Thrift Supervision (OTS)
Timothy J. Stier
Chief Accountant
1700 G Street Northwest
Washington, DC, 20552

**Securities and Exchange Commission,
  Washington DC**
Robert Uhl
Professional Accounting Fellow
Pascal Desroches
Professional Accounting Fellow
John W. Albert
Associate Chief Accountant
Scott Bayless
Associate Chief Accountant
Office of the Chief Accountant
Securities and Exchange Commission
450 Fifth Street, NW
Washington, DC, 20549

**Securities and Exchange Commission,
  New York**
Robert A. Sollazzo
Associate Regional Director
7 World Trade Center
12th Floor
New York, NY 10048

**Securities and Exchange Commission,
  Boston**
Edward A. Ryan, Jr
Assistant District Administrator
  (Regulations)

Boston District Office
73 Tremont Street, 6th Floor
Boston, MA 02108–3912

Microsoft
Dr Gordon Bell
Senior Researcher
Bay Area Research Center of Microsoft
  Research
455, Market Street
Suite 1690
San Francisco, CA 94105

American Bankers Association
Dr James Chessen
Chief Economist
Mr Douglas Johnson
Senior Policy Analyst
1120 Connecticut Ave NW
Washington, DC 20036

International Monetary Fund
Alain Coune
Assistant Director, Office of Internal
  Audit and Inspection
700 19th Street NW
Washington DC, 20431

Financial Accounting Standards Board
Halsey G. Bullen
Project Manager
Jeannot Blanchet
Project Manager
Teri L. List
Practice Fellow
401 Merritt
Norwalk, CN 06856

Henry Kaufman & Company
Dr Henry Kaufman
660 Madison Avenue
New York, NY 10021

Soros Fund Management
George Soros
Chairman
888 Seventh Avenue, Suite 3300
New York, NY 10106

Carnegie Corporation of New York
Armanda Famiglietti
Associate Corporate Secretary, Director
  of Grants Management
437 Madison Avenue
New York, NY 10022

Alfred P. Sloan Foundation
Stewart F. Campbell
Financial Vice President and Secretary
630 Fifth Avenue, Suite 2550
New York, NY 10111

Rockefeller Brothers Fund
Benjamin R. Shute, Jr
Secretary
437 Madison Avenue
New York, NY 10022–7001

The Foundation Center
79 Fifth Avenue
New York, NY 10003–4230

Citibank
Daniel Schutzer
Vice President, Director of Advanced
  Technology
909 Third Avenue
New York, NY 10022

Swiss Re
David S. Laster, PhD
Senior Economist
55 East 52nd Street
New York, NY 10055

Prudential-Bache Securities
Bella Loykhter
Senior Vice President, Information
  Technology
Kenneth Musco
First Vice President and Director,
Management Internal Control
Neil S. Lerner
Vice President, Management Internal
  Control
1 New York Plaza
New York, NY

Merrill Lynch

John J. Fosina
Director, Planning and Analysis
Paul J. Fitzsimmons
Senior Vice President, District Trust
  Manager
David E. Radcliffe
Senior Vice President, National
  Manager Philanthropic Consulting
Corporate and Institutional Client
  Group
World Financial Center, North Tower
New York, NY 10281–1316

Permal Asset Management

Isaac R. Souede
President and CEO
900 Third Avenue
New York, NY 10022
(telephone interview)

HSBC Republic

Susan G. Pearce
Senior Vice President
Philip A. Salazar
Executive Director
452 Fifth Avenue, Tower 6
New York, NY 10018

International Swaps and Derivatives Association (ISDA)

Susan Hinko
Director of Policy
600 Fifth Avenue, 27th Floor,
  Rockefeller Center
New York, NY 10020–2302

Standard & Poor's

Clifford Griep
Managing Director
25 Broadway
New York, NY 10004–1064
Mary Peloquin-Dodd
Director, Public Finance Ratings
55 Water Street
New York, NY 10041–0003

Moody's KMV

Askish Das
Analyst
Michele Freed
Analyst
160 Montgomery St, Ste 140
San Francisco, CA 94111
Marc Bramer
Vice President, Strategic Clients
130 South Main Street
Suite 300
South Bend, IN 46601

State Street Bank and Trust

James J. Barr
Executive Vice President, U.S. Financial
  Assets Services
225 Franklin Street
Boston, MA 02105–1992

MBIA Insurance Corporation

John B. Caouette
Vice Chairman
113 King Street
Armonk, NY 10504

Global Association of Risk Professionals (GARP)

Lev Borodovski
Executive Director, GARP, and
Director of Risk Management, Credit
  Suisse First Boston (CSFB), New
  York
Yong LI
Director of Education, GARP, and
Vice President, Lehman Brothers, New
  York
Dr Frank Leiber
Research Director, and
Assistant Director of Computational
  Finance,
Cornell University, Theory Center, New
  York
Roy Nawal
Director of Risk Forums, GARP
980 Broadway, Suite 242
Thornwood, NY

Group of Thirty
John Walsh
Director
1990 M Street, NW
Suite 450
Washington, DC, 20036

Broadcom Corporation
Dr Henry Samueli
Co-Chairman of the Board, Chief
  Technical Officer
16215 Alton Parkway
P.O.Box 57013
Irvine, CA 92619–7013

Edward Jones
Ann Ficken (Mrs)
Director, Internal Audit
201 Progress Parkway
Maryland Heights, MO 63043–3042

**Teachers Insurance and Annuity
  Association/College Retirement
  Equities Fund (TIAA/CREF)**
John W. Sullivan
Senior Institutional Trust Consultant
Charles S. Dvorkin
Vice President and Chief Technology
  Officer
Harry D. Perrin
Assistant Vice President, Information
  Technology
Patty Steinbach
Investment Advisor
Tim Prosser
Lawyer
730 Third Avenue
New York, NY 10017–3206

Sterling Foundation Management
Dr Roger D. Silk
Principal
14622 Ventura Blvd
Suite 745
Sherman Oaks, CA 91403

Grenzebach Glier & Associates, Inc.
John J. Glier
President and Chief Executive Officer
55 West Wacker Drive
Suite 1500
Chicago, IL 60601

Massachusetts Institute of Technology
Ms Peggy Carney
Administrator, Graduate Office
Michael Coen, PhD Candidate,
ARPA Intelligent Environment Project
Department of Electrical Engineering
and Computer Science
Building 38, Room 444
50 Vassar Street
Cambridge, MA, 02139

**New York University, Stern School of
  Business**
Edward I. Altman
Professor of Finance and Vice Director,
  NYU Salomon Center
44 West 4th Street
New York, NY 10012-1126

**Henry Samueli School of Engineering
  and Applied Science, University of
  California, Los Angeles**
Dean A.R. Frank Wazzan
School of Engineering and Applied
  Science
Prof. Stephen E. Jacobson
Dean of Student Affairs
Dr Les Lackman
Mechanical and Aerospace Engineering
  Department
Prof. Richard Muntz
Chair, Computer Science Department
Prof. Dr Leonard Kleinrock
Telecommunications and Networks
Prof. Chih-Ming Ho, Ph.D
Ben Rich- Lockheed Martin Professor
Mechancial and Aerospace Engineering
  Department

Dr Gang Chen
Mechancial and Aerospace Engineering
  Department
Prof. Harold G. Monbouquette, Ph.D
Chemical Engineering Department
Prof. Jack W. Judy
Electrical Engineering Department
Abeer Alwan
Bioengineering
Prof. Greg Pottie
Electrical Engineering Department
Prof. Lieven Vandenberghe
Electrical Engineering Department

**Anderson Graduate School of
  Management, University of
  California, Los Angeles**
Prof. John Mamer
Former Dean
Prof. Bruce Miller

**Roundtable Discussion on Engineering
  and Management Curriculum
  (October 2, 2000)**
Dr Henry Borenstein, Honeywell
Dr F. Issacci, Honeywell
Dr Ray Haynes, TRW
Dr Richard Croxall, TRW
Dr Steven Bouley, Boeing
Dr Derek Cheung, Rockwell
Westwood Village
Los Angeles, CA 90024

University of Maryland
Prof. Howard Frank
Dean, The Robert H. Smith School of
  Business
Prof. Lemma W. Senbert
Chair, Finance Department
Prof. Haluk Unal
Associate Professor of Finance
Van Munching Hall
College Park, Maryland 20742–1815

Gartner Group
David C. Furlonger
Vice President & Research Director,
  Gartner Financial Services
5000 Falls of the Neuse Road
Suite 304
Raleigh, NC 27609

Accenture
Stanton J. Taylor
Partner
Dr Andrew E. Fano
Associate Partner
Dr Cem Baydar
Analyst
Kishire S. Swaminathan
Analyst
Accenture Technology Labs
161 N. Clark
Chicago, Illinois 60601

Index